SECOND FRONT
NOW
1943

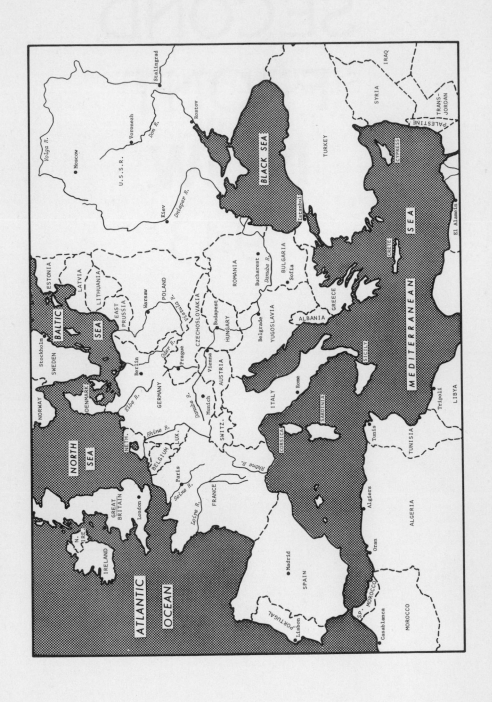

SECOND FRONT NOW 1943

WALTER SCOTT DUNN, JR., *1928*

The University of Alabama Press
University, Alabama

Library of Congress Cataloging in Publication Data

Dunn, Walter Scott, Jr.
  Second front now—1943.

  1. World War, 1939–1945—France. 2. World War,
1939–1945—Amphibious operations. 3. World War, 1939–
1945—Germany. I. Title.
D761.D923   940.54'012   78-32063
ISBN 0-8173-0008-2

CONTENTS

TABLES AND CHART

FOREWORD

In this provocative and wide-ranging essay, Dr. Dunn addresses head-on the central issue of invasion timing in the Allied European strategy of World War II. His reconstruction and comparison of the actual military situations of the several combatants are the most detailed and ambitious efforts in these directions I have seen. Drawing on a vast and growing body of American, British, and German memoirs and secondary sources, as well as on newly available archival materials in Washington and London, he has constructed a persuasive case for the feasibility of invasion in 1943.

Judging in retrospect the many intangibles that influenced the decisions of the various Allied leaders is of course a controversial business, and Dr. Dunn's judgments will doubtless be challenged on many levels. It is difficult to argue with success: the campaigns we and our Allies undertook in the European area did in fact succeed—at least in the sense that Axis power eventually was shattered—and thus the burden of defending theoretical versions of "what might have been" rests with the critics.

As a strategic planner in the War Department in the early years of the war, I was fully convinced of the operational feasibility as well as the military and geopolitical wisdom of an early, all-out invasion of the continent from Britain. Instead of concentrating their strength for such a decisive blow, however, the Western Allies permitted themselves to be diverted. As Dr. Dunn relates, the diversion included time-consuming and force-consuming operations in North Africa and even in the Pacific. For example, costly and indecisive campaigns in Sicily and Italy were undertaken. As a consequence, the planned buildup in Britain was delayed, and the invasion of Western Europe that had been planned for early or mid-1943 at latest—a time when the mass of the German forces was still irretrievably committed far to the East—was postponed until June of 1944. By that time, Soviet forces were well on their way to Berlin, and German defenses along the Atlantic coast had been strengthened.

I have never changed my earlier views of these matters. Consequently, I welcome Dr. Dunn's corroborative findings. Had the Western Allies faithfully adhered to their plan for assembling appropriate forces in the United Kingdom and for launching the invasion in 1943, I believe they would have succeeded. They, instead of the Soviets, could have seized and occupied much of Central Europe. Postwar history could then have unfolded under political and economic conditions much more favorable to the interests of the Free World.

September 1979   A. C. WEDEMEYER
                                                                     General, U.S. Army (Ret.)

PREFACE

Facing every writer of history is the need to make a choice between simply describing events in a cold, scientific manner or interpreting facts and presenting the alternatives with the inescapable intrusion of bias. This study is concerned with what might have been—a dangerous ground to tread. The focus, however, is not on what might have happened if, but rather on examination of the facts leading up to the decision not to open the second front in 1943 and the impact of that decision.

I have made a determined effort to provide the pertinent details, attempting to avoid the pitfall of being carried away with the rhetoric and ignoring the basic facts. In a source describing the arrival of the 858th German Infantry Regiment at the Normandy Front in 1944, the author stated, "One unit starting out at eleven in the evening of 6 June arrived near Caen at noon on 8 June, having madly cycled over 65 miles with no sleep, no food and no halts en route." The time elapsed was thirty-seven hours, and the actual distance moved by the unit was about sixty-five miles, but even a fair cyclist would have had no trouble covering that distance in about three hours on the excellent roads available on a moonlit night free of air attack. Either the facts were wrong or some part of the explanation was omitted.

My primary objective has been to present the data that supported the decisions (numbers of landing craft, tanks, airplanes, ships, and divisions) and to provide some interpretation of these facts. In addition to any other merit it may have, the work presents in one source a descriptive account of the armies of Britain, Germany, and America in World War II.

Comparing the characteristics of tanks and planes provides perhaps a more acceptable insight than relying solely on the biased comments of the participants. I have thus attempted to support my own interpretation by using the enormous amount of cataloged material on the physical aspects of World War II that has been collected in the past decade. This information is gathered in tabular form as well as discussed in the text. Wars may not have been won by the use of such tables, but graphs and charts do give a picture of the way the war was fought.

Inherent in the entire work is the application of production management and cost accounting to warfare. If sufficient resources are put into the process, for example, the result will be a victory, followed by a feedback to analyze the cost, which in turn would be used to determine the imput for the next process. Many of the men directing the war thought in such terms. Before 1943, they had invested hugh amounts of resources in risky ventures, yet they would not let the second front be opened in 1943, despite the availability of adequate resources. At the Casablanca Conference in January 1943 and at TRIDENT in May 1943, the decision to invade France was postponed. The reason for that procrastination is my subject.

CODE NAMES

ABC-1	American British Conversations 1, plan of March 1941 for cooperation, including lend-lease
ANAKIM	plan to reconquer Burma
ARCADIA	Roosevelt and Churchill conference in Washington, December 1941
BOLERO	plan for the build-up in England of one million Americans for the invasion of France
ELKTON	King's plan for taking Rabaul
GISELLA	German plan to invade Spain
GYMNAST	early name for the invasion of French North Africa
HUSKY	plan to invade Sicily in July 1943
OVERLORD	plan to invade France in 1944
RAINBOW 5	plan of March 1941 setting Germany as the first priority over Japan
RENO	MacAuthur's plan for taking Rabaul
ROUNDUP	early name for the large-scale invasion of France
RUTTER	the Dieppe Raid, August 1942
SLEDGEHAMMER	plan for limited invasion of France in 1942
TORCH	final name for the invasion of French North Africa in November 1942
TRIDENT	Roosevelt and Churchill conference in Washington, May, June 1942
ULTRA	series of highest classified messages relating the information from intercepted German messages

1

STRATEGIC PLANNING,

1941–1942

"Second Front Now," chanted the crowds in London's Trafalgar Square in 1942. Yet the attack on France was not launched until nearly two years later. Was an earlier attack militarily possible, as claimed by some Western military men and the Russians, and was the second front, in fact, delayed for political reasons? From early 1942, this question was hotly debated.

The delay of the invasion would have enormous political impact on the postwar world, and for that reason political factors overshadowed military possibilities. If the invasion had been launched in 1943, when the German army was still deep in Russia, the Allied armies would have penetrated deep into Germany and forced her surrender before the Russians reached the German border on the East. It was nearly four hundred miles from the front line in July 1943 at Kursk to the prewar Polish border and a further five hundred miles to the German 1939 frontier. The distance from Normandy to the Ruhr was less than four hundred miles. It is possible that Germany could have been defeated before the Russians had completely occupied Poland, providing the West with the opportunity to return the Sikorski government-in-exile. At the least, a Western hold on most of Germany would have given Churchill and Roosevelt a far stronger hand to play in negotiations in 1944.

The British were willing to deal from a weaker position rather than sacrifice the lives of additional British troops, which would have resulted from an earlier invasion, when a greater proportion of the initial invading force would have been British rather than American. Delaying the invasion involved more Americans earlier. Although Churchill was committed to the invasion of France, some of his advisers, such as Oliver Lyttelton, the minister of production, opposed a confrontation with the German army at any time, suggesting instead the continuation of the air war and "invasion of countries on the periphery" to bleed the German resources, "just as French resources were bled by Wellington in Portugal." If Britain had supported the Balkan campaign in World War I, rather than reinforcing the western front, Lyttelton wrote, "There would have been many more Englishmen alive today . . . and the result would have been the same."[1] Churchill replied to Lyttelton on November 9, 1942, that he should not get involved in strategy.[2] The men in senior positions in Britain had seen many of their friends die in France in World War I and were reluctant to allow a repetition.

Reinforcing the opinion that delay would save lives was belief in the Mediterranean strategy forcefully supported by Lyttelton's letter quoted above. The theory was that by pecking away at the periphery, Germany would waste her energies trying to protect her conquests. The net result, however, was that Britain dispersed her resources far and wide, making it difficult to obtain superiority anywhere, while Germany, with interior lines of communication, was able to move her troops from place to place at a leisurely pace and, through stubborn withdrawal battles, to pin down large British forces in Tunisia, Sicily, and Italy.

The war was extended a year, Russia gained control of eastern and central Europe, and British losses in Italy probably exceeded any additional losses that would have been sustained in an earlier invasion of France.

Unfortunately, much of the information needed to support or deny the possibility of an invasion in 1943 is still classified in 1979 (such as most of the intercepts of German messages made by the British) or buried in the tons of minutiae in government warehouses. Nevertheless, in recent years, more information has become available in usable form. Intelligence summaries based on intercepted messages, in-depth studies on the German army during World War II, and the papers of the leading figures provide evidence warranting another examination of the timing of the second front that finally took place on June 6, 1944.[3]

The timing of the second front was influenced by both political and military considerations. The attack could not have been launched until the Allies had the means to place in France a force superior to the defending German forces. There are reasons to believe that this military requirement was met by April 1943. Politically, it was expedient that the second front be launched at a time that would provide the Western Allies with the best possible position at the conclusion of the war—with Germany destroyed and Russia weakened and confined to the smallest possible area, without undue loss of British and American lives. Karl von Clausewitz long ago pointed out that war was merely an extension of politics. In the 1930s, the great powers were in a dilemma as to how to deal with Germany. Would Germany ally herself with the West against Russia or with Russia against the West? Or would the West be compelled to join with Russia to contain Germany? When Hitler revealed his unlimited aggressive intentions after the occupation of Austria in March 1938, he upset the uneasy balance of power created after the failure of the Western democracies to defeat bolshevism in the 1920s. From 1933 until 1939, Germany had exacted territorial gains from the West while hurling propaganda against the Red menace. Although Hitler appeared concerned about communism, he was an opportunist. The Russian-German pact signed in August 1939 enabled Germany to smash Poland and then, with a secure eastern boundary, turn to the West to defeat the armies of Britain and France.[4]

In May 1940, Britain turned for leadership to Winston Churchill, a man noted for his inconsistencies and tenacity. Churchill rejected Hitler's proposals for accommodation and instead declared a national struggle against the Germans. Hitler realized his inability to cross the channel after failing to win control of the air in September 1940 and turned east and struck at Russia in June 1941.[5] At that time, the traditional role of England in the never-ending game of balancing powers came into play. Churchill accepted the fact that neither Russia nor Germany made a suitable ideological partner because both openly avowed the destruction of the British imperialists as part of their national goal. The wise move for Britain's future political position was to support the weaker side, hoping that at the end of the war, both would be worn down, and the weaker would have won because of Britain's help. As a price for this help, Britain might have demanded concessions payable after the war.[6] For example, even though Churchill concluded correctly that, in 1941, Russia was the weaker of the two parties and decided to send aid, he erred in not extracting a guarantee of the independence of the Baltic states and Poland. Conversely, Russia demanded that Britain guarantee Russia's conquest of the Baltic states in exchange for remaining in the war against Hitler. Russia continually plagued the West for promises and immediate aid. The first Russian request for a second front came on July 18, 1941, only six days after the Anglo-Russian Treaty had been signed. The Russians were also playing the balance of power game, supporting the weaker side, Britain, in exchange for favors, with the hope that after the war both Germany and Britain would be weakened.[7]

After the Germans failed to take Moscow during the winter of 1941–1942, Churchill became less generous in his support of the Russians. A new partner was then in the game—Roosevelt—who has been charged with believing that generous aid to Stalin would make him less aggressive in the postwar world. Roosevelt provided a massive flood of material aid to the Russians and, in May 1942, promised a second front in Europe before the smoke had cleared from the tunnels on Corregidor, America's greatest defeat by a foreign power.[8] Many historians have considered Roosevelt naïve for urging action in Europe in 1942, while considering Churchill wise for making noncommittal statements. In making final decisions, however, especially those related to the second front, Roosevelt was as hard a realist as Churchill. Both preferred to see a weakened Russia in the postwar world, but they disagreed on the method. After months of heavy pressure from the British, Roosevelt made the final decision in July 1942 to attack North Africa rather than prepare to invade France in 1943 to relieve the Russians.[9]

The purpose here is not to prove that the second front should have been launched in 1942, in 1943, or even in 1945, but that the decision was political, not military. Germany could not have lasted long when faced with a two-front war, but if the second front had been launched too early, many additional British and American lives would have been lost and with little compensation. The gains might have been surrendered at the conference table. If it were made too late, the Russians could claim the real victory and would have physical control of most of Europe and could ignore the wishes of the West in setting up a new Europe.[10] Politically, 1944 was the best year—the initial landing involved little loss of life or material on the part of the West, and yet the West was left in control of nearly half of Europe when Germany collapsed. On the basis of military capability, according to American military leaders, the second front was possible in 1943, if not in 1942. A German surrender in late 1943 would have saved Germany from the heavy bombing of 1944 and 1945 and spared Russia much of the devastation that resulted from the battles during those years.

Would the invasion have succeeded in 1943? The chances of any venture are determined by comparing the two contending forces. The possibility of a successful invasion was a matter of weighing the number of German troops and their capabilities against the number of Allied troops that could be delivered on the French coast. Many half-truths were told concerning the military situation, for example, the problem with landing craft was not that there was a shortage, but that the equipment had been needlessly sent to the Pacific theater. Furthermore, the British had cracked the most secret codes of the Germans, and from 1940 the British had a complete knowledge of the German plans and troop movements. Certainly the West knew its own resources and, with full information concerning the enemy, could have struck a neat equation.

In the opinion of General George C. Marshall, the equation was balanced in favor of the West for an invasion in 1943. On the other hand, the British chief of the Imperial General Staff, Alan Brooke, having the same information, saw the balance against the West even as late as 1944. The following chapters will examine in detail the factors in the equation. The conclusions drawn from the facts will indicate, first, that Marshall was not being unduly influenced by procommunists in Washington as General Albert C. Wedemeyer thought.[11] Second, Western ability to launch an invasion in 1943 and Roosevelt's decision not to insist on one would indicate that he was more of a realist politically than some have suggested. In presenting the case for an earlier invasion, the Americans were not military amateurs; they interpreted the political situation differently.

The timing of the assault was the crucial issue. Militarily, 1943 would have been a better year for the attack because the Germans were at a disadvantage and the Allies had sufficient resources to make the attack. The delay enabled the Germans to rebuild from April 1943 until June 1944. The time lapse from the date of the encirclement of Stalingrad and the defeat in Tunisia until D-Day worked to the advantage of the Germans. The Germans gained relatively more military capability than did the Western Allies during that period. The German army in France was very weak from April 1943 until February 1944.[12] By June 1944, the Germans had increased their strength in the West considerably, while the Allies had fewer troops on hand, inasmuch as there were fewer British divisions available. The Germans moved men to the West during 1944, but no new American divisions were formed after 1943. In effect, while the Allies sat for a year, the Germans rebuilt.

The military reasons presented to the decision makers for not proceeding with the invasion plan were not valid. Shortages, poor training, and other missing elements were often presented in terms of current conditions, rather than in terms of conditions that would exist at the time of the planned event. For example, the supply of landing craft that would be available in the summer of 1943 was the crucial figure, not the quantity available in July 1942 at the time these plans were being made. The British military apparently could not comprehend the ability of the Americans to estimate needs and then produce the required quantities of machines, trained men, and supplies on a predetermined schedule. The poor performance of the British production planners gave the British generals some cause for this lack of confidence.

Was there need to be concerned with time or was time the inexhaustible commodity that General Brooke seemed to believe? Warfare revolves around the concept of expressing destructive military force while, at the same time, reducing one's own vulnerability to the enemy's destructive force.[13] Punch, but keep your guard up! Both sides have the same time in which to perform these two functions. To prepare an attack, four steps were necessary: preparation (production, organization, and training forces in the use of weapons), logistics (moving men and equipment to the area of battle), maneuvers (movement in battle), and the actual use of the weapons against the enemy.[14] By 1943, the Allies had completed the first two phases, but refused to move on. By hesitating, they sacrificed the time gained during the enormous buildup that took place in America and Britain in 1942.

Time is money—it is also life and death. Productivity is measured in time units—so many pieces per minute. Travel is measured in so many miles per hour, and the efficiency of an army is measured in so many square miles gained and in the number of enemy soldiers killed or captured in a certain number of days. The German army conquered Poland in twenty-two days and France in thirty-eight. West Russia took ninety-five days.[15] Time was one of the major factors in the theory of lightning war. Two of the often-quoted theorists on warfare as practiced during World War II were Basil H. Liddell Hart and J. F. C. Fuller. Both of these men advocated swift, decisive war, as opposed to the bloody battles of attrition fought during World War I on the western front and in World War II on the eastern front.[16] Fuller listed the principles of war: (1) direction: having a definite objective; (2) concentration: bringing the maximum amount of force to bear at the crucial point; (3) distribution: the manner in which available forces were disposed; (4) determination: having once decided on a plan, launching it and following through; (5) surprise; (6) endurance: having the ability to maintain one's forces through to the finish; (7) mobility: having the ability to move troops quicker than the enemy; (8) offensive action: taking the initiative; and (9) security: keeping one's base of operation safe and offering no easy opportunity for enemy attacks to succeed.[17] All of these principles were taught at the United States Army Command and General Staff School, but the British army was reluctant to accept these concepts both in 1926 when Fuller first published them and in 1943.

In Germany, on the other hand, General Heinz Guderian adopted the ideas readily and developed the blitzkrieg, which had as its objective the paralysis of the command function of the enemy.[18] Unfortunately, the Allied concept of blitzkrieg became entangled with the idea of overwhelming numbers of tanks supported by clouds of airplanes, which was believed to have caused the German successes of 1939 through 1941. But that was not the point at all, for in a drag-out battle of attrition, the thirty Polish divisions would have held much longer, and, in fact, the French expected them to hold because the Poles had been trained by the French. Furthermore, in May 1940 the British and French not only had more tanks, but better tanks, as indicated by the brief moment of British supremacy in the Battle of Arras in May 1940. The real point of a blitzkrieg was concentration rather than overall numerical superiority. The Germans conducted the war to paralyze the opponent—preferably by never fighting a serious battle—as occurred in the second phase of the conquest of France. In a war based on the theory of paralysis, one takes many prisoners and kills very few. The target is not the destruction of the enemy forces (an often-quoted phrase in British and American directives), but rendering the foe incapable of resisting by striking before he has time to regroup, reorganize, reform, and present a new front.[19] Blitzkrieg was only a name for a decisive form of warfare to bring the matter to an end in days, not months. The superior party—the one able to express a greater military force in a given space and time—won quickly.

Fuller's principles may be applied to the situation in 1942 from a purely military point of view: (1) The objective was the removal of Germany from the war. (2) The crucial point was the center of German arms production, the Ruhr Valley, and the quickest route to this point was northern France. (3) The largest possible number of troops should have been concentrated in the British Isles. (4) The invasion should have been launched with the single objective of breaking through to the Ruhr and sweeping on to Berlin. (5) Surprise was possible because of the number of available beaches, and the date could have been concealed by creating false alarms through deceptive activity. (6) The large reserves of forces in the United States provided amply for endurance. (7) The Allied navies and the overwhelming number of vehicles gave the Allies far greater mobility. (8) The initiative was in the hands of the Allies. (9) The Royal Navy and Air Force provided ample security to the home base.[20]

All of the pieces were available, but the Allies chose to delay for political purposes. In doing so, they sacrificed a military advantage and gave Hitler a year in which to strengthen his forces. Time is the same for both sides, and the good general does not waste it. Hitler had wasted time from May 1940 until 1943 in the areas of preparation and logistics, sacrificing his lead developed between 1933 and 1939. By the end of 1942, Britain and America had made up the time lost and had surpassed Germany in production, as will be shown in the later chapters.

Britain and America converted their factories and produced an amazing amount of war material in 1942. Germany made little use of the war potential of the conquered countries until 1943, when time began to work once again for Germany under Albert Speer's direction. German production improved both in quantity and in quality, because the captured nations' industry was utilized and millions of non-Germans were recruited into the war effort as workers, service troops, and even combat soldiers. Even though Germany could not overcome the preponderance of the Allies, the invasion in 1944 was more difficult than it would have been a year earlier.

The British and Americans ignored the value of their lead in 1943 and misjudged the Germans' relative use of time. When the balance was heavily in favor of the Allies, they failed to apply the maximum military force at the crucial point with the object of paralyzing the German war effort. Instead, they allowed most of their war potential to remain idle, while the Germans rearmed and shifted forces to meet them. By wasting opportunity, the Allies lost the chance for a clean, quick end to the war.

The Allies were well aware of the opportunity. An early return to Europe had been given first priority for over two years, but was delayed by offensive action in North Africa and in the Pacific. Allied leaders competed for resources for their respective favorite programs. A hasty thrust at France in 1942 was favored by the Russians. An indirect attack on Germany through Italy was favored by the British. Commitment of forces to Japan first, leaving Germany until later, was favored by General Douglas MacArthur, commander of the Allied forces in the Southwest Pacific, as well as by Admiral Ernest J. King, commander of the United States Fleet, by the Australian government, and by American public opinion. A major attack on Germany through France in 1943 was Marshall's strategy. Roosevelt was undecided but wanted action.

As early as January 29, 1941, British and American planners began meeting secretly to discuss overall strategy in the event that America entered the war. On March 27, 1941, the ABC-1 agreement was adopted, which included collaboration on a lend-lease basis. RAINBOW 5 was the plan developed for this agreement, which would make Germany the first target, while the United States defended the Pacific with limited naval offensives. The army hoped to defend not only Hawaii, but the Philippines as well, while the navy protected Wake, Samoa, Guam, and Midway.[21] Again, in August 1941, the staffs met at the Atlantic Conference and reaffirmed that the first objective in the event of American entry into the war was to be Germany.[22]

As a side effort, the British and Roosevelt had expressed interest in the invasion of French North Africa throughout 1941, Roosevelt's purpose being to forestall German infiltration into Brazil from Dakar, which at that narrow point in the Atlantic was only sixteen hundred miles away. On December 11, 1941, Churchill cabled Roosevelt urging a meeting so that the case for North Africa could be presented.[23] Various British plans had long been under study for this invasion to support the British campaign in Libya. During the sea voyage to the United States, Churchill's advisers worked on strategic plans for the conduct of the war based on multiple landings on the Continent in 1943 after Germany had been weakened by air attack and blockade. As a prelude, the Americans were to take part in the cleanup of Africa in late 1942, as well as provide four divisions to garrison Northern Ireland. Churchill and Roosevelt discussed some form of action in Africa on the evening of December 22 and, having agreed, presented their ideas to the Joint Chiefs of Staff at the beginning of the ARCADIA Conference on December 23, 1941.[24]

At that conference, the planners were given the task of examining the various courses of action in Africa and the related problems. The American army was opposed to action in Africa as being a diversion of effort, and Marshall feared the results of the personal influence that Churchill was imposing on Roosevelt. The British supported the African adventure, despite the objections based on shortages of shipping and doubts of the French attitude. Early accomplishment, however, was dependent on British success in Libya, which by January 9, 1942, was not in the cards. By January 25, General Erwin Rommel was once more driving back the British. On the same day, an approach to the French for cooperation had been rejected. These events forced the Allies to abandon plans for landing in North Africa in May, and the conference turned to a more general statement on strategy. The final statement was a triumph for Churchill. The American plan calling for a slow buildup leading to an assault in northern France was replaced with a plan for immediate action in several areas based on the peripheral strategy sponsored by the British.[25]

The grand strategy for the war was formally stated by the British and American Combined Chiefs of Staff at the ARCADIA Conference in December 1941: (1) Secure the major areas of war production in the United States, Britain, and Russia. (2) Defeat the submarines to keep open communications. (3) Close the ring around Germany by supporting Russia, building up the Middle East, and occupying North Africa. (4) Wear down Germany by air bombardment, blockade, sabotage, and propaganda. (5) Return to the Continent in 1943 via the Mediterranean, Turkey, the Balkans, or western Europe. (6) Go on the defensive in the Pacific.[26] The final paper on strategy echoed Churchill's memorandum that had been prepared on December 18, 1941.[27] The agreement was based almost completely on the British draft—the Americans made little comment.

The British had been planning offensive action from 1941, and plans had been made for landings all over the map. The first British plan prepared in detail to invade the Continent was presented to the British Chiefs of Staff on January 3, 1942, during the ARCADIA Conference. Twelve divisions were to land on the French coast between Deauville and Dieppe in April 1943. The assault force would consist of five brigade groups (each equal to about one-third of a division). The follow-up would bring the force to five armored and seven infantry divisions. The plan called for a daily landing schedule of six thousand vehicles and eight thousand tons of supplies, which would require fifty tank landing ships. This plan for Europe was discarded because the British considered it impossible to complete fifty tank landing ships in time.[28]

The Americans, nevertheless, wanted immediate action. They wanted to finish Germany as quickly as possible in order to get back to defeating Japan to satisfy the navy and the public demand for revenge for Pearl Harbor. The United States wanted to mobilize a large force, meet Germany head-on in Europe, and decide the issue.[29] Dwight D. Eisenhower wrote on January 22, 1942, as deputy chief of the United States Army Operations and Planning Staff: "We've got to go to Europe and fight—and we've got to quit wasting resources all over the world and still worse—wasting time. If we're to keep Russia in, the Middle East, India and Burma, we've got to begin slugging with air at Europe, to be followed by a land attack as soon as possible."[30]

Before Eisenhower could go on the offensive, however, he and his associates in the War Department had to plug extensive leaks in the defensive structure. The Japanese were spreading in many directions, and the Australians were fearful for their own safety. The United States dispatched troops to Hawaii, to Caledonia, and to Australia. Regiments and smaller units were assembled, shipping was found, and they were sent off to islands around the Pacific, to the Canal Zone, and to Alaska. At the same time, the British were also pouring forces eastward. General Brooke was irritated with the struggle to bring stability to the Far East at the cost of the Middle East. He had little patience with grandiose plans for an invasion of France put forth by the Americans, whose failure at Pearl Harbor had created the mess in the Pacific. In May 1942, Brooke thought that the Americans were taking a long time getting "into their swing" and blamed them for the defeat in the Pacific: "It arose out of initial American unpreparedness and carelessness in the one sphere where they might have been expected to restrain Japanese power. . . . Because of the surprise, in the face of every warning," the British had lost so much![31]

In Britain, agitation for a second front was mounting. Unlike the American system, the British government was subject to dismissal by Parliament at any time, and with the steady stream of defeats being inflicted on British forces in the Pacific, Churchill was in political difficulty. Refusal to provide more aid to the Russians was especially bitter to the Labour party, and there was urgent need for a military success.[32] Believing that nothing could be done in Europe, the British searched elsewhere for a victory. To clean up Libya and protect India, the British planned to send three hundred thousand men overseas between February and May 1942, taking them away from the potential European invasion force.[33]

The Americans were still concerned with the second front. By March 1942, the defensive structure in the Pacific was in place, and Roosevelt and Marshall wanted action in Europe. They feared the collapse of Russia during the coming summer campaign. Some form of help had to be offered by the Western Allies.[34] Marshall presented his idea for a major attack on Germany through France to Roosevelt on March 5, 1942. Roosevelt approved and on March 9 informed Churchill of the hope to aid the Russians with a second front. On March 25, Marshall presented further arguments to Roosevelt, who ordered the preparation of a plan that was delegated to Eisenhower.[35]

After Eisenhower outlined all of the arguments, he, too, favored an early assault on Europe. In considering the Mediterranean route, he realized that neither Sicily nor Italy could be attacked directly because of the threat of land-based aircraft, which meant that French North Africa would have to be acquired first. He therefore rejected the Mediterranean approach for the following reasons:

(1) The scene of action was too far from Germany. (2) Italy's collapse would not bring down Germany. (3) It would be difficult to attack Germany across the Alps after Italy was taken. (4) It would be difficult to concentrate forces in the Mediterranean for lack of a substantial base. Only the United Kingdom could provide a base for over one million troops. (5) The forces defending England, especially aircraft and naval forces, could be used in an attack on France, but not for an attack elsewhere. (6) The attack on France posed no natural obstacles as compared to the mountains in Italy. (7) The shortest convoy route was to England, and ports were available to receive the ships. Since we had to maintain the convoy route to England, why not use it rather than add an additional route to protect?

The factors against the French coast landing were also considered: (1) German fortifications would be difficult to overcome. (2) The German air force was concentrated in western Europe. (3) Considerable German naval and submarine forces were concentrated in northern France and Norway. (4) The approaches were already well mined. (5) Because of the power of the Germans, we would have to await a break in their morale before attacking. Nevertheless, weighing all these factors, Eisenhower decided that France was the best target for an attack in 1943.[36]

Two plans emerged, a new version of the British SLEDGEHAMMER, a small-scale attack in 1942, and a new plan, ROUNDUP, a major invasion. The SLEDGEHAMMER concept was to place from eight to ten divisions in France to relieve pressure on the Russians during the summer of 1942. American participation would be limited to two and a half divisions; Britain was to provide most of the troops. The problem was the lack of landing craft in early 1942 to supply the divisions over the beaches because there were no major ports in the area selected for the attack. The planners believed that it would take at least eight weeks to open a port to ships, resulting in an extended period of supply by landing craft. A detailed plan was worked out, however, for a landing near Boulogne if the Germans did not reinforce the area and if all German reserves were committed in the East.[37]

Eisenhower's new plan, ROUNDUP, called for a major invasion in Europe in April 1943 by eighteen British and thirty American divisions, 2,250 British and 3,550 American planes, and 7,000 landing craft. The area chosen was the coast between Le Havre and Boulogne.[38] The Americans would provide one million men and their supplies. The British would contribute at least four hundred thousand men to be returned from the Mediterranean plus other forces in England. The plan was presented to Roosevelt by Marshall and Henry Stimson, the secretary of war, on April 1, 1942. Roosevelt accepted it and, on April 4, 1942, sent Marshall and Harry Hopkins to England to present the idea to Churchill and the British military leaders. On April 3, Roosevelt had cabled Churchill to announce the arrival of the mission: "What Harry and George Marshall will tell you all about has my heart and mind in it."[39]

Although the British had been considering such an attack, Brooke's reaction

was that it was a complete reversal of American policy and the program set at
ARCADIA of tightening the ring rather than delivering a frontal blow. Churchill
accepted the concept with some hedging—the Middle East must not be left
unguarded—but he promised to get his staff to agree. Hopkins doubted Churchill's sincerity, but Marshall was impressed. Brooke raised the point of a need
for adequate shipping to get the American divisions over as well as the lack of
landing craft. He thought ''it was not possible to take Marshall's . . . castle in the
air . . . too seriously.''[40] The dislike was mutual, for Marshall felt that Brooke
might be a good fighting man but did not have ''Dill's brains'' (Sir John Dill,
British military representative in Washington).[41] Brooke considered Marshall
easy to get on with but ''rather over-filled with his own importance. But I should
not put him down as a great man.'' Brooke thought, ''in fact, in many respects he
is a very dangerous man whilst being a very charming one.'' Admiral King and
General MacArthur were merely considered as threats by Brooke for their constant attempts to drain resources to the Pacific.[42]

After the meeting with the General Staff on April 9, Brooke questioned Marshall privately about the plan and concluded that the Americans had insufficient
knowledge of modern warfare, of logistical problems, and of ultimate objectives.
Even if the Americans did bring over thirty divisions in 1943, there would not be
enough landing craft to carry them over the channel and maintain them. Brooke
believed, ''Even by 1943 the most that could be looked for in landing craft would
only suffice to create a two division front,'' and the attack could be made only
after Germany had been weakened by Russia.[43] Although he thought none of the
conditions needed for success could be met in 1943, in fact all of them were.

In England, at the Defense Committee meeting with parliamentary leaders on
April 14, Marshall and Hopkins again presented their plan, hopefully for
SLEDGEHAMMER and certainly for ROUNDUP in 1943. The plans still met
with favor, but Brooke and Churchill urged that aid be sent to the British in the
Indian Ocean and in the Middle East to prevent an Axis juncture in the Caucasus.
Inconsistently, Brooke found twenty miles of the channel an insurmountable
obstacle for the Allies, but feared that the Germans could join with the Japanese
more than ten thousand miles away! Again the problems of shipping and landing
craft were brought out, but Marshall tried to give reassurance that by 1943 the
United States could provide for a full-scale assault on a six-division front. The
British technically agreed on April 14, 1942, to accept the large shipments of
American troops and to start preparing joint plans for an invasion when it became
practical.[44]

The major objection of the British was the fearsome power of the German
army. An examination of the actual extent of this force will be covered in several
chapters, but at this point it will suffice to introduce the unrealistic British fears.
In April, Brooke believed that the invasion force would have to face thirty to
forty German divisions.[45] Churchill was a little more conservative: ''The Germans had left 25 mobile divisions in France.''[46] Brooke thought that the Germans
would be able to bring in fresh divisions at double the rate that the Western Allies

could land them over the beaches: "His [Hitler's] formations were fully trained and inured to war whilst ours were raw and inexperienced."[47] Brooke had little faith even in the British divisions. Stalin sensed the British military leaders' fear of the German army when he commented ironically at the Moscow Conference in 1942 that the British should not be afraid, "that fighting the Germans was not so bad," even though the Germans were then hammering away at Stalingrad.[48] Despite Brooke's fear of German power, he wrote to General Sir Archibald Wavell on May 5, 1942, "I cannot see where the Germans are to raise a large enough mass of manoeuvre [reserve] of reasonably fresh troops to launch the full-scale offensive to finish off Russia and penetrate to the Caucasus. The forces may be there, but they are hard to find and there are very few signs of them at present."[49] This statement shows that Brooke underestimated the German army less than three weeks after taking the opposite position, but that Brooke was fully apprised of German plans for 1942.

Nevertheless, Brooke was correct in questioning the validity of SLEDGE-HAMMER with its limited involvement. The Germans did have rebuilt divisions that were able to defeat the Russian offensive at Kharkov on May 19, 1942, and then immediately launch the massive drive into the Caucasus. The British had landing craft sufficient for only four thousand men in May 1942, and they were uncertain of American production. There were twenty-five German divisions in the West, but Britain considered only ten of her divisions equipped and trained for an invasion, and the Americans could supply only two at that time. Brooke wrote on March 3, 1942, "What can we do with some ten divisions against the German masses." He refused to foresee that many of these problems would be eased by April 1943 and certainly all of them by September 1943. Instead, he was gloomy regarding the prospects even for 1944.[50]

The British apprehensions were unwarranted for the war was changing in favor of the Allies. By June 1942, the Japanese had overreached themselves. Their plan called for the conquest of the Aleutians, Fiji, Samoa, New Caledonia, Midway, and more of New Guinea, cutting the direct line of communication between the United States and Australia. Early in May 1942, however, the Battle of the Coral Sea had frustrated their attack on Port Moresby, and although the outer Aleutians fell, the attempt on Midway was beaten back on June 3 and 4 with heavy Japanese losses—four large aircraft carriers and hundreds of planes and highly trained pilots. The Japanese Combined Fleet was no longer capable of offensive action.[51]

The position in the Pacific was stabilized, and the Allies could have concentrated on Europe, but even there diverting factors existed. Russia's problems were a major worry in the determination of policy. Today it is difficult to understand the constant concern of the Western Allies over the fate of the Russians. After the fall of France, the British realized that Russia was the only source of the massive manpower needed to defeat the German army. Britain courted Russian favor just as Germany continued to supply Russia with manufactured goods in exchange for raw materials. Both Churchill and Hitler had deep ideological differences with Stalin, but both swallowed their convictions in the face of reality, each hoping that Russia would defeat the other. Stalin grew more and more cautious during 1941 and discredited British information about German plans to attack Russia. He had so thoroughly inured himself against British propaganda that he refused to believe the attack when it was actually launched. Once the Germans invaded, it appeared the Russians would collapse as had the rest of Europe. Hundreds of thousands of Russians were captured as the German panzers broke through the Russian lines. Western generals forecast the end of Russia in a period of weeks and were pleasantly surprised when the German attack faltered in front of Moscow and was then driven back during the winter of 1941. Space and cold, however, not Russian valor, had saved Stalin, and as the summer of 1942 drew near, German forces were six hundred miles into Russia within easy striking distance of Moscow, Leningrad, and the Volga. Another six-hundred-mile advance during the summer of 1942 would have left the Russians clinging to the slopes of the Ural Mountains unable to keep the attention of more than a fraction of the German army. It was questionable whether the Russians would be able to withstand another onslaught of the caliber of the 1941 campaign and whether the Germans would be able to mount such a campaign. The Russians themselves had doubts and dispatched Vyacheslav Molotov to London and Washington to plead for help by insisting on a second front. Stopping first in London, Molotov received no promises, but in May 1942 he had far better luck with Roosevelt.[52] Although Molotov demanded a second front to take forty divisions from the Russian front, Roosevelt promised a front of only indefinite size in 1942.[53] On May 31, 1942, Roosevelt cabled Churchill demanding that he assist in fulfilling this promise with an invasion of France in August 1942. Far from being willing to support the second front, Churchill was on the verge of canceling the supply convoys to Murmansk because of the heavy losses to German aircraft and U-boats. In June the convoy lost twenty-three ships out of thirty-four dispatched, and the convoys were canceled until the winter, when shorter days along the northern route and poorer flying weather would make it more difficult for the Germans to locate and destroy the ships.[54] Because of this disavowal of England's solemn promise to aid Russia with tanks and planes at a time when the Germans were driving through the Ukraine, Churchill saw the need to provide some action.

Churchill's decisions regarding the second front were heavily weighted by the attitude of the Russians. In the plan for the war discussed at ARCADIA in Washington in December 1941, Churchill pointed out that the Russians had stopped the Germans, but that the only assistance the West could provide was supplies: "In this way alone shall we hold our influence over Stalin and be able to weave the mighty Russian effort into the general texture of the war."[55] Another method of placating the Russians was to continue to promise a second front. Though Roosevelt was genuine in his promise to Molotov in June 1942, Churchill hedged.

A third method of cooperation was through the sharing of intelligence. Stalin's

spies on the German General Staff informed him of all German plans and dispositions so he knew of the weakness of the Germans in the West. A British military
mission was sent to Moscow to exchange information with the Russians. The
course of these meetings forms a good index of Anglo-Soviet relations. On June
16, 1942, the Russians were cooperative, promising weekly meetings and immediate information regarding the identification of German units on the eastern
front. On June 23, 1942, the British expressed reluctance to provide information
on their airborne radar, but the Russians proved cooperative until July 20, 1942,
when they refused to continue the meetings.[56]

Churchill abandoned the idea of an immediate second front in Europe by the
summer of 1942 and turned to GYMNAST, the plan to clear North Africa
preliminary to the French invasion. On June 3, 1942, Vice Admiral Lord Louis
Mountbatten arrived in Washington to discourage further consideration of
SLEDGEHAMMER, the limited invasion in 1942, because, though the Russians
were in great need (one of the prerequisites for SLEDGEHAMMER), the operation would be a pointless sacrifice. The plan for a 1943 invasion was still alive.
Roosevelt wanted "early action" in 1942, however, and the British promoted the
attack on North Africa.[57] The persuasive Mountbatten was followed by Churchill
himself, who arrived in Washington on June 18.

Matters looked very bleak to Churchill when he arrived. A convoy to Malta
had been lost to enemy action, and it was questionable whether the island fortress
would hold.[58] The British had taken a serious defeat in North Africa and were on
the run. Coincidentally, the fall of Tobruk was reported on June 21, while
Churchill was in the Oval Office with Roosevelt and Marshall.[59] Although the
Americans were no longer pressing SLEDGEHAMMER, they were reluctant to
follow the Mediterranean strategy because it would delay ROUNDUP in 1943.
Some action had to be taken. The Russians demanded help and needed it badly.
The Western Allies could not stand idly by while their essential partner was
ground into the dust. The situation in North Africa was frustrating—after enor-
mous efforts to build up the Eighth Army, Rommel with inferior forces had put
the whole lot to rout, taking Tobruk in a few days and chasing the remnants of the
Eighth Army back to Egypt. A massive descent on French Algeria and Morocco
seemed to provide an answer. It would assist the Russians; it would help the
Eighth Army; and it would open the Mediterranean shipping route and ease the
shipping shortage by removing the need to go around Africa to reach the Middle
East and India. All Churchill had to do was to convince the Americans.

Brooke removed suspicion when he agreed with the Americans that no operation should be conducted that would delay ROUNDUP and joined them in
questioning the wisdom of GYMNAST (the attack on North Africa). The Combined Chiefs of Staff agreed that GYMNAST was the worst of alternatives because it would disperse the base organization, the lines of communication, and air
strength.[60] Despite this advice, Churchill, although still firmly behind ROUND-
UP and agreeable to the continuation of the American buildup in Britain with a
hope for SLEDGEHAMMER, tenaciously stressed that the Allies should exam-

ine the possibility of GYMNAST in 1942.[61] Stimson and Marshall continued to see GYMNAST as a fatal threat to the future of ROUNDUP.

To relieve the situation in Egypt, Marshall promised and delivered promptly three hundred new Sherman tanks and one hundred self-propelled 105mm howitzers to the Eighth Army that would give them overwhelming superiority over Rommel in numbers and an edge in quality as well.[62] This action would put matters right in Egypt, while the main effort was held to the channel, either in late 1942 or 1943.

Roosevelt could not ignore the pressures for a second front in 1942. He had promised Molotov action, and the American public needed evidence that the United States was in Europe to fight.[63] Something had to be done, and both Roosevelt and Churchill agreed that GYMNAST seemed to be the answer if the British General Staff vetoed SLEDGEHAMMER. In favor of the North African attack were the principles advocated by Churchill, providing a second front and at the same time aiding the Eighth Army. An additional bonus would be the opportunity for American divisions to gain combat experience against a soft target.[64]

The decision was not finalized in Washington, but when Churchill returned to London, he asked his staff for comments on the possibility of success of the current plan to attack France. C. T. Paget, commander of the Home Forces, W. S. Douglas, commander of the Fighter Command, and B. H. Ramsay, commander of the Naval Command, replied on June 29, 1942, with a long list of objections: lack of landing craft, limited capacity of British ports, heavy German defenses, and the limited range of British fighters that restricted the assault to the Pas de Calais. The maximum force that could be landed with the landing craft scheduled for April 1, 1943, would be 270,000 men and 30,500 vehicles by D-Day plus seven. If the weather turned bad, the totals would be reduced by as much as 33 percent.[65]

The British Chiefs of Staff decided on July 2, 1942, that SLEDGEHAMMER could not succeed because the troops would be driven off by strong German forces.[66] On July 6, Churchill told the English cabinet that an invasion of France was off for 1942 and recommended that GYMNAST be undertaken, even at the sacrifice of the buildup program and ROUNDUP.[67] On July 8, Churchill cabled Roosevelt that SLEDGEHAMMER was impossible and GYMNAST was the best bet because it would offer an opportunity for both nations to work together and the French in North Africa could be less difficult opponents than the Germans.[68] This cable created a crisis in Washington.

Sensing the change in British attitude, Marshall and King changed the directives to the Pacific commanders on July 2, instructing them to go on the offensive. The decision to attack Guadalcanal was made on June 25, the day that Churchill returned to England.[69] After receipt of Churchill's cable, with firm evidence in hand, Stimson, Marshall, and King reacted strongly. If the British had no desire to fight the Germans in France, why not drop the matter and turn our efforts to the Pacific, they told Roosevelt.[70] The British representative in

Washington, Sir John Dill, must have informed Churchill of the stir, for on July 12, Churchill cabled Dill that SLEDGEHAMMER would hurt ROUNDUP, but that GYMNAST would not, as it would merely divert six American divisions that could be easily replaced from the United States. It was essential that the Americans support GYMNAST because of the hope that the French would not resist an American invasion as strongly as one by the British, for whom the French held a grudge because of the British attack on their fleet in 1940. If Roosevelt said no to GYMNAST, nothing would be done. Nevertheless, Churchill urged Dill to reaffirm point four in his cable: "4. There could be no excuse in these circumstances for the switch of United States effort and I cannot think that such an attitude would be adopted." On July 14, Churchill cabled Roosevelt that no one thought SLEDGEHAMMER would succeed, whereas everyone thought GYMNAST was the best possible effort. Under no circumstances would GYMNAST interfere with plans for ROUNDUP, which "should proceed at full blast." On the fourteenth, Roosevelt rejected the Pacific plan and two days later ordered Marshall, Hopkins, and King to go to London to meet with Churchill and the British staff to settle the matter. On the fifteenth, Dill warned Churchill that the Pacific plan had been presented to Roosevelt and that Churchill must convince Marshall that the British would attack France as soon as possible; otherwise "everything points to a complete reversal of our present agreed strategy and the withdrawal of America to a war of her own in the Pacific."[71]

When Marshall, Hopkins, and King arrived in London, they were given an intensive briefing on the British position. Churchill objected strenuously to the limited measures of SLEDGEHAMMER because he believed that the Germans would send fifty or sixty divisions to France to destroy the invasion force. He also feared that the submarine campaign would cut off the supply line to Britain and leave the troops stranded. Consequently, Marshall and the new commander of the United States forces in Europe, Eisenhower, accepted the fact that SLEDGEHAMMER was not possible in 1942.[72] Eisenhower concluded that the British could not muster any more than fifteen divisions because of commitments elsewhere. For example, the Royal Navy was tied up waiting for the German battleships to come out of their ports and could not provide a bombardment force. Furthermore, the Royal Air Force was neither equipped nor trained for supporting ground forces.[73]

Even though SLEDGEHAMMER was off, Marshall and Eisenhower still opposed GYMNAST.[74] On July 22, Hopkins cabled Roosevelt from London telling him that he must make the decision. Roosevelt replied, "GYMNAST," and on July 24, the Joint Chiefs of Staff (British and American) announced the plan to go into North Africa.

The memo from the American Chiefs of Staff to their British counterparts on July 24, 1942, agreed that North Africa was acceptable if SLEDGEHAMMER was impossible; however, the Americans concluded in the document, Combined Chiefs of Staff 94: "That it is understood that a commitment to this operation renders ROUND-UP, in all probability impracticable of successful execution in

1943 and therefore that we have definitely accepted a defensive, encircling line of action for the *Continental European Theater*, except as to air operation."[75] Paget, commander of the British Home Forces, was of the same opinion: "If a decision is taken to despatch operation 'TORCH', it should be accompanied by a further decision to cancel for the time being all preparations for operation 'ROUNDUP' other than planning."[76]

Eisenhower wrote at the time that the date of the decision could go down as "the blackest day in history." Forrest C. Pogue, the biographer of General George C. Marshall, wrote concerning the decision, "On no other issue of the war did the Secretary of War and Chief of Staff [Marshall] differ so completely with the Commander-in-Chief."[77] On July 26, Marshall told Eisenhower he was to command the North African landing under a new code name—TORCH. His staff was to come from the ROUNDUP planning staff, and all thoughts of invading France were dropped.[78] On August 1, Dill cabled Churchill that the Americans had abandoned ROUNDUP in 1943 as a result of the preparations for TORCH and suggested that Churchill not argue the point.[79]

As Churchill had hoped, Roosevelt still refused to divert resources to the Pacific, but the threat to do so still existed. In fact, the threat was carried out, and during the last six months of 1942 an increasing number of airplanes were diverted to the Pacific. At the British Chiefs of Staff meeting on November 20, 1942, Mountbatten reported that Eisenhower had informed him that Marshall would send no more American troops to Britain until the British sponsored a plan to attack France on a set date, regardless of a "crack in German morale."[80]

While the movement of American troops to Britain practically ceased, the Pacific received additional divisions.[81] The Pacific policy was definitely changed from a defensive stance to an offensive drive. During the first half of 1942, limited instructions were sent to MacArthur and Admiral Chester Nimitz: (1) to hold bases essential to maintain communication with Australia; (2) to support operations that would contain the Japanese; (3) to defend North America; (4) to protect sea and air communications in the Pacific; and (5) to prepare for major amphibious operations in the future.[82] These instructions were altered radically by a joint directive of Marshall and King on July 2, 1942, placing the Southwest Pacific forces under MacArthur and the remainder of the Pacific forces under Nimitz on the offensive. The defeat of the Japanese navy at the Battle of Midway had deprived it of striking power, thereby giving the initiative to the Americans.[83] The United States Navy was directed to take the islands of Tulagi and Guadalcanal and, despite some delay, the landing was made on August 7, beginning a lengthy battle of attrition that lasted until February 1943. The Japanese committed 36,000 men and lost 24,000. The Americans sent in 60,000 and lost 5,850 killed and wounded plus many more sick. Four American divisions (First Marine, Second Marine, Americal, and Twenty-fifth Infantry) were worn down but obtained valuable combat experience. They had learned how to defeat the Japanese in the jungle.[84]

In the interim, acting under the instructions of July 2, 1942, MacArthur began the bloody task of taking Buna on the northern coast of New Guinea from the Japanese. The campaign was a long and bloody one that burned up two American divisions (Thirty-second and Forty-first) along with elements of four Australian divisions (Fifth, Sixth, Seventh, and Eleventh) with questionable results. The objective of both campaigns was to envelop the Japanese base at Rabaul.[85] Rabaul was bypassed and neutralized from the air later in the war.

What had caused the abrupt turnabout in American policy in the Pacific? Stimson wrote in his diary on July 10, 1942, "As the British won't go through with what they agreed to, we will turn our backs on them and take up the war with Japan."[86] The British were not the only ones who turned the hoped-for single thrust of Allied strategy into a diverse random spray of enterprises around the globe. Admiral King, General MacArthur, and Roosevelt were not certain that the Americans would complete BOLERO, the plan to move a million troops to England, and be ready to invade France in 1943.[87] Admiral King placed unrelenting pressure for more resources and broader directives for the navy in the Pacific.[88] King supported ROUNDUP only as long as there was promise that the European war would come to a quick close, permitting a shift of forces to the Pacific. When this hope for a quick victory faded, so did his support for all-out concentration on ROUNDUP.[89]

Another major influence on the shift to the Pacific policy was Roosevelt, who as commander in chief made the major policy decisions, sometimes against the judgment of his military advisers.[90] Roosevelt listened carefully to public opinion and to Congress and tempered his decisions according to what he heard. The public wanted action in the Pacific. Corregidor fell in May 1942, and, despite the demand for revenge, the military forces were doing nothing. Although Roosevelt rejected the complete abandonment of the European theater in favor of the Pacific, he permitted an ever increasing diversion of resources to that area during 1942 and 1943.[91]

Others contributed to the diversion from the main thrust. MacArthur was the hero of the right-wing press, and his desire for more forces to begin his battle back to the Philippines had widespread support. The Russians were pressing for immediate action and were not favorably disposed toward waiting almost a year before the Western Allies would even begin to tackle large forces of Germans. Everyone seemed to have an alternate to the attack on France in 1943. The decision to invade North Africa was prompted by political motives to give the Russians and the American public immediate action.

On military grounds, the Allies should have focused on France. The Western Allies would have the ability to conduct a quick, clean campaign in Europe in 1943, which the Germans fully expected but were incapable of stopping in view of their commitments to the battle front in Russia. Instead, the energy of the European forces was siphoned off into a campaign that could only end in the Alps and offered no serious threat to the German industrial vitals. Although promises were made that ROUNDUP was still on, the Americans were not convinced and turned their attention to the Pacific. The loss of the time gained by prodigious production and training efforts in 1941 and 1942 gave the Germans an additional year to build up their defenses and made the final invasion more costly. The delay left the Russians to fight the greater part of the German army for an additional year. Even though TORCH was politically wise and offered such advantages as shorter shipping routes, release of the Eighth Army for other tasks, and battle experience to American divisions, these gains could have been turned to the accomplishment of the thrust to the heart that would have finished Germany. Such was not the case, and even more time was frittered away at Casablanca.

2

THE DIVERSION

TO SICILY

The successful entry into North Africa (TORCH) should have been followed by a quick return to planning the crucial campaign—the invasion of France (ROUNDUP). Instead, one diversion led to another, and the conquest of Sicily was the logical next step, inasmuch as the troops would be in Tunisia less than a hundred miles across a calm sea from Sicily. The first matter, however, was to clean up North Africa, a task that proved to be more difficult than expected.

The decision to land in North Africa had been supported by the false belief that the French would not resist[1] and therefore the campaign would be relatively easy compared to the alternative cross-channel invasion. The British argued that invasion of France could not be considered for many reasons: the German strength in France, the lack of landing craft, the poor state of training of the American troops, the inadequacy of Allied tanks and aircraft compared to German equipment, the lack of logistical support, and the excellent German communications system in France compared to the relative isolation of North Africa.[2] (The facts and fancies of each of these issues will be discussed in later chapters.)

The struggle in North Africa proved that conditions were no easier there than in France, and yet the Allies succeeded in Africa. Until the cease-fire was called by Jean Louis Darlan, some of the Vichy French troops fought tenaciously. The Vichy French launched a naval sortie at Casablanca with cruisers and destroyers, supported by the guns of the battleship *Jean Bart,* that was a far more powerful action than any launched by the Germans in June 1944. The Allies were able to land on the beaches in North Africa, although they were physically poorer than those in Normandy and the surf was worse. Furthermore, the Germans had good communications in North Africa and were able to move troops to Tunisia faster than the Allies could muster strength during the early months.

The North African campaign validated American strength and capability in the face of tough opposition. The attack proved our logistical capability—compared to a short trip across the channel of perhaps fifty miles, the ships were loaded in Scotland and in England more than fifteen hundred miles away and in the United States three thousand miles away from the North African coast. The state of American training was better than the British had maintained. The Americans fought well, except for the setback at Kasserine described in chapter 13. In succeeding invasions, new divisions with no battle experience were used for the initial landings, proving that combat experience was not essential. In fact, the

American infantrymen had far more training than either the German riflemen in North Africa or those occupying France at the time. In regard to equipment, although the German tanks were marginally superior to the British tanks in 1942, they were not superior to the American tanks. The American Shermans were equal to the Panzer IV German tank in 1942, were better than the Panzer III, and were inferior only in gun power and armor to a handful of the Tigers that were still suffering from mechanical difficulties.

In summary, although military reasons were given for the rejection of the invasion of France in 1943 and the substitution of the November 1942 invasion of North Africa, the true reasons were political—the need for a quick, easy victory. One can understand Roosevelt's desire in those crisis-laden months to take the spectacular early plunge in North Africa with its assumed low risk rather than to invade France in September of 1942 or the spring of 1943—a high risk but a more decisive play.[3]

The planning of TORCH did not proceed without a hitch. A great deal of controversy arose over where the landings should be made. The Americans advocated a cautious approach on the Atlantic, fearing that the Germans might come down through Spain and cut the communications behind a landing in the Mediterranean (a move the Germans indeed were planning). The British urged landings as far east as possible to prevent the Germans from taking the major port of Tunis and using it as a depot for the defense of the crucial narrows between Sicily and Tunisia.[4]

Marshall did not have much concern for the Mediterranean. Once that route had been opened to British shipping, there would be little need for it because by that time the war in Africa would be over. The Germans could close the Mediterranean at any time by invading Spain (operation GISELLA, which they had carefully planned even to the selection of the units to take part). The Mediterranean was useful only for an attack on Sicily and Italy that, even if all went well, could only end futilely at the mountain barriers separating Italy from Germany, which indeed was the final outcome. Marshall argued for the safe course—the occupation of the west coast of Africa followed by a gradual move east with the help of the French. That plan would have satisfied Roosevelt's need for a "no-risk" invasion and guaranteed that American troops would enter battle with no fear of loss. The British were more concerned with a rapid cleanup of Algeria and Tunisia (before the Germans could react), followed by an attack on one of the Mediterranean islands.[5] The result was a compromise with strong landings made by American troops on the Atlantic and landings by the British, with some American aid, at Algiers and Oran, but not far enough east to seize Tunisia before its acquisition by the Germans.

Even before the landing, the Allied leaders were considering the next move after North Africa was conquered. The agreement to begin the offensive there had come only after agonizing months of discussion by means of transatlantic flights and a flurry of cables lasting from ARCADIA in December 1941 until the final decision on July 24, 1942. The next objective could not wait for a similar period of seven months of debate. The new plan, however, would have to take into consideration the American disagreement regarding North Africa that indicated their lack of interest in the Mediterranean. As a protest against TORCH (which Marshall believed was merely diverting attention from the main theater), the Americans weakened the buildup plan (BOLERO) in order to support the Pacific operations beginning in August 1942.[6] Another factor to be considered was the attitude of the Russians if the West refused to attack the Germans.

By the fall of 1942, the tide was turning against the Axis. General Bernard L. Montgomery was ready to follow up the victory in Egypt at Alam El Halfa in September. In the Pacific, Guadalcanal was being secured despite bitter Japanese resistance; and at Stalingrad, the Russians had halted the German Sixth Army. In view of this favorable situation, in late October 1942, Churchill drafted a policy for the future conduct of the war. The document gradually evolved into a paper numbered COS (42) 345 that outlined Churchill's strategy and eventually formed the basis for the decision at Casablanca to continue the war in the Mediterranean. The draft that he sent to Major General Hastings L. Ismay, Chief of Staff of the Minister of Defense, on October 22 indicated that Churchill was having second thoughts about France. He wrote in paragraph five, "Personally I have never believed that the assault on Pas de Calais where the enemy is strongest could be done either in 1942 or 1943" unless German morale cracked. Therefore, he had opposed SLEDGEHAMMER (the 1942 invasion plan) and had promoted instead the attack on North Africa to delay matters. The delay in ROUNDUP was not expected to break faith with the Russians because, as Churchill wrote, Molotov knew even in June 1942 that the April 1, 1943, date for ROUNDUP was "obvious moonshine."[7] Seeking to reinforce his argument, Churchill added in longhand to this paragraph that the tides and beaches on the Pas de Calais were unfavorable and that the ports were shallow, mined, or destroyed.

In paragraph seven, Churchill noted that the Russians were ignorant of amphibious warfare and were "wilfully closing their eyes to the German strength on the French northern coast" while continuing to clamor for a second front. Churchill recommended that the Western Allies clear North Africa, open up the Mediterranean with air cover, "and attack the under-belly of the Axis at whatever may be the softest point"—Sicily, southern Italy, perhaps Sardinia, the French Riviera, or, with Turkish aid, the Balkans. He predicted, "our war from now on till the summer of 1943 will be waged in the Mediterranean theater" but added that BOLERO must go on "to pin down large forces on the northern coasts of France."[8]

The Chiefs of Staff made some significant changes in the printed version of Churchill's paper COS (42) 345, dated October 24. More technical reasons were substituted for Churchill's personal belief regarding the decision to delay. Instead of "personally I have never believed" (which was stricken), a sentence was inserted in paragraph one regarding the shortage of landing craft. In paragraph two, to the sentence, "It soon became apparent in 1942" that the operation would not have a chance of success unless the Germans cracked, was added,

"Personally I was sure that the newly raised U.S. formations . . . and British forces could not establish themselves on the beaches . . . in the teeth of well-organized German opposition." These few phrases show that three of the reasons for delaying the invasion were added to the basic documents as afterthoughts. Had Churchill believed on October 22 that the reasons for the delay of the invasion were lack of landing craft, poor state of American training, and certainty that the Germans would be "well-organized" in April 1943, these three reasons would have been included in his earlier draft. Instead, these words were added later to improve the sound of the paper. Likewise, in paragraph seven, the phrase about Molotov knowing that the date April 1, 1943, was moonshine was changed to state that when Molotov returned in June 1942, he knew "exactly how we stood about invading Northern France."[9]

Churchill commented that the printed version was too long, repetitious, and badly written. The major points remained, however. Shipping was considered the problem requiring first priority to preserve Britain's lifeline and to permit the United States to bring in her army. According to Churchill, the British and the Americans could not challenge the bulk of the German army on land. A large army could not be established in France "until German military power has been undermined" with bombing and by the Russian army. Because the Russian front was the greatest single contributor to the wearing down of Germany, Churchill believed that the West must stimulate the Russians with supplies, by attacking the Germans by sea and air, and possibly by providing direct military aid to the Russians in the Caucasus. Churchill's plan was that only limited amphibious operations would take place in 1943 in the Mediterranean with Sardinia or Sicily as the target.[10]

While the plan was being discussed in London, a British mission was in Washington discussing production goals for 1943 with the American Chiefs of Staff. The leader of the mission was Lyttelton, who was strongly opposed to the second front. On November 7, Lyttelton wrote to Churchill asking permission to show plan COS 345 to the Americans as the strategic basis for production schedules. Churchill refused permission on the grounds that the plan was not yet perfected, nor had it been approved by the War Cabinet. Much to Churchill's dismay, Dill, on his own authority, showed a digest of COS 345 to the American Chiefs of Staff. Churchill was concerned that the plan as it stood in November was "in my opinion, unduly negative" because the West would not fight the Germans except on an island separated from the German lines of communication by salt water. The islands mentioned in the plan, Sicily and Sardinia, he felt were insignificant for a year's effort. Churchill wanted to include Italy and possibly the Balkans as targets. What was needed, he wrote, was "a very large scale offensive on the under-belly of the Axis in 1943. . . . Can we really expect the Russians will be content with our lying down like this all during 1943." Churchill felt that a greater attempt should be made.[11]

When Churchill demanded that the digest of the less aggressive plan COS 345 be withdrawn from the American Chiefs of Staff,[12] Dill responded that the

Americans had found "little to which they did not agree." Dill thought it was good that the Americans knew the thinking of the British and that Churchill should soon propose a formal strategy statement to the Americans before any misunderstanding developed in the Mediterranean.[13] When he saw the digest that Dill had prepared, Churchill's comments were devastating. With reference to Dill's stretching the Germans, Churchill commented that perhaps the Germans should be invited to Dakar because "this would certainly 'stretch' them. . . . Are we going to tell the Russians that the policy of 'Keep salt water between us and the German Army' will rule in 1944 as well as in 1943." Churchill stated that it was entirely contrary to Britain's plan to say that no overseas offensive against Germany was contemplated in 1943. Even if the Allies could not invade Europe, he said that "it would be most unwise to state this at present." He believed that not only did the Russians resent doing all the fighting, but the American Pacific school would rejoin: "If this is all they can do in Europe, we must develop our offensive against Japan." He felt that by showing the digest to the Americans "grievous harm has been done."[14]

A far more aggressive plan was needed for 1943 than the one drafted in COS 345 because of pressure for a second front, as well as lack of American support for the Mediterranean strategy and the Russian reaction. Pressure for a second front was growing in Britain. Explaining his position to the House of Commons on November 11, 1942, Churchill gave the classic list of reasons for the delay: a second front against France would require a vast number of landing craft and divisions trained for amphibious warfare, the preparation of which would take time, and the German army in France was as large as the British army in the United Kingdom, excluding the Home Guard. Although Churchill admitted that the Germans were not as well equipped as the British and Americans, he pointed out that the Nazis had many battle-experienced officers as well as "ample weapons of the latest type" and immense fortifications. On top of all that, the weather was unfavorable. He claimed that his promise of a second front to the Russians had deceived the Germans and caused them to hold thirty-three divisions in the West to protect themselves against an invasion.[15] These explanations served to quiet the opposition in Parliament, but the matter was not closed, and a plan of action was needed.

The rate of buildup in England for the invasion of France had been sharply reduced because of the American dissatisfaction with TORCH. Marshall believed that the diversion of troops and war potential from the main theater for the sake of quick, spectacular victories over small bodies of enemy troops in North Africa made good headlines, but did little to bring the war to a close, and as a result, the buildup in England slowed almost to a halt. Ships were available in New York harbor but had no cargoes to carry to England. To fill these ships and clear the warehouses, various miscellaneous items were sent; for example, Britain was supplied with enough frozen beef to last eighteen months. Available, but seldom called on, were the two liners, the *Queen Mary* and the *Queen Elizabeth*, each of which could carry a division of troops across the Atlantic in less than ten days. The delivery rate to the United Kingdom was cut sharply to provide more landing craft for the Pacific. At the same time, the production of landing craft was being reduced in order to build more warships. During the last three months of 1942, only 37,000 American troops went to England. In August 1942, only 100,000 tons were shipped. By December 1942, only the Twenty-ninth Division was left in England as part of a total of 105,000 American troops, less than half the number present in October of that year.[16] Churchill questioned this slowdown of the American buildup in England. He was still committed to the cross-channel attack and demanded an all-out effort to complete the preparations that he had compromised by demanding the diversion to Africa.[17]

On November 20, 1942, the British Chiefs of Staff met to consider the American actions. The BOLERO target had been cut to only 350,000 troops in the United Kingdom by April 1943, with 930,000 promised by August 1943, and there was small chance of the latter goal being achieved. Mountbatten reported that Marshall had told Eisenhower that no more American troops would be sent to the United Kingdom until the Combined Chiefs of Staff approved an attack that was not dependent on the collapse of the German army.[18]

On November 19, 1942, American General Russel P. Hartle, deputy commander of the European theater, wrote to the British Chiefs that accommodations for only 427,000 would be required in 1943.[19] This letter caused a considerable stir, to say the least. Churchill cabled Roosevelt the next day stating that if only 427,000 men were to be sent, it appeared that BOLERO had been abandoned along with the plan for a second front. Churchill reminded Roosevelt that although the attack had been delayed by TORCH, all agreements with Stalin were based only on postponement, not abandonment: "But never was it suggested that we would attempt no second front in Europe in 1943 or even in 1944." Churchill believed that there was still a chance for a 1943 attack if the Russians were successful in the Ukraine or if the Italians collapsed. He suggested coming to America to talk it over.[20] Roosevelt replied on November 26 that ROUNDUP had not been abandoned by the Americans, only that there was doubt about 1943, and that the rate of buildup had been slowed down primarily because of TORCH. Roosevelt said that the defense of Spain required more troops and also that the Americans were "more deeply in the Southwest Pacific than I anticipated." BOLERO would continue, he added, "as our shipping and other resources permit."[21]

At the British Chiefs of Staff meeting on November 25, American General Walter Bedell Smith said that Marshall had telephoned him that day regarding the misunderstanding over the Hartle letter and the 427,000 figure.[22] This call must have assured the Germans that the second front was off for 1943—they were tapping the transatlantic cable and were deciphering the scrambler telephone.

Stalin's concern for the second front became more acute as the Germans pressed at Stalingrad. Stalin expressed realization that the invasion of North Africa might prohibit the French invasion in a cable on November 28, 1942: "I hope that this does not mean that you changed your mind with regard to your promise given in Moscow to establish a second front in Western Europe in the spring of 1943."[23] Previously, Stalin had done little to dissuade the Allies from embarking on the North African side show. Perhaps he was overly confident in September 1942 as his reserves grew and the front held at Stalingrad, believing that he did not need the extensive diversion of Germans demanded by Molotov in May 1942. But by December, Stalin was angry. The British representatives in Moscow sent a long message to Churchill on December 14, 1942, outlining the expected Russian reaction to the refusal to attack in 1943. Unless the British did something quickly "all the old suspicions about the second front will be revived."

> It is impossible to say exactly what form these suspicions may take. It might be anything from a relatively innocuous belief that something had gone wrong with our plans, that as usual we were hopeless bunglers, etc. etc., to a far more danger-ous belief that because threats to Stalingrad and the Caucasus seemed less, we now felt that we need no longer make the same effort, and had even better not make that effort too soon, for fear that the U.S.S.R. might emerge too strong at the end of the war. . . . No suspicion is too fantastic to be entertained.[24]

Churchill wrote on this message that rather than tell Stalin there would be no second front, why not state that we have to work out the time and place? Churchill wrote that the reason for the delay "should be hung on to some plausible peg." Churchill ignored the advice of the Embassy in Moscow to do something and instead suggested that the message be placed "in the locked box." The policy of inventing reasons for the delay was accepted among the British policy makers.[25]

Only because of pressures from the pro-Soviet English, the Americans, and the Russians did Churchill try to work out a more aggressive plan for 1943. On November 14, he sent a plan to Eisenhower for comment that included as objec-tives the clearing of the North African shore, the opening of the Mediterranean to Allied shipping, and then a "strike at the under-belly of the Axis in effective strength and in the shortest time."[26] Italy was to be the target for 1943 and perhaps northern France later in the year. To his Chiefs of Staff, Churchill wrote on November 18, 1942, that TORCH was not a substitute for a second front; it was only a thirteen-division effort, and the planning for a second front called for forty-eight divisions. Churchill hedged by adding that plans for an attack on France might be dropped if events proved it to be impossible.[27] The first priority was to be the Mediterranean. Churchill wrote on November 29 that invasion along the south coast of France was possible in July 1943 in view of German trouble in the east. "Hitler will not be able to bring back any large force from the east to the west," and German setbacks have "greatly modified and may funda-mentally change the situation."[28]

The British Chiefs of Staff remained conservative. Although they did not intend to abandon "any resolute effort to form a second front in Europe in 1943 if an opportunity occurred" (meaning if the Germans were weakened), the Chiefs believed "that our resources in manpower, shipping, and landing craft are wholly inadequate to build up 'TORCH', re-open the Mediterranean for military traffic, and carry out the operations which are contemplated in the Mediterranean next spring and summer, in addition to 'ROUNDUP' in July, 1943." They felt that the Allies did not have enough strength to "fight 40 German divisions now in France, apart from other divisions which they might be able to bring from elsewhere." Even if the Mediterranean projects were given up, there would not be enough resources to attack France and certainly not enough to do both. The British Chiefs reminded Churchill that the American Chiefs had assumed that ROUNDUP was off for 1943 when TORCH was adopted on July 24, 1942.[29]

The front-line generals were divided in November 1942 on the issue of the second front. Eisenhower's reply to Churchill's Mediterranean plan favored Sardinia over Sicily because it would be easier and was a more strategic location.[30] Montgomery wanted to go directly from Tunis to the channel coast and wrote to Brooke on November 27, 1942: "This obviates all difficulties of shipping, air-support and so on: we should be developing the offensive from a firm base. It would be costly but it would bring off a fight with the Germans. I am quite certain that the way to deal with the German is to face up to him in battle and fight him. . . . Given a large number of Americans I believe the invasion of Western Europe could be brought off successfully next summer about June, when the weather is good."[31] Some of the British generals were "far from convinced of the fighting value of the United States Army."[32] German resistance in Tunisia had discouraged Brooke, and, because there was no end in sight in December, the British Chiefs of Staff could not envision bringing the troops back to England in time for a summer attack.[33]

Churchill still did not accept this line of reasoning, according to his memo of December 2, 1942, in which he summarized the military position as follows. In North Africa, there were twenty-two British, American, and French divisions plus nine divisions in the Middle East, for a total of thirty-one. In the United Kingdom, there were fifteen British divisions available for the attack, and twenty American divisions could be brought over by August or September 1943. Fifteen more U.S. divisions were available in the United States, for a total of eighty-one divisions. Against these forces, the Germans had thirty-three divisions standing opposite Britain in northern France, and eleven of these had been withdrawn to protect southern France. He felt that some offensive action must be taken.[34] This memo was printed as COS (42) 429 for discussion by the Chiefs of Staff on December 3, 1942. It urged the prompt conclusion of the Tunisian effort by March 1943, followed by the occupation of Sardinia in June and the return of the landing craft to England by June 30. He noted that rehearsals for the invasion could be held in July and the actual attack launched in August or September. He sincerely believed that if no effort were made in 1943, there was danger that Stalin would make a separate peace with Hitler.[35]

The Chiefs began to make changes in the memo. Brooke increased the number of German divisions from thirty-three to forty. (The total in September was actually thirty-three, but by November, six more divisions were beginning to form, increasing the number to thirty-nine.) In other papers, Brooke said forty or forty-one. (The Third SS Panzer and 161st Infantry Divisions came from Russia for refitting in November, raising the total to forty-one.) The quality of all of the divisions, however, was very poor, and southern France was occupied by ad hoc divisions formed from the training units in France.

Brigadier Ian Jacob, the military secretary to the War Cabinet, made a change in language from "are also being compelled to find 4 to 6 divisions for Italy" to "They will probably be compelled to find." Jacob noted that the Germans had not yet moved the divisions: "It is our estimate of what the enemy will almost certainly have to move."[36] Though not stated, Jacob and Churchill knew of the orders to the divisions to move, but felt it was not wise to state this knowledge as fact in a document that would be circulated widely. The information came from intercepted German messages relayed to Churchill via a series of intelligence reports called ULTRA described in chapter 12.

The Chiefs of Staff discussion on December 3, 1942, was revealing. Churchill maintained that the Allies must engage the Germans, at least in Sardinia, and through bombing. He had told Stalin that there would be an offensive in 1943. Brooke said that Churchill, while in Moscow, had held out North Africa as the alternative to France. Churchill suggested "that the German strength in France was over-rated. It should not be judged merely by the number of Divisions." He did not think that the invasion would be formidable. Brooke countered with figures showing that the British could provide only ten to fourteen divisions and the Americans could bring no more than fifteen, which was not enough. Both Churchill and Lord Frederick Leathers, minister of War Transport, saw the Pacific as a threat—the Americans had the bulk of their shipping there, and it was being "wastefully used." The Pacific was receiving all of the new American construction, and the Americans had even failed to meet their share of PQ 20, the convoy to Russia.[37] Discussion continued on COS 429 for eleven days. On December 14, Churchill had about given up hope for the second front in 1943: "I am as you know at present thinking along both lines, 'Brimstone' [Sardinia] and 'Roundup,' but it will almost certainly be necessary to choose. Personally, I should only choose 'Brimstone' etc. if I were satisfied after intense efforts that 'Roundup', was impossible in 1943."[38]

Finally, on December 15, 1942, the Chiefs stated their views in COS (42) 452 that the maximum buildup of forces in Britain in 1943 would be thirteen British divisions and twelve American divisions. To build up such a force, the following would have to be given up: (1) any major increase in the bomber force; (2) attacks on Sardinia and Sicily or any other Mediterranean target; (3) aid to Russia; (4) any threat to Italy; and (5) an amphibious assault in Burma to aid China. Even omitting all of these goals would provide not the forty-eight divisions promised in the original ROUNDUP, but only twenty-five divisions, and the earliest date would be August 1943. The Chiefs recommended instead: (1) attacks on Sardinia, then Sicily, Corsica, or the toe of Italy; (2) increased bomber offensive; (3) a threat to invade France to pin down the German divisions; (4) sending two more convoys to Russia before the Mediterranean demands removed the ships; (5) bringing Turkey into the war; (6) launching ANAKIM in Burma to help the Chinese; and (7) still have twenty British and American divisions available in England by late summer 1943 to exploit any advantage if the Germans suffered a setback.[39]

The Chiefs met with the War Cabinet on December 16 to discuss both COS (42) 429 and 452 and how to convince the Americans that a second front could not be launched in 1943. Those present were Churchill, Anthony Eden, Brooke, Sir Dudley Pound, Sir Charles F. A. Portal, Mountbatten, and Ismay. Brooke made an elaborate presentation with maps and charts, indicating that limited capacity of British railways and ports would limit the inflow of American forces to 120 ships per month. Meanwhile, he went on, the Germans would be able to use the railways to move many divisions from east to west to France, but could move only a limited number of divisions to Italy with only the two rail lines. Rail service to Greece was reduced to one single track at Nish. Therefore, Brooke advocated knocking out Italy "and perhaps enter[ing] the Balkans."

Pound wanted American naval aid to fight submarines, but said, "There was a tendency at present for all American new construction to disappear into the Pacific." Eden wanted an attack on France in 1943, but, depressed by the figures, was convinced that the Mediterranean strategy was the only possible way. Churchill still wanted ROUNDUP but felt that there weren't enough forces. He still questioned the Chiefs' figures because the Americans had been able to land two million men in France in five months in 1918. If the Americans refused to provide more forces, however, he feared that ROUNDUP had to be abandoned. Sicily was to be taken, followed by Italy, "preparing the way for entry into the Balkans and bringing Turkey into the war on our side." The final decision was to be made after Roosevelt sent his ideas over; however, general agreement on COS 452 (which was not to be shown to the Americans) would form the basis of plans for 1943.[40] On December 16, Brooke expressed relief that he had convinced Churchill to forego any thought of attacking France in 1943.[41]

On December 23, the British received JCS 167/2 (later numbered CCS 135, December 26, 1942) from the American Chiefs recommending a different plan—that the Allies go on the defensive in the Mediterranean and transfer excess forces to Britain as part of the buildup for a 1943 landing in northern France; the building up of an American air force in Britain, keeping Turkey neutral, supplying Russia, attacking in Burma to aid the Chinese, and maintaining the initiative in the Pacific.[42] Marshall was still intent on a second front in 1943. Churchill, however, objected to the idea of transferring forces from Africa to Britain and suspected that the phrase "consistent with needs of other theaters" used by the American Chiefs meant that the United States would give the Pacific priority.[43]

The War Cabinet continued to discuss the plans for the next four days, making minor changes. Churchill deleted any favorable references to daylight bombing in the British proposals, hoping that the Americans could be converted to night bombing. Aid to Russia was restored to the British proposals. Sicily was defined as the target, and Sardinia was dropped. Lord Leathers requested that the idea that the British ports could not handle the buildup of American forces be deleted.[44]

From Washington, Dill cabled that the implications of the American proposal meant greater priority for the Pacific. He said that already the Pacific allocation of LSTs and LCI(L)s by June 1943 was greater than the total requirement of the Sardinia plan and indicated that the Americans were set against the Mediterranean strategy because "it is a too indirect approach." He indicated that the Americans wanted to close down the Mediterranean after Tunisia was taken and concentrate on northern France.[45]

The final position of the British Chiefs and Churchill was contained in COS (42) 466, December 31, 1942, which was, in essence, the strategy adopted later at Casablanca—defeat the U-boats, bomb Germany, attack Sicily, then attack Italy, send aid to Russia, and limit operations in the Pacific. Only on the last item did the Americans change the intent of the British at Casablanca.[46]

A conference of the three heads of state was needed, but Stalin refused to leave Russia at a crucial time because he, in fact, commanded the army. Therefore, Roosevelt and Churchill met without Stalin at Casablanca. The American party was small and divided internally over the issue of the Pacific campaign. Needless to say, they were not well prepared. The British, on the other hand, came with a large staff complete with a headquarters ship to provide facilities for an ULTRA team and instant communication links. The British had worked hard and long preparing their papers and conferring with Churchill.[47]

The decisions made at Casablanca in January 1943 would be crucial for the future conduct of the war. To adhere to the concept of defeating Germany first, the decision must be made to concentrate all energy against the Germans in France. The further flow of troops to the Pacific could have been stopped and supplies reduced to a minimum for the troops already there. Troops in Africa could have been returned to England and the invasion launched with thoroughly trained British and American forces.[48] But Churchill was no longer convinced of the potentiality of ROUNDUP and, as we have seen, had turned his mind to the Mediterranean. His change of heart was explained on the basis of the military situation—lack of ships, poor weapons, and German strength.

The British claimed at Casablanca that the submarines were still a dangerous menace and that concerted effort was needed to control them. Because of the heavy losses to the U-boats, they felt it would be impossible to bring enough men and supplies across the Atlantic for a major invasion. The British also argued that insufficient landing craft, tanks, and divisions were available to match the powerful German army in France. Therefore, General Brooke urged instead that the Allies strike in the south at the weakest point in the Continental fortress.[49]

When General Marshall continued to press for ROUNDUP at Casablanca, Brooke countered with planning studies, indicating that no more than twenty-one divisions could be landed in France during 1943 and that these would be overwhelmed by the forty-four German divisions already there. At a meeting on January 2, 1943, the British Chiefs of Staff had estimated that as many as twenty-five divisions could be landed, a figure that Brooke revised downward to discourage Marshall. Brooke presented a fairly accurate count of the number of divisions in France, but said little about their quality. The British planners conceded, however, that enough landing craft were available for the initial assault of six divisions.[50]

The availability of a maximum of twenty-one Allied divisions seems conservative in view of the actual placement of thirteen divisions in Sicily in fewer than thirty days, and several months later, sixteen divisions in Italy in about thirty days. Given a reasonable error in staff planning, Brooke's twenty-one division maximum remains an incredible miscalculation which well-trained British staff officers seldom made in logistical matters. How could they honestly have erred so badly in underestimating the Allied ability to land troops and in overestimating the number and quality of Germans who would oppose them?

In contrast to the large staff Churchill brought to Casablanca, Marshall had only a few officers, and he had no intelligence service to warn of German weakness. Nevertheless, he believed an invasion of France was possible by the fall of 1943.[51] Despite his optimism, Marshall was forced to compromise, and, in exchange for British approval of Pacific offensives, he accepted the British plans to go forward in the Mediterranean by attacking Sicily.[52] Roosevelt and Churchill presumably accepted the plan presented to them by the Combined Chiefs of Staff, but Churchill had much to do with its formation.

Sicily was chosen because the troops and supplies were idling, and the leaders feared taking the Germans head-on in France. The British believed that the Germans would be weak in Sicily, because of the difficulty of moving troops to the island under Allied air attack. There were few railroads south of Naples, and the Strait of Messina created an additional bottleneck. After Sicily was taken, an attack on Italy would knock her out of the war and deprive Germany of the fifty-four Italian divisions being used for occupation duties.

In reality, however, there was no strategic objective. Italy was ideally suited for defense with its many mountains capped off by the Alps. The ultimate goal was pointless because removing Italy from the war would have only a negligible effect.[53]

Casablanca was a trade-off—the British wanted to stay in the Mediterranean, and several American leaders had vested interests elsewhere. Admiral King wanted to go on the offensive in the Pacific, and General Henry H. Arnold wanted a major air offensive against Germany. General Marshall alone was a proponent of the cross-channel attack.[54] Casablanca was a series of vague compromises, all of which diverted effort away from Germany toward British interests in the Mediterranean and American interests in the Pacific.[55] The final report was written by British Brigadier Ian Jacob, who was quoted as follows: ''If before the conference he had had to write down what he hoped its decisions would be he could never have written anything so sweeping, comprehensive and favourable to British ideas as in the end he found himself writing. . . . Our ideas had prevailed almost throughout.''[56]

The plan agreed on at Casablanca centered on the reopening of the Mediterranean to make better use of shipping by reducing the length of the voyage to the Middle East and the East. The Mediterranean would also provide air bases from which Germany could be attacked from the South. In addition, the operations in the Mediterranean would distract the Germans and draw some forces from the eastern front. The destruction of Italy was an early objective, compared to the long-term goal of the general reduction of the German potential. The invasion of Sicily would have satisfied all of these objectives, but the further step of invading Italy was left for future conferences.[57]

In return for that shift of emphasis from northern France to the Mediterranean, a comprehensive American plan for offensive action in the Pacific was also approved. The objectives were to retake the Aleutian Islands, to advance northwest from Samoa to protect the line to Australia, to make diversions in the Malay barrier, and to advance through the central Pacific by way of the Marshalls toward Truk and subsequently to capture it. There was to be no advance toward Rabaul unless forces were available to follow through. Operations in Burma were to be carried on to hold China in the war.[58]

The British had no wish to go that far in the Pacific and even opposed operations in Burma as being of no strategic importance. Agreement was finally reached when the British were assured that the program would be carried out with the resources already available in the Pacific and, therefore, would not detract from the needs of the European theater. The plan had been to limit American additions to the Pacific of 250,000 army and air force personnel and 500 planes, plus most of the newly constructed warships and 1,250,000 tons of shipping—a very modest demand. In fact, during 1943 much more was sent. The Americans added five additional divisions (Sixth, Seventh, First Cavalry, Thirty-third and Third Marine) to the nine army and two marine divisions already there.[59]

The unfortunate result of the Casablanca Conference was that the previous concept of concentrated effort toward the defeat of Germany was abandoned. In its place was a strategy that served only to divide Allied efforts, diluting our forces on every front to the point that little of any substance was achieved in 1943.

As the British had predicted, the conservative approach to the North African landing, placing most of the troops too far west, stretched out the campaign far longer than planned. The Germans had the time to bring in new divisions from France, and the Italians supplied additional forces. The methodical advance of Montgomery across Libya gave Rommel ample opportunity to withdraw into Tunisia. As a result, the battle for Tunisia developed into a stalemate in early 1943. The Americans continued to pour additional unneeded divisions into North Africa. The American Thirty-sixth and Forty-fifth Infantry Divisions arrived shortly after the Axis forces surrendered. The First Armored, Second Armored,

First Infantry, Ninth Infantry, Thirty-fourth Infantry, and Third Infantry were all in North Africa, making a total of eight American divisions present or in transit by the end of the campaign.

The British also had an enormous force in the Mediterranean and in the Middle East: the British First Army, comprised of the IX Corps (First Armored, Sixth Armored, Seventh Armored, and Forty-sixth Infantry) and the V Corps (First Infantry, Fourth Infantry, Seventy-eighth Infantry); and the British Eighth Army, comprised of the XXX Corps (New Zealand Division, Fifty-first Infantry, Fiftieth Infantry, Fifty-sixth Infantry, and First French Infantry) and the X Corps. In Libya, Egypt, and the Middle East there were the Tenth Armored, Eighth Indian Infantry, Sixth South African Armored, Fifth Infantry, four tank brigades, and twelve infantry brigades. The total was equal to six armored divisions and sixteen infantry divisions. In addition, there were three infantry divisions in the French XIX Corps, plus the eight American divisions, making a grand total of thirty-three divisions available.

All of that might was opposed by what equaled seven German divisions (334th, Fifteenth Panzer, Hermann Goering Panzer, Tenth Panzer, Twenty-first Panzer, 164th Infantry, and Ninetieth Panzer Grenadier) and five Italian units, none of which was equal to a division. The German divisions averaged about five thousand men per unit, except the Hermann Goering and the Tenth Panzer, which had ten thousand men each. In other words, thirty-three Allied divisions were available to fight the enemy strength of two German divisions, five reinforced regiments of Germans, and five regiments of Italians. Needless to say, when the British finally gave the order for the troops to attack the Germans in Tunisia, the contest was over within a few days.

Although taking unnecessary risks is not ordinarily sanctioned, the measure of safety used in the Tunisian cleanup was apparently excessive. Rather than turning the well-trained, experienced forces in Tunisia to the major objective, France and then Germany, the main thrust in 1943 was made in the Mediterranean, and the campaign bogged down in the Appenine Mountains in Italy. The Pacific was given limited resources, none of which were used for strategically significant purposes until early in 1944. MacArthur nibbled at a few more outposts, and the navy neutralized Rabaul, reducing the distance to Tokyo by only a few miles. The most significant event in the Pacific was the conquest of Tarawa in November 1943. The British, who had seen little strategic value in Burma, pursued that campaign with little enthusiasm. The air attacks on Germany, according to Albert Speer, reduced the potential war production by less than 10 percent. German output was actually greater in 1943 than in 1942. The concern for the antisubmarine war was not a grand strategic objective, but rather a matter of continuing procedures that had already shown evidence of coping with the menace.

Considering the enormous military potential at the disposal of the British and American leaders, little was achieved in 1943. Why was such an indecisive and conservative program of defense adopted? On the political side, the Russians were doing very well in January 1943, and there was no need to risk all to assist them. Nor, on the other hand, were the Germans yet weakened to the point that the Western Allies should have rushed in to pick up the pieces before the Russians took over. Under these conditions, there was little urgency in committing large forces on the Continent. Politically, it appeared wise to sit out 1943 in Europe and clean up the raw edges in the Mediterranean, with the hope that in due course something might develop, such as a German collapse on the eastern front. Meanwhile, the large navies and air force could be given a year to practice their own forms of war to protect the Allies from further territorial losses and to wear down the Axis powers.

3

THE COMPROMISE

OF 1943

Despite the phrase "defeat Germany in 1943," Roosevelt and Churchill opted at Casablanca for a do-little or nothing strategy in 1943. The Mediterranean strategy projected only the conquest of Sicily, and then the situation was to be reviewed again. The hope was that Germany would collapse under the stress of the battle in Russia and the Allied air raids. If not, perhaps France would be invaded in 1944.[1] The TRIDENT Conference in May 1943 continued the policy of procrastination, and for lack of any constructive policy, the Allies began to think of invading Italy. The surrender offer of the Italian government had opened the way for complete involvement in Italy.

The Mediterranean strategy was based on opportunism. The invasion of North Africa had been launched to provide Roosevelt with what he considered a necessary quick military victory in the Atlantic to direct American public opinion away from an overwhelming concern for the Pacific. North Africa offered an easy way of getting some of the available troops into action with minimum effort, minimum risk, a minimum objective, and a minimum possibility of achieving anything substantial. It was also a maximum waste of precious time, which was working against the Western Allies. The opportunists said "we need action, we have some troops, so let's use them in a spectacular manner but with a minimum risk." The answer was North Africa and the "soft underbelly" of Europe.

The Combined Chiefs did not see the Mediterranean strategy as necessarily committing them to the attack on Europe by way of the soft underbelly. Their thinking was more in terms of the Mediterranean providing a theater into which the Germans could be drawn under conditions more favorable to the Allies than those offered by the beaches in northern France.[2] Certainly the Mediterranean offered an ideal opportunity for the British to make use of their navy to dilute the German defenses along an unbelievably long coastline, while the ships enabled the British to strike where they wished. The regrettable aspect of the theory was that the advent of air power and the limited range of 1943 fighter planes severely restricted the areas where an attack might be launched without the help of aircraft carriers. The Germans were able to select a limited number of danger areas and concentrate their forces on the few suitable beaches within range of Allied air bases. The forces gathered to resist the invasions of Sicily and Italy were more concentrated than the forces along the French coast, where there were many choices of beaches and the availability of widespread fighter cover further extended the number of areas.

The Combined Chiefs of Staff were not attuned to the goal of beating the Russians to the Balkans or to Vienna. The American objective was to divert Germans from the Russians, who were in need of help during the summer of 1942.[3] By the time of Casablanca, however, the Russians did not appear as desperately in need of help as they had been six months before. In fact, in January 1943, the Russian tank forces were running rampant in the Ukraine and were closing in on the skeleton of the German Sixth Army around Stalingrad. Except for the brilliant work of Field Marshal Erich von Manstein in February and March of 1943 in the Ukraine, the Russians could have held their gains in the South and launched their attack against the Dnieper River many months sooner. As the planners met in Casablanca, the Russians looked stronger than ever and had little need of any sacrificial aid.

At Casablanca there had been persistent pressure by Admiral King to divert more resources to the Pacific. The obvious defeat of the American plan for an invasion of France in 1943 left General Marshall, its major proponent, less resistant to this diversion. Part of the Casablanca compromise had been that if the British had their way with the invasion of Sicily, the Americans would be permitted more aggressive action in the Pacific. General Brooke thought that the offensive that followed was beyond the terms of the agreement.[4]

The Americans had great plans for the Pacific. In late February 1943 in San Francisco, Admiral King met with Admiral Chester Nimitz, commander of the naval forces in the Pacific. The meeting followed a speech by Roosevelt on February 12, 1943, in which he objected to the "inching" from island to island in the Pacific and advocated bolder strokes.[5] As King and Nimitz reviewed the situation, the Japanese were being cleared from Guadalcanal, Task I in the program. The next step, Task II, was seizure of the northeast part of New Guinea, which was MacArthur's job. Task III was a joint venture combining MacArthur's forces and those of Nimitz to take the central point of the Japanese strength, the fortress of Rabaul, located on the eastern end of the island of New Britain.

In preparation for this task, Admiral William F. Halsey, commander of the South Pacific theater, planned to work his way up the Solomon Islands toward Rabaul, while MacArthur proceeded from the west by way of New Guinea. After taking Rabaul, the combined force would strike toward the northeast to cut Japan from the East Indies.

In Australia, MacArthur had completed his part of this plan called ELKTON, but had not agreed with the concept. Adding another attacking force from the central Pacific under Nimitz to those under his and Halsey's command would require considerable juggling of troops. The attacks by sea would be costly in warships and merchant shipping and would have to be conducted without the support of land-based aircraft. For these reasons, MacArthur deemed the plan unwise and substituted his own plan—RENO.

RENO called for the capture of Rabaul, as did ELKTON, and then turning directly about to attack westward along the northern coast of New Guinea and eventually approaching the Philippines on the island of Mindanao. The remainder of the East Indies would be neutralized, while all effort was concentrated in the Philippines.[6]

Nimitz was not in complete agreement either. He feared the bold strokes advocated by King because of the remaining strength of the Japanese air bases in the Gilberts and Marshalls. American fighter bases were still too far in the rear, and the army had not provided as many aircraft as had been promised. Nimitz also feared the power of the Japanese ground forces, which he believed might recapture islands not strongly garrisoned and protected. Rather than drive for the heart at that time, Nimitz preferred to concentrate on the submarine war against Japanese shipping and air attacks.[7]

King had grander ideas and demanded assaults on the islands leading to Rabaul. He promised to obtain more army planes and bring to the Pacific all navy planes not needed for the antisubmarine warfare in the Atlantic. King pointed out that the Americans had to maintain the initiative as the best defense. The Joint Chiefs of Staff had provided resources for an attack, and attack they would.[8]

The matter was resolved in a high-level meeting in Washington in March. All of the Pacific theaters were represented at the Pacific Military Conference. To take Rabaul the planners had estimated would require twenty-two divisions and two regiments, plus forty-five air groups, but only fifteen divisions and two regiments and twenty-some air groups were available in March 1943. Therefore, on March 21, 1943, the Joint Chiefs of Staff decided to neutralize Rabaul by air and bypass it. A circle of islands were taken around Rabaul during 1943 to provide air bases and to isolate the Japanese fortress. Meanwhile, MacArthur turned his attention to the westward drive toward the Philippines, while the navy independently began preparations for the island-hopping course across the central Pacific—two nearly parallel drives toward the China coast.[9]

The British viewed the increasing scale of diversion to the Pacific with alarm. After the King-Nimitz meeting in San Francisco, Brooke noted in his diary a concern about the preparation of new plans for offensives in the Pacific, which he blamed on the visit of Madame Chiang Kai-shek to the United States in February. He believed that her influence was the basis for the moves to seek ways to help China. Already on February 17, Brooke saw that something had gone wrong with the planned buildup in England because only fifteen thousand Americans had arrived since January 1 out of a scheduled eighty thousand. These fifteen thousand had come on British ships while American ships went to the Pacific.[10]

Throughout the period between February 17 and April 15, Brooke's diary contains entries about the American bad faith in breaking the Casablanca agreement and neglecting the buildup in Britain in favor of further aid to the Pacific. The Americans were even shipping material to the French at the cost of their own buildup, which Brooke saw as part of Marshall's tactic to cut off American participation in the Mediterranean. To Brooke, the real culprit was Admiral King, who was diverting shipping, landing craft, and equipment to the East under the guise of merely holding Japan.[11]

Meanwhile, Stalin was running into difficulty in the Ukraine. The Germans had switched twenty fresh divisions from France to Russia, and these divisions had stopped the Russians and driven them back, retaking Kharkov. Brooke refused to acknowledge Stalin's accusations that lack of Allied efforts had enabled Hitler to concentrate all of his forces against Russia. In his diary Brooke wrote: "This was untrue. But in accordance with their normal winter routine, the Germans had merely used their excellent west-to-east communications to rest tired divisions from Russia by exchanging them with fresh ones from France and the Low Countries."[12]

German moves in February and March and the number of so-called "tired divisions," having the same numbers as those captured at Stalingrad, reveal a lack of reality on Brooke's part. The Russians needed at least a show of Allied intent to invade France to force the Germans to keep some divisions in France.

To provide some response to Stalin's prodding, Roosevelt and Churchill wanted to move up the invasion of Sicily to June, but Brooke objected on the grounds that the weather in Tunisia was delaying matters. Tunisia would not be cleared until May 1, according to Eisenhower, who had hoped to delay the next step until July. Marshall suggested that the Allies go on with the Sicily landing before the conclusion of the Tunisian campaign in order to conclude matters in the Mediterranean and get the troops back to England for a late summer attack in France. Though Churchill liked the idea, Brooke thought it "quite mad and quite impossible."[13]

Rather than seeking to close off the Mediterranean, Brooke and Churchill were already discussing the invasion of Italy on April 13, 1943, with the hope of further activity to bring Turkey into the war. Brooke advised moving all available landing craft to the Mediterranean and concentrating all of Britain's effort there.[14]

By May of 1943, another conference of the Combined Chiefs of Staff and the Western leaders was urgently needed to plan the follow-up to Sicily. The conference, known as TRIDENT, opened on the happy note of the conclusion of the Tunisian campaign. The British proposed the immediate occupation of Italy south of Rome after Sicily had been taken. From Italy, landings were to be made on the Dalmatian coast, opening a front in the Balkans and bringing Turkey into the war. These two fronts would divert German troops from the West and prepare the way for the 1944 attack in France.[15]

General Marshall, however, was taking a very hard line, demanding that seven divisions be returned to England from the Mediterranean and that May 1, 1944, be set as the final date for the second front. The loss of the seven divisions would prevent any grandiose schemes in the Mediterranean which Marshall believed would have taken more and more resources and delayed the invasion.[16]

By April 17, 1943, Churchill had abandoned any attempt to make a landing in France in 1943. In a letter to General Ismay suggesting that the planning staff under General Frederick E. Morgan be reassigned, Churchill blamed the Americans for not providing the troops needed, as well as blaming the lack of landing craft and the strength of the Germans. Morgan's staff was to be reduced greatly but utilized for a series of raids, along with a more gradual approach to the projected landing in 1944. All of this activity was to be "wrapped up in a vast scheme of cover and camouflage" to keep the Germans on guard.[17] At the TRIDENT Conference, Churchill further procrastinated and talked of an invasion as soon as there were "reasonable prospects of success," but preferred not to set a date.[18]

At the TRIDENT Conference, Roosevelt also was convinced that the invasion was off. He wanted desperately to continue on the offensive, but saw no chance to attack France. The army in the Mediterranean tempted him, even if he feared that invading Italy would jeopardize an attack in France in 1944, just as North Africa had compromised the attack in 1943.[19]

The reasons for continuing in the Mediterranean centered around three issues: the dangers involved in the major invasion, American preference for dividing the resources with the Pacific, and British hopes for the Balkans. Brooke summarized the conflicting points of view in his diary on May 24, 1943:

May 24th. Washington. To-day we reached the final stages of the Conference, the "Global Statement of our Strategy." We started with a C.O.S. at 9 a.m. to look over our proposals and followed up with a long Combined Meeting at which we still had many different opinions which were only resolved with difficulty.

Our difficulties still depended on our different outlook as regards the Pacific. I still feel that we may write a lot on paper, but that it all has little influence on our basic outlooks which might be classified as under:

(a) King thinks the war can only be won by action in the Pacific at the expense of all other fronts.

(b) Marshall considers that our solution lies in a cross-Channel operation with some twenty or thirty divisions, irrespective of the situation on the Russian front, with which he proposes to clear Europe and win the war.

(c) Portal considers that success lies in accumulating the largest Air Forces possible in England and that then, and then only, success lies assured. . . .

(d) Dudley Pound on the other hand is obsessed with the anti-U-boat warfare and considers that success can only be secured by the defeat of this menace.

(e) Alan Brooke considers that success can only be secured by pressing operations in the Mediterranean to force a dispersal of German forces, help Russia, and thus eventually produce a situation where cross-Channel operations are possible.

(f) And Winston? Thinks one thing at one moment and another the next moment. At times the war may be won by bombing, and all must be sacrificed to it. At others it becomes necessary for us to bleed ourselves dry on the Continent because Russia is doing the same. At others our main effort must be in the Mediterranean directed against Italy or the Balkans alternately, with sporadic desires to invade Norway and "roll up the map in the opposite direction Hitler did." But more often than all he wants to carry out all operations simultaneously, irrespective of shortage of shipping.[20]

The Balkan plan was closest to Churchill's heart. On July 16, 1943, he wrote to General J. C. Smuts, prime minister of South Africa: "The situation in the Balkans is most hopeful . . . we must take Rome and N. Italy and also give succour to the Balkans patriots. In all this there is great hope, provided action is taken worthy of the opportunity. I am confident of a good result, and I shall go all lengths to procure the agreement of our Allies. If not we have ample forces to act by ourselves."[21] Smuts was one of Churchill's closest advisers, if not the closest, and he would not have expressed himself so strongly, threatening even to break Allied unity over the subject, had he not been sincere. Eisenhower, according to his aide, in the summer of 1943, "felt that the Prime Minister was obsessed with the idea of proving to history that invasion of the Continent by way of the Balkans was wise strategy and would repair whatever damage history now records for Churchill's misfortune at the Dardanelles in the last war."[22] Even after the compromise at TRIDENT, Churchill upset the cart by inserting the Balkans as an objective after the fact. Hopkins managed to persuade him to delete it once again before the American military saw it, but this did little to allay American suspicions.[23]

The Germans believed that an amphibious invasion of the Balkans was possible and had a great chance of success. Germany could not defend Greece and the entire Adriatic coast against a major landing. If such an invasion were combined with an attack by the Russians from the East, the Germans could have been driven out eventually despite the mountainous terrain. Churchill wanted a Balkan campaign, even after the compromise had been worked out, which specifically did not mention the Balkans but permitted the invasion of Italy. On July 19, 1943, he told his Chiefs of Staff that the proper strategy for 1944 was to occupy Italy as far as the Po "with option to attack westward in the South of France or north-eastward towards Vienna, and meanwhile to procure the expulsion of the enemy from the Balkans and Greece."[24]

Despite his postwar statement that he had never wished to send "armies" to the Balkans, Churchill wrote again to Smuts on September 3, "We should immediately take Southern Italy and move on to the Adriatic, and from a suitable point there launch a real attack on the Balkans and set its resurgent forces going. This will bring Turkey into the picture and carry our Fleet into the Black Sea." The British fleet in the Black Sea would have been a most undesirable sight to the Russians. On September 5, Churchill was still enthusiastic in writing to Smuts: "I have always been most anxious to come into the Balkans which are already doing so well."[25]

Churchill's generals joined him in this infatuation with the Balkans. Brooke was heartbroken in early 1944, when he thought of the missed opportunity by not continuing on in full force toward the Balkans. General Sir Harold R. Alexander thought his troops could fight their way through the Ljubljana Gap to Vienna if they were not weakened by diverting troops for the invasion of the south of France. Driving beyond Italy into the Balkans would have been difficult. The physical restrictions imposed by the terrain that lay between Italy and Vienna made it unlikely that the Allies could have launched an attack of sufficient force to drive the Germans back more rapidly than in Italy. Added to the physical problem was the staunch reluctance of the Americans to involve themselves in the Balkans.[26] In July 1943, Roosevelt firmly rejected any Balkan venture: "I cannot agree to the employment of United States troops against Istria and into the Balkans, nor can I see the French agreeing to such use of French troops."[27]

Although this strong American stand ended any real hope of an Allied threat to Vienna, as in any meeting of equals, such a stand resulted in compromise on others. In fact, the Americans took two such stands. While Marshall opposed the Balkans, Admiral King fought strongly for increasing the commitment to the Pacific.

The plan for the Pacific was submitted to the TRIDENT conferees on May 20, 1943. The basic objective was the unconditional surrender of Japan, if possible by sea control alone or by control of the sea plus air bombardment. If neither were sufficient, a landing was to be attempted. The air offensive with China providing the bases was highly regarded. First, however, the navy had to fight its way to Hong Kong to provide a port of entry to China. The basic question was how to get to Hong Kong by way of the central Pacific under Nimitz or the southwest Pacific under MacArthur. Admiral King advocated the central Pacific route because it was shorter and required fewer resources. If the Japanese fleet were destroyed in the interim, the navy could strike directly at Japan without reliance on land-based aircraft in China. The southwest route was considered unhealthy and gave the Japanese an opportunity to stall the drive with large numbers of troops in the Philippines.[28]

In opposition to King's advocacy of the central Pacific, the southwest route would result in the capture of the oil fields of the Dutch Indies, and, furthermore, the drive was already under way. In typical style, the American Joint Chiefs of Staff approved of both drives, a decision confirmed by the Combined Chiefs. Even though additional men and supplies were required, the Chiefs were willing to provide them from the shipping, troops, and material that had been slated for the attack on France. By the end of December 1943, there were eighteen American plus Australian and New Zealand divisions in the Pacific, only a few of which would be used in January 1944.[29]

While the divisions and material flowed to the Pacific, the greatest obstacle to attacking France were the words "Allied lack of . . . " or "too many German. . . . " Churchill considered the invasion too risky on May 12, 1943, because the beaches were uncertain, the tides were extreme, the German defenses were too strong, the German reserves were too numerous, and more reserves could be brought in because communications were good.[30] None of these factors would turn in the Allies' favor in another year, but Churchill's reasoning was based on the fact that the Italian beaches were easier, the Mediterranean tides were less extreme, there were fewer defenses or reserves, and the rail communications in Italy were poor. In other words, the arguments were created to support invasion of Italy. His basic reason was more plainly stated to the Chiefs of Staff on July 19: "I do not believe that 27 Anglo-American divisions are sufficient for OVERLORD in view of the extraordinary fighting efficiency of the German Army and the much larger forces they could so readily bring to bear against our troops even if the landings were successfully accomplished."[31] Churchill feared the terrible casualties that might result from a head-on clash with the Germans in France, and from the summer of 1943 on, he was not an advocate of the invasion.[32] Even on April 15, he had written to Brooke that an invasion in 1943 was off but that, for deception purposes only, the buildup and planning should go on to tie some Germans in France. However, he went on, the deception should not waste effort for a plan impossible in 1943 "and about which there is no fixed plan for 1944."[33]

As each and every qualification was met for the descent on France, the British talked less of any real matters and referred only to the power of the German army, which, as they well knew, was exaggerated. Even though Churchill himself stated that a British or American division was worth two German divisions, which were "little more than a glorified brigade group," the British began to talk of the advantages of the Italian campaign.

Churchill summed up the advantages of the Italian plan. It would dishearten Germany to lose an ally; it might bring Turkey into the war; it would remove more than twenty-five Italian divisions from the Balkans; it would eliminate the Italian fleet and permit the British to send ships to the Pacific; it would take pressure off Russia as German divisions were drawn into Italy; and we had a good army in North Africa with nothing to do (but which could not travel more than a few hundred miles).[34]

Eisenhower was willing to go along with the attack on Italy if the conquest of Sicily proved easy.[35] Marshall objected to Italy on the grounds that there was no strategic objective. He saw no value in striking at the soft underbelly and believed that the diversion of Allied troops would only delay further the necessary confrontation with the German army that, he felt, would lead to a speedy end of the war.[36]

The most powerful objection to the attack on Italy was that it led nowhere. Italy was easy to invade from the sea because not all of its many good landing beaches could be fortified. The only defensive option was to guess on the basis of fighter plane range (or to intercept enemy plans, which the Germans did) and then move reinforcements rapidly to the point of landing. The poor Italian roads and railroads did not make this task easy. The mountains required many tunnels and bridges that were subject to air attack. Even the telephone system was inadequate.[37] These same conditions would slow the advance of the highly mechanized Allied forces. The British generals were aware of this defensive advantage, but thought they could fight their way through regardless. Churchill, who saw Italy not as an end but as a means to reach the Adriatic, had underestimated the obstacles.

All of these arguments were put forth at TRIDENT. Brooke wrote that the Joint Chiefs of Staff meeting was getting nowhere; the Americans believed that the British had "led them down the garden path" into North Africa, then to Sicily, and then wished them to go to Italy. Eisenhower was suspicious of British intentions on the basis that the promises of 1942 at Casablanca had been broken. Whether or not there was an intent to deceive cannot be determined from the records. Certainly Brooke consistently and Churchill at times believed that the major effort on land should be left to the Russians. When Roosevelt indicated that he had abandoned the 1943 attack and would go ahead in the Mediterranean, Brooke wrote, "At last the first stage of my proposed strategy was accomplished in spite of all the various factors that have been trying to prevent it."[38] The final outcome of the conference was not a complete defeat for Marshall. The bombing offensive, as well as the Pacific and Burma, all received some priority. Operations after Sicily were to be decided after the event, with Italy as a strong contender. The cross-channel attack was put off until May 1, 1944, but it was definitely to take place then.

Eisenhower was left as the arbiter as to whether or not Italy was to be invaded, although at that point it made little difference, because the major invasion had been put off for another year. The real struggle that followed was to ensure that once involvement in Italy began, resources would not be devoured to the point that the cross-channel attack would be delayed for still another year. At the TRIDENT Conference in May 1943, the British had succeeded in convincing Roosevelt that nothing could be done in France after Sicily and that the logistical problems of moving the armies from North Africa to England were insurmountable. Therefore, the Allies went into Italy.

Despite all of these arguments to the contrary, the Allies would have met weaker forces in France in 1943 than were met in Italy. They did have the landing craft needed to stage a major invasion in France. American troops were well trained and a match for the best that the Germans had thrown against them and were superior by far to the caliber of troops occupying France. Furthermore, the forces available to the Western Allies (with the addition of forces from the Mediterranean) would have been sufficient to defeat the German army in the West in September 1943. Allied equipment was equal to the best German equipment and superior to the limited amount of second-class equipment available.

The rationale behind the decision to carry out the more defensive program was explained away in military terms. The West was not strong enough to confront Germany for various reasons—lack of ships caused by the U-boat attacks, lack of landing craft, the poor quality of American troops, inferiority of Allied tanks compared to those of the Germans, insufficient air support, lack of service units and logistical support, and the superior strength of the German army in the West. In the following chapters, an examination of all of these factors will show that the true reasons for the course of action in World War II were political rather than military.

4

THE

SUBMARINE MENACE

One of the most frequently mentioned reasons for delaying action in Europe was the fear that the German submarines would reduce the flow of men and supplies across the Atlantic to a point that an army in France would be compromised. Churchill remarked that the U-boat attack was the only true threat to Great Britain.[1] Throughout the war, the attention of the Royal Navy was riveted on this problem.

Regarding the timing of the second front, the question is whether the U-boat could indeed interfere with the buildup and support of forces in Britain once they had landed in France, and, if so, at what point did the Allies contain this threat? The U-boat did seriously threaten Britain's life line until August 1942, but after that time it could not hinder the buildup or support of forces in Europe. If shipping shortages did exist, they were caused by diversion to the Pacific rather than by sinking of ships.

A review of the records shows that in September 1939, Germany had only fifty-seven submarines, of which thirty-nine were operational. The remainder were used for training. All but five of the thirty-nine were of the coastal variety, the Type IIs. The Type II weighed only 250 tons, had a radius of action of only four hundred miles, and a cruising speed of five knots, less than that of a merchant ship. The five oceangoing U-boats were Type VIIs, which became the standard U-boat throughout the war, though it was improved in later years. The Type VII weighed 770 tons and had a cruising range of nine thousand miles at ten knots. It had a top speed of seventeen knots on the surface and eight knots submerged. It could remain at sea for five weeks and reach any part of the North Atlantic. Nearly seven hundred were built during the war. In addition, about two hundred larger boats from 1,000 to 1,700 tons were constructed. These large underwater cruisers were designed for minelaying and supplying the smaller boats at sea or for long-range operations, for example, in the Indian Ocean. The mainstay, however, was the Type VII, which had speed, agility, and range, besides being cheaper to make than the large boats.[2]

Construction of new U-boats did not progress rapidly during the first year of the war. An average of fourteen were at sea during 1940.[3] By January 1941, there were only eighty-nine U-boats, practically all Type VIIs, in service, of which only twenty-two were at sea. These few boats had spectacular success and devastated British shipping.[4] The period from June to October 1940 was known as the "happy time" for the raiders. Despite such obstacles as the conventions of international law, the long trip around Great Britain to reach the open sea and the convoys, torpedoes that did not function, and the agonizingly long time taken by the shipyards to refit the boats between tours, these few boats sank 715,000 tons of shipping during the first six months of the year and, combined with surface raiders, such as the *Graf Spee,* were sinking an average of nearly 450,000 tons per month from June until December 1940.[5]

Even though Britain and the United States were building new ships at an average of 100,000 tons per month during this same period, the net loss per month was nearly 350,000 tons, a steady erosion of the shipping supply.[6] These were indeed happy times for the U-boats; they were welcomed home with bands and crowds, and each commander was made a hero as he added to his score. The total loss in shipping from all causes by the end of 1940, after sixteen months of war was nearly 4 million tons at a cost of only thirty-one U-boats.[7]

And yet 1941 was to prove even more costly to the British. After the fall of France in June 1940, the U-boat bases were moved to convenient French ports jutting out into the Atlantic to reduce the travel time from base to the area of operations in the mid-Atlantic. The German air force was also moved to France and, with long-range, four-motor Focke Wulf 200 bombers, was able to range far out to sea, attacking ships and spotting convoys for the U-boats. The German pilots were not adept at reconnaissance because of their poor navigational skill. Even though they spotted the ships, the coordinates that they broadcast were too inaccurate to be of use to the U-boat captains. The Germans also used Stuka dive bombers to attack shipping in the English Channel, forcing the English to abandon the use of that route. As a result, all of the convoys from the Western Hemisphere approached the British Isles through the northern entrance to the Irish Sea between Ireland and Scotland. That practice aided the U-boat because all of the ships were funneled into one narrow stream and were subjected to a concentrated attack.[8]

The British were forced to reduce the protection offered by destroyers and other escorts even though to do so made their ships more vulnerable. Because of the continued threat of invasion to England from September 1940 until the Germans turned to attack Russia in June 1941, the Royal Navy diverted destroyers from convoy duties to protect the southern coast of England. The result was fewer escorts for the convoys and greater opportunity for the U-boats. Another advantage for the U-boat commander was the development in late 1940 of a better system of refitting boats between voyages. Though U-boats were still low in priority for men and materials, the time spent in the French bases was reduced, and a higher proportion of the boats were at sea. By July 1941, about one-half of the 150 U-boats available were operational.[9]

The rate of construction of new U-boats increased slowly, and by the end of 1941 there were more than 240, of which about 100 were operational. About 15 new U-boats were completed each month during the spring of 1941; during this time, the British sank about 3 per month.[10] The increase in sinking, from 23 in

1940 to 35 in 1941, resulted from the strengthening of the convoy escorts after October 1940, when the invasion threat was eliminated by winter weather.[11] The destroyers were able to return to the convoys at the very time when the rough seas made it most difficult for the U-boats to operate. In January 1941, the antisubmarine forces began to receive deciphered German messages from ULTRA. As each U-boat reported its position at night, the Admiralty was provided with the information and could both direct convoys away from the path of concentration and detail destroyers to attack individual boats. At the same time, the Germans had cracked the British naval codes and were reading the Admiralty messages, so that each side jockeyed its ships across the Atlantic like a gigantic chess game, each trying to react to decoded information in such a manner that the other would not know that its messages were being deciphered.[12]

On May 7, 1941, the British captured the U-110 complete with an Enigma code machine, along with the current keys, which provided instant decoding of U-boat messages without the code-breaking process until the Germans changed the keys. With the aid of this information, the British sank ten German supply ships and four U-boats in June 1941. The Germans suspected a security leak, but placed the blame on either traitors or taps on telephone lines.[13]

Meanwhile, the number of escort vessels was increasing rapidly. British shipyards completed 39 destroyers in 1941. The United States transferred 50 World War I vintage destroyers to the Royal Navy during the fall of 1940, and these ships were rapidly refurbished and assigned to convoy duty. British and Canadian shipyards were turning out corvettes, 70 in Britain alone in 1941, which were smaller than destroyers but powerful enough to remain at sea with the convoy and fight it out with the U-boats.[14] In June 1941, the Royal Navy had 248 destroyers and escort destroyers in commission plus 157 building; 99 corvettes in commission plus 44 building in Britain and 52 in Canada; 300 trawlers and antisubmarine yachts with 47 building; and 48 sloops and cutters with 3 building.[15] In the spring of 1941, some of the destroyers were returned to defense duty against a possible invasion, but the attack on Russia removed the threat completely, and once again the escort forces were reinforced. Of the 35 U-boats sunk in 1941, 25 were sunk after June 22, 1941.[16]

More help came from the air. The Coastal Command of the Royal Air Force was placed under the control of the Admiralty, which made more effective use of the long-range Sunderland flying boats. The number of squadrons was increased greatly over 1940. The intensive air patrol of the Bay of Biscay made the crossing of this body of water at the beginning and end of each voyage a harrowing experience for the U-boats, though few were sunk.[17]

The American navy was also becoming more troublesome to the U-boats. In December 1940, the United States agreed to protect shipping in the Atlantic before war was declared on Germany. The Lend Lease Act of March 11, 1941, was followed by intensified American naval action under the National Emergency Declaration of May 27, 1941, which had begun with the neutrality patrol in 1940.

On April 18, 1941, the United States declared that German U-boats crossing the 26° west longitude would be considered engaged in unfriendly acts against shipping. American ships then began actively to search out submarines and report their locations to the British.[18] In June 1941, Hitler ordered his U-boat commanders to avoid contact with the American navy. No warships were to be attacked at night unless the commander was certain that the ship was not American, which was practically impossible to determine. In effect, this order gave immunity to all warships guarding convoys.[19] In July, the United States was convoying ships to Iceland, where they were transferred to the British for the final half of their journey to the British Isles. On September 4, 1941, a German U-boat tried to sink the American destroyer *Greer*, and on October 31, the destroyer *Reuben James* was sunk by a torpedo. Despite Hitler's order to avoid contact, the Germans were provoked into action by America's undeclared war against the U-boats.[20] Surprisingly, the purposeful sinking of one of America's warships by another nation resulted only in the lodging of a protest.

Despite all the additional obstacles, the U-boats turned in a good record for 1941—about 4.3 million tons sunk, slightly more than in 1940. These losses were inflicted by comparatively few raiders; an average of only eighteen boats were at sea during the first six months of 1941 and thirty-three in the last six months.[21] The heaviest shipping losses came during the first six months of 1941 (nearly 500,000 tons per month with U-boats claiming about half); a maximum of 690,000 tons were lost in April 1941, during the evacuation of Greece and Crete due more to air attack than to U-boats. At the beginning of May 1941, matters looked very bleak from the British point of view.[22] Some of the losses were made up from foreign sources. As Norway, Holland, France, and Greece fell, many of the merchant ships belonging to those nations were taken over by the British. Churchill noted that up until December 1941, Britain had recouped its losses by acquiring control of ships from countries taken over by the Germans. Thereafter no further windfalls were available.[23]

Germany's invasion of Russia relieved the British of the threat of invasion and released destroyers for antisubmarine work, but it also imposed greater risks to shipping in the Murmansk convoys. Could Russia withstand the Germans, or would she fall as had all the rest? Britain had to do her best to help by sending war material. In October 1941, an agreement was made to deliver to Russia 1,822 fighter planes, 2,443 tanks, and 3,000 trucks during the next twelve months. The best delivery route was through Murmansk, which meant sending convoys through the Arctic Circle, where they could be attacked by air or by surface vessels and U-boats based in Norway. The British plan was to send one or two convoys of twenty-five ships each month, but the losses were tremendous and were to increase in 1942. Of the original agreement, one-sixth of the fighters and one-fifth of the tanks were lost at sea, but the British maintained the effort.[24]

These first years were but a prologue to the disastrous year of 1942. Eight million tons of shipping were sunk during twelve months from all causes, the worst year of the war for the Allies.[25] Only 2 million of the 4 million lost in 1941 were replaced, but over 7 million of the 8 million lost in 1942 were replaced as American shipyards hummed.[26] In April 1942, Admiral Karl Doenitz, commander of the German U-boats, estimated that 700,000 tons a month must be sunk to keep pace with American shipbuilding. His estimate was nearly correct, and his commanders responded.

During the first eight months of 1942, the Allies lost 5,337,000 tons of shipping from all causes, an average of 667,000 tons. The heavy losses in the first eight months resulted from the lack of antisubmarine measures in American coastal waters. Previously, this area had been left free of German attention, in keeping with Hitler's order not to provoke the Americans. When America entered the war, the U-boat commanders found a happy hunting ground, sinking unescorted ships silhouetted against the lights of American coastal cities.[27] During the first six months, losses, mostly in American waters, exceeded construction by over 3 million tons.[28] When the convoy system was finally extended to the Gulf of Mexico in July 1942, losses dropped sharply.[29]

The turning point in the battle of production versus sinkings came in August 1942, the month when production exceeded losses for the first time during the war—a major net gain of 300,000 tons. Net gains in increasing dimensions continued for the remainder of the war, except for November 1942, when a net loss of 250,000 was suffered as a result of pulling escort vessels from the convoys to participate in the invasion of North Africa.[30]

The long-term impact of the losses was leveling out. In 1939, the United Kingdom had imported 54 million tons of cargo; by 1941, the tonnage had dropped sharply to 30 million. In 1942, the drop was only 6 million tons, down to 24 million tons. The result was a shortage of some items and rationing of practically every article that the consumer purchased. Food rations remained adequate and, in fact, were higher in some categories compared to those made available to the British public during the postwar austerity days of 1947–1949, when Britain was trying to close the adverse balance of trade by reducing consumption at home.

The lowest level of the British ration was reached in August 1942. At that time, the ration per week for each individual was slightly less than a pound of beef, veal, mutton, or pork; 4 ounces of bacon or ham; 8 ounces of sugar; 8 ounces of fats including 2 ounces of butter; 8 ounces of cheese; 4 ounces of jam or marmalade; 2 ounces of candy; one and a half dried eggs; 2 pints of milk during the winter; and a whole egg every other week.[31] Fish, rabbit, and poultry were not rationed and were reasonably plentiful, as were bread and potatoes. This was not a starvation diet, especially when one considers that children received many of the adult allotments and food was apportioned by the family. A family of four, for example, was able to obtain a half pound of butter and one and a half pounds of margarine each week. In comparison to the pound of meat and 8 ounces of fats, the German ration for garrison-duty soldiers provided only 8.6 ounces of fats and 13.8 ounces of meat.[32] The average British worker at the bottom of the rationing scale was eating better than soldiers in the German army.

Table 1. **Comparison of Rations and Consumption of Food**

Food type	Quantity allowed or consumed per week per person in ounces		
	British ration 1942	German army ration Garrison	U.S. consumption 1942
Beef	16	13.8	21.4
Pork	4		19.6
Fish	unrationed	7.4	3.8 (1974 amount)
Rabbit	unrationed		
Poultry	unrationed		6.4
Sugar, Jam, Jelly	14	7.4	25.2
Fats	8	8.6	13.8
Cheese	8		6.0
Eggs (number)	1½ dry, ½ shell		6
Milk (pints)	2	6.2 oz. condensed	6.8
Bread	unrationed	148.0	48.3 (flour)
Potatoes	unrationed	79.0	39.0
Vegetables	unrationed	62.0	48.6

SOURCE: Lyon, *Eisenhower*, p. 222; Calder, *People's War*, p. 231; U.S., War Department, *Handbook of German Military Forces, Technical Manual-Enemy 30-451*, p. VI, 19; U.S., Department of Commerce, *Historical Statistics of the United States, Colonial Times to 1957* (Washington: Government Printing Office, 1960), pp. 186–87.

Churchill insisted that, in fairness, the British public should not be forced to "make a greater sacrifice of standard of living than the American People" by cutting imports for civilian purposes.[33] A report provided to Churchill on October 30, 1942, compared the food available for consumption in Great Britain for 1942–1943 to prewar averages. In the categories of cheese, potatoes, fresh vegetables, liquid milk, and cereals, the supply was greater than before the war by as much as 80 percent. The supply of fats, meat, sugar and fish was less by as much as 40 percent. The shortage of eggs in the shell, only at half supply, was made up by dried eggs. The major lack was fruit, which was down to 33 percent of the prewar average. The general position in October 1942 was considered reasonable. Reserve stocks had been run down by two million tons in 1942, but this was not considered serious.[34]

The tide turned in August 1942. After that time, the rations improved as more shipping became available. In December 1939, of the 18.5 million tons of shipping under British control, 11.5 million tons were used mainly to carry civilian cargoes to the United Kingdom and less than 2 million tons were used for military purposes. By September 1942, 19.7 million tons of shipping were under British control, of which nearly 4.5 million tons were used for military purposes and only 7.5 million tons were used to carry civilian cargoes to Britain. By March 1943, the civilian tonnage had increased to over 8.5 million tons, although this figure declined gradually down to 7.5 million tons by September 1945.[35] One interpretation of these figures is that the civilian needs had been gradually tapered down, beginning in June 1940, reaching a point in September 1942 where they were maintained until the end of the war, regardless of the total available shipping.

The amount of shipping available to the United States Army in the Atlantic in 1942 rose sharply from 750,000 tons in May 1942 to 2.5 million tons in September 1942. By mid-1942, the army had adequate shipping to move large masses of troops and supplies without interfering with the British civilian economy.[36]

Even though the situation was improving, the preparations for the landing in North Africa in November took a toll on available ships because they were tied up in ports in America and England loading troops for the combat landings. The Murmansk convoys became more and more costly during the summer of 1942, as the long summer days exposed the convoys to German air attack for twenty or more hours per day. Although Churchill hoped that the Russians and Germans would wear each other down, he believed that continued aid to the Soviet Union was essential. On the one hand, aid would enable Russia to continue fighting, and, on the other, it would prevent Stalin from seeking an accommodation with the Germans that would place Britain in danger of attack. Therefore, despite the losses, the convoys continued. In April and May, only fifty-eight ships reached Murmansk out of the eighty-four dispatched.[37] On June 21, 1942 (the longest day of the year), a convoy of thirty-six ships, plus three rescue ships, set out from Iceland for Murmansk. Of these, only eleven convoy ships and two rescue ships survived the onslaught by German surface vessels, aircraft, and U-boats.[38]

Such a loss was too great to sustain at a time when ships were needed for North Africa. Churchill reluctantly canceled the July convoy and informed Stalin that he would try to develop some way of delivering the goods by way of Iran. The problem with that alternative was that Iran did not have an adequate port facility, railways, nor even good roads to deliver large quantities of goods. Less than 25 percent of the supplies could be carried by that route, and considerable time would be needed to improve the roads as well as to build docks and railroads.[39]

The Russians were furious over this defection. In July, the Germans were forcing the Russian armies to retreat in the Ukraine. Compared to the enormous losses being suffered daily by the Red Army, the losses suffered by the convoys seemed insignificant. Yet the Russian attitude was ambivalent. They demanded aid, but consistently downgraded the value of British and American tanks and planes. A photograph of either British or American tanks in action on the eastern front is a rare item. Perhaps the Russians did not routinely take such pictures, preferring to photograph their own vehicles. Reinhard Gehlen, then chief of the German army intelligence unit for the East, estimated in June 1942 that the Russians had received twenty-eight hundred American and British tanks and with them had equipped thirty tank brigades. He had reports that the Russians disliked them, however, because their tracks were narrow, their engines stalled on the low-octane Russian fuel, and they were generally inferior to the T34 tank.[40] Certainly none of the Western tanks in 1942 were comparable to the Russian T34, and the Allied tanks were probably used for training purposes or to equip the Siberian Army defending the far eastern border against Japan. The Soviets did photograph and release pictures of the Bell Airacobras being supplied by the United States, and American two-and-a-half-ton trucks were practically the only trucks seen in Russian photographs.

Despite their bad-mannered denigration of obvious British sacrifice in sending the supplies, the Russians must have found the aid of some value. The British were sending 20 percent of their aircraft production and nearly half of their tank production to Russia. By July 1942, the British had shipped two thousand tanks to Russia.[41] An indication that the Russians did find this aid helpful was the irritation they expressed in July 1942, when the convoys were halted until autumn so that longer nights would protect the ships from the German planes.[42]

The summer of 1942 was indeed difficult for Britain. In addition to the disaster to the Murmansk convoy, one sent to replenish supplies on Malta was all but destroyed. Lacking supplies, the aircraft and submarines based on Malta could not block the Italian convoys from reaching Libya. With ample supplies, Rommel was able to overrun the Eighth Army, chase it back to El Alamein, and come within a whisker of taking Alexandria and the Suez Canal. Mussolini was so confident of victory that he had his white horse brought to Tripoli in readiness for the triumphal march through Alexandria. Fortunately, the Eighth Army held.[43]

Matters took a dramatic turn for the worse for the Germans by July 1942. During the first six months of 1942, the rate of loss of U-boats was not excessive; the Germans lost only 21 while building 105, a very desirable ratio. Beginning in July, the rate of destruction of U-boats increased sharply because of the effect of the improved countermeasures. Escort vessels, by then, had radar sets that led them to the U-boats on the surface.[44] There were sufficient destroyers and long-range aircraft to take advantage of the information in the decoded radio messages. High-frequency direction finders were placed on the convoy ships for close detection. Previously, even though the British knew where the boats were, they had no means of attacking them. With larger numbers of escorts, the U-boats could be pursued. Furthermore, the Royal Air Force began bombing the submarine base at Kiel, and Coastal Command was by then providing air surveillance farther out to sea.[45] By July 1942, the U-boats had to travel nearly a thousand miles before they were clear of land-based aircraft.[46] The Bay of Biscay was closely patrolled by long-range bombers with radar able to detect a U-boat on the surface at night, even in heavy seas. The Germans developed the METOX that intercepted the pulses given out by the meter wave radar sets and provided some warning to their U-boats. The warning was sufficient to make crash dives just before the bombers could attack. Additional antiaircraft guns were mounted on the submarines to give them a chance to protect themselves if they were caught on the surface.[47] Despite the German countermeasures, the heavy cordon in the Bay of Biscay meant that the U-boats could not travel on the surface at night as they had in the past. Instead, most of the trip had to be made underwater at only seven knots compared to seventeen knots on the surface,[48] barely allowing time to recharge the batteries before the planes would attack again.

When they reached the open sea, the U-boats experienced far more difficulty. The Allied bombers reached nine hundred miles out to sea from Northern Ireland and from Newfoundland. Their radar sets enabled them to attack any U-boat near a convoy. Thus ended the classic high-speed chase on the surface at night to outdistance the convoy and lie in wait either on the surface or submerged. After July 1942, the U-boat commander had to guess the direction of the convoy and hope that it would pass by—a far less efficient method of attack.[49]

The number of aircraft available to battle the U-boats increased greatly in September, when attack groups were formed by the Allies. The attack group consisted of a squadron of destroyers and an escort carrier, the latter a merchant ship converted into a comparatively slow aircraft carrier (seventeen to twenty knots) that had little armor and carried about thirty planes. The escort carriers were cheap to build, and by the end of 1942 the United States had constructed over 20 of them, leasing 3 to Britain.[50] In March 1942, there were 383 British and 122 American escort vessels in the Atlantic.[51] More destroyers and other antisubmarine vessels were coming out of the shipyards at a rapid pace. More than 80 American destroyers were built in 1942, along with 73 British destroyers and 28 corvettes and frigates.[52] In October, British estimates predicted that 475 British antisubmarine craft would be available on January 1, 1943 and that an additional 129 would be completed in 1943; losses were estimated at only 64, leaving 640 available at the end of 1943.[53] In addition, the Americans were building up their forces, and the Canadians also built additional corvettes. By January 1, 1943, 481 British and Canadian escort vessels were on duty in the Atlantic.[54] Attack groups then were given the task of searching out and destroying the wolf packs, rather than waiting for them to attack the convoys. Escort carriers also formed part of the force guarding the convoys, which meant that the U-boats would have to contend with planes equipped with radar any time a convoy was approached.[55]

By the end of August 1942, 106 U-boats had been sunk since the beginning of the war, an average loss of 5 percent of the operational boats each month. More than 3,800 men had been killed or captured—38 percent of the seagoing personnel each year.[56] That was a shattering rate of loss, and one marvels at the courage of the men who continued to volunteer to man the U-boats against such odds. The number of operational boats still continued to grow, but at a much slower rate. The crews were no longer the highly trained experts of 1940, and new, inexperienced captains made fatal mistakes that cost the lives of their entire crews. During the last four months of 1942, 44 more U-boats were sunk, a total of 150 after September 1939, and in practically all cases the entire crew was either killed or captured. The newly trained officers and captains on their first command had little chance of competing with the then highly trained crews of the Allied destroyers and corvettes, as well as with the increasing number of planes. An error of a few seconds, a delayed command, or a slow response on the part of a crewman could strand a U-boat on the surface to be spotted by a plane or warship and ruthlessly pursued for hours or even days once contact had been made. Finally, the U-boat would be forced to surface to be destroyed or would be caved in by depth bombs beneath the sea. Only a few were lucky enough to escape once they were spotted.

Churchill reported the turning point in the war on shipping in his speech to the House of Commons on July 2, 1942. The United States was currently building four times as much shipping as Britain and would build eight to ten times as much as Britain in 1943. Strenuous efforts had been made to reduce losses, and masses of escort vessels were under construction: "These measures . . . should result in a substantial gain in tonnage at the end of 1943 over and above that which we possess, even if, as I cannot believe, the rate of loss is not substantially reduced."[57] On September 8, 1942, Churchill observed that though the losses at sea had been heavy, July and August had seen improvement. Building was exceeding losses, and warfare against the U-boat was more successful than ever.[58]

By the end of 1942, the net loss in shipping was still seven million tons from the beginning of the war, but this deficit was rapidly made up in 1943, most of it in the first six months. The British civil authorities were aware of the shift and, in early 1943, demanded sharp increases in the amount of goods for the civilian economy at the expense of military shipments. Richard M. Leighton describes the situation: "Civilian shipping authorities had always contended that statements of military requirements were inflated, that they reflected both wasteful scheduling and loading practices and excessive margins of safety."[59]

In May 1943, General Morgan, in charge of planning the coming invasion, though rebuffed by the supposed shortage of shipping, was informed "in circumstances of complicated anonymity" that the shipping shortage was "bunk," that losses were light, and that construction was increasing. From January 1943, shipping resources had been growing at the rate of over one million tons per month.[60]

During 1943, life became more and more difficult for the U-boats. On May 14, 1943, Josef P. Goebbels wrote in his diary that the submarine had failed; he blamed poor scientific development in Germany. Though the U-boats were able to contact the convoys, they were driven off by the escorts.[61]

The effect of the countermeasures was apparent in April 1943, when ship losses were down by 50 percent and U-boat sinking was up 400 percent.[62] More Liberator bombers, with advanced radar systems, were assigned to antisubmarine work. The U-boat was in potential danger every time it surfaced in the North Atlantic. Such conditions placed a heavy strain on the U-boat crewmen.

The changing fortune of the U-boats was described by the commander of U-230. The boat had left Norway in January 1943 and was attacked by aircraft six times in two days. Although the METOX device alerted the crew in time to dive, the depth bombs came close. For other boats with less alert crews, these attacks were fatal, but only because of the good fortune of U-230 has the record of its voyage survived. Finally, U-230 reached its station, six hundred miles east of Newfoundland, beyond the practical range of land-based bombers that were unable to patrol at length that far from shore. The U-230 joined a group of from twenty to forty boats patrolling zones in the North Atlantic, but it had no luck until February, when Convoy SC 118 was intercepted by twelve U-boats. The attack on the convoy continued for three days and nights. Nine ships were sunk as well as three U-boats, a very costly victory.[63]

No more ships were sighted until March 8, 1943. Convoys were less frequent than in 1942, but were larger in number of ships and escorts. Convoy SC 121 with more than 60 ships was sighted and attacked by 18 U-boats, again for three days and nights. Six of the ships were sunk at no loss to the U-boats.[64] On March 11, the U-230 stopped its attack on SC 121 to join 40 U-boats in setting up a screen to intercept Convoy SC 122. Coincidentally, just as the Allies had broken the German code, the Germans were decoding Allied messages and were well aware of the general route and size of the convoys. Contact was made on March 16, and all U-boats were ordered to attack. Within two days, 22 ships had been sunk and 6 damaged. On March 18, convoy HX 229, heading east, bumped into the battle that by then involved more than 130 ships, more than 30 destroyers and corvettes, and 38 U-boats. The battle continued for two more days, and a total of 38 ships were sunk, plus 9 damaged. Only one U-boat was lost, making that the greatest victory of the war.[65]

It was to be the last U-boat victory. On the return trip through the Bay of Biscay, the British patrol bombers were using an improved radar device. On the night of March 26, 1943, U-230 was attacked six times and forced to crash dive each time. During the daytime, hunter-killer groups, destroyers supported by an escort carrier, kept the boat under the water all day. With luck, U-230 finally reached Brest.[66] The Allied defense was steadily improving as the British and Americans perfected escort techniques for the convoys. The new corvettes and destroyer escorts were faster and more maneuverable, and land-based air cover was extended even farther.

The ill-fated German U-230 set out again after refitting at Brest on April 24, 1943. It traveled six days under constant attack night and day to reach the mid-Atlantic, which was still free of land-based aircraft. From May 5 to 7, seven U-boats were lost. On May 11, a convoy of 100 ships was intercepted with an escort of more than a dozen destroyers, 24 corvettes, and an aircraft carrier. From 11:00 A.M. until 4:30 P.M., U-230 was attacked seven times. On the seventh attack, she was located by a destroyer that depth-bombed her from 4:30 P.M. on May 12 until 3:30 A.M. on May 14—thirty-five hours of continuous attack—certainly a nerve-shattering experience. During the attack on the convoy, three U-boats were lost, but not a single ship was sunk. On May 14, another convoy was sighted, but attacks on the subs from the air and from destroyers with depth charges continued throughout the night. Three more U-boats were lost on that day, and again not a single ship was sunk. During the next few days, seven more U-boats were destroyed, but no ships sunk. During May 1943, 38 U-boats were destroyed, and two thousand crewmen were killed or captured. The U-230 reached Brest on May 28, 1943, after five weeks at sea, heavily damaged without having sunk a single ship.[67]

The U-230 was not alone in its troubles. Adversity was shared by all of the U-boats, and 84 had much worse luck, being sunk in four months. The direct result was that Allied shipping losses by submarines dropped sharply from 540,000 tons in March 1943 down to a scant 28,000 tons in June 1943, probably representing about four ships.[68] By June, Admiral Doenitz realized that he could not continue under the new conditions. He recalled all of the U-boats in the North Atlantic and sent the few boats still serviceable far afield into distant oceans with the hope of finding less well-defended ships.

The intensive surveillance of the Bay of Biscay made even this maneuver difficult. The U-boats could not travel in or out of the bases in Brittany. In July, 37 more were sunk. Out of a group of 17 trying to cross the Bay of Biscay as a unit to disperse the attacks, 10 were sunk. In four months, 60 percent of the operational U-boats had been lost. During 1943, 237 were sunk. By the end of the year only 175 were operational. Although there were still boats available, the captains and crews were by then inexperienced young men.[69]

No group of men could take losses of that magnitude for long. By the end of the war, thirty-nine thousand men had gone to sea in U-boats. Of this total, twenty-eight thousand were killed in action, and five thousand were taken prisoner. Of the 842 U-boats that saw action, 781 were sunk. Even though there were many still in service in 1943, the real spirit was gone, and the raiders became more cautious because the slightest error would result in loss. Even the invention of the snorkel device that permitted the sub to operate under water for long periods and to recharge batteries without surfacing could not cope with the Allied countermeasures.[70]

Shipping losses in 1943 dropped to only 3.6 million tons, the level of 1940, and most of that loss occurred during the early part of the year. Production of new shipping totaled 14.5 million tons, a net gain of over 10 million tons, more than the U-boats had sunk during the first four years. Monthly losses never exceeded 170,000 tons from all causes after July 1943. The battle between the shipyards and the submarine had been decisively won.[71]

The important question then arises: at what time was the situation sufficiently stabilized to permit a major invasion of Europe? The war at sea had to be won first in order to provide secure transatlantic shipping lanes to bring troops and supplies from the United States. According to the above statistics, the turning point was reached in August 1942, when new construction exceeded losses to the U-boats by over 250,000 tons.[72] In only one month did losses exceed construction after that time. By the end of May 1943, the U-boats were withdrawn from the North Atlantic because of their heavy losses. Therefore, though shipping may have been short in 1942, it was sufficient to launch a large-scale invasion of North Africa from embarkation ports thousands of miles away from the beaches. By

1943, the U-boat could not have prevented the massive buildup of forces, first in England and then in France.

The Americans never lost a large troop ship to enemy submarines in the transatlantic crossing during the war. One transport on its way to Greenland lost six hundred men, and three hundred were lost on a ship bound for Iceland.[73] The fast passenger liners converted to carry the troops were speedy enough (twenty-six and a half knots) to evade the U-boats, which moved at slower speeds (seventeen knots) even on the surface, and only through incredible luck would a U-boat find itself in a position directly on the course of one of the liners and have time to launch a torpedo. For this reason, the liners crossed in five days without escorts and gave the Allies tremendous troop-carrying potential. In fifty-five days from May 5, 1943, to June 25, 1943, the *Queen Mary* (three trips), the *Queen Elizabeth* (three trips), the *Scotland* (one trip), the *Andes* (two trips), the *Pasteur* (two trips), the *Mariposa* (one trip), and the *West Point* (one trip) were scheduled to carry 124,000 Americans and Canadians to Britain. Ninety thousand were to go on the two Queens.[74]

Cargo-carrying capacity was available, but much of it was used to carry civilian goods to England and to other Allied nations. The wartime ration was high to maintain morale, and large stocks were on hand in warehouses. Ships were also diverted to the Mediterranean and to the Pacific from where they never seemed to return. In January 1942, there were a million tons of American army-controlled shipping in the Pacific, compared to half that amount in the Atlantic. In July 1942, both areas had 1.5 million tons, and in August, the Atlantic finally forged ahead.

With far smaller forces to maintain, the Pacific still held 40 percent of the shipping tonnage. The islands of the Pacific and Australian ports were not prepared to handle the vast amount of material dispatched to them without adequate attention given to where it would be unloaded. The ports of Australia were clogged with ships waiting for dock space. At one point, more than a hundred ships were waiting to be unloaded at an Australian port with berths for only eight. The waiting ships were equal to two transatlantic convoys with a capacity of up to one million ship tons or two months' total shipment of military supplies to Britain during the last half of 1942.

The islands had no facilities whatsoever, and cargo had to be laboriously loaded by the ships' own winches into lighters that would then carry the cargo to shore, where it was transferred by hand to open storage. The result was a tendency to use a cargo ship as a floating warehouse, unloading materials from her hold as needed. This was lunacy in the face of a shortage of shipping, but there was no other solution. On occasion, supplies at the bottom of the ship's hold covered with thousands of tons of unneeded supplies would be reordered from the United States rather than unloaded from the ship already at hand. On September 28, 1942, Admiral Nimitz found eighty cargo ships (possibly as much as 800,000 tons of shipping!) in Noumea harbor in New Caledonia. The ships could not be sent to Guadalcanal because they were not combat-loaded. They could not be reloaded at Noumea because of the lack of piers, cranes, barges, trucks, and dock labor. They could not be sent to New Zealand for reloading because of a longshoreman's strike. Consequently, the ships stayed where they were for weeks on end.

Even if labor and equipment were available to unload the ships, there was no warehouse space to protect the goods from damage. Eventually, warehouses were built and dock crews were organized, but such work took many months. Meanwhile, much-needed ships lay at anchor for months partially unloaded or were loaded with goods that were not needed. On more than one occasion, the manifest, a list of items on a ship, was misplaced, and no one knew what the ship contained. The management of shipping was so poor and the distance from home so great that two or three times as much shipping was needed to maintain a division in the South Pacific as in Europe.[75]

Despite the wasteful practices in the Pacific and the continuing efforts of the U-boats, the supply of shipping in the Atlantic continued to grow. The requirements for BOLERO were being met by June 1942 and would have continued except for the invasion of North Africa. With more attention to several matters such as a more parsimonious attitude toward the Pacific, shipment of divisions to England rather than to the East, and full-scale utilization of ships available, there would have been an ample supply. But decisions were made at the highest level, and diversion to the Pacific had priority.

After mid-1942, diversion to the Pacific, not the U-boat, created the shipping shortage. Even in 1941, British countermeasures were hampering U-boat operations. The first half of 1942 brought heavy losses as a result of the American refusal to institute convoys until mid-1942. American shipyards went a long way to replace these losses, and by August 1942, more ships were being built than were sunk. Allied countermeasures in 1942 resulted in the sinking of more and more U-boats, and Churchill himself declared July 1942 as the turning point.

5

LANDING CRAFT

Were there enough landing craft for the invasion of France? General Frederick Morgan, the chief of the planning team for D-Day, had the most appropriate answer. There was no such thing as "enough landing craft"—any force commander always wanted more. The proper question, according to Morgan, was, were there enough craft to lift the minimum force necessary to give a "reasonable prospect of success"? The answer in 1943 was yes, there were enough to lift this minimum force.[1]

The story of the development and production of landing craft is typical of the creation of the entire Western Allied war machine. A need was recognized, a solution sought, and temporary expedients found. Long-term solutions were based on the experience gained from the temporary expedient. After an effective design was accepted, production was begun, using all available facilities, including those that had never been used for that kind of product.

The primary need was to land troops and tanks on an enemy shore. The existing harbors and docks could not be used because they would be the most heavily fortified, and, furthermore, the docks could be destroyed and the harbors blocked with scuttled ships. If landings could be made on the open beaches, the enemy would not know where along the coastline the landing was to occur and would have to dilute his defenses. In addition to protecting the harbors, the enemy would have to cover every mile of the shore.

Diluting the defense was not enough. The invading force had to have the ability to land quickly large numbers of troops, tanks, and guns because a few men in rowboats would be quickly driven off. Therefore, the attacker had to capture a port or develop special craft to land on open beaches. The British tackled the problem in 1938 and came up with the idea of the Landing Ship Infantry (Large) (LCI[L]), as it was later designated. Four of these vessels were in use by 1940, the "Glen" class (*Glengyle, Glenearn, Glenroy,* and *Breconshire*). Each ship could carry a battalion of infantry, along with a number of landing craft to be unloaded by davits, like lifeboats on a passenger vessel.[2]

These smaller landing craft were needed to take the troops and equipment from the ships to the shore. The British wanted a quiet armored craft that would carry a platoon of about forty men. The result in early 1940 was the Landing Craft Assault (LCA) to land the infantry. Close support fire was to come from the Landing Craft Support (LCS), equipped with mortars that could be fired as the troops approached the shore. Tanks were to be landed on a third type of boat, the Landing Craft Mechanized (LCM), designed to carry the heaviest tanks, but still light enough to be lifted from merchant ships with ordinary derricks.[3]

Fast ships of the "Glen" type were to carry the troops to the coastal area, where small craft would put them ashore. The total capacity of the four British infantry landing ships, however, was only four battalions plus some vehicles (a far cry from the two invasion corps being planned in October 1941 for the attack on France that would require 380 LCAs and 15 infantry landing ships). To increase the total capacity, two Dutch cross-channel ships and five Belgian cross-channel ships were selected for conversion to landing ships because of their high speed of twenty to twenty-two knots. In addition, orders were placed in August 1940 for 150 assault landing craft.[4]

Landing craft had a low priority in England in 1940. The U-boat was the leading menace, because it created an ever-present danger to her very survival. If landing craft were built, antisubmarine vessels would be overlooked; therefore, few landing craft were constructed, and the British turned to America. Based on British experience with the Glens and the Belgian and Dutch ships described above, plans were made for the LCI(L). These plans were shown to the Americans and, by May 1942, the design had been completed and production was under way.[5] Because the LCI(L) lacked suitable living quarters for more than two days, it could not be used as a troop transport for crossing the ocean, even though it had a cruising range of eight thousand miles at twelve knots. Unlike the Glens, it could be beached and two hundred troops unloaded directly on the beach by two gangways on either side of the bow. It had a draft of only three feet forward and five feet aft.[6] In May 1942, the Joint Chiefs of Staff ordered a large fleet of the craft to be ready in February 1943. The first LCI left the ramps in September 1942. More than 150 had been completed by January 1, 1943, and 70 more were finished during that month.[7] On January 12, 1943, twelve LCIs left the United States; they arrived at Gibraltar on February 9, 1943. By May 1943, 103 LCIs had been delivered to the Mediterranean, a sufficient number to land more than a hundred companies of infantry or about seven divisions.[8] The total number of LCIs used by the Allies on D-Day was only 72. These statistics reveal that there was an ample supply of LCIs as early as January 1943, and most of them were already in the European theater.

One of Churchill's major concerns was how to place tanks ashore with the assault wave. Under his prodding, in July 1940, Roland Baker of the Royal Navy designed the Landing Craft Tank (LCT), Mark I, that had a ramp to allow the tanks to roll off onto the beach. Although thirty were ordered, they proved to be poor sea boats when the first two were tried in November 1940. The craft was hard to handle and could not sustain a long trip at sea. Churchill was not satisfied and demanded a ship that could carry sixty tanks (a full tank battalion) across the sea and launch them right on the shore.

The Royal Navy devised the Winettes, the Landing Ship Tank, Mark I (LST [1]), that could carry twenty tanks at a speed of sixteen knots and disembark the tanks over a 124-foot ramp at the bow. Three of these were completed (the *Boxer, Bruiser,* and *Thruster*) by early 1943, but at a cost of nine badly needed corvettes.[9] The craft took too much time to build and deprived the navy of needed antisubmarine vessels.

An expedient was tried. A type of ship was used on shallow lakes in Maracaibo in Venezuela that drew only four feet of water at the bow and could be beached. Three of these were taken over (the *Misoa, Tasajero,* and *Bachequero*) and were provided with a sixty-eight-foot bow ramp that made it possible to unload more than twenty tanks on steep beaches, though not on shallow ones. These ships were ready by June 1941 and did not compare too unfavorably to the LST(1)s that were still under construction.[10] But there were only three, and, even when added to the three LSTs, there was lift enough for only a little more than 120 tanks—less than one-third of an armored division. Many more were needed.

In November 1941, the British Combined Operations staff sent a team to the United States with sketches of what was to become the LST(2).[11] After a month of discussion, an order was placed for delivery in April 1943 of two hundred of the new LSTs and other smaller craft. In view of the large number of LSTs required and the limited amount of traditional naval material available, the craft was designed to use eight locomotive diesel engines for power rather than a traditional ship engine.[12] While at sea, the LST(2) drew eight feet forward and fourteen aft, but it had the capability of blowing its ballast tanks and reducing these depths to three feet forward and nine and a half aft. Such a design enabled the ship to go aground on the beach, unload its cargo over the huge ramp, lowered after the clamshell doors at the bow were opened, and then pull itself back off the beach.[13]

The American chief of naval operations, Admiral Harold R. Stark, was doubtful that the orders could be filled without sacrificing antisubmarine construction. The solution suggested by Admiral Edward L. Cochrane was that the craft be built on the rivers (Mississippi, Ohio, Missouri) and the Great Lakes, rather than in the seacoast shipyards. The regular shipyards could then continue to build warships, while the landing craft were built by firms having little previous experience in ship construction.

In December 1941, the ARCADIA Conference gave production of landing craft high priority. The United States agreed on January 7, 1942, to complete the landing craft program, but Admiral King was not enthusiastic. (His biography fails to mention landing craft in his description of the ARCADIA Conference.) On February 28, 1942, Admiral J. W. S. Dorling found that the landing craft program was tenth on the priority list of naval construction.[14]

In March 1942, Roosevelt was very concerned about the landing craft program. The planners had not set the accurate number needed, and the war production staff complained about the lack of lead time to begin construction. The navy was reluctant to use shipbuilding capacity for what they considered an army task. None of them took too seriously Roosevelt's orders for landing craft and simply marked time on the program.[15] Churchill's visit in May 1942 and the definite plans for a second front created more interest. By the end of May 1942, production on the landing craft was under way with a priority second only to aircraft carriers.[16]

The landing craft program was continually opposed by the navy. At the Combined Chiefs of Staff meeting on June 2, 1942, the planners still had not set definite numbers required.[17] In July, TORCH ended the possibility of a 1943 invasion in the minds of the Combined Chiefs, and they began discussing cancellation of landing craft in August. Dill reported to the British Chiefs of Staff on September 22, 1942, that landing craft were to go to the Pacific instead of Europe, "on main ground that no BOLERO movement was now necessary." No American landing craft crews were to be sent to Britain until a full-scale ROUND-UP was ordered. The priority for landing craft was lowered because construction of LSTs delayed naval shipbuilding. Both Marshall and King agreed that craft were to be either "laid up" or sent to the Pacific, but not sent to Europe.[18]

In September 1942, the Joint Chiefs of Staff, under King's urging, decreased new orders for landing craft. One hundred LSTs and 48 LCI(L)s were cut from the program. A greater number would have been eliminated, but inasmuch as construction was already under way, it was easier to complete the craft than to stop and clear the way for other production. This left 390 LSTs and 252 LCI(L)s still in the 1943 program in addition to 84 LSTs and 109 LCI(L)s in the 1942 program. Most of the craft were to be sent to the Pacific, but Dill convinced the Americans to send some to Europe for use by the British. The Americans would provide craft for their own assault troops, "when their policy in the European theatre is decided."[19]

After the invasion of North Africa, Eisenhower appealed to the Combined Chiefs of Staff for more landing craft, and promises were made for large numbers of smaller craft. The British were to get 24 LSTs and 24 LCI(L)s. The total European allocation for 1943 was to be 128 American-manned LSTs and 75 manned with British crews.[20] From November 1942 to February 1943, 169 LSTs were completed: November 1942, 19; December 1942, 43; January 1943, 46; and February 1943, 61. By January 27, 1943, 10 LSTs had left the United States for North Africa, and by March 27, 21 more had passed Bermuda. Against strong British opposition, more than half of the craft were sent to the Pacific during the period January through May 1943.[21] In February 1943, the first 12 LSTs left the East Coast for Guadalcanal. The shortage of landing craft that was to plague all future plans in the Mediterranean, and later in the Atlantic, had its origin in the production cutback during late 1942 and in the diversion to the Pacific in early 1943. The shortage of LSTs, often a matter of top-level discussion in 1943 and 1944, was not the fault of the American shipyards.[22] By May 1943, 96 LSTs had been delivered to the Mediterranean, and by the end of June 1943, 241 had been built, compared to only 233 LSTs required for the OVERLORD operation. The problem was the diversion of the craft to the Pacific and to the Mediterranean, where they were used for other tasks once Admiral King was convinced that there would be no invasion of France in 1943.

Tanks could also be carried in ships and unloaded on LCTs. That method was cumbersome, however, because of their heavy weight and was dangerous during the first phase of the assault, when the ships would have to remain at anchor for long periods under enemy fire. Nevertheless, for the first assault wave, a few tanks had to come ashore in the less vulnerable LCTs.

Early in 1940, the British were working on an LCT and, in July, developed the LCT(1), described above, which was designed to carry three tanks. To speed production, the British turned to America in 1941 and asked her to build the LCTs. In September 1941, a British naval mission under Rear Admiral J. W. S. Dorling came to the United States with a lend-lease proposal for 1,300 LCTs. In October, the order was increased to 2,250 to be delivered by the spring of 1943. The Americans said that the best they could provide would be 800. That was not enough, so the planners substituted the LST; therefore, there was a reduction in the need for LCTs, and the order was reduced to 200 in November 1941.[23] In August 1942, 45 LCTs were completed in the United States, followed by 409 during the next three months. Then production practically ceased because of the cutback referred to above.[24]

The first American-built LCT was delivered to the Mediterranean in January 1943. Crossing the Atlantic was a problem. A highly untraditional solution was to place the LCT on the top deck of an LST with a large crane, and then the unique ballast controls of the LST were used to tip the LST to one side until the LCT slid and dropped into the water with an enormous splash. The procedure was dangerous but spectacular, and it worked with little damage to either craft or ship.[25] By the end of May 1943, 69 LCTs had been delivered to the Mediterranean by that method, and 90 had been delivered to England. Manufacturing was comparatively simple, and consequently production figures were well ahead of needs. During 1942, the British built 521 in addition to the American production of 470. The total requirement for LCTs on June 6, 1944, was only 835, less than the number available in April 1943.

The shortage of landing craft apparently was caused not by the lack of production in the shipyards, but by the allocation made by the United States Navy. On July 1, 1943, the three major types of craft were distributed as follows:[26]

Area	LST	LCT	LCI(L)
Pacific	84	180	70
Atlantic	92	139	102
Total	176	319	172

The landing craft had been built, but about half of them were in the Pacific, where no major need was planned for them until November 1943.

Whereas in the development of the larger craft the British had provided the Americans with leadership, in the case of the smaller boats the Americans had forged ahead. From 1935 on, the navy and Fleet Marine Force had been conducting joint landing exercises. In January 1941, these exercises had been worked up to a point of a two-division landing, using older navy-designed landing boats, and for the first time, the Higgins "Eureka" boat. Later termed the LCP— Landing Craft Personnel—this craft was designed and built by Andrew Higgins, a New Orleans shipbuilder who had gained experience building fast, small draft boats for use in the bayous by merchants who wished to avoid the more public waterways.[27] The British were also interested in this boat, a good sea craft in rough water, that could beach without damage. It later came in a ramped version over which the men could quickly debark, or it could carry either a jeep or a piece of light artillery. The British ordered 136 early in 1941, and the United States Navy accepted it as the standard LCP in 1941.[28] The LCP was manufactured in hugh numbers. By December 1942, 2,434 had been built, although only 1,382 were used on D-Day.[29] More than 500 could be loaded on a single Liberty ship, so delivery was not a problem. The LCP, used as part of the ship-to-shore movement, was the basic method available for the landings in North Africa and continued to be used for the long-range assaults in the Pacific. At no time after January 1943 was there a shortage of this type of craft.

In addition, there was a wide variety of special craft. The development of the LCM by the British, basically a boat to carry a single tank and used for ship-to-shore landings, came along quite well, and although more than 1,380 were available in January 1943, only 315 were used on D-Day, because the LCT and LST were far superior carriers of tanks and vehicles. Other craft such as the Landing Craft Support, which provided close-in fire from mortars and later from rockets, were basically landing craft converted for this special purpose. The Landing Ship Dock (LSD) was a huge ship that could carry smaller craft afloat within it. Only 22 were built, most of which went to the Pacific.[30]

One special development was the LVT, the Landing Vehicle Tracked, an improved amphibious tractor that could carry twenty-five men ashore at four knots. Later versions were armored and carried heavy-caliber guns, making them truly amphibious tanks. All of these were diverted to the Pacific theater, even though they would have been very useful in an attack on Europe. Another special development, the DUKW, was a two-and-a-half-ton cargo truck with a hull that enabled it to travel in water. This remarkable craft became available in large numbers early in 1943. During the Sicily landing, the DUKW brought supplies directly from the landing craft inland to the point of need.[31]

In general, the total picture for the availability of landing craft early in 1943 was so good that, in January 1943, landing craft production was reduced from Priority II to III.[32] In March 1943, Admiral King, who had already reduced the LST program, refused to provide more because the quantity already available was not needed. Nevertheless, King saw that most of the craft went to the Pacific.[33] By the end of 1943, the United States had built 19,482 landing craft of all types. Inasmuch as only 2,493 were used on D-Day, if there was a shortage, it was caused by allocation and not by availability. The navy wanted lavish allotments for its program in the Pacific. For example, whereas only 148 LSTs were used in a seven-division landing against the Germany army in Sicily, the navy allotted 47 LSTs for a landing of elements of three divisions to battle the equivalent of one reinforced Japanese division at Saipan and 51 LSTs for the Hollandia landing.

To better understand the use of the boats and the techniques developed, it would be well to review the two basic kinds of landings, ship to shore and shore to shore. The ship-to-shore type transported the troops, landing craft, and vehicles in carge ships to an area offshore, removed the landing craft from the ships and loaded the troops and vehicles for the final run to shore. In shore to shore, the troops and vehicles were loaded into large landing ships and landed directly on the opposing beach. In 1942, few large landing ships were available, which meant that North Africa had to be staged as a ship-to-shore movement. The only exception were the tanks on board the Maracaibo LSTs. With the arrival of large numbers of LSTs and LCIs early in 1943, a profound change took place in the ability of the Allies to assault a beach. Then, for the first time, a major part of the assault force could be loaded on the friendly shore, and the problem of handling small boats at sea was reduced.[34] In the European theater, the occupation of the small island of Pantelleria was the first shore-to-shore operation. The Third Division was loaded for shore-to-shore landings in the Sicily invasion, but the remainder of the troops were landed ship to shore.

The other factor of some concern was the loading of the cargo ships. Normally, a ship was loaded in a manner that would make the most efficient use of the available space, for seldom was a military cargo heavier than the maximum weight per cubic foot that a ship could carry. Therefore, the space on a ship was at a premium, not its ability to float a given weight. On the other hand, the most efficient packing of the ship was not necessarily the order in which the items were needed, and when an assault landing was made, time could not be spared until a ship was entirely unloaded to reach the ammunition at the bottom of the hold. Therefore, an alternate plan called "combat-loaded" was devised. On a combat-loaded ship the troops were carried on the same ship that carried their vehicles and supplies. The material would be loaded in reverse order of need, that is, supplies of ammunition would be loaded last and therefore be near the top of the hold. Loading a ship in this way was wasteful in terms of maximum cargo but was more practical for actual use of the equipment.

The total amphibious attack force consisted of troop transports, cargo ships, landing ships, and naval ships for protection and also for bombardment of the enemy coast. To coordinate the movement of such a complicated assortment of ships and men required considerable skill. Once on shore, what happened? Although army commanders soon took charge of the troops, unique and complex problems were involved in transferring the mountains of supplies from the ships to the depots to be ready for use by the combat troops. All of these problems had to be solved.

As early as 1938, the British were working on the problem of landing on hostile shores. They developed the concept of carrying the troops and special landing craft on fast ships especially fitted for the tasks described above. These ships and craft formed the basis for the landing at Narvik, where hasty and inefficient planning resulted in loss of all of the craft. The withdrawal from Dunkirk gave the British some reverse experience, but despite the heroic pictures of small boats rowing out to sea, most of the troops were actually loaded on destroyers from docks in the port of Dunkirk. Little was learned at Dunkirk, although eight of the LCAs and one LCM performed very well.[35]

The low state of the art of landing a force by the British was revealed in the abortive attempt to take Dakar in 1940. The force assembled for this task included 2,500 Free French troops and a brigade of Royal Marines, but not enough landing craft. The only craft available were fifteen LCAs, two LCMs, and one LCS, enough to lift five small companies and a few vehicles to shore. Because of the reinforcement of the Vichy French naval forces and their energetic resistance, the British withdrew without even attempting to land.[36]

Despite the lack of success up to that time, some basic decisions had been made. One decision was that the Royal Navy should handle the boats and the army should take over at the shore line. A further step was the creation of Combined Operations under the leadership of young Lord Mountbatten. Although this command, including navy, army, and air force, is best known for the commando raids on Europe, its development of landing skills played a far more important part in the war. By August 1941, the British had advanced to the point where they could assemble the ''Pilgrim'' force, a fully equipped amphibious force, designed to take the Canary Islands. It conducted a practice assault landing in Scotland later in 1941, landing twenty thousand men on a mock enemy beach. Although matters went badly because of the weather, the technique and equipment were essentially workable. By October 1941, the British planners had conceived two invasion corps, complete in every detail, except for the aircraft, which the Royal Air Force refused to assign to any operation without a definite mission.[37]

During the summer of 1942, the most expensive form of training was acquired. The Canadian First Division was landed at Dieppe with the intent of remaining one day, as a test of the ability to conduct such operations and to try out German defenses. The disastrous result is described in chapter 12. Montgomery questioned whether anything was learned, but certainly some value was gained from the great sacrifice. The Germans learned two false lessons, the first that because of the need for a port to support the buildup of the forces landed, the attack would finally come at a port. For that reason, they heavily fortified the ports along the channel. The second error was that some of the Germans believed that the invasion could most easily be defeated on the beach.[38] This was a vital issue because the disposition of mobile reserves depended on whether the invading force could be defeated by relatively small forces at the beach or whether large reserves would have to be accumulated to fight the major battle before the invader had time to land additional troops. In 1944, Rommel believed in the fight on the beaches, while Field Marshal Gerd von Rundstedt held out for centralized reserves that could be moved more easily to a wider variety of locations from centers of transportation. The result was that the reserves were divided; half were at the coast and half were inland. There were neither strength enough to defeat the Allies on the beach nor readily available reserves to drive them back during the crucial first week.

The British learned some positive lessons, first, that a direct assault on a port would be too costly. Also there would be a need for heavy bombardment of the defenses by ships and aircraft. Furthermore, close coordination of supporting fire was essential, as well as heavy fire from close-in support ships to quiet enemy defenses that had escaped the bombardment. Beach obstacles must be cleared before tanks were landed—most of the tanks at Dieppe were stopped at the water line. Good landing crews were essential, as well as a specially designated party of men to unload the craft. To provide command facilities, a specially fitted headquarters ship was needed. Another requirement was that a permanent assault force be created to control the landing craft. This group was organized as Force ''J,'' which later served as a parent for future landing forces for the Mediterranean and D-Day.[39] By September 1942, detailed instructions based on the Dieppe experience had been drawn up and were ready for the troops who took part in the TORCH landings in North Africa.

Also in 1942, the British began to develop a successful shore party technique. Once on the shore, the landing came under the control of a ''Beach Group'' for each division. The group included an infantry battalion, a naval beach commando, and an RAF beach unit. The first Beach Group to control the beach was used in the landing on Madagascar. For TORCH in November 1942, this basic concept was expanded into a highly sophisticated unit called a Brigade Brick, consisting of more than two thousand men, including an infantry battalion, an antiaircraft unit, a medical section, a signal section, military police, a ration store, water supply trucks, and bicycles for messengers. The Brigade Brick could maintain an infantry brigade ashore for four days, unloading three small ships per day. The Brigade Brick was completely responsible for the delivery of men, vehicles, supplies, and all other services over the beach to a point inland where needed by the combat troops.[40]

American experiments with landings had begun as early as the 1930s. During the winter of 1939, the Third Division was in amphibian training at Fort Lewis and in January 1940 began training with the navy at San Diego.[41] On June 26, 1940, after the fall of France, both the First and Third Divisions were ordered to train in amphibian landings.[42] By December 1940, the emergency expeditionary force was formed, consisting of the First Infantry Division and the First Marine Brigade (later the First Marine Division). In January 1941, it participated in Fleet Landing Exercise Seven at Culebra Island near Puerto Rico. There the navy first used the Higgins boats, and the marines were carried in three newly equipped Assault Transports. The force had a week of preliminary training before landing five thousand men. Plans went askew, however, for the army used old motor launches and the navy obsolete boats in addition to the new Higgins type. Despite all of the problems, men were landed, but still the army observers were critical.[43]

A few weeks later, King approached General Marshall regarding continued joint training, but Marshall was not enthusiastic, believing that landings were easily managed with some special training. King disagreed and advised the use of highly trained units of landing specialists rather than hastily trained army units.[44] King's views prevailed, and on June 21, 1941, the First Joint Training Force was formed on the Atlantic Coast, including the First Infantry Division and the First Marine Division. On September 9, 1941, the Second Joint Training Force was formed in the Pacific with the Third Infantry Division and the Second Marine Division. In July 1941, the First Force held exercises at New River, North Carolina, and in August 1941, it staged a two-division landing. Although King noted great improvement over the landings made six months previously, others were critical of the performance. The major faults were lack of preparation time, inexperience of the troops, lack of planning, and a complicated chain of command.[45]

After Pearl Harbor and the ARCADIA Conference with the British, the entire approach to amphibious training changed. The British had laid out the enormous task ahead—to put an army on the French shore—and Eisenhower at the War Plans Division was working on a scheme to put forty-eight divisions in France in 1943. Serious efforts were necessary. In January 1942, another maneuver on the Atlantic Coast by the First Infantry Division was judged unsuccessful. The First Marine Division went off to Iceland for occupation duty, and the Ninth Infantry Division was brought into amphibian training.[46] In February 1942, the Joint Chiefs of Staff appointed Rear Admiral Roland M. Brainard to form the first amphibious force, and in March the Atlantic Fleet Amphibious Force was activated.[47]

In May 1942, discussion began regarding who would operate the landing craft, unload the boats, and move the material across the beaches. The navy questioned whether it wished even to man the small landing craft and certainly did not want the responsibility of unloading them and moving cargo. The outstanding advantage of the Combined Operations Headquarters, assembled by the British, was that both services together managed the three tasks. Instead, in the United States, a decision was made regarding the point at which one service would relinquish control to the other. The first decision was that the navy would handle the landing ships and large craft, while the army would operate the smaller craft.

In June 1942, Captain William P. Clarke was given the task of training navy crews for eighteen hundred large landing craft, a total of twenty-two hundred officers and twenty-two thousand men. The plan called for an eight-week training cycle beginning on July 1, 1942. Every two weeks a thousand men and a hundred officers were to begin training. For the sake of expediency, the men were drawn directly from "boot" camp, the navy version of basic training, and officers who had experience handling small boats were given direct commissions from civilian life. The Coast Guard supplied some officers and men as well, and new reserve officers were brought into the organization. The program began well, and more than four thousand men were trained by August 1942.[48]

Meanwhile, the army was assigned the duty of manning the small boats and had to enter the boat business on a large scale. On May 9, 1942, a Boat Training Center was established at Camp Edwards, Massachusetts, ready to begin training a division for landings by July 15, 1942. Colonel Daniel Noce of the Corps of Engineers (the only branch with any small boat experience) was ordered to form eighteen boat operating regiments and seven boat maintenance battalions. After a review of the need to handle the supplies on the beach, Engineer Special Brigades were formed, each consisting of a boat regiment to operate the boats; a shore regiment to control the supplies on the beach and to unload the boats; a boat maintenance battalion to keep the boats running; and other miscellaneous troops including signal, medical, quartermaster, and ordnance as required. Each of these brigades was to provide landing capability to an infantry division. On June 5, 1942, authority was given to activate eight such brigades.[49]

Between June 1 and August 15, 1942, 400 army officers were commissioned, among them yachtsmen and others familiar with small craft, as was true of the navy. By the end of 1942, nearly 3,000 officers and 39,000 men had been trained by the Boat Training Center. The First Brigade was activated on June 15, 1942, and by early 1943, four brigades had been activated.[50] The command had on December 31, 1942, 2,900 officers and 37,600 men. On July 15, 1942, as planned, the Forty-fifth Infantry Division came in for training with the First Brigade. In August, the First Brigade was sent to the United Kingdom, and the Second Brigade trained the Thirty-sixth Division. The First Brigade sailed with 335 officers and 7,500 men on August 6, 1942, only two months after the command had begun training. The First Brigade later played a significant role in the North African invasion.[51]

Both the army and navy had entered vigorously into the preparation of an amphibious force. From the time of the decision, in May 1942, when the form and shape of the landing craft were finally decided and training of the crews had begun, until the scheduled ready date of spring 1943, about sixty thousand men had been trained and were ready to support the landing of at least four infantry divisions. Actually, the force was capable of landing even more troops because of changes in the plan. During the summer of 1942, the navy, observing the success of its training programs, decided to resume the task of manning the small craft in the European theater. As a result, the engineer special brigades were not permitted to operate boats in Europe. The First Brigade in Europe had already used its boat regiment to perform dock labor rather than to man landing craft. The result of this change of responsibility was that the First Special Brigade, with some added engineer battalions, was then able to provide beach service for the entire Seventh Army during the landing on Sicily, with the navy operating the boats. The First, Fifth, and Sixth Brigades provided for the American First Army at Normandy.[52] The southwest Pacific area retained the right for the engineers to man the boats because many of its landings were short hauls. The Second, Third, and Fourth Brigades eventually saw service under MacArthur, manning the boats and operating the beach.

In any event, by the target date of April 1943, in addition to fifty thousand

British in Combined Operations, the United States Army and Navy had produced a team of sixty thousand trained men.[53] The Americans alone could have landed at least four, and probably eight, divisions simultaneously. Not being needed, however, most of these men languished in the United States, while a few put a procession of infantry divisions through amphibious training. In January 1943, the Second Brigade was sent to Australia to assemble landing craft.[54] In October 1943, the Third Brigade was finally embarked after waiting six months for shipping (obviously not a high-priority unit). The last element of the Fourth Brigade did not leave for the Pacific until June 1944. There was no lack of trained men to operate the boats—the navy's resumption of the boat operation function had resulted in an oversupply of trained men.

July 1942 was the month of decision that sent our forces into North Africa and, coincidentally, during the same month, a major shift in the role of the marines was decided. Up to that time, the marines had been considered the striking force in all projected landings and had played that role in the two joint training forces. Then, along with the decision of the navy to operate the landing craft came the decision to move all marines to the Pacific theater, leaving the European theater with amphibious-trained army divisions for landings. In August, the First Marine Division was transferred to California. The rationale for the change was that the marines were trained and organized to attack a beach and secure it until the army arrived to take over. Then the marines were to withdraw and prepare for another invasion. When divisions landed in Europe and Africa, they landed to stay, and withdrawal would have been difficult.[55] The airborne divisions, however, were also used as assault forces, and they certainly were not designed to stay, nor was their withdrawal considered a problem.

To obtain a better understanding of Allied capability to achieve a landing in 1943, one must take a closer look at the landings in North Africa and Sicily. The types of craft available for TORCH were the Higgins boats (including some with ramps), the LCM, and the LCS (see Table 2). Only three of the Maracaibo tank landing ships were available. In other words, most of the landing would have to be done in the Higgins boats.[56] With this comparatively primitive array of landing craft, the plan called for the landing of two-thirds of the Second Armored Division and the Third Infantry Division (the latter having taken amphibious training on the West Coast) brought by convoy from the United States. The First United States Infantry Division (which had trained in amphibious landings with the marines on the East Coast), one-half of the First United States Armored Division, one-third of the Ninth United States Infantry Division (trained by an engineer special brigade), and the Seventy-eighth British Division, made a total of five and one-half divisions (about ninety thousand men) that were to land more or less simultaneously at widely scattered points.[57]

Each landing was a different experience. At Fedhala, the Third Division and Sixty-seventh Armored Regiment landed 40 percent of the troops and 16 percent of the vehicles on the first day, using Higgins boats, including LCVs and LCP(R)s for the tanks and vehicles. All of the troops and 68 percent of the

Table 2. Major Types of Landing Craft

Designation	Length, feet	Width, feet	Cargo	Number available			
				April 1943	Sicily	Sept. 1, 1943	Overlord
LST(2) Landing Ship Tank	328	50	27 light tanks or 15 medium tanks or 220 men	200+	148	295	233
LCT Landing Craft Tank	120	32	5 light tanks or 3 medium tanks or 150 tons	991+	238	479+	835
LCI(L) Landing Craft Infantry (Large)	158	23	205 men and 32 tons	220+	235	343	72
LCP, LCVP, LCM, Higgins boats Landing Craft, Personnel Landing Craft, Vehicle and Personnel Landing Craft, Mechanized	36–50		1 light tank or 36 men or 1 jeep or 1 artillery piece	7,000+	991	?	1,697+

SOURCE: Dwight D. Eisenhower, *Crusade in Europe* (Garden City, N.Y.: Permabooks, 1952), p. 70; Karig et al., *Battle Report*, p. 166; Donald Macintyre, *The Naval War Against Hitler* (New York: Scribner's, 1971), pp. 356–57; Leighton, *Global Logistics, 1940–1943*, p. 684; Coakley and Leighton, *Global Logistics, 1943–1945*, pp. 41, 75, 212.

vehicles were unloaded by the fourth day, but up to 160 of the landing craft had been destroyed, mostly on the first day. More than two hours were required to load the boats as the troops, each man burdened with sixty pounds of rations and equipment, climbed slowly down the cargo nets. There was no opposition at first, and 3,500 troops were beached before dawn, when resistance began.[58]

At Mehedia, the Sixteeth Regimental Combat Team landed in 161 Higgins boats at night. All went well with no opposition until dawn, when resistance began from three French regiments and a French tank regiment. Again, the unloading was slow because of darkness and 70 of the 161 landing craft were damaged.

At Safi, Combat Command B of the Second Armored Division and the Forty-seventh RCT landed without difficulty in the face of only 450 defenders. The tanks were carried on the *Lakehurst,* an eight-thousand-ton ship that had been a train ferry. The Sherman tanks were too large for the LCMs, so it was planned to beach the *Lakehurst.* Because of the light opposition, however, the ship was unloaded at the dock in the port. Of the 121 used, only one landing craft was destroyed and eight damaged.[59]

The Center Task Force struck at Oran on four widely separated points. The First United States Infantry Division and half of the First Armored Division made up the force of 39,000 men. The landings took place at night, which called for slow loading of the landing boats but resulted in little initial opposition. The tanks were carried successfully in three Maracaibos, each carrying twenty-two. Two of the landings were strongly resisted. The First Division lost over 360 men, but the troops were probably the best trained and had the best landing craft, though an insufficient number.[60]

The Eastern Task Force consisted of the 168th RCT of the Thirty-fourth Division, the Eleventh British Brigade, and the Thirty-ninth RCT of the Ninth Division. The men faced little opposition but had great difficulty with the boats. Ninety-eight of 104 boats were lost in waters calmer than on the Atlantic Coast, where only a third of the boats had been lost. The men complained that the boats were poorly designed; however, the actual problem was the poor training level of the navy crews of the landing craft who had been rushed from the United States at the last minute to replace the army engineers as a result of the jurisdictional dispute described above.[61]

The general estimate of the landings was that the British crews had handled their boats better, although they had to assemble a large portion of their total supply of boats and crews for the operation. The beach organization was poor, and it was fortunate that ports were seized early, because otherwise the supply system might have collapsed. The major faults were the poor piloting of the boats and the overloading of the troops with equipment. The plus factors were the development of the beach organizations both by the British with the Beach Group and Brigade Bricks and the American Shore Regiment of the First Special Brigade. Coordination of the landings from a headquarters ship to gather army, navy, and air force commanders together on one ship was solved on two beaches with headquarters ships, but on others the practice was still used of stationing the navy and army commanders on a warship that was subject to call for combat duty. When the big guns on the battleship were fired, most of the radio contact with the shore was broken.[62]

One factor, often ignored, was the spirited defense at some of the landings. At Casablanca, the *Jean Bart* was still at dock uncompleted, but four of her fifteen-inch guns were used against the invaders. Early in the morning, eight French destroyers and light cruisers attacked the convoy at Fedhala, shelling the landing boats. The American navy counterattacked, sank four destroyers and eight submarines that had joined in the attack, and damaged the cruisers and another destroyer. A few days later, German U-boats arrived, sank four ships, and damaged two others. The naval attacks on the invaders were heavier at Casablanca than at Normandy, and more ships were lost. But the Allies were ready to counter these attacks in strong fashion.[63]

Although the North Africa landing was successful, it was an amateur production compared to the Sicily invasion. Furthermore, the careful preparation and available resources used in the Sicily operation should have proved to any skeptic the solid state of the Allied landing capability in 1943. No lessons were learned by HUSKY (code name for the Sicily landing). It was the "first Combined Operation in which the Lessons Learned could not have been taken direct from the report on any exercise," according to General Robert D. Q. Henriques, a British officer on the Seventh United States Army staff.[64] The HUSKY planners were able to benefit from the buildup of equipment and trained men designed for ROUNDUP.

The number of troops in the initial assault was impressive, seven and a half divisions, compared to six at Normandy. Only 160,000 men were to land initially on Sicily compared to 176,000 at Normandy because fewer auxiliary units were used. There were to be 14,000 vehicles, 600 tanks, and 1,800 guns landed compared to 20,000 vehicles, 1,500 tanks, and 3,000 guns at Normandy, fewer but certainly in the same league. Included on the troop list were the First and Third Infantry Divisions that had taken amphibious training with the marines. Other American divisions in the assault were the Forty-fifth Division that had been trained for landings by the engineers in America, elements of the Second Armored Division that had landed in North Africa, and a parachute division that had some experience in North Africa. All of the British units had been blooded in battle, the Fifth, Fiftieth, and Fifty-first Infantry Divisions. The First Canadian Infantry Division came from the British Isles, where it had been since 1940.[65] Certainly no claim can be made that these troops were not trained.

There was no need to be concerned about the capture of ports, as in Africa, because the landing craft were sufficient to supply the needs of the army group. Instead, the concern was for the capture of airfields to provide bases for fighter cover.[66] The supply of landing craft that was used to launch HUSKY in Sicily would have been more than sufficient to launch an invasion in France in 1943 (see comparison on Table 2).

The entire landing operation was carried off even though the caliber of opposing troops was superior to that met in Normandy in 1944 and greatly superior to the quality of the troops manning the coastal defenses in Normandy in 1943. The new LSTs and LCIs made possible a shore-to-shore landing by the Third Division. The delivery of the new DUKWs meant rapid and efficient transfer of cargo from the landing craft to the troops. Some of the DUKWs were loaded directly from ships anchored offshore. Landing craft losses by the British were only 1.5 percent and by the Americans, operating in a heavy swell, only 12 percent compared to the 90 percent and 33 percent losses in North Africa. The trick of getting the boats ashore had been well mastered.

The logistics, according to Samuel E. Morison, "were well taken care of in HUSKY."[67] Stockpiles of material had been shuttled across the sea in LSTs from North Africa. The beach organization of the British was functioning well, and the First Engineer Special Brigade, with added engineer battalions, was serving the American army well. The training and planning prepared for D-Day in France in the spring of 1943, though it was denied its true goal, was given an opportunity to prove its capability.

Despite diversion of large numbers of landing craft to the Pacific, few of them were used in combat during 1943. At no time during 1943 were more than two divisions landed simultaneously. Normally the landings in MacArthur's area were short hops by forces of less than a division. The first major landing assault in the Pacific area under the navy was the attack on the Gilbert Islands by the Second Marine Division and the Twenty-seventh Infantry Division on November 20, 1943, five months after Sicily. The Second Marine Division had been idle in New Zealand since being withdrawn from Guadalcanal in January 1943, whereas the Twenty-seventh Division saw its first action at Makin Island in the Gilberts. The reinforced Twenty-seventh Division with nearly 20,000 men attacked less than 800 Japanese, including 200 Korean laborers, and suffered 66 killed and 152 wounded in the effort. This task required nine LSTs, an LSD, and a number of smaller craft, including 48 LVTs and numerous LCVPs.[68]

The Second Marines had a far more difficult time against nearly 5,000 Japanese on Betio-Tarawa, suffering over 3,300 killed and wounded. Their landing craft needs were only 12 LSTs, one LSD, and numerous smaller craft, including 125 LVTs but mostly the Higgins-type LCVP. Neither of these ventures required the use of large numbers of assault craft; most of the larger landing craft were being used for service functions rather than the combat function for which they were designed, while the European theater was supposedly in dire need, especially of the LSTs.[69]

Despite the alleged landing craft shortage, successful landings were made in North Africa, Sicily, and Salerno. In North Africa, the Allies put five and one-half divisions ashore, admittedly with some problems. On July 10, 1943, the Allies staged a seven-division landing in Sicily. This total lift in terms of combat troops landed was more than debarked in Normandy a year later, and the turnaround time was longer, for the shipping and the staging areas were far inferior to those available in England. Two months later, showing a logistical and planning organization effective enough to mount two major invasions in a short period of time, the Allies placed seven divisions at three points in Italy. The times of the landings were staggered, allowing reuse of landing craft, but if seven divisions could be lifted in the Mediterranean, certainly seven could have been lifted in the English Channel.

General Morgan complained after the war that no one would ever know how many landing craft were actually available for use by the British and Americans throughout the world at any given time and that if the figure were stated it could not be checked.

The landing craft were available. Ample supplies of all types of craft were available from early 1943. United States production of LSTs was in stride by October 1942 and by February 1943, 150 had been built and about 50 were completed each month. The United States had manufactured more than 470 LCTs by December 1942, while the British had completed 521 by that date, well over the number required for Normandy. More than 150 LCI(L)s had been built by the United States by December 1942 and 70 more were finished during the following month—three times the number needed for Normandy. The necessary number of craft had been built by early 1943, but many had been sent to the Pacific. Even those available in Europe were sufficient to launch seven divisions in Sicily. These facts reveal that there was not a shortage of landing craft.

6

COMPARISON OF

ARMOR

The inferior quality of Allied tanks as compared to German tanks was cited not only as a reason for postponing the invasion but also as the primary cause for other defeats. In 1942, the British generals were convinced that German armored equipment was superior to British tanks. This bogey had its beginning as part of the excuse for the rout of the British and French in France in 1940—that masses of powerful German tanks had made resistance impossible. In 1942, Rommel chased the British back to El Alamein, and, again, one of the reasons given was the superiority of the German tanks. The question is, were the German vehicles truly better, or were they used more skillfully?

From 1939 until the Russian counteroffensive during the winter of 1941-1942, the German panzers were supreme, not because of their quality or numbers, but because of the decisive manner of employment. By the end of 1942, the Germans had been defeated in Russia and in Egypt by overwhelming numbers of opposing tanks, clearly indicating that any technical superiority of the German panzers could be overcome by the massive employment of mediocre tanks. By mid-1942, the Allies had sufficient numbers of comparable tanks to overcome whatever the Germans could muster in France.

Before comparing the capability and weakness of the host of armored vehicles available to both sides in 1943 and 1944, an analysis of the tactical employment of these weapons is essential. The Anglo-French armies in 1940 had more tanks and in some respects better ones, but they were widely dispersed, inadequately supplied with fuel and ammunition, and committed to battle piecemeal. Defeat resulted from poor tank employment by commanders, not from poor tanks.[1]

The two fundamental approaches to the employment of military power were lightning strokes to paralyze the enemy and massive battles of attrition. The Germans used the blitzkrieg in 1940, while the Allies plodded through a battle of attrition. Weapons sometimes reflect the prevailing philosophy of commanders who have influenced the design to carry out their favored method, as did the Germans in 1940. At other times, the commanders were forced to fight battles in a certain way because of the availability of weapons with particular characteristics. For example, it was difficult to launch lightning strokes with heavily armored tanks having a top speed of twelve miles per hour, or, on the other hand, to fight a battle of attrition with lightly armored tanks.

Allied leaders in 1942 were divided on the issue of lightning war versus attrition. General George Patton believed firmly in lightning war, and his dash across France in 1944 was a sterling example of the method. Enormous bags of prisoners were taken, losses were comparatively light, and an even greater victory might have been achieved had the basic dictum of all competition been followed—"reinforce success, starve failure." Eisenhower and Montgomery, on the other hand, were believers in the battle of attrition. The Battle of El Alamein was a classic. The British lost 840 tanks and thousands of men in breaking Rommel's front. The failure to follow up the breakthrough and achieve the envelopment that should have resulted reveals a lack of appreciation for the art of mobile warfare.[2] Did the Allied commanders have the proper tools for a lightning war, or were they restricted by their weapons to a battle of attrition?

The Allies were aware of the relationship of the type of tank available to the strategy that could be employed. On September 12, 1942, the British adopted a "General Staff Policy on Tanks" that defined the tactical role of tanks. The tank was to assist in obtaining a decision in battle: (1) by engaging enemy armor in battle; (2) by attacking administrative echelons of the enemy rear; and (3) by operating against enemy infantry. For this purpose, the British established in order of priority the following requirements: (1) absolute reliability; (2) a six-pounder or heavier gun to fire both armor-piercing and high-explosive rounds; (3) be equal in speed to the enemy; (4) have a "useful" radius of action; (5) have armor proof against enemy tank guns at normal battle range; and (6) have a good fighting compartment.[3] The British "attrition" concept emerges from this policy—the tank is to fight other tanks with a heavy gun and armor proof against German tank guns. Speed and range, the attributes of the exploitation tank, were slighted. Speed need be merely equal to the German and range "useful."

The M4 Sherman tank, the one most widely used by the British and the Americans, was best suited for lightning war—it was fast and reliable, though lightly armored. Its gun was in the intermediate range. In fluid conditions, it performed well, but in head-to-head confrontation against a screen of antitank guns, it was deficient. Efforts to upgun and increase the armor were only partially effective, so the Allied leaders should have either avoided heavy battles of attrition or developed a new tank. When the Sherman was used in a battle of attrition, its losses were heavy. El Alamein was one example. "Operation Goodwood" was another. In July 1944, Montgomery attempted to smash head-on into heavily defended German positions. The Germans waited behind a screen of antitank guns and tanks placed to fire from "hull down" positions (with only the turrent exposed to enemy fire). With very little loss to the Germans, more than 300 British tanks were destroyed out of the 1,350 used. One British tank battalion lost 41 tanks, 80 percent of its strength.[4] The Sherman was not designed for a slugging match with antitank guns and suffered heavily when used in that manner.

If the Allied leaders were to insist on attrition, they needed a new tank. Winston Churchill had long sought to develop what he termed a "break through tank," a slow, heavily armored one suited for the head-on battle. In 1943, he advocated the construction of two to four hundred heavily armored tanks, called Churchills, sacrificing speed, which was reduced to eight or even six miles per hour.[5] Speed often had a low priority with British tank designers. The British "infantry" tanks, the Valentine and Matilda, with heavy armor though low speed, were designed for battles of attrition, but their guns were too light to make them effective against other tanks. Not until late in the war did the Americans and British develop heavily armored tanks, with an adequate gun, to perform in a slugging match, but by that time the war had become fluid, and there was little need for the heavy tanks.

German opinion was similarly divided regarding the use of armored vehicles. Although Hitler had supported the proponents of lightning war among his generals during the early years, the first defeats at the hands of the Russians made him more conservative. His decision during the winter of 1941–1942 to create a more static defense probably was a wise one in view of superior Russian mobility in the snow, but his insistence on carrying through a static defense philosophy for the remainder of the war had little result other than prolonging battle, costing more German lives, and sacrificing the possibility of local victories that might have discouraged the Russians.

By 1942, both sides had accepted the battle of attrition and static defense, giving only lip service to lightning war. Under such conditions, the speed and reliance of a tank were far less significant than its armor and gun. Hitler chided his generals that the speed of a tank merely enabled it to run away, just as the speed of a destroyer enabled it to flee from a battleship.

Under the impact of an altered philosophy, the design of the German tanks changed radically. They grew heavier and slower, and most of the armored vehicles produced were not tanks with a 360° traverse turrent, but rather tank hunters, tank destroyers, antitank gun carriages, and assault guns—defense-oriented weapons with only a limited traverse of the main gun.[6] By eliminating the turret, heavier guns could be placed on the existing tank chassis and put in action immediately, rather than waiting years to develop a larger chassis to mount the larger gun in a turret. It was difficult to place a long 75mm gun in a comparatively small tank turret on the Panzer IV, compared to placing the 105mm howitzer in a simple box on the much smaller Panzer II chassis.

The assault gun and self-propelled artillery piece were defensive in nature, and their adoption indicated a change in German philosophy from attack to defense. Even though the Allies continued to think offensively, they, too, became more conservative. Both the British and Americans reduced the number of armored divisions after 1942 and abandoned the concept of lightning strikes, thinking more in terms of tank-supported infantry. No new armored divisions were created after 1942 by either the Americans or British, and the latter in 1943 disbanded several existing armored divisions and brigades, while converting others to special purposes. By 1945, there were only five British armored divisions and sixteen American ones.

Instead of forming tank armies to strike deep into the enemy's vitals, the

British and Americans used armored vehicles as the French had used them in
1940, as infantry support units. Each British and American division in the European theater had a tank battalion and a tank destroyer battalion attached, and
tanks worked closely with the infantry.[7] Armored divisions were scattered along
the front rather than being concentrated in corps and armies. The lavish supply
meant that there were more than enough to go around. The tanks and tank
destroyers were even used as field artillery.[8]

As the role of the tank changed, so did its design. In 1943, the trend in new
designs was toward thicker armor and bigger guns, sacrificing speed and range.
Each new design offered some advantage such as more armor, a better gun, or a
more reliable engine. The prototype was built and tested, and after a year or so,
the new tank would go into production, although by then the philosophy behind
its original design or the conditions that prompted it would have changed. The
Russians and Americans stayed with the T34 and the Sherman, but even these
basic vehicles were subjected to improved guns and changes in the engine and
armor.

It cannot be said that one tank was better than another. Each had its strengths
and weaknesses. Nevertheless, the characteristics that were most important to the
success of a tank can be compared, such as guns, armor, speed, and reliability.
Relative judgment can be made on the basis of these four attributes.

The comparison of guns is not as simple a matter as might be assumed. The
quality of a gun in fighting other armored vehicles is based on high velocity and
heavy projectile weight. Momentum is equal to mass times velocity, so that a
heavy shell moving at a slower speed may have the same momentum or overall
stopping power as a small shell traveling at high speed. Because the momentum
of the large shell is spread over a greater area, however, the large shell may be
unable to penetrate the armor of a tank, whereas the smaller shell would. The
three factors involved in the efficiency of a gun were, therefore, the velocity, the
weight of the shell, and the impact measured in foot pounds per square millimeter. The British two-pounder shell weighed only two pounds, but had a diameter
of 40mm and a velocity of 2,600 feet per second, which made it an effective
antitank weapon, slamming about 4.14 foot pounds of energy against each square
millimeter of armor. The German 50mm tank gun with the long (L60) barrel
provided 6.18 foot pounds of energy per square millimeter and was, therefore, a
superior gun to the two-pounder.

The velocity of a projectile determined its penetrative power. To increase the
velocity, the amount of powder used to drive the projectile had to be increased or
the size of the projectile decreased. The latter solution was developed in the final
year of the war through various methods of firing small shot from large guns.
Until 1943, the approach was to add powder and make the barrel longer to give
the powder more time to burn before the shell left the barrel. The long barrel was
the visible evidence of a high-velocity gun, but the breech and chamber also had
to be made much sturdier to withstand the larger amount of powder, all of which
made these large guns difficult to mount in existing tank turrets. As a convenient

reference guide, guns were referred to not only by the diameter of the bore, for example 75mm, but also by the length of the barrel, which was expressed in a number equal to the length of the barrel divided by the diameter of the bore. Therefore, a 75mm L43 gun had a barrel 43 times 75mm long, or 3,225mm (10 feet 7 inches) long. Generally speaking, the longer the barrel, the higher the muzzle velocity.

Once inside a tank, a shell bounced around, exploded ammunition, and caused general havoc. Even if the shell did not penetrate, it could chip off metal on the inside of the tank, causing the same reaction. It made little difference how large the penetrating shell was, as long as it produced flying metal inside the tank. The usual method of expressing the effectiveness of a tank gun was the millimeters of armor that it could penetrate at varying distances, which was determined by actual test. Inasmuch as the tests gave varying results, there were often minor differences in the sources.

Comparing armor was even more complex. Each tank had different thicknesses of armor at different points. The front of the hull and the turret were most heavily plated. The top and rear surfaces, not usually exposed to direct fire, were most often lightly armored. The side armor was in between. Generally, an antitank crew was faced with the front of an oncoming tank. Great courage was needed, therefore, to allow a tank to go by, hoping that it would not see you, and then try to destroy it by firing at its side. Russian antitank gunners were best at the side shots simply because they could not run away for fear of being killed for desertion. Allied antitank gunners were reluctant to risk a side shot at close range. Therefore, the usual comparison of armor is made on the basis of the maximum armor surface on the front of the hull and turret. Armor could not be added to heavily shield all surfaces because that would add to the weight of the tank. The heavier the tank became, the larger the engine became to propel it, and the slower it moved, making it an easier target. Underpowered tanks tended to break down more often because the engine was continually under stress. A larger engine required a larger tank with more area to cover, which again increased the weight. Early in the war, German tanks were fast, but lightly armored. Later, the Germans decided to add armor and decrease speed. The first Tigers were underpowered and thus had frequent breakdowns. The Americans, on the other hand, were willing to sacrifice armor to retain speed. The British infantry tanks were underpowered and slow with a high rate of breakdown; the cruisers were generally fast with light armor, but also had high breakdown rates resulting from poor design.

Unreliability could be expected when a tank was underpowered or if the engine design had not been tested thoroughly. A well-designed engine that had not been overly modified was essential for reliable performance. The Liberty engine, a World War I aircraft engine, was dependable in its original form and was used to power early British tanks. As it was changed to increase horsepower to adapt to its new role, it became unreliable. The Americans used a variety of engines to power the Sherman, but all of them were based on well-tried designs. The

Table 3. **Guns and Armor on Tanks and Tank Destroyers**

	German					
	Panzer III (J)	Panzer IV (H)	Panther	Martin III	Tiger I	King Tiger
Gun	KWK 39 50mm L60	KWK 40 75mm L48	KWK 42 75mm L70	PAK 36(R) 76.2mm L54	KWK 36 88mm L56	KWK 43 88mm L71
Shell (pounds)	4 ½	15	15	16 ½	21	23
Armor penetration						
mm at 500 yards	61	91	141	98	137	193
mm at 1,000 yards	50	81	121	88	122	170
mm at 2,000 yards		63	106	79	110	152
Armor in mm	70	85	110	25	100	150
Muzzle velocity						
(feet per second)	2,700	2,460	3,057	2,420	2,648	3,270
Speed	25	22	29	26	25	26
Reliability	good	good	fair	good	poor	very poor

SOURCE: Wheldon, *Armies,* Appendix; Von Senger, *German Tanks,* pp. 209–10; Peter Chamberlain and Chris Elli

Germans used a basic line of engines for the Panzer I–IV tanks, but ran into difficulties when they increased the horsepower to operate the heavier tanks. The use of the Czech T38 chassis with an extremely good engine gave them a dependable base for many smaller vehicles.

Therefore, as we examine tanks on both sides, we must compare guns, armor, speed, and reliability. A comparison of the tanks available in 1943 is pertinent to the allegation that Allied armored vehicles were so inferior to German tanks that an invasion was not wise in 1943. The comparison a year before, or later, is of subordinate interest.

The myth of Allied tank inferiority was revived in June 1942 after the calamitous defeat of the Eighth Army by an inferior number of German tanks.[9] But the British tanks really were not at fault. In 1942, the British two-pounder tank gun was better than the short 75mm gun on the German Panzer IV tank and the 50mm L43 gun on the Panzer III. The British tanks had better protection with 65mm to 78mm armor on the infantry tanks and 40mm on the cruisers, compared to a maximum of 50mm on most of the German tanks. The German advantage in June 1942 was not guns and armor, but good maintenance of more reliable engines and the skillful tactical use that made their tanks more efficient.[10]

The Germans were well aware of certain deficiencies of their tanks. In November 1941, they encountered the Russian T34 tank outside of Moscow. The Russian high-velocity 76mm gun, plus superior armor, made contemporary German tanks obsolete, and steps were taken immediately to find the answer.

British		United States				
Cromwell	Firefly	Stuart	Sherman	M10 TD	M18 TD	M36 TD
6 PDR	17 PDR	37mm	75mm	3 in.	76mm	90mm
57mm	76mm	L50	L40	L50	L53	L53
L52	L55					
6	17	1 ½	13	13	13	23
87	140	48	68	99	99	113
80	130		60	89	89	104
67	111		47	73	73	87
76	76	67	76	37	12	50
2,700	2,900	2,545	2,600	2,800	2,600	2,800
32	25	36	29	30	50	30
good	good	good	good	good	good	good

ritish and American Tanks of World War II (New York: Arco, 1969), pp. 200–08.

The Panzer III and Panzer IV were provided with heavier armor and larger guns. By October 1942, the Panzer IV was being armed with a 75mm L43 gun or a better version, the 75mm L48. To withstand the high-velocity Russian guns, the armor of the Panzer IV was increased to 80mm in June 1942, and similar improvements were made in other tanks.[11] Both the Panther and the Tiger were being developed by the end of the year, but the tanks available to the Germans in France in the spring of 1943 were still the Panzer III and Panzer IV, plus captured tanks. The Tiger and the new Panther were in production but not available in quantity. The characteristics of all of these tanks are outlined in Table 3.

In 1943, the Panzer III(J) with a 50mm L60 gun, and protected with 70mm of armor, was outclassed by both the American M4 Sherman and the Russian T34 and was barely a match for the British cruiser types. At the end of 1942, the Panzer III(N) was in production, equipped with a 75mm L24 gun, a low-velocity infantry support gun. Only about 660 of these were made during 1943, and few were involved in tank battles. The earlier versions of the Panzer III and the Panzer I and II were not considered combat tanks by the Germans in 1943. The Panzer III(J) and Panzer III(N), like the Panzer IV, were reliable machines with many years of production experience behind them. But production of the Panzer III ceased in August 1943, although the chassis continued in use for assault guns.[12]

The Panzer IV(H), with a 75mm L48 gun and 88mm of armor, was a good match for the Sherman; its gun was a little better and its armor was 9mm thicker than that of the Sherman. These two tanks were the basic protagonists in the battles of late 1942 and 1943.[13]

The Tiger I was the pride of the German panzer force. Although slow, heavy, and mechanically unreliable, the thick frontal armor of up to 100mm and the 88mm L56 gun made this tank a fearful opponent. Yet the side armor of the Tiger was no better than that of the British infantry tanks, and fire from concealed antitank guns into her flanks was sufficient to stop the Tiger. The Tiger Battalion used in Tunisia early in 1943 was not a success.[14]

The Panther was still a thing of the future in the spring of 1943. Only seventy-seven were made by March, and in May few were in the hands of the troops. The Panther had its baptism of fire in the Battle of Kursk in July 1943 and proved very unreliable. None of the Panthers were available for use in the West during the summer of 1943.

German development of tank destroyers attempted to combine the role of assault gun with that of tank destroyer, both vehicles differing from tanks in that they had no turrets. The German philosophy was in part dictated by existing conditions. They were continually faced, after 1942, by superior numbers of enemy tanks. The combined Russian, American, and British tank production far exceeded the output of German factories. Therefore, tanks could not be wasted. Infantry and armored divisions were assigned large numbers of towed antitank guns and improvised tank destroyers, using an amazing variety of captured guns and tracked vehicles in addition to the German products.

The regimental antitank companies were upgunned from 37mm in 1940 to 50mm in 1941 and 75mm in 1942. The divisional antitank battalions were converted to 75mm guns in 1942 and often included some 88mm guns and a self-propelled company. There were few nondivisional antitank units, although 88mm antiaircraft battalions were often used to form the antitank screen that was the key element in German defense against the mass use of tanks by the Allies. The essential nature of the 88mm guns, in this role, gave rise to the ironic saying that the infantry fought until the last antiaircraft man was killed—with great reason, for when the antitank screen was destroyed, it was prudent for the infantry to leave because they were defenseless against the Allied tanks.

The assault guns and/or tank destroyers were used in increasing numbers in German formations, filling the role of substitute tanks. The early assault guns used in France in 1940 were designed as mobile infantry support guns to take the place of tanks in this role. Closely related were the tank hunters, panzerjagers, that had a role similar to the American tank destroyers, but lacked the turret of their American counterparts. In the beginning, the assault guns had low-velocity guns of 75mm caliber or larger, while the panzerjagers carried high-velocity guns of 75mm or less. As the war progressed, classification became more difficult; many vehicles could perform both roles, just as a tank could serve as an infantry support weapon, as well as fight other tanks.

By 1941, the Marder II and Marder III were in action, using the chassis of the Panzer II and the Czech T38 tank. They were armed with either a Russian 76mm

L54 gun or a German 75mm L46, both excellent guns with high velocity. Although the chassis were reliable and provided good speed (over twenty miles per hour), the armor was thin and could withstand little more than machine-gun fire.[15] All of these vehicles were open topped and did not provide all-around protection of any kind to the crews. They were primarily designed as tank destroyers and only occasionally performed the assault gun role as a substitute tank.

Self-propelled guns were improvised on many different chassis. The Wasp, an open-topped vehicle with light armor mounting a 105mm howitzer, was produced in 1942 on the Panzer II chassis and was used as a self-propelled artillery piece. A variety of vehicles mounting a low-velocity 75mm gun on a Panzer III chasis, with a closed top and thicker armor, were designated as the Assault Gun III that was most often used in the infantry support role as a substitute tank. A variety of guns were placed on the Assault Gun III; the best was a 75mm L48 gun. More than three thousand of these vehicles were made in 1943 and five thousand in 1944.[16]

A very successful vehicle that combined the function of the assault gun and tank destroyer was produced in 1943. This was the Baiter, a well-armored (60mm of frontal armor), fast (twenty-five miles per hour), and well-armed (75mm L48) vehicle, using the proven T38 chassis. The outstanding feature was its low profile; it was only a little over six feet high, an important feature in the survival of a tank destroyer, whose safety depended on good concealment and cover.[17] Very few of these vehicles were available to the troops until 1944.

At the end of 1942, the Germans began a concerted effort to upgun, that is, to provide larger guns for existing tracked vehicles. The Panzer IV tank could not take a gun in its turret larger than the 75mm L48 because there was no room for the gun to recoil, when fired, and still have space for the men to load it. In October 1942, increased production of assault guns was ordered to provide larger guns on tracks at the front. A 75mm L70 gun, with very high velocity, designed to be used on the Panther tank, was mounted on a Panzer IV chassis (without a turret) to create the Jagdpanzer IV. This design immediately provided the firepower of the Panther on a reliable chassis at the sacrifice of the flexibility of the turret-mounted gun. In 1943, the Tiger I gun, the 88mm L71, was placed on a Panther chassis creating the Jagdpanther. The change from tanks to assault guns in German production was startling. In 1942, assault gun production was less than 1,800 compared to 4,200 tanks. In 1943, assault gun and tank production was almost equal at 6,000 each.

The immense variety of vehicles created many headaches in repair and maintenance. The best types were sent to the eastern front, the remainder (older types, captured tanks, and the results of ideas that had not worked out) were left in the West. Most of the tanks in the West in 1943 were Panzer IIIs of which more than half were the older version with the short 50mm guns, a few Panzer IVs, Czech T38s with 37mm guns, and French Soumas with 37mm guns captured from the French in 1940.

The assault guns were of the poorer type. Some were French 75mm guns of World War I vintage mounted on captured French and British tracked infantry carriers. Others were 75mm guns or 105mm howitzers placed on the T38, Panzer II, or Panzer III chassis with open tops and partial side armor.[18] The best of the assault guns was the Marder III.

The general tank quality in the West was equal to or lower than the equipment that Rommel had at El Alamein. The Sherman, the Grant, and the British tanks of 1942 had proved superior to the German types at that time, which indicates that the Allies would have had tanks superior to the German armor in France in 1943.

Whereas the Germans had been developing their armored vehicles from the early 1930s, the Americans had done very little research on tanks before the beginning of World War II. The American tank designers were heavily influenced by German concepts and the reports that came back from France in 1940. As late as 1938, the basic American philosophy was that the tank should be an infantry support weapon armed with many machine guns. The M2 developed in 1938 at the Rock Island Arsenal became the basic chassis for the future M3 Grant and the M4 Sherman.

The M2 was neither a heavily armored tank to break through defenses nor a fast cruiser to plunge into the enemy's vitals with high speed and thin armor. Instead, the M2 was designed to plod along with the infantry providing machine-gun fire from six 30-caliber machine guns plus a 37mm gun. In August 1940, one thousand of these M2s were ordered, but were canceled when reports of the Battle of France indicated the need for a heavier gun.[19]

Rather than abandon all the research and development that had gone into the M2 and await the lengthy developmental period of a completely new tank, the decision was made to modify the M2 by enlarging the right-hand machine gun sponson to take a 75mm gun and to eliminate the other three machine gun sponsons. The redesign, called M3, was completed in March 1941 and was in production by June 1941 in a huge specially built tank arsenal in Detroit constructed by the Chrysler Corporation.[20]

As early as June 1940, the British were trying to buy tanks in America. They ordered quantities of a special variation of the M3 with a large turret which they christened the Grant. By August 1941, large-scale production was under way in three plants. The M3 had a 75mm gun of medium velocity, a good 37mm gun, and three or four machine guns. Its maximum armor thickness was only 37mm, however, and its high silhouette (ten feet, three inches high) made it an easy target. (The British Grant version was only nine feet, four inches high.) Its speed of twenty-six miles per hour was adequate. Its major weakness was the limited traverse of the 75mm gun, which put it in the class of a German assault gun. Great numbers of M3s were available in 1942, and they played an outstanding role in the British victories in North Africa. The Grant 75mm gun was the best tank gun in North Africa in 1942. The basic adage of the Allies, including the Russians, was that a large number of mediocre tanks were far better than a limited number of high-quality tanks, the philosophy that the Germans developed during the last years of the war.[21]

From the beginning, however, the M3 was considered only an expedient. The design of the M4 Sherman was begun in 1940 around the basic need for a 75mm gun in a full-traverse turret to match the German Panzer IV. The accepted design incorporated all of the basic mechanical parts (engine and transmission) of the M3 but changed the hull and the turret. By September 1941, a pilot model had been accepted. In March 1942, three factories were turning out M4s, and by the fall of 1942, eleven plants were making them. The new tank had the same 75mm gun as the M3 (mounted in a full-traverse turret) and had three machine guns. Armor was increased to 76mm on the turret and 50mm on the hull. It had a maximum speed of twenty-nine miles per hour and a lower silhouette (nine feet). It was simple to maintain, reliable, rugged, uncomplicated, and easy to manufacture. More than forty thousand were made. The disadvantage was the thin armor on the sides, exposing the gasoline tanks and engine. The nickname of "Ronson" (a popular cigarette lighter noted for its ability to light every time) came from the ease with which a single shot could set the Sherman ablaze. As a result, numerous expedients were used to apply additional armor, including welding on extra plates and attaching racks for sandbags.

Nevertheless, the Sherman was a good match for the Panzer IV in 1942 and in 1943. Later models had the improved M3 75mm gun, and in July 1942 the development of the 76mm gun M1 was begun. Few of these tanks were available, even by June 1944. In general, the Sherman was usually just a little behind the German Panzer IV in the continuing race to increase the power of the gun and the thickness of the armor.[22]

In the German Panzer III class, the United States built the M3 light tank which the British dubbed the Stuart. Much smaller than the medium, weighing only fourteen tons, the Stuart had a maximum speed of thirty-six miles per hour. The final design was approved in July 1940 after the Battle of France had indicated the need for more armor. Production began in March 1941. The 37mm gun (L50) and the 51mm armor were comparable to the early versions of the German Panzer III and superior to the various captured French tanks used by the Germans in France in 1943. In July 1941, 84 of the Stuarts were sent to North Africa, and, by November, 163 Stuarts made up about a third of the British tank strength in North Africa. In February 1941, the Cadillac Division of General Motors suggested that the M3 be built using two Cadillac engines, which were readily available, instead of the scarce aircraft-type engines. The result was the M5 Light Tank, also called the Stuart because the only significant difference was the engine. The M5 was also heavier and had more armor. Production began early in 1943. Both the M3 and M5 light tanks were in ample supply in that year with over 9,000 M3s completed by mid-1943.[23]

The United States developed a long line of auxiliary armored fighting vehicles similar to the German assault guns. To perform the role of the assault gun, a 75mm pack howitzer was placed in a half-track early in 1942 and was called the

T30. By April 1942, the chassis of the M5 light tank had been adapted to take the 75mm pack howitzer, mounted in an open-topped turret. About two thousand were made, providing an excellent infantry support vehicle similar to the Panzer III(N).[24]

The M7 Priest, a self-propelled, 105mm howitzer, performed the role of self-propelled field artillery similar to the German Wasp. Faced with a need to replace the 75mm pack howitzer on a half-track, the Americans placed a modified 105mm howitzer on an M3 medium tank chassis. Although the Priest was an expedient to provide immediate production, it proved to be very successful and over two thousand were assembled.[25]

The tank destroyer had a confused beginning in America. During the summer of 1940, following the German victory in France, a solution to the problem of defending infantry divisions against tank attack took on an extremely high priority. Should the antitank forces wait for tanks or search for them was the question basic to the development of organizations and weapons.

Many of the experts believed that the best defense against a tank was another tank, but this was a very expensive solution and meant dispersal of the tank force to defend the infantry. A towed antitank gun was simpler and cheaper. The antitank gun was light and easily concealable, but was limited to use in a static role by the infantry. A third alternative was an antitank gun mounted on either a wheeled or tracked vehicle to act aggressively in destroying tanks.[26]

Another question was how large the gun should be. The 20mm had proved ineffective in 1940, but the larger towed guns were difficult to move and conceal. In June 1940, General Lesley J. McNair decided on a towed gun, either a high-velocity 37mm or a 75mm with a range of over fifteen hundred yards. Antitank guns were to be grouped in units of three battalions held in reserve, until large bodies of tanks were located, and then sent out to destroy the tanks. Defense from minor tank-supported attacks was to be provided by infantry regiment antitank companies.[27]

This doctrine was accepted for trial on September 23, 1940, and discussed at length in 1941. Regimental antitank companies and independent antitank battalions were formed and tested in maneuvers. The conclusion favored the more flexible approach with large groups of antitank guns, but the question of towed versus self-propelled guns remained to be solved. Until October 1941, there were no self-propelled guns, so the towed guns had to suffice.

Early in 1942, a 75mm gun M1897A, the French 75mm gun left over from World War I, was mounted on the M3 motor carriage. Both towed and self-propelled battalions were formed. In November 1942, the forces that landed in North Africa had regimental antitank companies with towed 37mm guns and independent antitank battalions with twenty-four self-propelled 75mm guns.[28]

Performance in North Africa by the high-silhouette half-track was poor. The doctrine of seeking out tanks and ambushing them was changed by commanders in the field. Tank destroyers were ordered to charge enemy tanks in open fields. Heavy losses resulted, and the towed gun regained favor. In view of the failure of the self-propelled 75mm gun, Marshall offered Eisenhower 150 90mm antiair-craft guns mounted on antitank carriages along with armor-piercing ammunition. Eisenhower accepted the offer on March 18, 1943, but they arrived too late to be used in Tunisia, and no information on their use later has come to light.[29] (At the end of the war, a 90mm T9 was being developed.) The 90mm was a little too heavy to make a good towed gun. In 1943, the towed three-inch gun mounted on a low-silhouette carriage, which could be easily concealed, was adopted as the standard weapon for the independent battalions. The concept of a static defense against the tank was in keeping with Eisenhower's philosophy.

Nevertheless, the concept of a mobile tank destroyer was not dead. The M10 tank destroyer was available in 1943, another adaptation of the basic medium-tank chassis. In April 1942, plans had been made to mount the three-inch anti-tank gun on the M4 chassis with an open-top turret. The gun was an obsolete antiaircraft weapon that could penetrate 85mm of armor on the Panzer IV(H) at a thousand yards. By September 1942, production had begun, and by the end of 1943, over seven thousand were made. They weighed thirty-three tons, had a maximum speed of thirty miles per hour, and had 37mm of well-sloped armor. The crew had enough protection to permit its use as a tank or assault gun. In November 1943, the policy was changed; half the tank destroyer battalions used the M10, and the rest used towed three-inch guns.

In July 1943, production began on the M18 Hellcat with the 76mm L52 gun. The finest tank destroyer of World War II, weighing only twenty tons, it had a speed of up to fifty miles per hour and a low silhouette (only eight feet, five inches high, including the antiaircraft mount). The M18 was reliable and could cross rough terrain, but was not available in quantity to the troops until early 1944.[30]

The tank destroyer that would finally provide a gun equal to the Tiger tank was the M36. In October 1942, plans were made to place the 90mm L50 in the M10, which required the design of a larger turret. In April 1944, production began, but the M36 was not available to the troops in Europe until late 1944. The 90mm gun was an obsolete antiaircraft gun that could penetrate the armor of a German Panzer IV(K) at two thousand yards and a Panther or Tiger at five hundred yards.[31]

Regardless of the delay in developing a good tank destroyer, few would have been required for an invasion in 1943 because most of the German tanks were in Russia. Even in 1944, the German army could send far fewer tanks against the Allies in the West than had been anticipated in 1942. With small tank formations to deal with, there was no need for the tank destroyer brigades with nine or more tank destroyer battalions plus attached service troops (the equivalent of an anti-tank division) that were formed in 1943. The number of American tank destroyer battalions was reduced from 224 in 1942 to 106 and then to 78 early in 1944.[32]

Even in 1943, the American army had a surplus of armored vehicles of all types—tanks, self-propelled guns, and tank destroyers. The quality of the weapons was comparable to the major types in use by the Germans, and the number of American tanks was sufficient to overwhelm the few Tigers that the Germans had in 1943.

In addition to the American armored force, the British also had some useful vehicles, though not equal to the American products. The British armored vehicles lacked the simplicity of the basic American designs. While the Americans concentrated most of their production efforts on the two basic chassis, the light tank and the medium tank, merely altering the hulls, turrets, and guns, the British came up with a long list of alternate designs, searching for a reliable tank with an adequate gun which they never really achieved. From 1942 on, many of their tank regiments were equipped with the Sherman M4.

During 1942, the British were using, in addition to the American tanks, the Matilda that had been developed before the war. It had proved extremely successful in North Africa in 1940 and 1941 against the Italian tanks. It was heavily armored, up to 78mm, and the two-pounder gun was quite effective. In 1942, however, it was outclassed, and the turret was too small to take even a six-pounder (57mm) gun. The Matildas were being used for training and special purposes by the end of 1942.[33]

The Valentine was the successor to the Matilda in the heavily armored infantry tank class. Production had begun in 1940, and it was first used in North Africa in June 1941. Its turret was large enough to take the six-pounder that was fitted beginning in March 1942. In March 1943, a medium-length 75mm gun was installed in the same turret, which gave the British a well-armored (up to 65mm) assault tank, but with very low speed, a maximum of only fifteen miles per hour, as a result of a small engine producing only 138 horsepower and its heavy weight (twenty tons). The Valentine was the most reliable of the early British tank designs, but suffered from the small turret that limited the size of gun that could be installed.[34]

In 1942, the British had two cruiser tanks, that is, tanks with lighter armor and higher speed than the infantry tanks. The Covenanter, the Cruiser Mark V (A13, Mark III), was the outcome of four years of effort to design a fast tank based on the Christie suspension (characterized by large road wheels that made higher speed practical). The Covenanter went into production early in 1940, and although it was used by the Ninth, Eleventh, Forty-second, and Guard Armored Divisions in the United Kingdom for training until 1943, it was never used in combat. Even though it had a speed of thirty-one miles per hour, the two-pounder gun, 40mm armor, and mechanical unreliability made it unsuitable for battle. The engine, despite many modifications, overheated and broke down. In combat, this would have been a serious problem.[35]

The other cruiser available in 1942, the Crusader, the Mark VI (A15), evolved from the same design development as the Covenanter. The Crusader went into production in 1940, and in the spring of 1941, it was the principal British tank in North Africa. The two-pounder gun was replaced by a six-pounder in 1942. The Crusader had 51mm of armor and a speed of twenty-seven miles per hour. By the end of 1942, 5,300 had been built, and they continued in combat until the end of the Tunisian campaign in May 1943. The Crusader suffered from mechanical breakdowns, and a great deal of maintenance was required to keep it running.[36]

The Churchill infantry tank was available in limited numbers in 1942, but suffered the same problem of unreliability as did the two cruisers. Production began in June 1941, but mechanical difficulties resulted in redesign and alteration. By April 1942, over a thousand had been made, the originals with the two-pounder gun and models after April 1942 with the six-pounder. The 102mm armor made it heavy (forty-four tons) and slow (fifteen and a half miles per hour maximum) even with a 350-horsepower engine. The Churchill was first used in combat at Dieppe and then in Tunisia. In January 1943, a medium-length 75mm (L37) gun was added, but the turret was not big enough for the more powerful long 75mm guns. Nevertheless, with the 75mm L37, the Churchill performed well for the rest of the war. Over 5,600 were built and used in a wide variety of special roles.[37]

During 1941, the British were trying to design a heavier cruiser tank, using a larger engine and mounting a heavier gun. The Cavalier was an unsuccessful attempt to use the Liberty engine with an improved Crusader chassis with heavier armor and larger turret. The first model was completed in January 1942, but most of the Cavaliers were used for artillery observation.

The Centaur was based on an improved Crusader chassis developed for the Cromwell, but used the improved Liberty engine designed for the Cavalier because the aircraft engines intended for the Cromwell were in short supply. The Centaurs were designed to exchange engines when the Rolls-Royce Meteor engines were available and become Cromwells. By the end of 1942, production was under way, and 476 were built by July 1, 1943. The Cromwell used a Rolls-Royce engine developing six hundred horsepower. In January 1943, production began with a version mounting a six-pounder gun. The Cromwell was a fast tank, thirty-two miles per hour, with 76mm of armor, and was comparable to the Sherman tank. However, the first Cromwells with the 75mm L37 gun were not delivered until November 1943, and, by then, the demand was for a longer gun.[38] The Cromwell, along with the Sherman, formed the main equipment of the British armored divisions in 1944. Both the Cromwell with the six-pounder and the Churchill were well developed by 1943 and were in the hands of the troops.

In November 1942, the British planned to equip five tank brigades with Churchills, while the five armored divisions then equipped with Covenanters were to receive Crusaders, Centaurs, and Cromwells no later than August 1943. All of these were battleworthy tanks.[39]

In the field of self-propelled guns, the British relied heavily on American models. The Sexton was made in Canada, based on a chassis very similar to the American M3 and mounting a British twenty-five-pounder gun. As they became available, the Sexton replaced the Priest M7 self-propelled 105mm howitzer in the role of artillery support for the armored divisions.

Most of the British antitank battalions were equipped with towed guns, moving from the two-pounder in 1940 to the six-pounder in 1942 and finally to the seventeen-pounder in 1943. These battalions were assigned permanently to each division with very few extra battalions at higher levels. Self-propelled battalions using American M10s were assigned to the armored divisions, and a few were held in reserve. At no time were large numbers of units created on the same scale planned for the United States Army. The British seemed more inclined to use tanks to fight tanks in the North African battles, rather than rely on screens of antitank guns. This philosophy cost them heavily in tank losses throughout the war.

To make use of the powerful seventeen-pounder gun as a tank destroyer, the British replaced the three-inch gun in the M10 tank destroyer and called it the Achilles. This vehicle, however, was not available until January 1945.[40]

The Archer also used the seventeen-pounder mounted on a Valentine chassis. Because of the large size of the gun, the chassis had to be redesigned, and, in the final design, the gun pointed to the rear with only limited traverse like the German assault guns, rather than the turret mounting that the Americans used. The vehicle did not go into production until March 1944 and proved successful, despite the awkwardness of having to turn the vehicles around to fire the gun.[41] Neither of these vehicles was ready in 1943, so the British relied on American products in the self-propelled gun line.

The tremendous production achievement of the Allies between 1940 and 1943 resulted in a complete reversal of philosophy. In May 1940, the Allies deployed both antitank guns and tanks in a thin, defensive screen which the Germans pierced with massed armor. By 1943, the Germans were relying on a defensive screen (slightly thicker, to be sure) of guns and tanks, trying to ward off massed Allied tank forces. The Germans placed great emphasis on heavy towed guns supplemented by tank destroyers or assault guns. The tank destroyers were designed to deliver heavy fire on enemy tanks from a concealed position, and, therefore, less emphasis was placed on speed, and the armor on the tank destroyers grew heavier. The old concept of a fast tank destroyer, with a heavier gun but with little armor, that could run away in the event of a pitched battle was maintained only by the Americans, who felt that high speed was necessary to catch the prey. Therefore, on both sides, there was division regarding the use of tank destroyers as well as tanks, dictated primarily by the numbers available.

The inferiority of Allied equipment compared to German equipment, especially tanks, was often expressed as a reason for delay of the invasion. In 1941 and early 1942, the British tanks had proved inferior to the tanks in the German Afrika Korps. By April 1943, however, the Sherman tank had completely replaced earlier models in American armored divisions and in some British armored divisions. There were ample quantities to supply the British, and even the Russians were sent a few thousand. The Sherman was about equal in armor and gun power to the German Panzer IV(H), the major tank. The Tiger I was the best tank around in 1943, but few were available, and they were not dependable. The Panther was still being developed and proved undependable when first used at Kursk in July 1943. The British Cromwell and Valentine were inferior to the

German tanks, but the Churchill was still a match because of its armor. Alexander praised the Churchill highly; in a report to the prime minister on March 23, 1943, he called the Churchill the only good British tank.[42] The ambivalent attitude of the British toward the fitness of their tanks can be shown by two papers, both prepared by A. Richardson, director of armored fighting vehicles, in a two-week period. The first, dated January 25, 1943, assumed the invasion was still on for April 1943 and indicated that the British could provide tanks for only one armored division plus 100 percent reserves, exclusive of Crusader IIIs and Valentines, which he considered not suitable for combat. He thought the Sherman had limitations and the Cromwell would prove superior.

Only twelve days later, on February 6, Richardson assumed that the invasion would not take place until 1944, and he then presented a more optimistic attitude toward developing types. The Cromwell and the Centaur plus the Challenger being developed would be adequate for 1944 needs.[43]

The German Panzer III(J) was better than the American light tanks M3 and M5, which were in turn superior to early Panzer IIIs and the French tanks used by the Germans in the West. The American M10 tank destroyer had a complete traverse turret; the German tank destroyers did not, which gave the former an advantage.

In comparing the long list of minor armored vehicles, the Allies based theirs on proven chassis, like the M3 medium tank and the M3 light tank, that were more mechanically reliable than those of the Germans. The Czech T38 chassis was the basis for many of the miscellaneous German weapons, but was in the weight class of the light tank and was often overweighted by its guns. The overall situation was favorable to the Allies in 1943.

Matters changed dramatically by June 1944. The Sherman was still the mainstay of Allied armor, but, by then, it was inferior to many of the German tanks in use. In 1944, the Panther was in full production, using the high-velocity 75mm L70 gun that could penetrate the armor on the Sherman at over two thousand yards. The Tiger I posed an even greater problem, with its 120mm of frontal armor and an 88mm L56 gun that could pierce the Sherman at well over two thousand yards. The King Tiger, which appeared in numbers in 1944, had an even more powerful gun. On June 13, 1944, two companies of Tigers, a total of only thirteen tanks, on a hill southeast of Caen, shot up most of the Seventh British Armored Division while suffering the loss of only three tanks. One Tiger destroyed twenty-five British tanks at a range of eight hundred yards.

The Germans developed several types of powerful self-propelled tank destroyers between 1943 and 1944. By June 1944, German tank destroyers were using 75mm L70 gun on vehicles such as the Hetzer and the Jagdpanzer IV. This gun was much more powerful and could penetrate double the armor of the Sherman at two thousand yards. The quality of German tank destroyers had greatly outpaced Allied development during the months between the summer of 1943 and the summer of 1944. Their ability to destroy Allied tanks was limited only by their ability to see them and aim their guns properly.

Table 4. Comparison of Numbers of Tanks Produced, 1942–1944

Country and Tank type	Production 1942	Estimated available Jan. 1943	Production Jan.–June 1943	Estimated available Apr. 1, 1943	Production 1943	Estimated available June 1944
United States						
Medium M3 tank	}14,049	6,258	0		0	
Medium M4 tank		9,000+	11,916	15,000	21,250	20,000
Light tank	10,947	13,000+	4,583	10,000	8,212	10,000
Self-propelled guns	10,644	10,000+	6,182	15,000	est. 12,000	20,000
Total	35,640	38,258+	22,681	40,000	41,462	50,000
Great Britain						
Crusader		2,000+	1,403	2,000	1,944	2,500
Churchill	2,000	2,000	877	2,500	1,346	3,000
Valentine		4,000+	1,004	2,500	1,794	2,500
Centaur			476	400	1,271	1,000
Cromwell			92	100	561	500
Miscellaneous		1,000+	329	500	560	500
Total	8,611	10,000	4,188	8,000	7,476	10,000
Total Britain and U.S.	44,251	48,000+	26,869	48,000	48,938	60,000+
Germany						
First-line tanks	6,189	6,643	4,541	4,234	10,747	10,484
Second-line tanks		1,284		1,391		1,867
Captured tanks		1,000		822		500
Total	6,189	8,927	4,541	6,447	10,747	12,851

SOURCE: William K. Hancock, ed., *Statistical Digest of the War* (London: H. M. Stationery Office, 1951), p. 148; Seaton, *Russo-German War*, p. 402; Mueller-Hillebrand, *Das Heer*, 3:274, 124; Richard M. Leighton, *Global Logistics and Strategy, 1940–1943* (Washington: Department of the Army, 1955), Appendix B; Great Britain, War Office, *War Time Tank Production, Command Paper 6865* (London: H.M. Stationery Office, 1946), passim; Chamberlain and Ellis, *British and American Tanks*, pp.108, 37, 60; Churchill, *Hinge of Fate*, p. 850; Tank Production, PREM 3/425, PRO.

In general, the German army was better equipped in 1944 than in 1943. During the same period, there were few improvements in Allied equipment, although better tanks and guns did become available at the end of 1944. Therefore, though some of the Allied equipment was inferior to certain types of German equipment in 1943, the disparity increased to a marked degree in favor of the Germans in June 1944.

The general philosophy of the American army toward tanks was that an ample supply of mediocre tanks was better than an inadequate supply of excellent ones. Thus, the United States placed the ungainly M3 Grant in production and stayed with the Sherman M4 long after it had fallen behind technologically. The Germans, on the other hand, were concerned with improving their tanks to match the quality of the Russian tanks. Therefore, production schedules were continually interrupted, resulting in very limited tank production in 1942 and 1943. Table 4 compares American, British, and German tank production during 1942 and 1943 and compares the number of tanks and tracked vehicles available on January 1, 1943, April 1, 1943, and June 1944. Even by January 1943, the Allies had an incredible number of tanks available. The final campaign in Tunisia and the occupation of Sicily demonstrated the impact that numerical tank superiority could make on a battlefield suitable for armor. The minor advantages that the Germans might have possessed in quality in 1943 could not make up for numbers. While Allied design and numerical strength remained static in 1944, the Germans, through massive production efforts, came a long way toward closing the gap by June 1944, and, by December 1944, were able to give the Allies a sharp lesson in tank warfare. Under any possible interpretation of these facts, an invasion in 1943 would have been more advantageous to the Allies than waiting until 1944.

7

TANK FORMATIONS

Tanks and other tracked, armored vehicles were the pride of the battlefield. Yet, because of their inherent weaknesses, as with all other weapons, they had to be organized in such a way that they could be supported, protected, and transported. Comparisons between opposing tank forces in western Europe in 1943 should be made therefore in terms of tank formations. The formation giving greatest impact to the tank was the armored or panzer division, a large formation of one hundred to four hundred tanks and ten thousand men that had a balanced collection of supporting units both to assist the tank in combat and to supply its needs out of combat.

Tank brigades and groups consisted of three tank battalions including up to 150 tanks, but without any supporting units. The brigades were used to provide tank support to infantry units, often being split up to provide one battalion each to infantry divisions. Separate tank battalions with up to 50 tanks were attached to infantry divisions to provide support. While the Germans concentrated most of their tanks in panzer divisions and used assault gun battalions to provide support for the infantry, the British created a number of tank brigades equipped with infantry tanks to fill this role. The Americans attached separate tank battalions plus a tank destroyer battalion to practically every infantry division in combat.

Therefore, a comparison of tank formations has to take into consideration the Allied policy of dispersing their tanks while the Germans kept most of their tanks concentrated in the panzer divisions. The Allies, however, had so many tanks they could afford to parcel out thousands and still have enough to outnumber the Germans decisively in armored divisions in 1943.

The German panzer division, in early 1943, had an authorized strength of 167 armored vehicles, whereas its American counterpart had 390 tanks plus other armored vehicles (see Table 5). The main components of the panzer division were the panzer regiment with two battalions and two panzer grenadier regiments with a total of four infantry battalions, of which one was mounted in half-tracks and the other three rode in trucks.

The panzer divisions in the West were far from being up to strength. After heavy losses in the East in 1941 and 1942, the Germans were short of tanks and other weapons. In April 1942, some of the panzer divisions on the eastern front had been reduced to one tank battalion, three motorized infantry battalions, plus field artillery and other support units.[1] A strenuous effort was made to rebuild most of the panzer divisions in the East for the summer campaign of 1942, leaving few replacement tanks for the remaining panzer divisions. An example of the drastic rebuilding required and the limited results achieved, even in 1942, is the Tenth Panzer Division. After hard fighting during the winter of 1941–1942, the Tenth Panzer Division was reduced to its service elements, two battle groups with a total of less than 750 men, the Seventh Panzer Regiment with only 650 men, and the Ninetieth Artillery Regiment with about 940 men.[2] The units of the division were scattered about the eastern front plugging gaps. On April 15, 1942, the division was ordered to surrender most of its equipment to the Twentieth Panzer Division, the Eleventh Panzer Division, and the 221st Infantry Division and to prepare to move to France.[3] The remaining 3,745 men and about 300 vehicles were loaded on ten trains and sent to the Laon-Soissons area in France between April 18 and 22, 1942.[4]

The division was filled with men recuperating from wounds and recruits with four to six weeks of training. Captured weapons, mostly French, were provided in May and French vehicles in June. The division was to be ready for coastal defense duties by July 1 and for combat by August 15. The authorized strength of the division was reduced; there would be no machine gun company in the infantry battalions; all four of these battalions were to be equipped with trucks, rather than one with half-tracks; and the panzer regiment was to have only one tank battalion; the other battalion was to be refitted for combat on the eastern front.[5]

On May 3, 1942, the division had 38 Hotchkiss tanks, 7 Somuas, 17 Panzer IIIs and 5 Panzer IVs. Many items of equipment were still lacking.[6] A second tank battalion was formed, designated as the III Battalion, Seventh Panzer Regiment, but, on May 25, this battalion was redesignated the III Battalion, Thirty-sixth Panzer Regiment and reassigned, once again reducing the division to only one panzer battalion.[7] On May 27, the division still lacked German tanks and was short over 600 specialists including motorcyclists, engineers, drivers, infantry gunners, and service troops as well as 51 officers.[8] On June 4, the division was moved to Amiens and on June 18 engaged in its first maneuvers.[9] On August 12, less than four months after its transfer from Russia, the division was declared ready for defensive duties in the West, six weeks behind schedule and still short 35 officers and 60 men, 250 trucks, 104 motorcycles, 7 tank destroyers, and 5 other armored vehicles.[10] On August 21, the Tenth Panzer Division was put on standby orders to be ready to march to defend the Calais coast within four to eight hours of an alarm. The division was not, however, considered fully fit for eastern front service.[11]

The threat of Allied invasion resulted in strenuous efforts in September 1942 to improve the equipment. By October 1, five and a half months after refitting began, the division had German weapons, including 20 Panzer IVs, 108 Panzer IIIs, and 2 assault guns. The antitank unit had only 9 self-propelled 76mm Russian guns, 9 towed 75mm antitank guns, and 8 88mm antitank/antiaircraft guns, plus 33 50mm and 37mm antitank guns. This list of weapons was not comparable to that of an Allied armored division, yet the Tenth Panzer was the

Table 5. **Comparison of Armored Divisions, 1942–1943**

Weapons authorized	U.S. Armd. Div. March 1942 authorized	Br. Armd. Div. 1942 authorized	10th Ger. Pz. Div. Oct. 1942 actual	24th Ger. Pz. Div. May 1, 1943 actual
Pistols	3,850	2,924		2,375
Rifles and carbines	7,670	7,601		9,402
Rifles, foreign				3,600
Submachine guns	2,160	866	1,077	1,390
Machine guns	394	868	1,078	824
Machine guns, foreign				43
Machine guns, obsolete				127
Mortars	84	78	30	72
Antitank guns				
37mm/40mm towed	68	36		6
50mm/57mm towed		183	21	
75mm towed			9	38
37mm self-propelled	}126		12	
75mm self-propelled			9	6
Assault guns				
75mm howitzer	42		2	6
150mm howitzer				

Self-propelled guns				
105mm/25 pdr.	54			
Towed field artillery				
75mm howitzer		24	20	18
150mm howitzer			16	4
105mm howitzer/25 pdr.		24	24	16
100mm gun			4	4
Antiaircraft guns				
20mm		52	26	66
20mm quadruple mounts			8	2
88mm				8
40mm self-propelled		36		
Tanks				
Light	158		108	
Medium	232	278	20	
Light, foreign				5
Armored cars	79		39 (incl. Pz II)	50
Half-tracks and carriers	733	151		
Other vehicles	2,186	2,782		}600
Foreign vehicles				250
Horses				98

source: H. F. Joslen, *Orders of Battle, Second World War, 1939–1945*, 2 vols. (London: H.M. Stationery Office, 1960), 1:129: Records of German Field Commands, Divisions, Tenth Panzer Division, Microfilm, Series GG65 T315, roll 570, frame 263; Ibid., Twenty-fourth Panzer Division, roll 805, frame 89; Robert R. Palmer, Bell I. Wiley and William R. Keast, *The Procurement and Training of Ground Combat Troops* (Washington: Department of the Army, 1948), p. 321.

best equipped German division in the West by a wide margin.[12] The Tenth
Panzer remained in France as an occupation division until December 1942, when
it was sent to Tunisia, because it was the only reasonably fit armored division not
committed to the eastern front.[13]

By April 1943, the Russian victories in the East and the loss of North Africa
resulted in heavy losses in tanks that could not be replaced. The number of
first-line tanks available decreased from 6,643 to 4,234 between January 1,
1943, and April 1, 1943. The available tanks were sent to the combat areas,
stripping the German army in the West. At the same time, the West was called on
to recreate the divisions that had been lost at Stalingrad. These paper divisions
made up much of the German army in France in April 1943. The panzer divisions
in the West were at a very low state, using mostly obsolete German tanks or
French tanks for training (see Table 6). Even these substandard weapons were in
short supply.

The First Panzer Division had fought in the East almost continuously from
June 1941 until January 1943, when it was sent to France to refit, absorbing the I
Battalion, 203d Panzer Regiment. The Fourteenth and Sixteenth Panzer Divisions
were reforming after the original divisions had been captured at Stalingrad.[14]

Three motorized divisions that had been lost at Stalingrad were also being
reformed, the Sixtieth using the 271st Infantry Regiment as cadre, the Twenty-
ninth using the units of the 345th Motorized Division, and the Third Motorized
using the 386th Motorized Division. The 345th and 386th had been formed in the
winter of 1942–1943 from training battalions.

The Twenty-sixth Panzer Division was a new formation that had been created
at Amiens in France in September 1942 as the Twenty-sixth Panzer Grenadier
Brigade using two regiments from the Twenty-third Infantry Division. The 202d
Panzer Regiment (formerly an occupation unit with French tanks) was added on
February 1, 1943, to form the Twenty-sixth Panzer Division.[15]

The Ninth and Tenth SS Panzer Divisions were also training in France in
April. Both were formed from recruits from the Hitler Youth, boys about eighteen years of age, and their training was proceeding at a leisurely pace.[16]

The Twenty-fourth Panzer Division, another Stalingrad division, can be used
as an example of the reforming procedure. After the surrender of the Twenty-
fourth Panzer at Stalingrad, the new division headquarters was established at
Lisieux, France, on February 21, 1943. The division was to be reformed from
remaining men of the old division, who had not been with the division in
Stalingrad, plus added units: III Battalion, Fifth Security Regiment; Fifth Company, Ninth Panzer Grenadier Regiment; Fifth Battery, Ninety-third Artillery
Regiment; a pioneer platoon from the Twenty-sixth Panzer Division; and elements of the Nineteenth Luftwaffe Field Division. The first elements of the old
Twenty-fourth Panzer Division (men who were returning from hospitals and who
had been on furlough when the division was surrounded) arrived in Lisieux
during the week of February 21, along with the cadre units mentioned above.[17]

By March 6, 1943, the division had 82 officers and nearly 6,000 men, equip-

Table 6. German Panzer Units in the West, April 15, 1943

Unit	Panzer II	Panzer III				Panzer IV		Captured	Command	Total	Men
		"F" Short 50mm	"M" Flame	"J" Long 50mm	"N" 75mm	"F" Short 75mm	"H" Long 75mm				
1 Pz	10						57		4	71	
14 Pz								35		35	7,008
16 Pz								18		18	10,080
24 Pz						4?		25		29	15,380
26 Pz	9		12	23	14	6	53		10	127	
9 SS											13,718
10 SS											14,343
Goering Panzer							20		2	68	
3 Mtr		5		39	4	12				61	
29 Mtr		21		13		9		7		65	
60 Mtr		29		8				28		28	
100 Pz Reg	2						2	153	1	158	5,000
213 Pz Bn								32		32	
505 Pz Bn				25			20			45	
Marseilles		6	2	3						11	
Total, April 15, 1943	46	61	14	111	18	31	152	298	17	748	
Total, June 20, 1943	107			351				400		868	

SOURCE: *Kriegstagebuch des Oberkommandos der Wermacht*, 4 vols. (Frankfurt am Main: Bernard und Graefe, 1963), 3:265–335; Mueller-Hillebrand, *Das Heer*, 3:125–26.

ped with 3,110 German rifles, 600 French rifles, 138 German machine guns, 86 Czech and French machine guns, 33 antitank guns (of which 14 were French 75mm guns from World War I), 12 105mm howitzers, and 8 88mm guns plus some other weapons. Though the division was supposed to be completely motorized, it had 186 horses and 28 horse-drawn carts to supplement its meager supply of motor vehicles.[18]

The division reported on March 6 that the veterans of the old division were battle-tested; they were training the newcomers and the Luftwaffe men, who were fit but needed training and battle experience. The cadre units were also performing training tasks. The greatest problem was the lack of truck drivers, a problem that would plague the division for months.[19]

By March 7, about a thousand men, recuperating from wounds, had arrived from Insterburg, the home station of the division and the location of its replacement battalions.[20] On the same date, more troops arrived from Russia along with the Achilles Antiaircraft Battalion. On March 23, the tanks arrived, 5 Panzer IVs with long 75mm guns, 24 French Hotchkiss, and one Somua.[21] On March 25, the 127th Signal Battalion arrived, was redesignated the Eighty-sixth Signal Battalion, and added to the division. By March 24, the division had 184 officers, 8,374 men, and 98 Russian Hiwis. Of the total assigned, however, 1,270 were still on furlough after having fought in Russia.[22] The equipment was inferior; many of the French rifles were in poor condition; the field artillery had only two batteries of French howitzers and two batteries of French 75mm guns; and many of the vehicles were French. On March 30, more German equipment arrived, a battery of 100mm guns, a battery of light infantry guns, some 50mm and 75mm antitank guns, antiaircraft guns, machine pistols, and German rifles. To provide tractors for the field artillery, 14 Renault tanks were delivered, along with 14 Panzer IIIs with flame throwers. Service units were created, including two truck companies with 96-ton capacity.[23]

The 127th Tank Battalion was ordered from Russia on April 6, to become the III Battalion of the Twenty-fourth Panzer Regiment on May 22. Because of the shortage of tanks, the new tank battalion was to be equipped with assault guns that were to arrive in May or June.[24]

Between April 11 and 13, the men of the 891st Panzer Grenadier Regiment arrived in six trains. This regiment had a full complement of men and noncommissioned officers recently graduated from schools, but the officers were inexperienced. The regiment was broken up; the headquarters and one infantry battalion became the headquarters and II Battalion of the Twenty-first Panzer Grenadier Regiment; the other infantry battalion became the I Battalion of the Twenty-sixth Panzer Grenadier Regiment; and the artillery battalion became the II Battalion of the Eighty-ninth Panzer Artillery Regiment; the remaining companies formed the Twenty-fourth Reconnaissance Battalion.[25]

Many of the new men still needed individual training. The Fifteenth Army established schools for tank and half-track drivers, and the division created an automotive driver school.[26] Other schools were set up to teach leadership, panzer tactics, and combat techniques. Emphasis was placed on combat rather than on close-order drill. Machine-gun training and Nazi ideology were also stressed.[27]

The division was inspected on April 21 by the commander of the XIV Panzer Corps, who made the following criticisms: 35 percent of the officers were over-age; Czech light machine guns were still issued to the service units; the assault guns in the III Battalion of the panzer regiment were only a stopgap; and absence of the I Panzer Battalion greatly reduced the combat effectiveness of the division. The inspector stressed the need for field training, which was not possible because no suitable training ground was available. Above all, stress was laid on the need for each man to know his weapon thoroughly.[28]

The division received some additional weapons in May. The panzer grenadier regiments received six 150mm self-propelled heavy infantry guns; the antiaircraft battalion received eight new 88mm guns, type 37.[29] By May 7, the division had reached a comparatively high level, both in manpower and equipment. The division had 17,429 officers and men. (The equipment of the division is given on Table 5.) Although the division had developed considerably, it was not compara-ble to an Allied armored division. The artillery, antiaircraft, infantry, and tank units all needed better weapons, even for training purposes. Only on May 23 was the division finally given enough trucks to rid itself of bicycles in the infantry battalions, and, although two of the tank companies rode in tanks, the rest were still on bicycles.[30]

In May 1943, the Twenty-fourth Panzer had only five modern tanks, and the troops had not taken part in battalion maneuvers. How, then, could this division be considered equal to the British and American armored divisions? The lack of equipment, the poorly trained troops, and the inexperience of the majority of the men of the Twenty-fourth Panzer were typical of all the panzer units in France in the spring of 1943. Even these weak units were drained away in the summer of 1943. The defense of Sicily took the Hermann Goering and First Parachute Divisions from the German army in the West. Most of the garrison for Italy also came from the West, including five more of the panzer and panzer grenadier divisions. The First Panzer Division went to the Balkans.

The only panzer units left in France in August 1943 were the Fourteenth Panzer, the Ninth and Tenth SS Panzer, and the Twenty-first Panzer Divisions. Of all of these units, the one probably in the best condition was the Twenty-first Panzer that was reformed, beginning on July 15, 1943, in Rheims. It included the 125th Motorized Regiment of two battalions, which had formerly been the motorized infantry regiment of the West Armored Brigade and, therefore, was well trained. The other motorized regiment, the 192d, was newly formed on July 15, 1943, from replacements. The Twenty-first Reconnaissance Battalion was the former Armored Reconnaissance School (Demonstration) Battalion and had highly skilled soldiers. The 100th Panzer Regiment had been formed in January 1943 from an independent battalion and a company, but was equipped with French medium and light tanks of 1940 vintage with 37mm guns. The 155th Artillery Regiment had been the self-propelled 931st Artillery Regiment, another well-trained unit. The antiaircraft battalion was new, but the service units were built on the remains of the rear elements of the old Twenty-first Panzer Division that had been captured in Tunisia in May 1943. In all, the division had two good infantry battalions, a good reconnaissance battalion on motorcycles, and three good artillery battalions. But, it had only one hundred tanks that were obsolete and incapable of meeting the Sherman and more than four thousand new recruits—it was not an imposing force compared to the Allied armored divisions.[31]

The other divisions were still in poor condition, some having given up tanks and men to divisions going to Italy. All of the armored units were considered "in formation" and were not formally assigned to armies in France until at least October and most not until December. Therefore, even though these units had 888 tanks in August 1943, none were considered fit for combat by the Germans during the late summer of 1943.

The British forces in the United Kingdom alone were more formidable than this German force. In April 1943, there were in Britain the Guard, Ninth, Eleventh, Forty-second, Seventy-ninth, First Polish, Fourth Canadian, and Fifth Canadian Armored Divisions, a total of eight, plus four mixed divisions (Third, Fifteenth, Forty-third, and Fifty-third) each with a tank brigade and two infantry brigades, and five independent tank and armored brigades (137th, Thirty-fifth, Thirty-sixth, First Canadian, and Third Canadian). Most of the brigades had more tanks than did German panzer divisions of the period.

The table of organization of the British armored divisions presented a powerful, perhaps overpowerful, unit with four tank battalions (including the reconnaissance battalion) and four battalions of infantry. In April 1943, the Type VII organization for armored divisions in Britain called for 278 tanks, including 34 antiaircraft tanks and 30 close support tanks. They thus were far stronger than the German divisions described above. The British armored division had 13,000 men, about the same as the German and American counterparts. The British armored units in the United Kingdom in 1943 were still using some Crusaders and Centaurs, which even though battleworthy, were armed with the six-pounder gun. Churchills and Cromwells from Britain and Shermans from the United States were available in increasing numbers. These divisions could have been reinforced with additional American tanks, as two-thirds of them were in June 1944.[32]

An examination of the armored units in Britain forces one to reevaluate statements that these units were not effective. The Guards Armored Division had been formed in June 1941. The Guards battalions were made up of selected men and officers and were amply trained by April 1943. The division consisted of the Fifth Guards Armored Brigade and the Thirty-second Guards Infantry Brigade, along with appropriate supporting units. The division completed training in June 1942 and by September 1942 was equipped with 200 Covenanters. In November, the plan was to issue Crusaders by March 1943. In June 1943, the division had 435 Shermans and Centaurs.[33]

The Ninth Armored Division had been formed in December 1940, consisting of the Twenty-eighth Armored Brigade and the Thirty-seventh Infantry Brigade, plus supporting units. The Twenty-eighth Armored Brigade had three tank battalions and an infantry battalion. The First Fife and Forfar Yeomanry was a converted territorial cavalry regiment that had fought in France in 1940 as a light tank regiment and had escaped at Dunkirk to be reformed and refitted. The Fifteen/Nineteenth Hussars and the Fifth Dragoon Guards were regular army regiments that also had fought in France as light tank battalions and were converted to cruiser tanks in December 1940. The Eighth Kings Royal Rifle Corps was a second-line territorial battalion formed in September 1939.[34]

The Thirty-seventh Infantry Brigade had fought in France as part of the Twelfth Infantry Division. When incorporated into the Ninth Armored Division, the brigade had a regular army battalion from the South Wales Borderers and territorial battalions from the Royal Sussex and the Surreys, all formed at the beginning of the war, combined to make a well-trained, experienced infantry brigade. The Ninth Armored Division completed training with Covenanters in March 1942. In September 1942, it had 180 Covenanters and in December began training with Cromwells and Centaurs. By June 1943, the division had 394 Cromwells and Centaurs.[35]

The Eleventh Armored Division was formed in March 1941. The infantry brigade was made up of first-line territorial battalions, and the armored brigade contained a regular army tank battalion, a territorial cavalry regiment, and a regular army cavalry regiment converted to tanks. The Eleventh Armored completed training in March 1942 with two-pounder Valentines. It still had 243 Valentines in September 1942, but by June 1943 it was equipped with 304 Shermans and Centaurs.[36]

The Forty-second Armored Division had been converted from the Forty-second Infantry Division in November 1941. The Thirtieth Armored Brigade was formed in December 1940 and contained regular army cavalry regiments converted to tanks and territorial cavalry. The Seventy-first Infantry Brigade had two battalions of Highland Light Infantry. The Forty-second Armored completed training in September 1942 and was equipped with 234 Covenanters. In November 1942, it was planned to convert the division to Cromwells, and in December training began. By June 1943, the division had 303 Cromwells and Centaurs.[37]

The Seventy-ninth Armored Division was formed in August 1942. The Twenty-seventh Armored Brigade had come from the Ninth Armored Division when the number of armored brigades in the division was reduced from two to one. The 185th Infantry Brigade had originally been formed in Lancashire in October 1940 as the 204th Brigade. In September 1942, when the 185th Brigade was assigned to the division, it had regular army battalions from the Warwickshire, Norfolk, and the King's Shropshire Light Infantry. The Seventy-ninth Division was reformed in April 1943 as a divisional headquarters to supervise the training of special-purpose armored craft. The Seventy-ninth had trained on Covenanters, having 200 in September 1942, and then switched to Crusaders in October 1942. By June 1943, the division had 527 special tanks.[38]

The Fifth Canadian Armored Division was training with 199 Grants and Rams

Table 7. Comparative Tank Status, United Kingdom

September 3, 1942

Armd. Div.	Armd. Bde.	Tank Bde.	Tanks	Type
6	26		326	Valentine
9	28		180	Covenanter
11	29		243	Valentine
42	30		234	Covenanter
Guard	{ 5 Gd / 6 Gd }		200	Covenanter
79	27		200	Covenanter
Polish			192	Covenanter
5 Can	137		199	Grant, Ram
	20		188	Covenanter
			169	Covenanter (?)
		21	267	Churchill

June 3, 1943

Armd. Div.	Armd. Bde.	Tank Bde.	Tanks	Type
9	28		394	Cromwell, Centaur
11	29		304	Sherman, Centaur
42	30		303	Cromwell, Centaur
Gd	5 Gd		435	Sherman, Centaur
79	27 Armd		247	{ Spec. duty: Church., Grant, Valen. DD
Polish			402	Crusader
4 Can			248	Ram, Sherman
5 Can		137	279	Ram, Sherman
			114	

Unit	Tanks	Type		Unit	Tanks	Type
25	190	Churchill		31	246	Churchill
31	143	Churchill		33	98	Churchill
33	163	Churchill		34	205	Churchill
34	99	Churchill		35	280	Matilda, Churchill
35	50	Matilda		36	61	
36	76	Valentine		10	141	
10	81	Churchill		11	113	Churchill
11	105	Churchill		1 Can	253	Sherman
1 Can	198	Churchill		6 Gd	252	Churchill
				3 Can	129	Ram, Sherman
Other Units	58	Matilda		Other Units	54	

Total Tanks, Brit. 3,561 4,556

Total Tanks, Mid. E. 2,848 4,236

Total, Britain and Middle East 6,409 8,792

SOURCE: Tank Return, United Kingdom, September 3, 1942, PREM 3/425; Armored Formations, United Kingdom, May 31, 1943, WO 193/540; Tank Return, United Kingdom, June 3, 1943, PREM 3/425; Tank Return, United Kingdom, June 3, 1943, WO 199/587.

(the Canadian-made version of the Sherman) in September 1942 and by June 1943 had 279 Rams and Shermans. By June 1943, the Fourth Canadian Armored Division was ready with 248 Rams and Shermans. The Polish Armored Division had trained with Covenanters and had 192 of them in September 1942. However, it was switched to Crusaders and by June 1943 had 402. The Polish troops were well trained and experienced.[39]

All of these divisions were made up of first-rate battalions with a great deal of training and experience. Many had combat experience in France in 1940. By April 1943, all of the armored divisions were equipped with British tanks that were equal to most of the German tanks in France at the time plus some American tanks.

The British mixed divisions (Third, Fifteenth, Forty-third, and Fifty-third) each had a brigade with a table of organization of 205 tanks. The Third and Fifteenth were regular army divisions; the Forty-third and Fifty-third were territorial divisions formed in September 1939. In addition, five independent tank brigades with a table of organization of 202 tanks had trained for more than a year. Most of them had Churchills armed with the two-pounder, which was admirably designed to carry out the role of infantry support. The actual strength of these brigades is shown in Table 7.

The total number of medium tanks assigned to units in Britain in June 1943 was 4,556, more than two-thirds the number of tanks in the total German army on that date. Actual tanks in the hands of units outnumbered the German tanks in France by nearly five to one.

In addition to the divisions in England, there were four British armored divisions (First, Sixth, Seventh, and Tenth) and six tank brigades (Eighth, Twenty-third, First, Twenty-first, Twenty-fifth, and Fourth New Zealand) in the Middle East. There were also two Commonwealth armored divisions and a Polish tank brigade. The total assigned tanks in June 1943 was 4,236 (see Table 8). Some of these units could have been used in northern France, as was the Seventh Armored Division in June 1944. The British armored forces were so large in 1943 that there appeared to be no foreseeable use for them. Some units were disbanded, and, by June 1944, the number of armored and tank brigades had been greatly reduced. The British did not need more time to prepare armored units in 1943.

The Americans did need time to train their armored divisions. In the haste to form armored divisions in 1940, the Americans had adopted the German table of organization of 1940 with little change—two tank regiments and an infantry regiment of three battalions, a strong reconnaissance battalion, and three artillery battalions.[40] As had the Germans, the United States would find this organization too large and unwieldy. The Germans dropped down to two or three tank battalions, while increasing the infantry to four battalions by June 1941. The United States remained with the larger armored division until September 1943, when most of the divisions were reduced to three battalions of tanks and three of infantry. In April 1943, the American armored divisions still had six tank battalions and three infantry battalions.

Table 8. Comparative Tank Status, Middle East

September 9, 1942					April 25–May 9, 1943				
Armd. Div.	Armd. Bde.	Tank Bde.	Tanks	Type	Armd. Div.	Armd. Bde.	Tank Bde.	Tanks	Type
1	2		46	Mixed	1	2		113	Sherman, Crusader
						26		152	Sherman, Crusader
7	22		165	Grant, Stuart	7	22		91	Sherman, Crusader
8	24		33	Mixed					
10	8		108	Grant, Crusader	10	9		95	Sherman, Crusader
					6 S.Af.			47	Sherman, Crusader
31 Indian	4		99	Stuart	31 Ind.	4		130	Grant, Stu., Cru.
			67	Stuart		7		none	Shermans in transit
	9		69	Crusader		8		112	Sher., Cru., Grant
	23		120	Valentine		23		49	Valentine
		1	53	Valentine			1	134	Sherman, Grant
							21	162	Churchill
							25	152	Churchill
							4 NZ	53	Crusader, Sherman
							Polish	100	Valentine
Other			368		Other			535	
Total Fit			1,128					1,925	
In Repair*			1,259					1,553	
In Transit			461					758	
Total			2,848					4,236	

SOURCES: Tank Return, Middle East, September 9, 1942, WO 193/540; Tank Return, Middle East, May 9, 1943, PREM 3/284/9.
*In repair inlcudes tanks temporarily laid up for routine maintenance in units.

Whereas authorized strength meant little to the Germans, the Americans had reserves of tanks in depots so that a division seldom went into battle at much less than full strength. In January 1943, there were 241 replacement tanks in North Africa (more than the total German tank strength). On February 17, Eisenhower had more than a hundred medium tanks in depots to replace losses in the First Armored Division.[41] On September 15, 1944, after a dash across France that would have left German panzer divisions at one-third strength, the Twelfth Army Group, in its seven armored divisions and twenty-four tank battalions and mechanized squadrons, had 2,147 medium tanks, compared to a table of organization of 2,279, only 132 short. Of the 2,147, only 182 were under repair; the remaining 1,965 were ready for action after an advance of up to 350 miles in fifty days, a phenomenal replacement program. In comparison, the Germans were seldom at full strength after the first few days of an engagement; they had no reserve stocks—only tanks that came out of repair shops and an occasional delivery of fresh tanks, but the latter usually went to new divisions or to divisions in the process of rebuilding.

In addition to having more tanks, the Americans had more infantry in half-tracks, all three battalions, whereas the Germans had only one battalion in half-tracks and three in trucks, not all of which had the four-wheel drive of the American two-and-a-half-ton truck. This inadequacy meant that the German infantry would often be separated from their tanks because the trucks could not leave the paved roads. Even the American supply vehicles were four-wheel drive, which gave them traction on the poorest roads and cross-country in all but the worst weather.

All of the American divisional artillery (fifty-four self-propelled 105mm howitzers) was on tracks, meaning that it could keep up with the rest of the division and perform as assault guns. The German divisions had only eighteen self-propelled artillery pieces; the other thirty-four were conventional towed weapons, though some were of heavier caliber than the American. In practically every aspect, the American armored division of April 1943 was much stronger than the German panzer division.

In contrast to the hastily reformed panzer divisions in France, American armored divisions were composed of higher quality manpower and received better training with more equipment for a longer period. The First Armored Division was activated at Fort Knox, Kentucky, on July 15, 1940, with regular army units, including two tank regiments, an infantry regiment, and a field artillery regiment, plus several thousand recruits. The division trained for a year at Fort Knox, during which time it was constantly stripped of experienced men to cadre other divisions and provide candidates for officer schools.[42] By August 1941, training had progressed to a point that the division was ready for maneuvers in Louisiana and later in North Carolina, where the men had experience living in the field and in simulated combat.[43]

In August 1941, the division had a plentiful supply of M3 light tanks and enough of the M3 medium tanks, half-tracks, trucks, and lighter weapons to conduct meaningful exercises. During the winter of 1941–1942, the division had complete equipment for two battalions of light tanks and four battalions of Grant medium tanks. The division was also equipped with 75mm antitank guns mounted in half-tracks and M7 Priests in its field artillery battalions.[44]

In April 1942, the division moved to Fort Dix, New Jersey, to prepare for overseas movement. The men received individual training to toughen them, while replacements arrived to bring the division to full strength. The division sailed on the *Queen Mary* on May 10, 1942, reaching the British Isles on May 16. During six months in Northern Ireland, one battalion of Grants was replaced with Shermans. The First Armored Division landed in North Africa in November 1942 and engaged the Germans in early December, suffering heavy losses in equipment. By February 1943, the division had been rebuilt, but was still equipped partially with Grants when it was beaten at Kasserine by three German panzer divisions.[45] By May 1943, the shortage of Shermans at the front had been solved, and the Grants were relegated to second-line units. By the end of the Tunisian battle, the First Armored was a well-equipped, seasoned division with combat experience.

Typical of the newer armored divisions was the Sixth, authorized on January 15, 1942. Within four weeks, an officer cadre had been assembled at Fort Knox. On activation on February 15, 1942, the division had 324 officers and 1,390 men, most of whom came from the Fifth Armored Division. Schools were established for mess sergeants, medical, and other technicians. The Sixty-eighth Armored Regiment, formerly part of the First Armored Division, and the Sixty-ninth Armored Regiment, formerly part of the Second Armored Division, were reactivated with new personnel to form the tank regiments of the Sixth. The remainder of the units were newly created for the division in February 1942.[46]

On March 4, 1942, the new division was ordered to move to Camp Chaffee, Arkansas. The tracked vehicles moved by rail, but the remainder of the vehicles and personnel traveled by road. At Camp Chaffee, recruits filled the division from induction centers all over the country. By April 13, the division had 11,218 men and had started training the recruits. The last month of the thirteen-week training cycle included unit training at the regimental level. Training was conducted with obsolete M2 light tanks and Grant medium tanks.[47]

After completing the basic training schedule, the division went to the Louisiana maneuver area to conduct exercises and to receive new Shermans. The artillery battalions were attached in September 1942. All of the artillery battalions were former National Guard units with a minimum of eighteen months of active service. In October 1942, the division was sent to the Desert Training Center in California, where it underwent five months of rugged training in field conditions, operating as part of the IV Armored Corps. In March 1943, the division moved to Camp Cooke, California, where training continued, mostly review of fundamentals, physical training, and sports to keep the men occupied. Finally, in October 1943, the division was alerted for overseas movement, but, at the same time, many able officers were transferred to the newer armored divisions. Beginning on November 29, 1943, the division was given a final test that included simulated combat against other units. The division received a "satisfactory" rating, which was a relatively poor grade. In January 1944, the division, without its vehicles, proceeded to Camp Shanks, New York. Within a few weeks, the men were on board navy troopships. The division had been ready for combat as early as March 1943 and had marked time until the call for combat arrived in 1944.[48]

The other regular army armored division, the Second, was formed in July 1940, primarily from existing regular units, plus recruits. After over two years of training, the division moved directly from the United States to North Africa in November 1942, but was assigned to guard duty on the Spanish Morocco frontier. The Third Armored, formed on April 15, 1941, took its cadre from the Second Armored and, in turn, provided the cadre for another division. The Fourth was formed on April 15, as well, but received few regulars as cadre. In October 1941, the Fourth provided the cadre for the Fifth Armored. This rapid expansion meant that little unit training could be accomplished. In February, March, and April 1942, the Sixth, Seventh, and Eighth Armored units were activated, followed by six more divisions between July and November 1942. Of the fourteen armored divisions, eight had been in existence for a year in April 1943, even though they had been weakened by providing cadres for the additional six divisions.[49] Athough only the Third and Fourth would have been available for the assault, the Fifth, Sixth, Seventh, and Eighth would have been ready within a few months. After that, a regular stream of one per month for the next six months would have completed their training and been ready for shipment.

Although there were only two American armored divisions in the European theater in April 1943 (both were engaged in North Africa), the American tank contribution to the invasion in April 1943 could not be discounted. On December 31, 1942, there were fourteen armored divisions, twenty-six tank battalions, and eighty tank destroyer battalions active in the American army.

The activation of separate tank and tank destroyer battalions progressed rapidly during 1943. By December 31, 1943, 65 tank battalions and 101 tank destroyer battalions were active; in fact, the number of tank destroyer battalions was considered excessive and reduction had begun. At one time during 1943, there were 103 tank destroyer battalions in the United States, about half of which were equipped with the M10 tank destroyers.[50]

With some concerted effort, the United States could have contributed four armored divisions, ten tank battalions, and twenty tank destroyer battalions to an invasion in April 1943. There would have been a total of 3,060 tanks and tank destroyers that, when added to the British total of 4,500, would have produced a figure of about 7,500, backed by thousands of replacements to cope with a German force of fewer than 1,000.

Even though the quality of the British and American tanks was not superior to the best of the Germans, they would not have met the Germans' best in France in

1943. The Allied tanks were superior in quality and in number to the captured French Hotchkiss and Somuas and to the Panzer IIs and IIIs with the short 50mm guns, and they were equal to the rest. The Allies had the tanks and the trained armored units to launch the invasion in 1943.

In June 1944, the invasion forces included three British armored divisions, a Canadian armored division, a Polish armored division, six American armored divisions, and a French armored division, plus eight British tank brigades and more than a dozen American separate tank battalions, totaling more than 5,300 Shermans, Churchills, and Cromwells.[51] Meanwhile, the German tank strength grew from 748 in April 1943 to 1,552 German tanks, 310 assault guns, and additional captured tanks by June 1944. Included in the German total were 102 Tigers and 663 Panthers. Numerically the odds dropped from a possible seven to one to three to one. Considering the improvement in quality, the Germans increased in power at least four times in the wasted year.[52]

In April 1943, the Allies had available in England and in the Mediterranean theater a total of fifteen armored divisions against which the Germans had only seven panzer divisions, none of which was equal to Allied units in men or equipment. In addition, the Allies had far greater numbers of tank brigades and battalions and more armored divisions waiting in America. The Allies had an overwhelming superiority in armor in 1943, far more than needed to launch a successful invasion of France.

8

THE QUALITY OF TRAINING

The combat readiness of the American army was a determining factor in the timing of the second front. Excellent training produced good morale, and both were essential for an army to obtain the full value of the weapons in the hands of the troops. If the men did not know how to use their weapons and did not have the courage to do so under frightening conditions, the weapons were useless. Was General Marshall able to train millions of raw recruits and form them into combat-ready divisions in time for an invasion in 1943? The first step was to turn the individual into an effective soldier; the second step was to weld these soldiers into functioning teams. To judge the success of this effort and to establish some form of criteria, similar efforts made by the Germans must also be examined.

How long did it take to train a rifleman, the essential members of the infantry division? On the eastern front, the Russians, immediately after capturing a village, enlisted all of the able-bodied men, gave them a day of training, and placed them in a rifle division. The Germans provided from eight to twelve weeks in replacement battalions in Germany. After this basic training, the recruit was either sent to a reserve division for further training or assigned to a training battalion attached to a combat division. There experienced officers and noncommissioned officers had the opportunity to judge the performance of each man and to determine when he was ready for a rifle company. Assignment to divisional training battalions provided the German replacement with a conditioning period that greatly reduced the shock of combat.

The American system in 1942 and 1943 was to provide the raw recruit with thirteen weeks of basic training given by the cadre of new divisions as they were formed or in schools set up by older divisions to train replacements. Later, basic training was provided in replacement training centers. After basic training, the recruit continued his training as part of the division.

Very little time was needed to train a man how to use a rifle and to follow simple commands. Much more time was needed to inculcate a man with the concept that he must continue to use that rifle and follow those commands, even though his entire intellect told him that to do so would probably result in his own death or wounding, but that not to do so would endanger the lives of his friends. A man who was backed into a corner with no means to escape except surrender to a foe who would probably kill him anyway did not require training or bravery. He had no alternative but to continue fighting to the best of his ability with the hope that he might survive. The untrained Russian villagers knew they would be shot if they ran back and realized that they had a better chance going forward against the Germans. The man who needed training to build courage was one who had the alternatives either of running away, with little chance of severe punishment if caught, or of surrendering to a foe who would give him adequate treatment in a prisoner of war camp for the remainder of the war. Only one American was shot for desertion in World War II, and the Germans promised comfortable prisoner of war camps. Only 4 percent of the British and Americans captured by the Germans died before their release.[1] With alternatives in mind, the American soldier's morale and training had to be higher than that of the Germans in Russia in order for him to continue fighting. In contrast, when the Germans were given safe alternatives in France in September 1944, hundreds of thousands surrendered, and more fled unorganized back into Germany, leaving only a few to fight the delaying action.

The individual training given the American soldier was equal if not superior to that given to any soldiers during World War II. Nevertheless, a man is never completely prepared for battle. Battle is a matter of life or death, and one can never be overtrained. American training met at least a minimum standard that enabled most individuals to make a positive contribution to the effort.

Warfare, however, had ceased to be purely a matter of individual courage and skill. Working together as part of a team was more important than the talent of any individual. Confidence in the unit and the conviction that one must stay with the unit and carry out the will of the leader was more important in the long run than individual acts of bravery. For that reason, though individual training was important, unit training developed the ability to fight effectively as teams. How long did it take to create a division-sized team of over ten thousand men?

Every nation had a different answer to the length of time required to train a division. The Russians assembled divisions within days—the people's divisions in civilian clothes that filled the gaps at Leningrad and Moscow in 1941. The Germans rebuilt divisions on the base of burned-out formations, fleshed out with hastily retrained sailors and airmen, within a few months in 1944. The Volks-grenadier divisions proved to be powerful opponents during the Battle of the Bulge. During the North African campaign, the British assembled divisions at will from independent brigades (and broke up long-established divisions with the same lack of feeling).

There was no established rule as to the length of time required to build a division or the ingredients needed. The matter was very subjective and was concerned with a complexity of interrelated factors, including the personality of the division commander, the overall morale of the men, the experience and ability of the field grade officers (majors and colonels), the technical skill and attitude of the company officers, the enthusiasm and physical condition of the privates, the availability of equipment and supplies, the quality of the rations, the suitability of the training areas, and the comfort of the barracks, to name a few. A weakness in any one of these areas could seriously inhibit the growth of a division.

A division was ready for combat when it had a fair chance of carrying out its battle assignments the same criteria that applied to the soldier. If the assignment was the occupation of a coastline with only a faint danger of invasion from a foe thousands of miles away, such as the defense of Hawaii in 1944, a division (and a replacement) could be considered ready with little preparation. If the assignment was to land on a heavily defended island, such as Tarawa, the training would have to be quite advanced because the men would be expected to absorb heavy casualties and to withstand confusion within minutes of the start of the battle. Conversely, if a group were to form the second wave to follow up a landing and be charged with protecting the flank, the state of readiness could be lower because there would be an introductory period, completely controlled, with few losses. Different levels of competence were required for different assignments.

The Germans created special divisions to perform high-risk and low-risk assignments. The American army adopted the philosophy of interchangeable parts, where every division was qualified to perform all tasks, perhaps with a minimum amount of special training for selected tasks. Every infantry division had to be exchangeable with every other—all had to be able to take on the most strenuous duties.

General Lesley J. McNair, chief of the Army Ground Forces, opposed the development of elite units or specialized training if it were carried to the "point of endangering the unity of the army or soldierly fitness." On March 10, 1941, he told the Third Division, then engaged in amphibious training, that its special training might continue, but not at the expense of basic combat training, because the latter was far more important, and landing was only an incidental first step.[2] The result was that every division was an elite division with the best men and equipment available. There were no limited-service divisions to do the routine work on the line.

After the war, the German officers asked where American infantry divisions were—meaning divisions of limited mobility and low-grade men such as made up the bulk of the German and Russian armies, divisions created and maintained at a level suitable for the performance of only limited assignments. Such divisions, and units of even lower quality, were easily created and were economically maintained in regard to men, vehicles, weapons, and supplies. They were used for defensive missions, freeing the elite troops for demanding tasks.

The American army (and to a high degree the British army) had only one standard—the best. The best men, the best equipment, the best service elements, the best supplies, and, of course, the highest cost in terms of men, equipment, supplies, and, most pertinent to our topic, length of training. Continental-style infantry divisions could be created in four months, but to create elite divisions of the American mold took a full year.

During 1942, a standard method of creating a division had been adopted. The process began with the designation of a parent division to the new division. A cadre was selected consisting of 160 essential officers and 1,200 men that would be used to organize and train the new division. Members of the cadre were sent to schools and given special training for their new assignments. About a month before the new division was activated, the cadre was assembled. About 450 additional officers were added during the month before activation, and, starting on the date of activation, about 13,400 raw recruits were sent to the division. Two weeks after the date of activation, basic and individual training of these recruits began. After seventeen weeks, the division began three months of regiment unit training, followed by three months of training as a division. A final two months of training was given in combination with tanks and aircraft, after which the division was considered fit for combat.[3] From ten to twelve months were needed, therefore, to prepare a division. During 1942, equipment was usually provided at a level of 50 percent of authorized allowances, which was ample for training purposes, but even that amount was not always available, and training was delayed in some cases. At the end of 1942, the training period was cut from forty-four weeks to thirty-five weeks, most often by reducing the time spent on individual training from seventeen to thirteen weeks.[4]

To provide a better understanding of the prescribed training program of the first three mass-produced divisions (Seventy-seventh, Eighty-second, and Ninetieth), the "March" divisions (so called because they came into being in March 1942), the experience of the Seventy-seventh Infantry Division will be outlined. Formation of the division was authorized on January 25, 1942. Its training plan called for the arrival of the first element of the cadre between February 18 and 25. From the War Department pool, 59 officers were drawn; another 113 came from the First Army. Major General Robert L. Eichelberger, later commander of the Eighth Army in the Pacific, was named divisional commander on February 10. Eichelberger was an experienced officer, though he had not been in combat in France during World War I. His previous assignment had been superintendent of West Point. Prior to his appointment, Eichelberger and 16 staff officers had attended a short course at the Command and General Staff School for new division staff, while 200 other officers had been at various service schools, preparing for new positions in the division.[5]

The division activation was ordered to take place at Fort Jackson on February 14. Eichelberger and his staff arrived on February 18, and 200 officers, more than the quota, arrived on February 25. Many of this first batch of cadre officers had been chosen by the division staff from men known personally—a great help in the task of creating the leadership core of the unit.[6] On February 25, the Eighth and Thirtieth Divisions, stationed at Fort Jackson, provided about 1,400 enlisted men as necessary specialists and top noncommissioned officers who would make the division function.[7]

The plan required the addition between March 3 and 5 of 452 young officers to the division from the War Department's officer replacement pool. Most of the 400 "filler" officers who arrived were reserve lieutenants, recently called to service, who had been trained in university Reserve Officer's Training Corps. The reservists had completed a six-week summer camp during college, and some had received a refresher course before assignment to the division, but otherwise they had little experience. The senior officers in the division—the artillery commander and the three infantry regimental commanders—were all regular army, but few other regulars were available.[8]

The cadre, then up to about six hundred officers and over twelve hundred men, had to prepare for the arrival of the bulk of the men. In three weeks, less than two thousand men had to become acquainted with each other, build a skeleton for each company and battery to make up the division, prepare the barracks, kitchens, offices, and shops, and also learn lessons that they would be teaching within a few weeks. Six officers and twelve men were assigned to each company or battery, soon to number about two hundred men. Barracks had to be cleaned, bedding drawn from warehouses, and kitchens put into working order. At the same time, the staff was preparing the training program that included schools for typists, radio operators, cooks, and others. Inasmuch as the Seventy-seventh was one of the first divisions to be mass produced, there was little experience on which to draw for the instant creation of all the training programs, or even men experienced in giving training, so classes were given to train instructors, while the physical preparation of the camp progressed.[9]

In mid-March civilians were drafted and reported to induction centers. From there, they went to reception centers at Fort Devens, Massachusetts; Fort Niagara, New York; Fort Dix, New Jersey; and Fort George Meade, Maryland. The average age of the new inductees who came to the Seventy-seventh was nearly thirty-two! Many had families and were taken by Selective Service Boards near the end of the first round of the draft, resulting in an average age much higher than normal. At the reception center, the new soldiers received uniforms and inoculations. Within a few days, the men were sent by train to Fort Jackson. The first trains arrived on March 25, the day the division was formally activated. The last recruits did not arrive until April 21, two days behind schedule. On arrival, the men were divided into groups of two hundred and temporarily attached to companies for about two days. During this time, their classification cards were examined, and an attempt was made to assign them to positions in which their civilian occupation might be of help. Most, however, became riflemen and gunners, for which there were no civilian equivalents.[10]

The official training program began on April 7, before the last of the recruits arrived. By then, however, the units had all been formed, and the men began ten-hour training days, six days per week. Misfits were weeded out; older men were transferred to less onerous duties; and unfit men were discharged. On May 16, Lieutenant General Ben Lear, commander of the Second Army, inspected the division and approved its progress. In late May, firing of weapons began, and by June all men had fired individual weapons.[11]

On June 15, Eichelberger was promoted to commander of the I Corps and was replaced by the assistant division commander. Other senior officers changed during the next few months, including the chief of staff and two infantry regiment commanders. The division was also drained of lower ranks. Many officers and men went to specialist schools for short periods—Infantry School at Fort Benning; Artillery School at Fort Sill, Oklahoma; Engineer School at Fort Belvoir, Virginia; and Command and General Staff School at Fort Leavenworth, Kansas. In addition, the Seventy-seventh provided a cadre of two hundred officers and twelve hundred men for the Ninety-fourth Division in July 1942, taking away a high proportion of trained men. Later in the summer, smaller groups went to provide partial cadres for the Ninety-ninth and 100th Divisions. More than a thousand of the best men went to officer candidate schools during the summer of 1942.[12]

Despite the drain on this unit, training went on. On June 8, men of the Seventy-seventh, along with the Eighth and Thirtieth Divisions, were assembled on a huge field for a long, hot day when they needed stamina just to keep on their feet. Finally, an inspection team, including General George C. Marshall, Sir John Dill, and Lord Mountbatten, arrived and saw the three divisions pass in review. Mountbatten complimented the commander of the Seventy-seventh for its appearance that day after only eight weeks of training, and Marshall was also impressed, a reaction that led to a subsequent inspection that will be discussed later in this chapter.[13]

Training intensified during July. More gasoline was made available, as drivers completed their instruction, and units began combined exercises. In August, the infantry battalions conducted three-day exercises in the field, followed by regimental exercises. The infantry were trained to march twenty-five miles in eight hours. In September, the divisional artillery went to Fort Sill for six weeks as "school troops," gaining much valuable experience.[14] By mid-November, the division began training as a complete force at Fort Jackson, and, on January 28, 1943, the division was sent to the Desert Training Center at Camp Young, California. Here, ample space was available for firing weapons, and the harsh climate further toughened the division, as it learned the art of desert warfare. The assignment was merely to keep the division busy—the formal training program had been completed. There was little likelihood that the division would see combat in a desert. On September 29, the division crossed the country to Camp Pickett, Virginia, for amphibious landing training. Finally on March 14, 1944, the division recrossed the country to Camp Stoneman in California for staging prior to overseas movement. The division had been training for nearly twenty-six months.[15]

In fact, the division had merely been marking time since April 1943, awaiting a call for action. The same experience was to befall the Eighty-fifth Division after completing its training cycle. The Eighty-fifth Division originated in January 1942. The division staff was selected and sent to refresher courses at Fort Leavenworth, Kansas, and by April 6, the division staff and some cadre had arrived at Fort Shelby. On April 14, the officer cadre arrived, followed by the enlisted cadre on April 17. The division then had a strength of 156 officers and 1,190 enlisted men.

The officers included 57 regular army officers, 48 from the National Guard, and 51 from the organized reserves. Between April 21 and 25, the rest of the officer cadre arrived, reserve officers, who had completed the three-month refresher course at Fort Benning, and recent graduates of Class 6 and 7 of the officer candidate school. On April 30, the division had 581 officers and 1,270 men. Many of the enlisted cadre came from the Second Infantry Division. The enlisted cadre for the III Battalion of the 338th Infantry Regiment came from the Ninth Infantry Regiment of the Second Division. Most of the cadre were regular army soldiers with many years of service.[16]

Following formal activation on May 15, 1942, the new recruits began arriving by the thousands. By May 31, the division had 634 officers and 13,062 men. Training began in June. Camp Shelby was a vast training camp, ninety miles north of New Orleans, with facilities for three full divisions. The men lived in tents initially, but these were soon replaced with wooden huts. Individual training came first, then physical training, close-order drill, instruction in the use of weapons and gas masks, map reading, digging fox holes, long marches, and going through obstacle courses.[17] Emphasis was placed on gaining familiarity with the infantry weapons and on the troop's ability to make marches as long as twenty-five miles in one day to build up their fitness. In July, the division spent two weeks on the ranges firing weapons. Meanwhile, special schools were established to train radio operators, linemen, drivers, mechanics, ordnance repairmen, and supply clerks. By September, the division had gained considerable ability.[18]

On October 6, 1942, the Eighty-fifth was required to provide the cadre for the 103d Infantry Division. The Eighty-fifth provided 137 officers and 1,260 men for the 103d and received 750 replacements fresh from induction centers, who needed an eight-week training program to enable them to join the rest of the division and continue training. At the same time, the division was subjected to a screening by the War Department to obtain candidates for officer training. By the end of December 1942, the division had sent 667 men to officer candidate schools. With other losses to the air corps, the parachute school, and elsewhere, the division was drained of nearly 4,000 men in seven months, or about 30 percent.[19]

Despite the turnover, in December, the division began small unit training combined with firing weapons by platoon. In January 1943, the division began battalion and regimental unit training and combined infantry-artillery exercises. The division completed the unit exercises by March 20 and was ready to act as a division.[20] On April 6, the division arrived at the Louisiana maneuver area to be subjected to conditions approximating combat. The division lived in the open, under canvas, for over two months and was continually on the move. After several weeks of simulated battle against an enemy represented by flags, the Eighty-fifth was pitted against the Ninety-third Infantry Division in mock combat, using blank ammunition. Lieutenant General Ben Lear gave the division good marks after an inspection trip on May 13, 1943. Its maneuvers were completed by the end of May 1943.

The division had completed its training cycle and was ready for use. In early June, however, the unit was shipped to the Desert Training Center in California.[21] The supposed purpose of the period in California, as described in the division's history, was to "train, maintain, and supply troops realistically, as in a theater of operations; to harden troops physically; to train troops mentally for the shock of battle; to conduct fire under realistic battle conditions; to develop tactics, technique and training methods suitable for desert warfare; and to test and develop equipment and supplies."[22] All of this had been done before except for the desert part, for which there was no foreseeable need. In fact, the division was sent there to keep it busy until it was needed.

The training was extremely demanding. In addition to range firing, infiltration courses were conducted with live ammunition fired over the heads of the troops. Platoon tactics were emphasized along with platoon leadership. One platoon sent out on a six-day problem lost its way and four men died. By mid-September, the division had its fill of desert training, especially as there was no prospect of ever fighting in a desert. The division was sent to Fort Dix, New Jersey, the last units arriving on October 7, 1943. Many of the men were sent on furlough prior to overseas duty. The division was brought up to strength with the addition of 2,216 replacements from the Eighty-fourth and Ninety-ninth Divisions. By October 31, 1943, the division had 919 officers and 14,002 men. Finally, on December 24, the first large contingent boarded ship en route to North Africa.[23]

When the Eighty-fifth sailed, it was more than ready for combat. The division had completed its training in May 1943, and the additional months were spent marking time waiting for a call.

There were some serious problems in the training program. Despite the efforts of the Army Ground Forces, the parent division sometimes used the cadre as a means of getting rid of undesirable men. The intent was that the parent division would select able men, who had teaching ability, and give them an opportunity in the new division to use their talents and also to obtain higher rank sooner. The ideal was to enable young privates with talent and corporals with ability, for whom no openings were available in the old unit, to transfer to the new unit and achieve the promotions they deserved. Instead of providing able men, old units sent to the new units some privates who were released from the guard house. The Ninety-seventh Division in the spring of 1942 reported that one of the cadre corporals was sixty-one years old and another over fifty.[24] This was the exception rather than the rule, however. In general, the cadre men were of high quality.

Another problem was loss of men through transfer to other units for a variety of reasons, including the demands of units slated for overseas shipment that needed additional trained men to fill their ranks. A division ending its training cycle would often be short of men and have to draft fillers from other divisions when its turn came to go overseas, recreating the same problem for the next division. To ease this situation, cadres were increased to over two hundred officers and nearly fifteen hundred men, and a 15 percent overstrength of recruits was permitted, or nearly two thousand extra men. In addition, after the third month of training, another twelve hundred recruits were made available to the new division.[25]

Some divisions were asked to provide several cadres. Providing even a single cadre was quite a blow to a division, but to provide two required the surrender of over 15 percent of its strength. Furthermore, cadre men often included the best corporals and privates. These men were replaced by recruits who needed training in the basic essentials, whereas the remainder of the division was ready for advanced training. To solve the problem, in the fall of 1942, two divisions were designated as replacement divisions, and the others were left alone to continue with their programs.[26]

The new divisions also suffered from a shortage of good officers. The National Guard and reserve officers were not always able and were often over age. The new graduates of officer training schools lacked experience, although they learned along with the men.

Regardless of the problems encountered, the training system worked well, although a few of the divisions in their learning process received what turned out to be an important examination before they were prepared. On June 24, 1942, only six months after Pearl Harbor, Winston Churchill, along with General Alan Brooke, chief of the Imperial General Staff, and others were invited by General Marshall to Fort Jackson to see the results of the army training program. Marshall wanted Churchill to observe for himself the quality of the American army and the advanced state of its training.[27] This momentous visit had a great impact on the future conduct of the war. Most of the British leaders recorded their impressions at the time and later in their memoirs. The occasion was similar to a graduation day ceremony, but instead of the invited guests making flattering speeches or handing out diplomas, they considered themselves as outside auditors, treating the exercise as a final examination to determine the fitness of the American army to fight in Europe at a time when the British were objecting to American plans for an early invasion. The British saw the Eighth Infantry Division, the Thirtieth Infantry Division, and the Seventy-seventh Infantry Division, plus some airborne troops. These troops had not completed their training and were below the standard of quality of troops that the Americans planned to land in France in April 1943.

The Eighth Division had been activated on July 1, 1940, mostly with draftees. The 121st Infantry Regiment, a National Guard unit called into service in November 1940, replaced one of the regiments in the division on November 22, 1940. The Eighth Division had been the major source of 1,400 cadre men for the Seventy-seventh Division in February 1942. Training the raw recruits that replaced the cadre men had delayed its progress.

The Thirtieth Infantry Division was a National Guard unit from North Carolina, South Carolina, Georgia, and Tennessee, called into service on September 16, 1940. By June 1942, the division had been on active duty for twenty-one months and had developed pride over the years as a Guard unit. But the Thirtieth was being stripped to provide some cadre for the Seventy-seventh Division and was being used as a replacement source for divisions going overseas. The total strength of the Thirtieth in June 1942 was only 12,400 men, compared to a table of organization of 15,514. By August, the Thirtieth was further reduced to only 3,000 men.[28]

The Seventy-seventh Infantry Division, as we have seen, had been activated only three months before the inspection. Instead of representing the army in a final inspection before foreign dignitaries, the division should have been teaching recruits how to shoot.

After the inspection, Churchill praised the troops publicly: "The faces of the men gave me the greatest and everlasting memory of the day. I have never been more impressed than I was with the bearing of the men whom I saw."[29] Privately, the comments were not as complimentary. The British did not distinguish among the three divisions, and Churchill expressed his disappointment to Harry Hopkins at what he had seen. He thought that the individual men were good, but that the units were poor. "It takes at least two years and a very strong professional cadre to form first-class troops" Churchill wrote later.[30] His real worry was that the divisions would not be able to compete against the Germans, whom, incidentally, Churchill had never seen in battle.[31] Brooke had seen and been beaten by the Germans in Belgium in 1940. He thought that the individual training was good, but that the unit training was not. General Ismay, another member of the party, felt it would be murder to put these troops against the Germans.[32] All in all, the American army was given failing grades by the top British leaders. Such a review was never repeated; no second chance was offered. Primarily on the basis of this exercise, Brooke held to his opinion at Casablanca in January 1943 that the Americans would not be ready for France in 1943.

The first test of American troops against the Germans came in North Africa. The Americans who landed were among the best trained units available. The divisions had been weakened by providing cadres to other divisions, but the men knew their jobs.

American commanders made adverse comments concerning the level of training, but they were directed at the quality of the replacements. The new men were in poor physical condition, lacked training, and were of lower mental capacity than the original men. Many of the replacements had never fired their assigned weapon or participated in field maneuvers. To overcome these difficulties, in July 1943, the basic training cycle for replacements was lengthened from thirteen to seventeen weeks. Despite the poor quality of individual replacements, the divisions proved to be soundly trained, "equal [to] anything the Germans ever turned out, at least as far as training is concerned," according to an American staff officer.[33]

German reaction to the ability of the Americans in Tunisia was mixed. After Kasserine, Rommel wrote, "The American had as yet no practical battle experience, and it was now up to us to instill in them from the outset an inferiority complex of no mean order." In this objective he failed, and he later wrote: "I do not think that there has been any other front where we [the Germans] have been opposed by a command with such excellent qualities and by such well-trained troops—not to mention their equipment and armament—as the British and later the Americans in North Africa."[34] Field Marshal Albert Kesselring did not think much of the fighting value of the Americans, but he did not have a field command. He thought, however, that the Americans made up for their lack of experience with their equipment that was far better and more plentiful than either the British or German. American tanks and antitank guns spelled doom for Germany in future tank battles.[35]

Goebbels, in his diary, made many comments about the Americans in Tunisia. On March 20, 1943, before the Germans were defeated, he wrote, "The American soldiers, too, are considered by our troops to be the worst possible, not only because of the fact that the American soldiers have had no combat experience but also that they are not cut out to be soldiers." On April 9, he wrote that the American prisoners were no match for the Germans. They were savages, spiritually empty, and knew nothing of German geography. On May 18, one of his agents reported that the Germans considered the Americans "very inferior and mediocre" and that they would lose if faced with Germans on an equal basis.[36]

General Siegfried Westphal, who commanded German forces in Italy in 1943, commented that the British troops had combat experience and that although the Americans were at a disadvantage at first, "they soon recovered."[37] American divisions in Italy were products of the mass-production scheme. The men of the Eighty-fifth and Eighty-eighth Divisions commented that their first battles were no worse than the maneuvers in the United States. Only battle could produce battle-wise divisions; nevertheless, training could make the acquisition of that wisdom far less costly.[38]

Therefore, despite the harsh words of the Germans and British, the American training system worked well. Divisions were created within a year that were able to stand alongside the far more experienced British divisions and fight the best German divisions.

In comparison to the well-organized standardized procedure used to create American divisions, the Germans in 1942 were resorting to pure opportunism, often mortgaging the future ability to train replacements for the immediate availability of a few divisions. The Sixty-fifth German Infantry Division has been selected as an example because of its long service in the West, from July 1942 until July 1943, covering the period when a second front was under discussion. Of all the divisions in the West during this period, the Sixty-fifth should have been the best in 1943 because it had the longest time to organize and train.

The formation of the Sixty-fifth was part of the Twentieth Wave of divisions that included the Thirty-eighth and Thirty-ninth as well. These divisions were formed from Walkure II companies and battalions created on paper in 1942 from the personnel engaged in training recruits. Given the code word, Walkure, the units were to assemble in prearranged larger units and move on short notice into action. A training battalion, for example, would be required to list the names of men available to form a rifle company and gather them together for practice from time to time. Otherwise, they went on with their regular duties of training recruits. In July 1942, these alarm companies were called to form the three divisions permanently. Led by highly skilled instructors, the units quickly formed into divisions.

The Sixty-fifth Division came mostly from southern Germany, rather than from a single military district or Wehrkreise, as was customary in the German army. The recruits who formed the bulk of the division were available as a result of the early drafting of younger men to replace the heavy losses suffered during the winter of 1941–1942. The class of 1922, boys who would reach twenty during 1942, were drafted between February and April 1942, about six months before their normal period. Then in March and April 1942, the class of 1923, boys who would reach their nineteenth birthday in 1942, were also drafted. Additional manpower came from seventy thousand seventeen-year-olds who volunteered for the army.[39] The youngest men went to reserve divisions; the others were sent either as replacements to Russia or to the Twentieth Wave divisions, including the Sixty-fifth.

The Sixty-fifth Division consisted of the 145th and 146th Infantry Regiments, the 165th Tank Destroyer and Reconnaissance Battalion, the 165th Artillery Regiment, and service units. The II Battalion, 145th Infantry, was formed by the 109th Replacement Battalion in Karlsruhe in WK V; the III Battalion, 145th Infantry, came from the 320th Replacement Battalion in Ingolstadt in WK XII. The other troops came from various units in WK VII, XII, and XIII.[40] Early in July, a cadre of 22 officers, 13 warrant officers, 42 noncoms, and 193 men arrived in Camp Bitsch in Alsace-Lorraine to make quarters ready and begin putting the division together. Between July 7 and 15, the mass of men arrived, and on July 15, 1942, the formal activation order was issued to create the division.[41]

The equipment had been gathered in preparation for the division, and the only shortages reported on July 17 were fourteen gun tractors, the machine shop trailer for the divisional vehicles repair unit, vehicles for the postal unit, a field kitchen, and practically all of the engineer equipment.[42] That the level of supply was this good was remarkable when compared to American divisions being formed at the same time that often found themselves with only 50 percent of their organizational equipment during their early days of training. This report is open to question, however, when compared with the shortage statement for July 27, only ten days later. The ordnance workshop was still lacking, but also listed were vehicles for the antitank company, antitank rockets (none were available), eighty-six motorcycles, three 37mm guns, and twenty-two trailers.[43] Still the division had an excellent supply of equipment for a new formation.

Only three days after the division was formally activated, it was moved to Antwerp for training. Weaknesses began to surface. Although the men had moved by train, the vehicles had come by road and were much the worse for wear.[44] The condition of the division's motor vehicles was universally poor, and there were no tools to repair them. The lack of training of the drivers added to the difficulty. More than 50 percent of the individual weapons (rifles and pistols) were in poor condition, and again the tools were lacking for repair. Only 80 percent of the allotted ammunition was available. Grenades and machine pistol ammunition were very short. The result was that it would be difficult to conduct realistic training.[45]

The quality of the German manpower was mixed. Half of the regimental and battalion commanders were not physically fit for combat, but most of them were well fitted to provide combat training. Five of them had served in Poland and France, six in France and Russia, two in Russia, and only three lacked combat experience. The younger officers had recent battle experience. The division was missing only six junior-grade combat unit officers, five medical officers, and seven veterinarians by July 22.[46]

Most of the enlisted men came from training units in the south of Germany. The breakdown by percentage was as follows:[47]

Bavaria	25	Baden and Wurtemburg	15
Rhineland	15	Mosel and Western	7
Palatinate	7	Styria	7
North Germany	3	Central Germany	6
Silesia	12	Sudeten Germany	2
East Frontier	2	Volksdeutsche (Polish)	1

The total number of enlisted men included 113 surplus privates, but the division was short 415 noncoms. When the division was formed, about 25 percent of the privates were nineteen years old. Germans returning to duty who had been wounded in Russia made up about 33 percent.[48] This mixture of recruits and experienced combat soldiers was conducive to the rapid completion of training.

The infantry battalions had 810 men; the light artillery battalions 644; the antitank battalion 499; the engineers 339; and the signal battalion 431. The division was up to strength, but the report of July 30 listed its battleworthiness as fit only for a limited defensive role. They lacked special equipment, needed more training, and had inexperienced officers and headquarters units. This was the official report to Berlin when the division first appeared on the list of divisions in the West.[49]

On August 1, the division received bad news from Fifteenth Army headquarters: it was to surrender 6,236 young soldiers whose training (less than four months) had been completed and 657 returning wounded, a total of 6,993 men out of 8,837 privates. These men were to be transferred to units going into combat and replaced by lower quality men and recruits.[50] On September 12, the division was selected for coastal defense with the secondary mission of training recruits.[51] For the next nine months, men flowed constantly in and out of the division.

During the week of September 20, 1942, the Sixty-fifth Division received 3,255 new recruits. Nearly 1,500 were only nineteen years old or younger—an entire class of schoolboys. An additional 500 were Poles who spoke little or no German. A Polish-speaking officer was assigned to each battalion to lecture the Poles on the glories of National Socialism and to act as a security officer for the battalion.[52] The exchange of this large number of men destroyed the training schedule of the division that just the week before had attained the level of fitness for combat on the Russian front.[53]

The rapid training and development of this German division had been the result of the high quality of the officers and noncommissioned officers. These leaders had been taken from units of the replacement army in Germany in July as part of the crash program to form the three divisions,[54] but these leaders did not remain with the division. A good profile of the quality of the officers of the division is shown on a report of January 4, 1943, filed on the battalion and regimental commanders, all but two of whom were now from forty-four to fifty-five years old. Two captains commanding battalions were thirty and thirty-two years of age, indicating that all but two of the officers had probably served in World War I. The civilian occupations were listed for all except six, who were presumably regular army officers. The occupations included the upper and professional echelons of society, as one would expect—magistrate, social worker, physical education teacher, landowner, notary, and brewery owner (the supply unit commander).[55] A list of the officers on the division staff, including many lieutenants and warrant officers, indicated that most of them were in the age bracket of thirty to forty-nine with four older and four younger. The younger officers were former students; the older ones included a university professor, an export merchant, a businessman, a bank officer, and a clock and optical engineer. All of the occupations listed were of the professional class, and only two were specifically listed as regular army officers, though the occupations of six were not listed.[56] Again this background was what one would expect. The army was still controlled by professional soldiers and upper and professional classes. The technical training needed for staff positions was most easily found in the professional classes, many of whom had served probably as junior officers in World War I. The new generation of officers had come directly out of the universities into the army. Despite the belief that the German army drew its officers from all classes based on loyalty to the Nazi party, in fact, the senior commanders and technical officers seldom included members of the working class.

Beginning in September 1942, there was a rapid turnover of enlisted men, primarily because of the need for replacements on the eastern front. The division had been formed at full strength, but more trained men were being transferred out than could be replaced. Rather than a surplus, as in July, by October 9, the division was down to 10,095 men with only 7,855 fit for combat duty. The division was short 58 officers, 407 noncommissioned officers, and 273 men.[57] The loss of the junior officers and noncommissioned officers was especially troublesome because these were the men needed to train the new recruits, although many men recuperating from wounds could impart their knowledge. On November 28, 1942, Russian campaign medals were awarded to 1,490 men in the division, indicating the high percentage with combat experience.[58]

The German Sixty-fifth Division was used as a reservoir from which combat-fit men were drawn, on short notice, to replace nonfit men when another division was ordered to Russia. In November and December, more than a thousand fit men were sent to the Thirty-ninth Division in exchange for nearly six hundred men with frostbite.[59] The unusually severe winter of 1941–1942 caused many German infantrymen to suffer from various degrees of frostbite which, though painful when the man was exposed to cold weather, did not incapacitate him from further military service. Those with third-degree frostbite, however, were considered ineligible for duty in Russia. Before a division moved from France to Russia, all such men were exchanged. In one group of replacements, ten had to be sent immediately to a special hospital in Paris for frostbite cases. Another exchange gave up eighty combat-fit men, aged twenty-five years or younger, to the 167th Infantry Division for eighty men of the Volksdeutsche List III category, Poles who had been drafted into the army because they had German ancestors, but who were not considered reliable for service in Russia.[60] Six men came to the Sixty-fifth Division directly from the guard house of replacement units. A variety of special categories of exchange continually nibbled away at the combat level. Neither last surviving sons nor those who were the fathers of five or more children were to be committed to combat, so seven of these were received from another division. Another nine men were sent away under the program to comb older men out of combat units for placement in service units.[61] Even though only a few dozen of these miscellaneous transfers were reported each week, they caused a constant erosion in the quality of men and a disruption of the training schedule of the new recruits received in September. In January and February 1943, another six hundred men with third-degree frostbite were received from the Thirty-ninth in exchange for over eight hundred fit soldiers.[62]

The Sixty-fifth served not only as a depot for replacements but also as a source for cadres. On February 19, the order came to begin providing cadre for the Forty-fourth Division, one of the Stalingrad divisions, which was being reformed near Antwerp. On February 20, two rifle companies, two and one-half machine-gun platoons, a battery of light artillery, a self-propelled antitank platoon, and a towed antitank platoon were sent to the Forty-fourth Division. These men represented about 8 percent of the combat troops in the division. To prevent the Sixty-fifth from hedging on this request, strict orders were given that these cadre units were to be at full strength and fully equipped with weapons, equipment, wagons, and horses in good condition. All cadre units were to consist of fully trained men. In place of these men, the Sixty-fifth received more nineteen-year-old recruits.[63] On February 19, the Sixty-fifth was ordered to provide training personnel for the Seventeenth Luftwaffe Field Division. In exchange for privates and junior officers, the Sixty-fifth was to send an infantry battalion commander, an artillery battalion commander, a machine gun company commander, five infantry platoon leaders, and fourteen squad leaders, about 10 percent of its leadership.[64] Between the two requests for cadres, the Sixty-fifth lost nearly a fifth of its leaders. On February 21, 1943, the division had 278 officers and warrant officers plus 9,571 noncoms and privates, of which only 5,332 were combat-fit, a loss of almost one-third of the combat-fit men. Most of the remaining combat-fit men were recruits undergoing training.[65]

The quality of the manpower of the Sixty-fifth Division had dropped considerably. Whereas the officers had been 50 percent fit back in October, by March 4, 190 of the 266 officers were not fit for combat. Many of the senior officers had been lost during the same period. There were only 18 officers above the grade of captain and only 16 captains. The other 232 officers were first lieutenants, lieutenants, and cadet officers.[66]

The drain in trained personnel of this division continued in March and April. Nearly 900 fit men were sent to the Thirty-ninth Division, for which the Sixty-fifth received either unfit men or recruits from replacement battalions. In addition, 21 men were sent to train the Croatian divisions and 21 were sent to the Mechanized Brigade West. A total of over 900 of the remaining 5,300 combat-fit men were lost.[67] In April, another 220 men went to the Thirty-ninth Division and 680 to the Forty-fourth Division, for which the Sixty-fifth received only 100 recruits and 500 noncombat-fit men from the Forty-fourth Division.[68] On April 1, 1943, the Sixty-fifth had 5,233 combat-fit noncoms and privates, but many of the latter were new recruits.

While this continual turnover was taking place, the division was expected to carry out its two major missions—training recruits and guarding a sector of the coast in addition to building fortifications. A school was set up to teach driving to newcomers. Young officers and newly promoted noncoms were also in need of continuous training. The main task of the division was the individual training of the recruits who kept coming in.[69] On October 17, 1942, the division marched from Antwerp to the Walcheren Island sector and took on the coastal assignment. The unit marched nearly fifty miles; there was no pool of trucks around for such a move, as would have been the practice in the American army. In November and December, the unit was actively building concrete emplacements to upgrade the defenses.[70]

The Sixty-fifth Division on February 1, 1943, consisted of two infantry regiments, each with a headquarters company, an infantry gun company, an antitank company, and three infantry battalions, each of these with three rifle companies and a machine gun company. The artillery regiment had two battalions of twelve 105mm howitzers and one battalion of eight 150mm howitzers. The signal battalion had a radio and telephone company. The pioneer battalion had two engineer companies, and the mechanized battalion had two antitank companies (one with towed 75mm guns and the other with self-propelled tank destroyers) and a rifle company on bicycles. In addition, there was a reduced-service establishment armed with Polish light machine guns.[71]

Also attached to the Sixty-fifth Division in its coastal defense role was the 202d Naval Artillery Battalion with five batteries of obsolete naval guns and captured French guns; the 810th Naval Antiaircraft Battalion with five batteries, each with four 105mm antiaircraft guns; the 847th Luftwaffe Light Reserve Antiaircraft Battalion with 23 20mm antiaircraft guns; and the 668th Luftwaffe Light Antiaircraft Battalion with nine 37mm, four 88mm and 15 20mm antiaircraft guns.[72]

The division itself was equipped at a lower scale than the normal infantry unit with roughly about two-thirds as many weapons as a fully equipped division. Yet in terms of its authorized strength, it was well equipped at about 90 percent of authorized weapons with a generous supply of additional defensive weapons that were placed in the concrete bunkers.[73]

On February 21, 1943, the Sixty-fifth Division reported the following list of weapons:

Type	Authorized number	Actual number
Light machine gun, Type 34	305	261
Polish light machine gun	34	31
Heavy machine gun, Type 34	78	66
Mortar, 50mm, Type 36	57	51
Mortar, 80mm, Type 34	36	36
Antitank gun, 37mm	6	6
Antitank gun, 50mm, Type 38	8	11
Antitank gun, 75mm, Type 97/38	9	9
Self-propelled antitank gun 75mm, Type 40	9	6
Howitzer, 105mm, Type 16	24	19
Howitzer, 150mm, Type 18	8	8
Infantry gun, 75mm	8	6
Flamethrower	4	4

In addition, the Sixty-fifth Division had the following weapons installed in fortifications: twenty-three French light machine guns, thirty-two Polish heavy machine guns, six French 37mm antitank guns, twenty-two obsolete German 50mm guns from tanks, six 105mm infantry guns, three 75mm infantry guns, eight French 155mm howitzers, six French 75mm guns, and other miscellaneous weapons.[74]

Although this was heavy armament, indeed, and each month more and more concrete pillboxes were installed, the multiplicity of types of arms led to ammunition problems of the greatest magnitude—three kinds of rifle and machine-gun ammunition and over a dozen different types of artillery ammunition, exclusive of the attached units. The vehicle situation was quite good with about 80 percent of the table of organization running. The only serious shortage was in four-wheel-drive personnel carriers and tractors for the artillery. The division had 2,557 healthy horses, about 150 sick ones, and was short about 150.[75] Compared to the rest of the German divisions, the Sixty-fifth was quite mobile, with over five hundred trucks and personnel carriers and nearly three hundred motorcycles, but it was not in the league with a British infantry division having over three thousand trucks and vehicles and nearly a thousand motorcycles.

By June 1943, the progressive weakening of the Sixty-fifth by exchanging poor quality men for the recruits as they became trained was apparent. Over 900 men with third-degree frostbite, 375 Volksdeutche of List III, and 72 men recuperating from wounds were on the rolls. There were 198 men listed as missing. The division as a whole, however, was short only 80 men on June 1 and had 90 percent of its equipment, including a surplus of trucks.[76]

The growing threat to Italy after the fall of Tunisia brought a sudden change to the men of the Sixty-fifth Division. An army was needed immediately to reinforce Italy, and the high command could find divisions only in the units guarding the West. In early June, the Sixty-fifth was selected to receive better men and equipment in preparation for a combat assignment. Matters moved very swiftly. On June 6, 932 nonfit men were transferred to form cadres for fortress units, that is, units made up of overage men, and a further 450 nonfit soldiers were transferred to the Nineteenth Luftwaffe Division. Undoubtedly, many of the undesirable soldiers were disposed of in this way.[77] All officers not fit for combat were transferred out during June, including the commanders of one infantry regiment, the artillery regiment, the mechanized battalion, the engineer battalion, the service unit, and three infantry battalion commanders, in fact, eight of the sixteen major unit commanders. They were replaced by new physically fit officers from other divisions. The unit also transferred 866 frostbitten men to the 265th, 348th, 711th, and 712th Divisions. To preserve future leaders from untimely death in combat, 62 soldiers were sent off to officer training schools. Thirty-two "unreliable" Poles were sent to the Forty-fourth and 712th Divisions in exchange for more reliable Poles. A total of 2,101 replacements were transferred into the division in June to replace those sent away.[78] On July 18, 300 more replacements arrived from Germany, making the division overstrength. On July 20, the unit had an assigned strength of 229 officers, 66 warrant officers, 1,477 noncoms, and 8,880 men, a total of 10,652 of which 7,552 were considered completely fit and available for duty.[79]

The Sixty-fifth Division once again became predominantly south German (58 percent), with most of the men from Silesia, Bavaria, Rhineland, and Wurtemburg-Baden. About 12 percent came from Prussia. Only 1 percent of the men were then Volksdeutsche.[80] On June 10, the division table of equipment was upgraded. The Polish light machine guns were to be replaced with German types. Under the new table, the regimental infantry cannon company received two 150mm howitzers each and two additional 105mm howitzers. The regimental antitank companies received six 75mm antitank guns in exchange for 37mm guns. The mechanized battalion was divided into an antitank battalion with three additional 75mm antitank guns and a reconnaissance battalion with an added cycle company and a motor company with heavy weapons. The artillery regiment received a battery of four 100mm guns. The service unit was built up to full status, including doubling the size of the bakery and butcher units. The engineer battalion received an additional company. All equipment was to be of the latest type, and vehicles were to be provided on a first-priority basis.[81]

Despite the orders, the complete upgrading of equipment was not accomplished. By July 20, 1943, the division was still short of machine guns, was still using Polish machine guns and substandard antitank guns, and had not received the additional weapons ordered. Its vehicle situation was good, missing only fifty-five tractors. Though not all improvements had been completed, the unit was in its best condition since its formation. On June 8, it was relieved of its coastal defense sector by the Nineteenth Luftwaffe Division. The Sixty-fifth was in the Fifteenth Army reserve at St. Omer for only a short time. On July 31, 1943, it was ordered to Ferrara in Italy.

The story of the Sixty-fifth German Infantry Division reveals a great deal about the German army in the West during 1942 and 1943. The Sixty-fifth was given the dual assignment of guarding Walcheren Island and training. In addition to the recruits undergoing training, it was filled with frostbitten men from Russia, Poles, and overage soldiers, along with recuperating wounded. The equipment was either foreign or obsolete and in very short supply under a reduced table of organization. The quality of the men assigned went continually downhill from September 1942 until June 1943, as more and more combat-ready men were shipped back to replacement depots in Germany or to other divisions and replaced with more recruits or substandard men. If this were happening in an infantry division, what must have occurred in the occupation units that had no possibility of being used in the East and, therefore, were at the lowest priority?

The Sixty-fifth was also used as a source of cadres for the new divisions, which was evidence of the severe strain that reforming the Stalingrad divisions placed on the army in the West. In February, the Sixty-fifth was crippled by the loss of cadres to the Forty-fourth Division and the Nineteenth Luftwaffe Division. The extent to which it had been stripped is indicated by the need for 2,400 replacements to bring it up to 75 percent combat readiness in June and July of 1943.

The shortage of weapons faced by Germany in 1942 and 1943 before the effect of Speer's production revolution is indicated by the wide variety of weapons issued to the division. Even easily manufactured light machine guns were in short supply, although, by making use of captured equipment, the unit was adequately armed if the weapons in the fortifications are included. Although captured weapons make an impressive list, the problem of supplying a variety of ammunition limits their use in mobile warfare. On coastal defense, one assumed that by the time the ammunition that came with the weapon was fired, the enemy would have been driven back into the sea or the position would have been captured. In either case, it was felt that resupply of ammunition was not needed.

Both the quality of the manpower and the captured weapons point out strongly that the German army in the West in 1943 was not fitted for mobile combat. Once driven out of their positions, the German divisions would have been unable to fight effectively. Even their service units were curtailed by about one-half. Needless to say, these divisions were not equal to those of the Allies.

Table 9 compares the development of the two American and one German divisions. The greater opportunity for the American divisions to train in progressive steps is obvious. The American divisions did provide cadres to other divisions, but did not suffer the constant withdrawal of replacements on the scale

Table 9. Comparison of Divisional Training

Activity	Sixty-fifth German Division	Seventy-seventh U.S. Division	Eighty-fifth U.S. Division
Date formed	July 15, 1942	January 25, 1942	April 6, 1942
Cadre: Officers	22	172	158
Enlisted men	248	1,400	1,270
Cadre officers	mostly overage WWI veterans with combat experience	few regular army and National Guard, most ROTC and OCS	one-third each, regular, National Guard, and ROTC
Enlisted cadre	mostly returning wounded	reg. army from Eighth Div.	reg. army from Second Div.
Recruits	about 10,000	over 13,000	nearly 12,000
Joined the division	July 7–15, 1942	March 25–April 12, 1942	May 1942
Recruit quality	18- and 19-year-olds and limited-service men	average age 32, all A-1	21 to 30, all A-1
Losses during training:			
Provided cadres	Feb. 1943: 800 to 44 Div. Feb. 1943: 200 to 17 GAF Div.	July 1942: 1,200 to 94 Div. some to 99 and 100 Div.	Oct. 1942: 1,400 to 103 Div.
Other losses	Sep. 1942: 7,000 as replacements Nov./Dec. 1942: 1,000 to 39 Div. Jan./Feb. 1943: 800 to 39 Div. Mar./Apr. 1943: 1,800 to 39 & 44 Div.	1942: 1,000 to OCS	1942: 667 to OCS 2,000 other losses
Training	Continual recruit training and constructing fortifications	Nov. 1942: cycle completed Jan. 1943–Mar. 1944: adv. tng.	Mar. 1943: cycle completed Apr.–Sep. 1943: adv. tng.
Combat-ready men	10,652	15,000	15,000
Date ordered to combat	June 1943	Mar. 1944	Dec. 1943

that the German division did, though some American units had a small taste of providing fillers for overseas movement.

The American recruits were better qualified. All incoming American inductees were first-class physical specimens. At no time were unqualified men, disloyal foreigners, frostbite cases, or men in their forties forced on the American divisions. Above all, the turnover was slight; the American infantry divisions, with a few exceptions, were not used as replacement training centers, as were those of the Germans in the West in 1943.

Not only did the American divisions have a longer period of training, free of any other duties, but they also had better training facilities, whereas German divisions were required to construct coastal defenses and had no training grounds to receive realistic training. In contrast, the Americans had the use of large camps for training up to the division level and then maneuver areas and training centers where two or more divisions could be employed simultaneously.

Although short of weapons during training, the Americans left the United States with a full complement of first-grade equipment, whereas the Germans trained with substandard equipment and even fought in Italy with captured weapons.

Only in having combat-experienced officers and noncoms did the German division have an advantage over the Americans. When the final test was made in June 1944, this advantage did not prove effective, nor would it have been sufficient to make the Sixty-fifth German Infantry Division better than the Seventy-seventh or Eighty-fifth American Infantry Divisions in April 1943.

9

A COMPARISON OF INFANTRY DIVISIONS

To compare the strength of military forces, comparable units or common de-
nominators must be found. Traditionally, in World War II, the number of divisions was compared, but not all divisions were identical. Infantry divisions
varied not only from country to country, but even within one army. Germany
tended to create elite infantry divisions for attack and maintained large numbers
of substandard divisions for defensive purposes, whereas Allied divisions were
more uniform in quality.

The division was originally used under Napoleon to denote a large unit that
had complete administrative and tactical capability, could act as an independent
fighting unit, and could maintain itself in the field. The division changed radically as warfare changed. In World War I, the American division was a huge,
cumbersome unit with over twenty thousand men in four infantry and three
artillery regiments. In the late 1930s, the American division was streamlined by
reducing the number of infantry regiments from four to three and the field
artillery from three regiments (including six battalions) down to only four battalions.

The new triangular division consisted of three infantry regiments, each having
a battalion of light field artillery in direct support, plus a battalion of medium
artillery in overall support. Two of the infantry-artillery teams (regimental combat teams) would normally be fighting while the third was in reserve. The
soundness of this concept becomes obvious when one considers the alternatives—with four infantry regiments, either two were in combat and two in reserve,
which was wasteful as too many infantrymen would be required to cover a
front, or, if three regiments were up and one back, the reserve would be insufficient. A division of only two regiments, one up and one in reserve, would
also be wasteful, and if both were in combat, nothing would be in reserve.
Providing divisional reserves by withdrawing individual battalions from the regiments, as the Germans did frequently on the Russian front when they reduced
the size of their divisions, weakened the command structure and delayed response at critical times. All of the major armies in World War II used three
regiments in some of their infantry divisions.

The American infantry division, as authorized on July 15, 1943, is described
on Table 10. The major difference compared to the Germans was its large size,
over fourteen thousand. An efficient replacement system kept the American

Table 10. Comparison of American, British, and German Infantry Divisions

	American	British	German	German Panzer Grenadier
Infantry regiments	3	3	3	2
Cannon company (guns)	6	0	8	8
Antitank company (guns)	12 57mm	18 6-pdrs. in Bn AT Pl.	12 50mm	3 companies at 3 75mm, 6 50mm
Other	0		0	Engineer company LAA company
Infantry battalions (men)	3 (871)	3 (780)	2 (700)	3
Rifle companies (men)	3 (193)	4	3 (142)	4
Light machine guns	11	9+	16	18 + 4 heavy
Mortars	3	3	2	2
Weapons company	1	1	1	1
Heavy machine guns	8	0	12	0
Mortars	6	2	4	0
Other	0	6 6-pdr.	0	6 assault guns
Divisional artillery battalions	4	3	4	3
105mm howitzers	36	0	36	12 SP, 12 towed
155mm howitzers	12	0	12	8
25-pounders	0	72	0	
Antitank battalion (guns)	50 tank destroyers*	32 17-pdr.	12 75mm 12 assault guns 12 20mm AA	4 88mm guns 6 50mm AT guns
Antiaircraft battalion (guns)	36 50-cal. MG*	54 40mm	0	8 88mm 30 20mm

Other battalions	tank: 50 Shermans*	tank: 50* machine gun 36 H.M.G.	fusilier (4 inf. co.)	tank: 48 Mark IV
Reconnaissance	company	battalion	0	battalion: 5 co.
Total infantry battalions	9	10	7	6
Rifle companies	27	36	21	26
Weapons companies	15	13	13	12
Men	14,253	18,347	12,772	14,000
Pistols	ca. 1,200	1,011	1,981	2,678
Rifles and carbines	ca. 11,000	11,254	9,069	9,926
Machine pistols	unknown	6,525	1,503	1,230
Machine guns	636	1,262	656	924
Light mortars (50–60mm)	90	283	0	0
Medium mortars (75–81mm)	54	60	48	64
Heavy mortars (105–120mm)	0	16	28	26
Antitank rockets	557	436	108	0
20mm antiaircraft guns	0	71	12	58
40mm antiaircraft guns	0	36	0	9 (37mm)
40mm antiaircraft guns SP	0	18	0	0
25-pounders	0	72	0	0
105mm howitzers	54	0	36	37
155mm howitzers	12	0	12	12
100mm guns	0	0	0	4
Infantry guns (105–150mm)	0	0	24	8
57mm antitank guns	63	78	0	0
75mm antitank guns or	0	0	21	19
17-pounder	0	32		
88mm gun	0	0	0	12

continued

(Table 10, continued)

	American	British	German	German Panzer Grenadier
Motorcycles	0	983	168	475
Cars or quarter-ton trucks	637	495	136	1,440
Three-quarter-ton trucks	159	881	0	0
Two-and-a-half-ton trucks or over	457	1,056	370	944
Tractors	0	205	0	115
Trailers	0	226	40	117
Armored cars	13	31	0	17
Light armored cars	0	32	0	0
Tracked vehicles	5	595	60	179
Ambulances, etc.	775	52	9	72
Total motor vehicles (excluding motorcycles)	2,046	3,347	615	2,884
Bicycles	0	0	678	0
Assault guns or tank destroyers	50*	0	14	42 and 31
Tanks	50*	0	0	5
Horse-drawn vehicles	0	0	1,466	0
Horses	0	0	4,662	0

SOURCE: Table 1, Table of Organization and Allied Tables, July 15, 1943 in Greenfield et al., *Organization*, p. 274–75; *ROTC Infantry Manual*, 3:698; Joslen, *Orders of Battle*, 1:131; Mueller-Hillebrand, *Das Heer*, 3:227, 235; Keilig, *Das Deutsche Heer*, 1:15, pp. 15–16, 2:102, p. V, 9; Records of the Oberkommando des Heeres, Reforming Units, 1943–1945. Microfilm, Series GG30 T78, roll 398, frame 36241; U.S., War Department, *Handbook of German Military Forces, Technical Manual-Enemy 30-451* (Washington: Government Printing Office, 1945), p. II, 10–11.
*Normally attached units.

division close to authorized strength. The American division was not as heavily armed with automatic weapons as the German or British counterpart. American theory placed greater emphasis on aimed shots than on spraying the battlefield with bullets. The M1 rifle, the basic squad weapon, gave semiautomatic fire, that is, the rifleman had only to pull the trigger to fire eight shots after placing the first bullet in the chamber. In contrast, the Germans and British used a bolt-action rifle that required the soldier to manually pull back the bolt and push a fresh round into the chamber after each shot. The major advantage of the M1 was that the semiautomatic action eliminated the movement to operate the bolt that often revealed the position of a concealed rifleman. For this reason, the Germans developed a semiautomatic rifle for use by snipers. Though the semiautomatic rifle gave a higher rate of fire with less discomfort, the bolt-action rifle in skilled hands was nearly as effective. The official rate of fire for an M1 was sixteen to twenty-four rounds per minute; for a bolt action, ten to fifteen.[1]

The Americans used the Browning automatic rifle as the automatic weapon in the rifle squad. The British used the Bren light machine gun and the Germans, the belt-fed MG34 or MG42. The Browning automatic rifle (BAR) was not heavy enough (eighteen pounds) to perform as a light machine gun. It had a low rate of effective fire, about forty to sixty rounds per minute, and a small twenty-round magazine in keeping with the American idea of encouraging the soldier to aim his shots at visible targets.[2] The British Bren was heavier (twenty-two and a half pounds) and, with a thirty-round magazine and a cyclic rate of fire of five hundred rounds per minute, made an excellent light machine gun. The German MG42, however, was the best infantry weapon of the war. It had a high cyclic rate of twelve hundred rounds per minute and was belt fed. Because its barrel could be changed in a matter of seconds, the weapon could deliver enormous amounts of fire when needed, yet could be used for short bursts normally expected of an infantry squad automatic weapon. It weighed only twenty-five pounds, and its belt feed meant that far more ready ammunition could be carried than the awkward boxes of the BAR and Bren.[3] Whereas the Germans and the British conceived of small infantry units built around the light machine gun that could produce a large volume of fire, the American squad was a group of well-trained marksmen who would pick their targets rather than spray the general area. The BAR was added as a heavy rifle for special use, rather than as the basic offensive weapon.

To provide some automatic fire in the rifle company, the Americans attached two Browning light machine guns to the rifle company. The light machine gun was mounted on a tripod with a slow cyclic rate of fire, five hundred rounds per minute, but using belt ammunition. It had a heavy barrel that could sustain some prolonged firing, but the barrel could not be changed in combat, and when the barrel heated up, the gun was out of action. The official rate of sustained fire was only sixty rounds per minute.[4] It had many disadvantages: it was too heavy for use as an infantry squad weapon, had too slow a rate for mobile warfare, and was too inefficient to perform as a support machine gun. The rifle company also had three 60mm mortars that were far better than the 50mm models used by the Germans and British. The American mortar fired a three-pound shell nearly two thousand yards, and the tube and plate together weighed only forty-two pounds.[5] The antitank rockets that came into use in all armies in 1943 gave the infantry some defense against tanks if the soldier were brave enough to move close to the tank and place the rocket at a vulnerable position, such as the tracks, or, even better, the engine housing at the rear.

The regimental antitank company was the major source of antitank defense for the infantry. By 1943, the American divisions were using the 57mm antitank gun, a direct copy of the British six-pounder gun. This gun could fire a shell slightly more than six pounds in weight to penetrate 81mm of armor at five hundred yards, quite enough to cope with the German Panzer IV and the side-plates of the Panther and Tiger, but it took a great deal of courage to wait for the German tanks to move that close before firing. The first shot revealed the position of the gun and led to counterfire from the tank.

The British distributed their six-pounders in a divisional antitank battalion and in antitank platoons in each infantry battalion. The Germans used a 50mm antitank gun in the regimental antitank company that could penetrate only 59mm at five hundred yards, not enough power to trouble the 76mm armor on the Sherman until it came closer than one hundred yards. The Germans had 75mm antitank guns in divisional antitank battalions that were capable of dealing with the Sherman.

Pooling of specialized units made the American division potentially more powerful than its counterparts. Although not carried out to the fullest, pooling prevented the weighting down of the division with specialized units that were not always used. Examples are the antitank and antiaircraft battalions that were assigned to German and British divisions. These battalions would have been pointless in the Pacific theater, where even the regimental antitank companies had to be retrained for other duties. Independent battalions of special troops were created, including tank destroyers, tanks, antiaircraft, artillery, and reconnaissance that could be attached to divisions as needed. Special battalions were assembled into groups of two or more battalions when large numbers were called for. The result was that the army commander had a varied inventory of battalions that could be used to reinforce the infantry division.[6]

Under conditions in the European theater, each division often had a self-propelled tank destroyer battalion, a tank battalion, and an antiaircraft battalion attached on a long-term basis. In effect, the American infantry division had the same armored component as many German panzer divisions—fifty tanks and fifty assault guns. No division could possibly have all the special units it needed for every event, so pooling was essential. The drawback was that the needed unit might not always be available, and the receiving division might not have had personal contact with the attached units for a period long enough to develop teamwork.[7]

The Germans created a special type of infantry division that eliminated the horses and substituted motor vehicles. Called the motorized division in the early years, it was later referred to as a panzer grenadier division, indicating its tank component. After a brief trial, the Americans abandoned the motorized division. The question that led to abolishing the motorized division was not one of using trucks to move the infantry. In fact, the infantry division already could dump its load of supplies, use its trucks to transport the men, and then go back for the supplies—operating a shuttle. The question was whether to assign permanently enough trucks to move men and supplies simultaneously. With six quartermaster truck companies, each with forty-eight two-and-a half-ton trucks, there would be no need to dump the supplies, and both men and material could move together. The six truck companies plus a regular division took far less shipping space than a motorized division. No one really missed the motorized division. All divisions were trained to move with extra trucks. In fact, in Europe it was found that by putting men on self-propelled artillery, tanks, and tank destroyers, the entire division could move with its supplies at a rate of thirty miles a day and still be ready to fight at any time.[8]

Another form of infantry was the airborne. The American airborne forces began with the formation of four parachute battalions in the fall of 1940. In August 1942, the Eighty-second and 101st Airborne Divisions were formed.[9] Each division had one regiment of parachutists (1,958 men) and two regiments of glider troops (1,605 men). There were three battalions of gliderborne artillery with 75mm pack howitzers. The division had only 408 vehicles, mostly jeeps and trailers.[10] The total strength was only 8,500 men. Three other airborne divisions were formed rapidly in 1943, the Eleventh in February, the Seventeenth in April, and the Thirteenth in August 1943. The last division was left on the vine and never saw combat, though it was shipped to Europe in January 1945. After some experiments with light divisions, the Tenth Division was designated as a mountain division. It was filled with the highest quality manpower and trained endlessly. In November 1944, the Italian theater finally agreed to accept the division. In December 1944, it reached Italy and took part in the final campaign.[11] The lessons learned from actual combat performance of the special divisions were that they were wasteful of high-quality manpower and that regular divisions could and did accommodate to conditions that usually were temporary in nature. It was better to store a few thousand trucks or convert antitank gunners into infantry rather than keep in reserve entire special-purpose divisions, filled with highly trained soldiers, waiting for special circumstances. The standard American division was capable of modification for all roles.

The British had a more flexible attitude toward the division. It was an ad hoc assembly of brigades and battalions that could be changed at will, though most divisions conformed to the authorized table of organization presented in Table 10. The full British division had eighteen thousand men, compared to fourteen thousand in the American division and twelve thousand in the German. In fact, however, the British division was often understrength because British battalions received replacements through a system of drafts of men sent to fighting battalions from related training centers, similar to the German replacement system. Because battle losses are not predictable, there was often a shortage of replacements that led to the disbandment of some battalions in 1943 and later.

The British battalion had four rifle companies, rather than three, giving the division a much higher percentage of riflemen, its real offensive force. The British battalion had thirty-six sections, each with 10 men armed with a light machine gun and rifles, compared to the American battalion with only twenty-seven squads of 12 men with a BAR and M1s and the Germans with twenty-seven groups of 9 men with a light machine gun and rifles. The British battalion in 1943 had 806 officers and men with forty-five machine pistols, fifty-four Bren guns, sixteen two-inch mortars, and six three-inch mortars, comparable to the weapons of the best German battalions.[12]

The British battalion support company had a platoon of six three-inch mortars, comparable to American equipment, and an antitank platoon of six six-pounders, in contrast to the German and American antitank companies that provided only four antitank guns per battalion. A platoon of engineers and another of Bren carriers (a small-tracked vehicle) completed the company.

The British division had double the number of light machine guns, over twelve hundred, compared to fewer than six hundred for the others. The British, however, provided only forty-eight heavy machine guns compared to ninety in the German and American divisions, but the heavy machine guns were concentrated in a single battalion and provided with adequate ammunition supply facilities so that they could perform in the true role of the heavy machine gun, laying down curtains of fire. The scattering of the heavy machine guns in battalion support companies led to their use as light machine guns, following the infantry and being used as close support weapons. Such employment was unwise. Why use a heavy weapon to perform a role suited to the lighter gun? The number of mortars was about equal, but the British used a startling number of Sten guns, cheap submachine guns copied from German designs, that gave the infantrymen the ability to spray a large amount of ammunition at an obscure or unseen target. More than sixty-five hundred were assigned to the division, compared to fewer than three hundred in the American division and only fifteen hundred in the German.[13]

At the division level, the British antitank battalion and antiaircraft battalion were permanently assigned. Tank support came in the form of attached battalions, similar to the American system. Often a brigade of three tank battalions was assigned to an army corps, and then a tank battalion would be designated to work with an individual division on a day-to-day basis.

In general, the British did not emphasize long-term association of units within a division to the degree practiced by the Americans and Germans. Battalions in a brigade would be changed for a variety of reasons: one might be detached for a special mission; another might become seriously understrength and be withdrawn for rebuilding or because of replacement shortages; separate battalions of the same regiment might be combined into one and an additional battalion from another regiment added to a brigade. This ebb and flow of battalions within the brigades was not universal, but it was frequent once a division entered combat.

The brigades assigned to divisions were also subject to change. A division might be reduced to two brigades on occasion. If all the battalions in a brigade suffered heavy losses and needed rebuilding, the brigade would be replaced by another. Some brigades were broken up to provide individual replacements in others. The entire approach and attitude was quite different from that of the other two armies, and by adopting this flexible approach, the British were probably able to give their infantry battalions more frequent relief from continuous front-line action than was possible in the other two armies.

The field artillery component was organized into three field regiments each with twenty-four twenty-five-pounder guns formed into four batteries of six guns each. The twenty-five-pounder was a cross between a gun with a high velocity and a howitzer designed to lob shells over hills at a lower velocity. The howitzer was used by both the Americans and Germans in the infantry division, but the British adopted the twenty-five-pounder compromise gun howitzer in the 1930s. The advantage was that with its high velocity, it had a range of 13,400 yards, compared to 12,200 yards for the American 105mm howitzer. It fired a lighter shell, only twenty-five pounds compared to the thirty-two and thirty-three pounds of the others, but being a lighter weapon it was more easily managed.[14] Its high velocity made it a good substitute antitank gun in the western desert in 1942, when the two-pounder antitank gun proved incapable of coping with the later German tanks. Also, because of its greater range, the British did not feel that they needed to assign heavier pieces to the division, as did the others, which simplified the supply of ammunition to the division because only one size of artillery shell rather than two needed to be stocked. There were seventy-two pieces compared to only forty-eight in the artillery component of the other divisions, but both Americans and Germans assigned cannon companies to the infantry regiments equipped with low-velocity howitzers. The total number of pieces in the three divisions was therefore equal, but the quality of the British artillery was higher.

The most remarkable difference in the British formation was the number of motor vehicles. The total of nearly 3,500 plus nearly 1,000 motorcycles was more than double that assigned to the American division. A unique vehicle was the universal infantry carrier, commonly, though inaccurately, called the Bren gun carrier. This tracked vehicle was a miniature tank with about 12mm of armor, sufficient to resist machine-gun fire, and armed with either a Bren gun or a .50-caliber Boys antitank rifle or both. There were 595 carriers assigned to the division and 38 to the infantry battalions. They served as combat vehicles that could move men across open terrain swept by machine-gun fire, though they were vulnerable against even the lightest antitank guns. As infantry battalion supply transportation vehicles, they were far superior in cross-country capability to the jeep and the horse carts of the Germans.[15]

Although the British had nearly two thousand trucks, their trucks were generally smaller than those of the Americans and lacked the four-wheel drive that made the American trucks usable on poor roads. The British trucks were tied to paved roads, as were the motorcycles. The net result, however, was that in the conditions of northern France and Germany, the British division was equipped to drive ahead with great speed, and its large infantry unit gave it great shock power.

In addition to British divisions, the Commonwealth forces contained Canadian, South African, African, Australian, New Zealand, and Indian divisions. The British army provided supporting arm and service units to the Indian divisions, which had three British infantry battalions joined to the six Indian battalions. Inasmuch as the machine-gun battalion, the three artillery regiments, and all of the other arms and services were British during the early years of the war, Churchill suggested that these divisions be referred to as British-Indian divisions. Later, Indian special units replaced some of the British, although the need to provide special units for the growing number of Indian divisions and supporting units for the other Commonwealth divisions led to shortages of overhead units. Possibly as a result of the shortage, the British created a number of lower-establishment divisions in 1941 for service in the United Kingdom only. The lower-establishment division had only two, instead of three, field artillery regiments, no antiaircraft regiment, a reconnaissance company instead of a battalion, and greatly reduced engineer and service units.[16] Lower-establishment divisions were assigned to coastal defense duties, and were sometimes called county divisions or beach divisions. Later in the war, some were disbanded and others turned into units for holding men returning from hospitals or for training new recruits.

The Fifty-fourth East Anglia Division is an example. It was formed in September 1939 as a first-line territorial division with a complete array of artillery, antitank forces, and infantry brigades. In January 1942, it was placed on the lower establishment, and most of the artillery, antitank, antiaircraft, and service units were transferred during the next four months. Three infantry brigades remained, the 162d, 163d, and 198th. The 162d was formed as a first-line territorial brigade in September 1939 and kept its first-line battalions until September 1942, when two were replaced with the Seventieth Foresters (made up of limited-service men fit only for home defense), the Sixteenth Foresters (assembled from young soldier training companies in September 1940), and the Seventh East Yorks, also a new battalion raised in July 1940 that had previously been assigned to coastal defense duties. The Sixth Bedford and Hertfordshire Battalion remained (a second-line territorial battalion), but the best men were probably taken from this battalion and replaced with inferior grade manpower.[17] The brigade later served as security troops on the line of communication for the Twenty-first Army Group in France.

The 163d Brigade was formed as a second-line territorial brigade on September 18, 1939. It retained two second-line territorial battalions until December 1943 and picked up another territorial battalion. It must be assumed that these battalions had been filled with limited-service men, because they were employed only on line of communications duties after January 1942. The same situation existed with the 198th Brigade.[18] Therefore, the lower-establishment divisions were, in fact, groups of infantry battalions without complete supporting arms and service units necessary to make them a division and were comparable, in many ways, to the German occupation divisions.

The British also organized two airborne divisions that had varying numbers of battalions of parachutists and glider troops assigned, depending on the need. In addition, the Fifty-second Infantry Division that had been originally trained for mountain fighting was reorganized as an airlanding division, because all of its equipment was transportable by air. The division never functioned in this way and was reformed to fight as a normal infantry division.

Both the British and the American infantry divisions were powerful formations organized to play a multitude of roles with their assigned or attached units and weapons. Comparatively few special divisions, other than armored, were formed by the Western Allies. For limited-service activity, the Americans formed a small number of independent infantry regiments that provided garrisons and guarded communications. The British formed a few lower-establishment divisions described above.

The Germans, on the other hand, formed a multitude of special divisions. Not all of these special divisions could be counted as equals to those of the Allies, which was the basis of the controversy as to when the Allies were strong enough to take on the Germans in France. German divisions were divided into "mobile" and "static" types. German army "mobile" divisions included panzer, panzer grenadier, mountain, infantry, cavalry, ski, and jager divisions. The SS created panzer and panzer grenadier divisions with German personnel and a score of infantry, mountain, and cavalry divisions using non-German volunteers from captured nations. The German air force created a panzer division, parachute divisions (which were actually heavily armed infantry divisions made up of young volunteers), and field divisions from retrained security and antiaircraft troops.

Of all the so-called mobile divisions, only the panzer and panzer grenadier divisions were fully equipped with motor vehicles. All of the others had horse-drawn and motor vehicles to carry their essential weapons and supplies, while the men marched. "Mobile" meant a division that could move at the speed of marching men, as compared to "static" divisions that could not move at all.

The static divisions were mostly occupation units organized to defend fixed emplacements on the coast. Some of their weapons were permanently emplaced in blockhouses. The occupation division did not have even horses in sufficient numbers to move its weapons and supplies without outside help. Security divisions were designed to protect rear installations from partisans and had few weapons other than rifles and machine guns. Field training and reserve divisions were assembled to provide advanced training for recruits. These divisions were given token amounts of weapons for training purposes only.

Because of the heavy demands for special tasks, the Germans freely created diverse forms of divisions in an effort to make the maximum possible use of available manpower. About three hundred divisions were created from about half again the number of men that the Americans used in creating ninety divisions; although few of these German divisions were comparable to the American counterpart. The major difference was that few German divisions were kept up to strength, whereas the Americans kept heavy reserves of manpower available to replace losses. In addition, the Americans had large numbers of small independent units, spare parts, of which the Germans had very few. The result was that a German division would seldom exceed ten thousand men and often fell nearer to seven thousand, whereas American divisions, with attached units, would frequently exceed fifteen thousand men. Because most losses occurred in the rifle companies, the actual loss in combat value was even more drastic than the gross figures indicated.

The Germans had begun the war with divisions comparable to those of the Americans and British, but the heavy losses sustained in the winter battles of 1941–1942 overstrained the German replacement system. As plans were made to refit the army in the east for the summer offensive in 1942, it became apparent that under existing guidelines from Hitler, all the losses could not be replaced. The army requested eight hundred thousand replacements, but Albert Speer, the minister for armaments production, claimed this many men could not be taken from the factories.[19] The decision was made to reduce the size of the German divisions in the two army groups on the Russian front that were not to take part in the coming campaign. After making the point that losses had been too heavy to be made up, the order of April 26, 1942, stated the obvious—that losses were heavier in the fighting units than in the service elements. To maintain the number of divisions and the existing replacement system, the decision was announced that the size of the regiment (the unit on which the replacement system was based) would be reduced from three battalions to two. As a result, the replacement and training battalion in Germany would then have to provide new men for only two battalions instead of three. If a division found that it had extra men, they were to be made available for filling other divisions in Army Group South.[20] To further economize on manpower, the divisional antitank battalion and the reconnaissance battalions were to be reduced to company size and the two joined together to form a new smaller reconnaissance battalion. These new reduced scales applied only to the North and Center Army Groups; the divisions in Army Group South were completely rehabilitated.

The campaign of 1942 made heavier and heavier demands on the replacement system. Even before the loss of the Sixth Army at Stalingrad, the steady drain of men had created a crisis. The Army High Command on October 29, 1942, ordered a 10 percent cut in the service elements to provide more men for combat. Russian volunteers replaced the Germans, and the scale of transportation made available to the infantry division was reduced from a load capacity of 240 tons (compared to over 3,000 tons in the American division) down to 120 tons. These changes not only lessened the combat value of the division, but also impaired its mobility. The division became dependent on the army depots on a day-to-day basis.[21] During 1943, as a result of further losses and the need to rebuild divisions, the two-battalion infantry regiment was established throughout the army. The small reconnaissance battalion was replaced by a standard infantry battalion called the fusilier battalion. On October 4, 1943, this seven-battalion division was designated as the infantry division (new type).

A major reduction was made in the infantry battalion. The old one had 820 men, and each rifle section had 14 men. Each of the new seven infantry battalions had 708 men with only nine men in the section. The battalion had fifty-one light machine guns, twelve heavy machine guns, six medium mortars, and four heavy mortars. Each of the three regiments had an antitank company with at least twelve towed 50mm antitank guns and a cannon company with eight short-barreled howitzers. The division had an antitank battalion with twelve 88mm or 75mm guns, perhaps eight to fourteen self-propelled 75mm antitank guns, plus some 20mm self-propelled antiaircraft guns. The artillery regiment had thirty-six 105mm howitzers and twelve 150mm howitzers. This new German divisional organization reflected a realistic attitude toward existing conditions. The number of men authorized per division was reduced by eliminating two of the previous nine infantry battalions, while at the same time increasing their allotment of machine guns and other heavy weapons.[22]

Most of the transportation was horse-drawn. Only the antitank guns and some of the service elements were motorized. Needless to say, even those so-called "mobile" divisions moved at the pace of the marching soldier. The only motor vehicles in the infantry battalion were five half-tracks to carry the 120mm mortars in the weapons company, three volkswagens, and a single three-ton truck. There were 281 horses and 74 horse-drawn vehicles to move most of the battalion supplies and heavy weapons.[23] In contrast, an American battalion had enough motor vehicles to transport all of its weapons and supplies. It had assigned four one-and-a-half-ton trucks, two three-quarter-ton trucks, and thirty quarter-ton jeeps, plus twenty-three trailers. The British army infantry battalion had even more transport than the Americans: twenty-three motorcycles, eleven cars, thirty-five three-quarter-ton trucks, fourteen heavier trucks, and twenty-one tracked carriers. In the German army, very little motor transport was available in the higher echelons, so the infantry division could move only on foot or by rail. Even if trucks were available for the men, the horses could be moved long distances only by rail.

Despite its lack of mobility, the German battalion had considerable firepower. The basic unit was the rifle group of nine men with one or two MG42 light machine guns.

On September 9, 1943, the 80mm mortar was substituted for the 50mm mortar. Each company then had two 80mm mortars, and the battalion machine-gun company was equipped with six 80mm mortars in addition to four 120mm mortars. Therefore, the battalion had more effective weapons than the Americans, who continued to use the 60mm mortar in the rifle company and the 81mm mortar in the weapons company.[24] Although the quality of equipment in the first-line units was high, not all of the units received their allotment. In the changeover of mortars, the high command accepted this fact and ordered the temporary substitution of rifle grenade launchers for the discontinued 50mm mortars.[25] Even the provision of a weapon so simple to manufacture as a mortar could not be promised, let alone be delivered. To provide light machine guns, captured French and Polish weapons were substituted for German weapons. Until 1944, the German arms industry could not supply sufficient arms.

In addition to regular infantry divisions, the Germans had motorized infantry divisions called panzer grenadiers. This division had no horses, and everyone rode in or on a vehicle. In February 1943, the organization table called for two infantry regiments, each containing three battalions with four companies. Each battalion had seventy-two light machine guns, sixteen heavy machine guns, eight medium mortars, and twelve rocket projectors. Each regiment had a cannon company with six assault guns and an antitank company with nine guns. The division had a reconnaissance battalion with seven armored cars and four infantry companies in volkswagens or on motorcycles. The antiaircraft battalion had eight 88mm and eighteen 20 mm antiaircraft guns. Also, the German panzer or tank battalion had eighty-eight medium Panzer IV tanks. The artillery regiment had twelve 105mm howitzers and eight 150mm howitzers, four 88mm guns, six rocket launchers, and twelve assault guns.[26] This rather generous table of organization was accompanied by a note to the effect that it was to be accomplished if material were available.

In September 1943, a new table was published which reduced the numbers of rifle companies in the battalion from four to three, while adding more light machine guns to each company (see Table 10).

A weapons company for each battalion was created by dividing the regimental antitank company, giving one platoon to each battalion, and adding a platoon of four 120mm mortars to create the unit. The real effect was the reduction of rifle companies in the division from twenty-four to eighteen, while adding six platoons of heavy mortars. In addition, each regiment received an antiaircraft company. The tank battalion received forty-two assault guns in place of eighty-eight Panzer IV tanks. A more powerful antitank battalion with twenty-eight Panzer II or T38 type assault guns and twelve 88mm guns replaced the panzer artillery battalion. Not all divisions received the divisional antiaircraft battalion; some had only a company of 20mm antiaircraft guns.[27] The net effect of the changes in 1943 was to supply more and heavier weapons to fewer men. And even then, few of the divisions received the full complement of equipment.

The quality of the manpower declined sharply as well. The Gross Deutschland Division was the elite division of the army as distinguished from the SS. The division had been rebuilt and retrained in early 1943 for the battle at Kursk. Even this division had a poor mixture of men in the rifle section. A firsthand description of a rifle group of the Fifth Company describes each man.

Our noncom was the head of the column. Behind him came Grumpers, the Grenadier, who was about twenty-two years old; then Hals [a machine gunner], just past eighteen, and Lindberg, not quite seventeen; then our three gunners: [probably riflemen] a Czech of indefinable age with an unpronounceable name, a Sudeten of nineteen whose name ended with an "a", and me. Right behind me was the veteran [a machine gunner] with his number-two man, another terrified boy, and finally Grenadier Kraus, who must have been well into his twenties.[28]

The narrator was an Alsatian who had a German father and had been drafted into the German army. The group had two MG42s, and two men were armed with machine pistols, which was better than the allotment in the average division, indicating that this was indeed a favored unit. The group had only three experienced soldiers in addition to the group leader. Three others were very young; three were non-Germans, and, of those, two were nineteen.[29] If this unit was the elite, what would a regular division have contained? The 260th Division, which was defending a stable part of the Russian front during 1942 and 1943, provides an example of an average division. During 1942 it received 9,800 replacements, more than replacing a total of 5,645 losses, of whom 715 had been killed and 99 were missing. By mid-February 1943, there were 2,548 men in one regiment and 2,664 in the other, very near the allotted strength of about 3,000 men each. In April 1943, one regiment was 25 percent below strength and the other 17 percent, while other units were in better condition. An "Ost" battalion of two companies of Hiwis had been formed to assist the division as well as a tank company equipped with captured Russian tanks and armored cars.[30]

The shortage of trained men was serious. In the beginning of 1943, the division lacked more than 10 percent of its officers and about 5 percent of its noncoms. The equipment situation was not as serious as might have been expected, with about 80 percent of vehicles and weapons in stock and no severe shortage in any weapon.[31] Compared with the equipment allotment of a Type 44 infantry division, the 260th Division was in good form—157 motorcycles assigned, compared with the table of allotment of 154; 515 trucks, compared with the authorized 537; 31 antitank guns (most of them 37mm), compared with 22 75mm antitank guns authorized; 36 howitzers, compared with 48; and 448 light machine guns, compared with 614. Although many of the vehicles were in repair, especially the motorcycles during January in Russia, this example indicates that the German army was not completely battered in numbers of men and weapons—the problem was quality.

The 134th Infantry Division also suffered in quality. On April 22, 1943, it had 14,100 combat-fit Germans, 1,100 limited-service men, 2,300 Russian troops in its service elements, and 5,600 Russian prisoners working as laborers. The totals included units attached to the division. The quality of the equipment was mixed. On July 17 and 18, 1943, the division lost to the Russians two 152mm Russian howitzers and four French 45mm antitank guns, indicating heavy use of captured equipment. The division also lost five 37mm antitank guns that were obsolete.[32] The commander of the Center Army Group, Gunther von Kluge, wrote to Hitler that the replacements being sent to the front in 1943 lacked training and soldierly qualities. Even the Russians noted the poor training of German infantry replacements.[33]

The interrogation of German prisoners of war of Polish extraction in Tunisia in 1943 gave ample evidence of the severe shortage of high-quality manpower for infantry replacements and for building new units. Conscripted Poles constituted a high percentage of men in the replacement units in Germany in early 1943. The First Company, Ninetieth Motorized Ersatz Battalion, was completely Polish. When these replacements were assigned to combat units, care was taken to assign no more than two to any one squad. Training in ersatz companies was abbreviated both for new recruits and for men released from hospitals. Both received from three to eight weeks of basic training, depending on the judgment of the company officers as to when the men were ready. After the men finished basic training, a small percentage, usually those destined for the Russian front, were sent to *Ausbildung* companies for advanced training. Others went for a few weeks of specialist training as heavy howitzer gunners, panzer grenadiers, or reconnaissance troops. At the camp at Küstrin, two men, who had been reservists in the Polish army, were given only three weeks of training before being sent to Africa. Even rifles were scarce in the training company, and little opportunity was provided to gain experience using them.

Communists and other political prisoners, along with those convicted of other crimes, were released to form the 961st Africa Regiment. The discipline was harsh, but in exchange for good conduct in combat, the men were promised reduced sentences. Obviously, foreigners and convicts did not make the best soldiers, especially when deprived of even the most basic training with a rifle.[34]

The breakdown in quality in 1943 was nowhere more evident than in the formation of the static or occupation division, the Bodenstandige Division. On May 12, 1943, the high command ordered a sorting out of the age groups. Combat troops in regular infantry divisions were to be from eighteen to thirty-six years old. Troops in service units were to be thirty-seven years or older, meaning that younger men were to be combed out and transferred to combat units. Combat troops in occupation divisions were to include men from eighteen to forty-three years, with an average age of thirty-six. To achieve this average, younger men were to be transferred from the static divisions to combat divisions. Even men recuperating from wounds were to be used to fill the ranks of divisions in the West, to make more men available for the East, although no more than forty-five thousand recuperating wounded per month were to be placed in divisions in order to maintain some semblance of readiness in the West.[35]

Men over thirty-six could not have functioned as infantrymen in mobile warfare, especially in the German army, where the infantry moved long distances on foot. During campaigns, infantry divisions were required to march twelve or more miles per day, day after day, because no motor transport was available. Therefore, these divisions were tied to their occupation duties or more often to coastline defense. Although these divisions provided a satisfactory substitute for the role of screening the coastline against small unit raids and as an initial line of defense against a major invasion, once that invasion came and the crust was broken, there was little chance of pulling them from their fortress areas after the Allies broke out of Normandy. Rather than retreating with the rest of the army, many remained bottled up in the channel ports for the rest of the war.

The creation of these static divisions began in September 1942. The initial table of organization called for two infantry regiments and all other elements on a reduced scale. They had far fewer motor vehicles and used a variety of captured weapons and equipment.[36] In September 1943, for example, the 716th Static Division, which was holding the Normandy coastline, had only two "fortress" infantry regiments, the 726th and 736th. The designation "fortress" indicated that the men were physically below standard and not considered fit for mobile combat. Most of them were in their thirties and forties. The regiments did not have sufficient vehicles to move their equipment, which was permanently installed in fortifications. Each regiment had three infantry battalions but only a single antitank platoon of four guns. The divisional artillery regiment had only three batteries totaling twelve obsolete French model 1897 75mm guns. There was only one self-propelled antitank company in the division. All of the service units were greatly reduced.[37]

By May 1943, there were five static divisions.[38] On May 12, 1943, the high command ordered the formation of eight more in France and two more in Norway, while two infantry divisions were to be reorganized as static divisions by exchanging younger soldiers for older men to bring the average age near thirty-six years.[39] The new divisions were to consist of seven battalions in three regiments with reduced-service elements. They were to be built on cadres of five to six thousand each provided by the remnants of the 323d, 340th, and 377th Divisions and of fewer than two thousand men each from the 298th, 385th, and 387th Divisions from the eastern front. These cadres were to arrive from the East on July 15, 1943, as most of the men were eligible for furlough after service against the Russians. Three divisions were to be formed two weeks after the arrival of the cadres on August 1, four more on August 15, and the final division on October 1. The two Norwegian divisions were to be formed from divisions and units in Norway. The conversion of the 326th and 338th Divisions from infantry to occupation status was to be completed by August 1, 1943. Nineteen static divisions were available by September 1943. Only four additional such divisions were formed by June 1944. After the invasion, nonmobile units seldom were formed, because they were of little use in the fluid warfare existing on both fronts for the remainder of the war.

In addition to the regular mobile infantry division and the static division, a third class existed in 1943, the reserve division. To make more manpower available for the divisions in Russia, reserve divisions were formed from the training battalions in Germany and assigned to occupation duties in France and Russia. Twelve such reserve divisions were sent to France in 1943 to replace infantry divisions sent to the East.[40]

The creation of the reserve divisions hampered the training of new men to a certain degree. If a new draftee were not selected to go into the air force or the panzer force, he received up to four months of basic individual infantry training in a replacement and training battalion located in a barracks near his home in Germany. He was then sent either to a reserve division in the occupied territories or to a training unit behind the lines in Russia, where he received another four months of training while performing occupation duties or fighting partisans. Finally, he was assigned to a division where he was taught more skills in the replacement battalion. In comparison, the American rifleman received three months of individual training, usually in the division to which he was assigned. The division then received at least six months of unit training and went on maneuvers for a test of skill.[41]

Assignment to reserve divisions, however, had some benefit to the German recruit. Those taking advanced training had an opportunity to fight comparatively easy opponents—the French underground and the Soviet partisans—a far more realistic form of training than any camp could provide. The partisans provided combat conditions, practice, and, above all, an intermediate stage in preparation for actual contact. Contrarily, the shock of actual contact proved fatal to a high proportion of American replacements, whose chances of survival increased greatly if they lived through the first three days of combat.

Another type of division that appeared on the order of battle in France in 1943, but had little combat effectiveness, was the reforming division. When a division was captured, leaving only its rear elements intact, or was severely reduced by losses, all of the remaining combat troops either as groups or as individuals, along with any remaining equipment, would be transferred to other divisions. The remaining one or two thousand specialists (signal men, medical, supply, ordnance, bakers, butchers, and veterinarians) would be sent to France to form the nucleus of a rebuilt division usually bearing the same number as the old division. Replacements, men returning from hospitals, and new inductees would be sent to the unit along with men from the navy and air force who had been retrained as infantrymen. From these, a new division was built. The first step was bringing the men together, which usually took about three months. Then, depending on their priority and availability, they received weapons, vehicles, and other equipment. Often they trained with captured French and Russian equipment and received new equipment just before being sent East, but sometimes they carried the substandard weapons into battle. Until the fourth month, these divisions had little combat value, but after the equipment arrived, they speedily gained ability, based on the experience of the returning wounded and the enthusiasm of the young men.

The German system of relating each division to a geographical area and to specific replacement and training battalions meant that many of the men in the reforming division would have common ties and even family relationships. The result was an extremely rapid development of unit spirit and combat efficiency. By 1943, however, this system was weakening, as men from different areas were thrown together in reformed divisions because replacement battalions could not provide sufficient men within a few months to refit a burned-out division having only a few thousand survivors.

An impressive number of divisions were reformed in 1943. The Battle of Stalingrad and subsequent battles in the Ukraine plus the surrender of Tunisia had resulted in the loss of thirty-two divisions by June 30, 1943. Between July 1943 and May 1944, a further forty-one divisions were lost on the eastern front, twenty-three of these in the last three months of 1943. The number of men left from the Stalingrad divisions was quite small, usually the bakery company and the butcher company plus perhaps a medical company. Returning wounded and those on leave would seldom bring the total number up to a thousand. The divisions lost in Tunisia left fewer men, perhaps a hundred or so per division. On May 26, 1943, the Sardinia Artillery Regiment had fewer than 140 men from five artillery regiments captured in Tunisia, and the Third Sicily Grenadier Regiment had gathered about 130 men from four infantry regiments and an artillery regiment.[42] To rebuild these divisions was tantamount to creating an entirely new unit—only the number and the replacement battalions were the same. Nevertheless, the German high command went about the task with great skill. By July 1, 1943, most of the twenty Stalingrad divisions had been filled with men, but they lacked vehicles, weapons, equipment, even horses, and were not ready for combat.[43] Many of the divisions that fought the Allies in Italy were rebuilt Stalingrad divisions. The infantry units were low on the priority list, which accounts for the lack of German infantry divisions in the early months in Italy. Hitler was relying almost entirely on the rebuilt units and new parachute divisions to defend Italy, and, because only the panzer and panzer grenadier units were even approaching combat strength by September 1943, these are the units that were used. Parachute divisions were about identical to mobile infantry divisions. Few of the men ever received parachute training, but they were eager young volunteers and were trained by the air force as an elite group. The table of organization does not reveal the real strength of the unit nor the enthusiasm of the young volunteers that made them a formidable foe in pitched battles of attrition such as Cassino. Their lack of experience and transport, however, reduced their value in more fluid situations.

Another type of division in France was the air force field division. In order to retain control of air force men needed for infantry combat duty, Hermann Goering insisted on the formation of air force field divisions made up of air force men but organized to fight as infantry divisions. Though they were tough young men, they lacked training and experience. General Hellmuth Reinhardt was especially critical of these divisions on June 17, 1943, when four were grouped as a corps on the Army Group North front. His fears were realized on October 6, 1943, when the Second Air Force Field Division broke up, leaving a ten-mile gap on the front through which the Russians poured.[44] These divisions were not comparable to parachute divisions and were, in fact, little better than the occupation divisions. Later, the field divisions were absorbed into the army and given cadres of infantrymen to improve their level of competence.

The most common forms of nonarmored German divisions found in France were occupation, infantry, air force field, reserve, and forming divisions. There were only a few panzer grenadier and parachute divisions. (During 1943, there were no mountain, ski, jager, or cavalry divisions in France.) Only the infantry, panzer grenadier, parachute, and air force field divisions were true combat divisions. The occupation, reserve, and forming divisions were not able to fight except under very special conditions and did not form a valid equivalent to an Allied division. Even at their best, the German infantry and panzer grenadier divisions were weaker than the British and American infantry divisions. In 1943, the Allied divisions were far superior to their German counterparts.

Few of the forty-six divisions at General Rundstedt's disposal as late as October 28, 1943, were fully fit. All of the twenty-three divisions placed on coastal defense were short of weapons and were using captured French, Russian, and other foreign weapons, which created grave difficulties in supplying ammunition in any prolonged battle. "Ost" battalions made up of Russian prisoners were already being assigned at the rate of one per division. Rundstedt rightfully surmised that the Russians would either surrender or run away as soon as the enemy approached—as did happen. Eleven other divisions were still forming in October. Rundstedt was concerned over the poor quality of the army in the West. The numbers on the map may have looked impressive, but they represented old men in static divisions along the coast, young trainees in reserve divisions on the coast and in French towns, and hastily assembled masses of men attempting to form divisions from the remnants of depleted divisions from Russia. Equipment was in short supply and of substandard quality. The tank battalions were equipped with French tanks that had proved inadequate in 1940; the artillery had guns taken from the Czechs in 1939. The infantry was using captured French machine guns and even water-cooled machine guns left over from World War I. These divisions could not be considered as equal to the Allied divisions at the time.

Simply to count divisions in 1943 is not sufficient; it is necessary to compare them. The comparison of the American, British, and German divisions reveals that all of the divisions slated for action by the British and Americans were of the highest quality, but few of the German divisions in France in 1943 were of comparative worth. Even the better infantry divisions had only half of the combat power of the Allied divisions. The only German infantry divisions comparable to the Allied units were the panzer grenadiers and parachutists, and there were few of these in France in 1943.

10

AIR SUPERIORITY

The tank and the airplane were the two dominant machines on the World War II battlefields. Although air superiority was needed for the invasion to succeed, the degree of superiority required was questionable. The Allied air forces had three tasks: to conduct a strategic air war against German industry and cities; to defend the land and sea forces from German air attack; and to provide tactical air support for the army. How essential were these functions for a successful invasion and to what degree could they be accomplished in 1943?

The need for a successful strategic air offensive was debatable. The proponents of strategic bombing anticipated great benefits—the destruction of German industry to deprive the Germans of weapons and the destruction of German morale to deprive the troops of the will to fight. Before an invasion was launched, the Allied leaders decided that a strategic air offensive was necessary to wear down the German war machine. At the ARCADIA Conference in December 1941, Churchill and Roosevelt gave high priority to air attacks on Germany.

The British bombing effort was feeble up to then because of the lack of suitable planes. To reduce losses, the British bombed mostly at night, which reduced accuracy to area bombing. In February 1942, most of the RAF Bomber Command squadrons were equipped with a medium bomber, the Wellington, carrying a small bomb load. The average number of heavy bombers, Stirlings and Manchesters, operational in February was only forty-four, and even these were of poor quality. The Manchester carried a heavy bomb load, but its engines were unreliable. The Stirling Mark I carried an even heavier load, seven tons, but again it was not a reliable airplane.[1] If powerful long-range air strikes were to be launched, new planes were needed.

On February 22, 1942, Sir Arthur Harris took command of the RAF Bomber Command and gave new direction to the air offensive. At the same time, improved bombers, the Halifax II and the Lancaster, were made available in significant numbers. The Halifax II carried six and a half tons of bombs and performed dependably. The Lancaster, carrying seven tons, with a range of 1,660 miles, was the best bomber the British produced.[2] With the new machines, the RAF began large-scale attacks on France and Germany.

On the night of March 28, 1942, 234 bombers destroyed much of Lübeck in a concentrated attack.[3] On April 24, 1942, a similar force struck Rostock. By

May, the average number of serviceable bombers in Bomber Command was up to 416. On May 30, the first thousand-bomber raid (which included Coastal Command and training planes) struck Cologne, damaging 20 percent of the city. The following night, Essen received a similar blow.[4] The bomber offensive by night was definitely on. By September 1942, twenty-five German cities had been raided by a thousand-bomber force.[5]

While the Bomber Command was demolishing German cities by night, even more trouble for Germany was developing across the Atlantic. The United States Army Air Force was wedded to the concept of strategic bombing. Two heavy bombers were developed, the B-17 Flying Fortress and B-24 Liberator, both powerfully armed to defend themselves and capable of carrying heavy loads of bombs long distances. Their defensive capability made possible daylight attacks, resulting in greatly improved accuracy compared to the area bombing of the night raiders.

The B-17E, the first model to be mass produced and used by the Eighth Air Force in Europe, could carry three tons of bombs a maximum of 1,100 miles. The B-17F, which entered combat in 1943, had an added turret for better defense and a maximum range of 2,210 miles.[6] The B-24 had a range of 1,700 miles with two and a half tons of bombs.[7] These two heavy bombers formed the backbone of the American strategic air force in Europe.

In June 1942, the bulk of the ground crew of the Eighth Air Force crossed the Atlantic on the *Queen Elizabeth,* followed later by the planes that were flown across.[8] On August 17, 1942, twelve B-17s hit Rouen in daylight escorted by four RAF Spitfire squadrons. The Germans then had to defend both by day and night. In November 1942, however, the invasion of North Africa seriously curtailed American participation in the air battle over the Continent. By the end of 1942, four fighter groups and two heavy bomber groups had been withdrawn from the Eighth Air Force to form the Twelfth Air Force in North Africa.[9]

The result was that the Eighth Air Force had few planes left to begin the attack on Germany. Nevertheless, on January 27, 1943, B-17s escorted by Lightning P-38s attacked Wilhelmshaven in daylight, the first attack on Germany by the Eighth Air Force.[10] Because of the weakness of the attacks, the Germans had ample time, in early 1943, to prepare daylight defenses against the Americans. The tremendous defensive firepower of the massed B-17s had set the Germans back at first and required the development of new techniques and heavier armament on their fighters.

The two most numerous fighters to oppose Allied bombers were the Messerschmidt 109 and the Fock Wolfe 190. The Me 109 was a prewar design that had gone through a continuing process of improvement. The early models of the Me 109 had only one 20mm cannon and two machine guns, not enough to stop a B-17. To improve its ability to shoot down B-17s, the armament of the Me 109G, which made up 80 percent of the fighter production in 1943, was increased to three 20mm cannon and two 13mm machine guns.[11] A more powerful engine was added, the 1,475 horsepower Daimler Benz 605A, giving it a top speed of

387 miles per hour. But with the heavy load of guns, the Me 109G could not maneuver effectively in combat with Allied fighter planes. When the P-47 and P-51 began to escort the bombers, the extra guns had to be removed on some of the planes to make them effective fighters again. The improved German Me 109 had a range of 615 miles, which meant that it could stay in the air for nearly two hours and still have fuel for a few minutes of combat. Production progressed rapidly with 6,000 built in 1943 and 14,200 in 1944. Although the Me109 was not as agile as the Spitfire and was overpowered by the P-47, in the hands of skilled flyers, the Me 109 could have held its own, but the quality of German fighter pilots was declining in 1943. Air battles over France dwindled to darting attacks by the Germans, followed by hasty withdrawal.[12]

The Fock Wolfe 190A was the outgrowth of a prewar design. By the end of 1942, it shared, with the Me 109, the role of fighter in the Luftwaffe. At the end of 1943, the FW 190A-8 had a maximum speed of 408 miles per hour and was armed with four 20mm cannon and two 13mm machine guns. Nearly twenty thousand were built during the war, most of them in 1944. Only four thousand of the fighter version of the FW 190 had been built by the end of 1943.[13] The FW 190 was superior to the Spitfire and the Thunderbolt P-47 at low altitudes, but over twenty-one thousand feet, it did not perform well. Below twenty thousand feet, it handled easily even at high speeds.[14] In the hands of a skilled pilot, it was a real threat to any Allied aircraft below twenty thousand feet, but above that the P-47 and P-51 had better speed, climb, and handling ability. In 1943, the FW 190 was still in limited supply, and the demands for the defense of Germany against daylight raids kept many of them occupied.[15]

The American bombers could not face the German fighters alone. The Allies lacked adequate fighters to provide escorts for their daylight raids within the borders of Germany. On the other hand, Goering was confident that a few German fighters could manage the American bombers. Two new German fighter wings, the First and Second, were stationed in Holland and along the German coast, with a total of 1,045 fighters by the end of January 1943,[16] but these measures were inadequate. The B-17 could fly around the defensive fighter screen in Holland while the Spitfires and P-47s had the range to fly to Holland and battle with the German fighters. The P-38s could go even farther, escorting the bomber to nearer targets. Two fighter wings were not enough to form a perimeter.[17]

The threat of heavy daylight bombing soon became a reality. The Eighth Air Force increased from one hundred bombers in March 1943 to three hundred in May. On April 17, 1943, a heavy daylight raid by the Americans, escorted by P-38s, hit Bremen, opposed only by small groups of German fighters. Though subsequent attacks were weak, Speer feared the effect of precision daylight raids on German war plants in the Ruhr. Hitler finally saw the need for more fighter protection. Field Marshal Erhard Milch, in charge of German fighter production, tried to meet the increased demands of the West, as well as the needs of the Russian front and the Mediterranean. In the first eight months of 1943, 7,600 fighters were delivered, but many were needed on the battle fronts as fighter bombers and reconnaissance, reducing the number used as interceptors for the Reich.[18]

Under pressure from increasing attacks during the summer of 1943, the Germans organized Fighter Wings 25 and 50 and Destroyer Wings 26 and 76 by assembling squadrons of day fighters withdrawn from the front lines to oppose the daylight raids. Even the night fighters, with their hands full of the British, were brought into the battle against the B-17s. The American bomber losses began to mount in 1943 from less than twenty per month (January to March) to seventy-two in May and eighty-two in June. The British lost a thousand bombers between September 1942 and March 1943.[19] These were prohibitive losses and could not be sustained indefinitely.

Some air attacks made an impression in the summer of 1943. The massive blow on Hamburg beginning July 24, carried on night and day by both the British and Americans, was a shock to the Germans. The use of aluminum strips called "Window" defeated the German radar, and the bomber stream was used by the British for the first time. Flying bombers in a continuous column over the defensive belt reduced the effect of the antiaircraft guns and the night fighters. All of the defense was placed on the shoulders of just a few people. The antiaircraft gunners simply tired and lost their effectiveness. The heavy bombardment created a wave of terror across Germany and a breakdown of control in Hamburg.[20] At the end of the attack on August 3, 250,000 homes had been destroyed, nearly half of the city, and 40,000 had been killed.

The German reaction was to launch a counterattack on England that was puny in comparison. The Germans also built up both their day and night fighter protection. By the fall of 1943, the defensive forces had formed the Air Fleet Reich that included the I Fighter Corps (First, Second, Third, and Seventh Fighter Divisions) and the Third Air Fleet that included the II Fighter Corps (Fourth and Fifth Fighter Divisions). To provide pilots for this expanded organization, training time was shortened. Newly graduated pilots were sent first to the eastern front to learn their trade against the inferior Russian pilots and then brought to the West. The high quality of Allied flyers required that pilots be expert in their first dogfight. Fighter pilots went into combat with only 150 hours of flying compared to 300 in the RAF and 450 for the Americans.[21] In October over Schweinfurt, an American pilot reported, "They were flown by green kids, were sloppy in their maneuvers, and they left themselves wide open for our gunners. They got the hell shot out of them."[22]

During the summer of 1943, the effect of the bombing and allocation of materials had reduced German aircraft production. Production of Me 109s fell from 725 in July to 536 in September to 357 in December, but by 1944, the reorganization of fighter production under Speer ended the shortage of planes. The problem in 1944 and after was the shortage of trained pilots.

On the other hand, the Americans still could not protect their bombers all the way into Germany. The German fighters could close in and fire away at the

B-17 formations, overwhelming the defense with sheer numbers.[23] By August 1943, 600 single-engine day fighters and 180 twin-engine destroyers were defending Germany plus nearly 1,000 night fighters.[24] In July, August, and September, about 100 bombers were lost each month, and in October, 181 were lost.[25] On October 14, 1943, the last deep raid by the Americans, again on Schweinfurt, was made by 291 B-17s and opposed by 300 day fighters, 40 twin-engine destroyers, and some night fighters. Only 25 bombers escaped undamaged; 60 were shot down and 142 damaged at the cost of 35 German fighters.[26] Such losses could not be endured by the Allies, so the deep raids by day were halted.

Nevertheless, that was the last such victory for the German pilots. Effective long-range American fighters were on the way. The P-38 Lightnings were used in 1942, but lacked maneuverability, range, and performance at high altitudes.[27] The first fighter group equipped with the P-47 Thunderbolt arrived in England in January 1943. The Thunderbolt was a most unlikely looking fighter plane, designed, in 1940, around the giant Pratt and Whitney eighteen-cylinder radial engine. Because of problems with the engine and the radio, the P-47 was not committed to combat until April 1943. The P-47D had a 2,300 horsepower engine and a speed of 433 miles per hour. Though the P-47 was not agile, when the Germans outmaneuvered it, the pilot merely put the plane in a dive and left the Germans behind. Because of its large size, the P-47 could mount eight fifty-caliber machine guns in its wings. (The early versions of the Flying Fortress mounted only ten of these hard-hitting guns.) With the addition of a drop tank in May 1943, the range of the P-47 was extended to 1,250 miles, half again as much as the Spitfire, though not enough to get beyond the Ruhr Valley as an escort fighter.[28]

To fill the need for a long-range escort fighter, the Americans commandeered the production of the Mustang, originally designed for the British in 1940.[29] In November 1941, the first models were delivered to England and were used as ground attack planes during 1942 because the Allison engine lacked sufficient horsepower to give the aircraft fighter performance. In September 1942, the United States received the first of five hundred of the underpowered Allison version of the Mustang for use as dive bombers and used them in Sicily and Italy in 1943. Over fifteen hundred of these Mustangs with a top speed of 356 miles per hour were built and used by both the British and Americans.[30]

In September 1942, experiments began with a more powerful British Merlin engine built by the Packard Motor Company. The result was an aircraft with a speed of 441 miles per hour, and an initial order was placed for 2,200. By June 1943, the plane was in full production, and in December the first P-51B was in action with the Eighth Air Force. In March 1944, the P-51s went 1,100 miles to Berlin and back escorting the B-17s. By the end of the war, nearly fifteen thousand P-51s had been made; in many ways they were the best fighter planes of the war.[31]

With the aid of long-range fighters, the bomber offensive by day and night grew in intensity. The objectives of the bomber offensive were twofold as spelled out at Casablanca—first, to attack the German warmaking potential: submarine construction, aircraft factories, the transportation system, and the oil industry; second, to destroy the morale of the enemy.[32] In the latter objective the bombing never succeeded. Despite the extreme physical discomfort of those that survived, German morale did not weaken. In fact, the bombing seemed to stimulate hatred and determination to resist; the civilian at home knew that he was facing dangers similar to those faced by the man on the front. Morale collapse does not result from a prolonged siege that grows slowly in intensity, as did the bomber offensive, where one has the opportunity to adjust and, in fact, to form some plan for resistance. Collapse of morale comes from the sudden, unexpected blow—the surrender in a matter of days of a fortified line that was expected to hold for years, which happened to France in 1940. This type of shock permits no time for recovery, destroys morale, and leads to accusations of betrayal.[33]

As a matter of fact, the bombing program in the first six months of 1944 did not produce any net loss in German production. Although the bombing caused enormous expense in time, materials, and lost production because of the need to rebuild destroyed factories and machines and to relocate highly concentrated industries, production in all areas increased steadily throughout the war. In 1942, the Germans produced slightly over 5,000 tanks and assault guns, in 1943 nearly 9,500, and in 1944, 17,843. In 1942, there was a balance between requirements and production of oil; in 1943, there was a surplus, and until the fall of 1944, there was an adequate supply of oil even for the navy. In December 1942, 96,000 rifles and 10,770 machine guns were produced; in December 1943, 190,000 rifles and 15,700 machine guns; and in July 1944, 249,000 rifles and 24,000 machine guns. Certainly, the bombers were not slowing down small arms production. In other types of armament, similar increases were consistent.[34] In the area of aircraft production, the figures are even more startling. In 1942, 15,409 planes were produced; in 1943, 24,807; and in 1944, 40,593.

The rate of production shows that the air offensive had not seriously weakened the German war effort and did not do so until the end of 1944, after the invasion, when land warfare also contributed to the weakening of the German war machine.

In comparison to the low rate of efficiency of the air offensive, the cost to the attackers was enormous. Only the best of the young men were considered fit to fly, men who would make up the ranks of elite units or become officers and noncoms. The rate of attrition was terrifying. Every time a bomber fell, ten men went either to death or into captivity. On a single raid, six hundred men could be lost in sixty airplanes. The raid on Nuremberg cost the British ninety-four planes. Sixty Flying Fortresses were lost on October 14, 1943, during the raid on Schweinfurt. The Americans required an airman to fly twenty-five times in combat before relief, so with losses of 10 percent, as occurred often in 1943, the mathematical chances of survival were less than zero. The British requirement of thirty trips before a rest placed the chances of survival even lower. One man in three in Bomber Command was killed. Only 20 percent survived thirty missions, the remaining 80 percent were killed, wounded, captured, or relieved because of mental breakdown. The loss ratio was equaled only by the crews of the German U-boats. The American rate of survival must have been comparable in 1943 and 1944.[35]

Despite this heavy cost, the impact of the bombing campaign was not significant enough to hasten or delay the invasion. The Germans were far better prepared on land to resist the invasion in 1944 than they were in 1943, despite the fact that far more bombs were dropped from June 1943 to June 1944 than from September 1939 to June 1943. Still the invasion was successful in June 1944, even though the air offensive had not completed its job. Would it not have been simpler to have launched an invasion against Germany in 1943, when it had not yet experienced the dramatic increases in war production that took place in 1944 and enabled Hitler to mount more and better equipped divisions to face the invaders?

Turning from the primary strategic task of the air forces to the tactical role, the airmen had the obligation to protect the army and navy from German attack. Control of the air was necessary during the amphibious portion of an invasion because ships anchored off beaches were especially vulnerable, although the degree of control did not have to be complete. In May 1940, at Dunkirk, the British were merely contesting the air space. The efforts of the Luftwaffe were hampered by bad weather except for two and one half days out of the nine days of heavy movement. The British were able to provide sufficient fighter cover to permit 338,000 British and French troops to escape at a cost of thirteen Allied destroyers and torpedo boats, plus many smaller civilian craft. About two hundred Hurricanes and Spitfires flew 2,739 sorties over the beaches during the nine days. Even this did not represent a maximum effort as the RAF Fighter Command was husbanding its resources, looking forward to the approaching attack on Britain itself, when every fighter would be needed.[36]

After the amphibious phase, the need for air mastery was sharply reduced. Friendly air cover made possible the movement of large numbers of vehicles both day and night; lack of it restricted movement to darkness. Otherwise it had little impact on the battle.

Germany had complete control of the air over Stalingrad, but was decisively defeated on land. The British controlled the air in 1942 in North Africa, but Rommel continued to chase the Eighth Army. In Italy in 1943 and in France, the Allies controlled the air, but the Germans fought highly successful withdrawal actions. In fact, once the air arm accomplished its self-proclaimed primary mission of destroying the enemy air arm, it had little to do but act as long-range artillery.[37]

Control of the air was basically a struggle between the fighter aircraft. That battle was fought by a few basic types from each side that went through a progression of improved versions during the war years. The major German and American fighters have already been discussed.

The most revered Allied fighter plane of World War II was the English Spitfire, which was primarily a defensive interceptor because of its limited range and
firepower. The Spitfire V came into service in March 1941, and more copies of
this version were made than any other. Nearly 6,500 were constructed, mostly in
1941 and early 1942. They were armed with a variety of weapons, but most
Spitfire Vs carried two 20mm cannon and four machine guns. They had more
powerful engines than the previous Spitfires and a speed of 375 miles per hour.
They could carry five hundred pounds of bombs and fly to thirty-seven thousand
feet.[38] In 1942, the improved versions of the Me 109 and FW 190 were superior
to the Spitfire V. After some experimental and special-purpose models, the
Spitfire IX was developed and delivered to a squadron in July 1942. It proved to
be almost as good as the FW 190 and better than the Me 109s. Over 5,600 of the
IXs were made through 1944.[39] The Mark IX carried the same variety of
weapons as the Mark V, though in the later stages, some were fitted with two
20mm cannon plus two caliber .50 machine guns. The ceiling was increased to
43,000 feet; the speed was increased dramatically with a more powerful engine
up to 408 miles per hour; its range of 434 miles with normal gasoline tanks was
extended to 980 miles by auxiliary tanks. The fact that the British Mark IX
looked identical to the Mark V placed the Germans at a disadvantage, because
although their aircraft was superior to the Mark V, still in use in considerable
numbers, the Germans could not tell the difference and were forced to treat both
types with caution.[40] The margin in quality between the Mark IX and the FW 190
was so narrow that the quality of the individual pilots made the difference. In this
category, the British were far ahead of the average German pilot and emerged as
victors in most contests. By the end of 1943, all of the British Spitfire squadrons
had surplus pilots with excellent training.

Although the Spitfire continued to be improved, none of the later models were
delivered in large quantities, and most were designed for special roles other than
as fighters. The only important development was the Spitfire XIV that entered
service in January 1944 with a more powerful engine and better vision for the
pilot. A thousand of these were delivered. The XIV had a top speed of 448 miles
per hour and a range of 850 miles with drop tanks.[41]

The basic problem with the Spitfire was that it was an interceptor designed to
meet and destroy intruding aircraft. Therefore, it had very limited range—about
two hours in the air combined with a few minutes of combat exhausted its fuel. It
was expected to fight over its own air space and return to its base to refuel. Small
fuel tanks meant a cleaner design and a more agile airplane. The addition of the
drop tank in 1943 extended the range, but as soon as a foe was sighted these tanks
had to be released because they slowed the plane and interfered with combat
functioning. The Germans could, therefore, force the Spitfires to drop their
auxiliary tanks by sending up a feint attack as soon as the British crossed the
channel. Thus the amount of usable fuel in drop tanks was limited to the quantity
used before meeting the first unfriendly aircraft.

The Spitfire squadrons had few responsibilities after 1940 other than escorting bombers as far as their limited range would permit and patrolling over convoys. Few German planes ventured over the British Isles during daylight. To keep the pilots sharp, and, hopefully, to destroy German planes that would otherwise be used in Russia, the Fighter Command of the RAF instituted sweeps of six or more squadrons flying boldly over France, daring the Luftwaffe to challenge them, on a mission to seek and destroy enemy aircraft.[42]

One of the objectives of the raid on Dieppe, described in chapter 12, was a continuation of the policy of bringing the Luftwaffe to battle to destroy a maximum number of German fighters and reduce the number available for the eastern front. The amphibious assault force was a tempting bait, but the Germans were slow to respond in the air. Over two and a half hours passed before a large number of German planes arrived at the scene, by which time the troops were beginning to withdraw. The British used about 800 Spitfires, Hawker Typhoons, and Hurricanes plus about 100 Blenheims and Bostons. The Germans used 610 fighters and 50 bombers. Some RAF pilots flew three and four missions during the day, returning to England, refueling, and returning to provide support for the troops. The RAF flew a total of 2,617 sorties over Dieppe. The Germans claimed that they shot down 112 British planes at a cost of only 37 of their own. The British claimed 91 German planes at a cost of 98 of their own. Other records show 106 British planes lost and 170 German losses. The conflicting numbers result from false claims of planes shot down and the inclusion or exclusion of planes lost from related accidents or damaged beyond repair. The British probably lost more than the Germans because damaged British planes were ditched in the channel, whereas German planes with similar damage might well limp back to nearby fields. Regardless of the score, the British controlled the air over Dieppe throughout the day, which was the prerequisite for a successful invasion.[43]

Fighter sweeps over France continued during the first half of 1942. Even though the FW 190 was the best individual fighter in the air, the superior numbers of British fighters made the sweeps possible. Fighter attacks on locomotives in France had become so frequent that on February 13, 1943, the Germans ordered the provision of armored locomotives with antiaircraft guns placed on platform cars.[44] Meanwhile, the Germans were diverting increasing numbers of fighters from the battlefronts to the West for defensive operations.[45] By the end of December 1942, there were two hundred single-engined day fighters defending the West, along with four hundred night fighters.[46]

These fighter sweeps and the Dieppe experience indicated that the Allies could protect an amphibious force even in 1942, and certainly in 1943. Both the planes and the pilots of the Allies were superior in the spring of 1943, and they improved steadily.

The third task of the air forces was to provide tactical support considered by the Germans to be of great value. The Germans were the first to use aircraft tactically to support ground troops. The Stuka became the artillery for the panzer attacks in 1939 and 1940. Britain and America were more inclined to use air power strategically far from the battlefront and gave scant attention to air support of the ground troops.

The defeat in France pointed forcefully to the need for tactical air power, for more cooperation between air and ground, if success were to be achieved. Support of the ground forces took several forms: direct attack on enemy troops, weapons, and positions in the combat zone, interference in the movement of enemy formations behind the lines, destruction of supplies in the combat zone, and reconnaissance to obtain information regarding enemy forces.

Compared to the strategic air war and the battle for control of the air space with enemy fighters, tactical air support was a prosaic task. The air forces universally assigned inferior planes to ground support roles. In Poland, the Germans gave this assignment to their only combat biplane, the Henschel 123.[47] When the British Hurricane could no longer compete as a fighter, it was used for ground support. The Americans also assigned inferior fighters to the tactical air commands.

The primary task of tactical air support was to attack the enemy ground troops. This task was necessarily difficult because of the problem of distinguishing between the enemy and friendly forces and the complexity of ground to air communication. Not only did the pilots have trouble identifying friendly forces, with the result that planes often attacked their own troops, but also the troops had difficulty identifying aircraft and often fired on friendly planes. Because of the identity problem, pilots were reluctant to bomb close to the front line.[48]

Communication between air and ground relied on the mutual understanding of the capability of each. A ground commander had little concept of the problems of the pilot in identifying targets while flying at over three hundred miles per hour. Nor could the pilot always interpret the map references given to him. Air commanders were reluctant to keep aircraft on call, waiting for a request, and believed that ground commanders did not know how to utilize air power to achieve the best results. Therefore, the requests for support were subject to review from higher headquarters, and a delay resulted between the time of request—the time of need—and the time of response—actual attack on the enemy. The solution to this problem for the Allies came in 1944 with the attachment of air liaison officers to front-line combat units and with the availability of large numbers of tactical aircraft, making possible "cab ranks" of fighter-bombers waiting overhead for orders from the ground.

The Germans were the first to solve the problem of providing the necessary accuracy with the dive bomber. Ironically, the Luftwaffe developed the dive-bomber technique in 1933 using the American Curtiss Wright F2C Hawk. On the basis of demonstrations by the F2C Hawk, the Junker 87 Stuka dive bomber was designed in 1934. The Stuka was tested in Spain in 1938 and played a major role in the conquest of Poland in 1939.[49] The Ju87B-2 carried either one 1,100-pound bomb or five small bombs. It was armed with three machine guns, had a top speed of 238 miles per hour, and a range of 370 miles.[50]

In Poland and later in France, the Stuka provided accurate bombing of military targets—bridges, roads and troops—and also shattered the morale of inexperienced troops through the frightening sound of sirens and the sight of a plane plunging directly at them.[51] On the other hand, British attempts at providing ground support in 1940 were ineffective. Ten squadrons of Fairey Battles were sent to France to support the British expeditionary force. The Battle was a light bomber designed to bomb tactical targets from a level approach at low altitudes. With a maximum speed of only 240 miles per hour, the Battle was an easy target for German antiaircraft guns. After catastrophic losses in May 1940, the Battle was withdrawn from daylight use. The British realized the need for tactical air support and formed the Army Co-operation Command in December 1940 to organize, experiment, and train in all forms of land-air cooperation.

Two Curtiss planes were used intially, the Mohawk P-36 and the improved version, the Tomahawk P-40. Nearly four hundred of the Mohawks were orginally ordered by France from the United States and diverted to England after June 1940, when England was eager to buy any available plane.[52] The Mohawk carried four machine guns and had a maximum speed of only 323 miles per hour at fifteen thousand feet, not up to combat standards even in 1940.[53]

The first Tomahawks to reach Britain, about 250 of them in 1940, also came as a result of diverted French orders. Slightly faster and with two additional machine guns, the Tomahawks were still not considered good enough to battle German fighters. Therefore, the British relegated the Curtiss planes to army cooperation use.[54]

Searching for more Tomahawks in 1940 for use as ground support planes, the British asked the North American Aircraft Company to produce P-40s under license from Curtiss. Instead, North American offered a new design, the Mustang, later called the P-51. By May 1941, six RAF squadrons had the Mustang, which, like the Tomahawk, was limited to low altitudes by its Allison engine that did not function well above fifteen thousand feet.[55] After the British substituted the Rolls-Royce Merlin engine, the Mustang became a first-class fighter, and the American air force took over all production. Several squadrons of Allison-powered Mustangs were used by the Americans as dive bombers in Sicily and Italy, but as the planes were used up, the squadrons were equipped with other types.

The Hawker Hurricane was outclassed as a fighter by the end of 1940 and was converted to ground support, armed either with 20mm or 40mm guns, plus up to half a ton of bombs.[56] In September 1941, the Hawker Typhoon, designed to replace the Hurricane, but lacking the performance required of a fighter, was developed instead as a ground support plane, with a maximum speed of 405 miles per hour at eighteen thousand feet. The Typhoon Mark IB carried four 20mm guns and two thousand-pound bombs.[57] The mark of a superior ground support plane was high performance at low altitude, combined with the ability to carry a heavy load of arms.

The Americans used the P-40 in Tunisia for ground support missions because it could not cope with the Me 109 and FW 190 above fifteen thousand feet. Five groups of P-40s fought in the Mediterranean theater, but the Hawks were gradually replaced by the A-36 (the dive-bomber version of the P-51) and the P-47.[58] The P-47 Thunderbolt, which began its career as a fighter, was a potent support plane with the added ability to defend itself against fighters at high altitudes. The huge P-47 had the power to carry a heavy load of weapons (eight .50 caliber machine guns and sixteen hundred pounds of bombs) and a rugged construction with an engine that could survive heavy battle damage.[59]

Including the Typhoon, Hurricanes, P-40s, and P-47s, the Allies had a plentiful supply of aircraft that could perform as fighter bombers in 1943. Even the short-range Spitfires were usable in ground support roles. The fighter sweeps that had begun earlier proved the ability of Allied fighters not only to control the air space behind the enemy lines, but also to attack military targets, disrupt transportation, destroy supplies, and feed information to the ground troops.

There was no need to delay the invasion because of lack of air power. Sufficient control was achieved both defensively as air cover for Allied troops and offensively as an effective tactical air force during 1943 through the quality of the pilots as well as the overwhelming numbers and quality of aircraft. While Germany completed nearly twenty-five thousand planes to fight on two fronts in 1943, Britain and the United States produced over one hundred thousand in the same year. Even if the antibomber defense fighters in Germany had been sent to France to resist the invasion, the total number of German fighters would still have been less than the number of British and American fighters.

The turning point in the strategic air war occurred in January 1943, with the heavy attack on Berlin. From then on, the ability of the Germans to resist air attack was never sufficient to bring the Allied raids to a halt. The raids attracted a large portion of the German air force to try to bring down the bombers and left the army without needed air support on the front. But the achievements of the Allied air assault were not as spectacular as expected. Though production had been interrupted, total German output continued to increase. Without the air attack, perhaps 9 percent more German weapons would have been made and production facilities would not have been diverted to the manufacture of antiaircraft guns and fighter planes. No matter how beneficial the results of the assault by air, delaying the invasion to await their achievement could not be justified. By July 1943, Hamburg and Essen, the center of Krupps arms production, had been severely damaged. Whatever was to be achieved militarily by the Allied air war was well under way by mid-1943. The terror bombing that followed probably did more to bolster than to weaken German morale, according to Speer.[60] An invasion in mid-1943 would have made attacks on targets easier by disrupting the German defense system. Few can argue that the Allies needed an eight-to-one margin in the air before risking an invasion.

11

THE SERVICE ELEMENT

The lack of sufficient service units in 1943 was presented as another reason to delay the invasion of France. The function of the service element of a military force was to make up its logistical support—to plan and provide for the movement, maintenance, and supply of the force. The successful operation of a logistical plan resulted in the maximum effectiveness of the available combat troops and weapons. Poor logistics, on the other hand, resulted in "too little, too late," or insufficient men and weapons at the proper place and time to win a battle. By 1943, the Western Allies had developed logistical support elements far beyond the needs of the combat forces. The trend was toward the reduction of service elements as the war progressed. Certainly the service forces were adequate to launch the invasion in 1943 under a rational requirement.

A nation had a limited capacity to make war—it could provide a finite number of men for the armed forces and produce a limited amount of war material. Therefore, the employment of each soldier and each weapon was relative to early success, to prolongation, or even to loss of a war. Theoretically, there were no surplus men or materials—if not needed in one area, they could have been employed in another. No military command was capable of 100 percent efficiency—having exactly enough resources to win a battle and no more—there were varying degrees of efficiency. Too little resulted in defeat, but a large surplus of unneeded men and material that could have been used elsewhere more effectively prolonged the war, although this error went relatively unnoticed. Nevertheless, both were the product of poor military management. Naturally, most commanders preferred to err on the side of surplus; yet by doing so, they mismanaged resources in the same way as the commander who had too little. Excessive resources in one area meant shortages in another, with resultant slowing down or actual defeat in the deprived area. The goal of an able commander was to have the barest surplus of resources available to ensure victory, while unneeded resources were sent to other areas.

How much material and how many troops were enough? Decisions regarding the number of troops and weapons required for an operation were reserved for the field commander, based on the estimate of enemy forces, but because of the complex nature of the task, determination of the quantity of supplies such as food and fuel was often delegated to a subordinate, the supply officer. The commander would require an ample margin of combat forces to ensure victory with minimum losses. The supply officer, on the other hand, was concerned not only with winning, but also with his own position. The only error he would be blamed for was to be short of some item, so the tendency was to request vast quantities of everything. Judgment of this factor is difficult because of the natural tendency in the military to ask for everything that might possibly be needed because the final objective was winning the battle. Comparing war to a profit-oriented industry, the company manager, in addition to manufacturing a product, continually strives to reduce costs by controlling the labor force and the quantities of raw material and components, thereby either increasing the profit margin or enabling a price reduction with the hope of increased sales. In war, when the only objective is winning, the military commander is usually concerned only with completing the product (winning the battle), regardless of the cost, and he demands the maximum input of labor (troops) and materials (weapons and supplies).

A lower-grade field commander might be excused for taking this position, but the higher-grade officer had to be concerned with the overall victory involving many engagements and therefore should have been concerned with the utilization of troops and supplies to reduce the "cost" (troops, weapons, and supplies) of each battle won to make possible a maximum number of successful engagements. The Allied commanders, Roosevelt and Churchill, were not insistent enough on "cost control," though Churchill made many efforts in this direction. By not doling out resources with a tight fist, the high command created its own logistical problems in World War II. The combined industrial and human potential of Russia, China, the United States, and the British Empire made Germany and Japan pigmies in comparison. Yet, because of the widespread dispersion of their resources, the Allies often found themselves outnumbered and outgunned on many battlefields during the early years of the war. By 1943, however, even with mismanagement, the tide had turned. The Allies had the means to deliver the men and materials to any field of battle. That these elements were not ready for the invasion of northern Europe in 1943 was an arbitrary decision, not a matter of potential availability.

Gathering the men and materials for a major operation was carried out under a logistical plan. The plan had three essential components: the availability of troops, weapons, and supplies; the means to move them; and the ability of service troops to implement the plan. The latter two parts will be the subject of this chapter.

For the Allies, the logistical problem was extraordinarily complex because many of the men and materials had to be shipped from the United States. Because of the immense quantities and distance, attention to even the minor details could result in tremendous savings. For example, over 60,000 ship tons were required to transport an infantry division with its vehicles assembled. In 1942, the American army developed the efficient technique of packing two partially assembled large trucks in four crates, or two smaller trucks in three crates, or a jeep in a single crate. Not only were the crates more compact, but they could be stacked in the hold of a ship. Using this method made it possible to ship an infantry division in only 22,000 ship tons, slightly more than two ships, rather than six. This example also points out the enormous share motor vehicles occupied in the total volume of a fighting force.

The initial movement of a division was but the beginning of the problem. The army normally shipped, along with a division, replacements for equipment needed during the next sixty days, ammunition for seventy days, and a sixty-day supply of gas and oil. These supplies required nearly 50,000 ship tons, increasing the total to nearly 70,000 ship tons to move a division overseas, even with crated vehicles. Service and combat support units that backed up each division required an average of 8 ship tons per man, compared to less than 5 ship tons per man in the division itself. The higher figure for non-divisional units resulted from the high proportion of motor vehicles in the supporting units. Each division was normally supported by twenty-five thousand service and nondivisional combat troops, requiring a total of 200,000 ship tons. Therefore, a complete infantry division, plus service and supporting units, required 270,000 ship tons to cross the seas with a sixty-day reserve of supplies. An armored division needed 186,000 ship tons, plus 200,000 for nondivisional troops, for a total of 386,000 ship tons, nearly forty ships, which equaled a normal transatlantic convoy.[1]

The BOLERO plan orginally called for thirty divisions to be delivered in England by April 1943. If six were armored and twenty-four were infantry, nearly 2.8 million ship tons would have been required for the divisions and 6 million ship tons for the service units, for a total of nearly 9 million ship tons over the period April 1942 to April 1943, a minimum of 900 ships in twelve months. In addition, there were the air units. The complete BOLERO schedule called for an average of one hundred thousand men and their supplies to reach England in 120 ships each month. Naturally, the plan had a slow start, but by August 1942, the army had sent 772,000 ship tons to England, and the British had established camps for fifteen divisions.[2] Four divisions had been delivered complete with supporting elements and supplies before the North African campaign disrupted the plan.

The plan was working during the summer of 1942 and was expected to continue, despite the diversion of some forces to North Africa. To provide what turned out to be an expensive safety margin, in case Patton's landings in North Africa on the Atlantic Coast were strongly opposed, the decision was made to "combat load" the entire convoy from the United States. All vehicles were shipped on wheels rather than in crates, and supplies were loaded in reverse order of their potential need, so that items would be on top that were needed in the early days of a resisted landing. The result of combat loading was less efficient use of space and the need for more ships. In addition, the ships were tied up in port while the convoy was being assembled. The total loss in potential delivery to England must have been over a million ship tons. At the same time, in England, the British convoys were being combat loaded, and more ships were taken out of the transatlantic run. In October 1942, the British loaded 185,000 men, 20,000 vehicles, and 220,000 tons of supplies for their part in the landing, at least another million tons of shipping.[3] The net result was disaster to the BOLERO movement, as all of these ships (over 2 million tons), or about 22 percent of the total BOLERO movement, were diverted from the transatlantic convoys. Churchill was surprised that the North Africa plans should have such a disruptive effect on the BOLERO plan. Not only did the initial convoys hurt, but the follow-up convoys continued to divert effort. In December 1942, BOLERO deliveries from America to England dropped to 97,000 ship tons, about ten ships, and less than 10 percent of the BOLERO plan.[4]

Yet, there was a reserve of shipping capacity had it been called on and effectively used. On January 26, 1943, faced with the need to move and supply an army in Tunisia over primitive routes, a requisition for five thousand trucks, four hundred dump trucks, twenty locomotives, forty flat cars, and other materials filling twenty-two ships was cabled from North Africa to the United States. Only twenty days later, the materials had been gathered at the ports and were loaded on ships by February 15, 1943. This was nearly enough shipping to move a complete infantry division and supporting units. Such was the capacity of American merchant shipping and the supply system to provide noncombat items that, though needed to increase the capacity of the supply line in North Africa, were not critical in the sense of being combat items. The extent of the reserves available was revealed again when all of the men and materials needed for the landing in Sicily, including seven divisions (one more than landed in France in 1944), were delivered and ready in June 1943, a full month in advance of the landing and a little more than four months after the decision was made to land.[5] This same shipping could have provided the necessary troops and supplies for a second front in France in 1943, but instead, Allied effort was diverted to a second-class objective.

The logistical problem did not end with the delivery of men and materials to Europe. That was the routine part, comparatively free of variables, that could be planned with a high degree of accuracy. On the Continent, combat conditions introduced many variables that worked against the planner, and logistics became far more complex. Transportation in the "zone of communication" to the combat zone was a critical factor. How were the troops and supplies to be carried to the front line once they had landed on the European shore?

The German army relied heavily on the railways in the rear area. To move an infantry division any considerable distance, the Germans, with very little motor transport, had to rely on the rails, the capacity of which was practically inflexible. From thirty-five to forty trains, each of about fifty cars, were required to move a division. An infantry division with its vehicles required sixty-six trains.[6] A double-track railroad could move only thirty trains in one direction per day, and a single-track only ten trains in each direction. In an emergency, a single track could be reserved for one-way traffic and move nearly thirty trains a day. In other words, it took at least two days to move a division by rail along one line. With trains moving two hundred miles a day, the Germans could theoretically move a division from any point in Europe within a week for each rail line available. Outside of Germany and northern France, however, the rail network was sparse, and in the mountainous country to the south, trains moved very slowly and only with the help of two locomotives up the steep grades. South of Rome, for example, there were only two through railway lines heading south. In the south of France, there were fewer than a dozen lines leading from the southern border and the Mediterranean to the north. In Russia, the rail lines had to be converted from the wider Russian gauge to the European gauge, which meant that only essential lines were opened, and the ones that were converted were under continual attack from the partisans. Therefore, few rail lines were available to Germany from the areas where most of her troops were stationed in 1943. On January 2, 1943, the British director of military intelligence presented the following chart, which verifies the estimate given above. Based on the available rail network and the supply of cars and locomotives, the chart listed the time needed to move divisions. In all cases, only one division could move at once except from Russia to France, when seven could move at once.

From	To	Days to move a division
Russia	France	13 to 14
Russia	Southern Italy	15
Russia	Greece	20
Russia	Bulgaria	14
Norway	Southern Italy	22
Norway	Greece	24
Norway	Bulgaria	23
France	Southern Italy	6

To move a second division simultaneously required two or three days more for the moves from Russia and eight or nine days for the Norway moves.[7]

Even if lines were available, it was difficult to assemble a minimum of forty locomotives and two thousand cars for a division without vehicles and half again as many for the vehicles. It was almost impossible to move more than a few divisions simultaneously. In April 1943, when divisions were desperately needed on the eastern front, the Seventeenth Infantry Division and the 257th Infantry Division were started on their way to Russia from France in 241 trains over a period of four days. This was almost double the textbook requirement of 66 trains per division and raises the question that changes in the organization of the German division such as additional weapons, attached units, and necessary supplies may have doubled the requirement.[8]

The rapid movement of divisions by rail was possible only in highly developed areas. Two to twelve hours were required to load each train. There seldom were enough platforms and loading equipment to load at the same time more than a few dozen cars with vehicles, guns, and horses. Although the rail system could work wonders on occasion with good planning (for example, the Russian buildup for their counteroffensive in November 1942), it was relatively inflexible and cumbersome for the rapid, simultaneous movement of large bodies of troops.

For distances of less than a hundred miles, German divisions were moved partly by rail and partly by road; the horse-drawn and motor vehicles were driven, the troops marched, and the supplies were shipped by rail. This part-rail, part-road movement had many disadvantages. The troops were separated from their weapons, supplies, and ammunition. If the division was moving into a combat zone, the simultaneous arrival of all three, though essential, was almost impossible. An infantry division with fit young men could march up to twenty miles a day over long periods during the early years of the war. By 1943, such was not the case because by then infantry divisions were filled with older men in poor physical condition. Furthermore, an infantry division on the march stretched out for twenty-five miles on a road and made an ideal target for the fighter bombers. Therefore, they could march only at night with strict road discipline and at a slower pace.

The panzer and panzer grenadier divisions moved more swiftly. They had sufficient vehicles to move everything with their organic (permanently assigned) equipment at the rate of seven to ten miles per hour by night, and, during the long nights of the winter months, they could move about a hundred miles in a twelve-hour night. The six hours of darkness in June cut this distance in half. The staff manual recommended a maximum of ninety-three miles in six hours.[9] The Tenth Panzer took ten hours to move its advance elements forty miles on the day of the Dieppe landing. A panzer division going from Paris to Caen would be halfway there by the time the last unit left Paris. During the extremely short nights of the European summers, a panzer division needed two days to reach Caen because the fighter bombers brought all traffic to a halt when the sun came up. The men, however, would arrive overnight, if the rails were open and the unit had been loaded by nightfall. Once the combat zone had been reached, there was a terrible scramble to unload and seek cover before daylight brought Allied fighter bombers.[10]

Obviously, the Germans did not have the highly flexible communications that were often mentioned in the planning papers. The Allies had far better communication. They could deliver divisions faster to the beachhead than could the Germans and move them about the combat zone with even greater speed. Compared to the German rail system, the Allies provided motor transport on a lavish scale once the troops landed. These vehicles gave the Allied combat forces rapid mobility and made them independent of either a railroad network or good roads, as the efficient two-and-a-half-ton truck with four-wheel drive and the jeep were practically cross-country vehicles. But this mobility was paid for in ship tonnage, mechanics, and supplies that reduced the number of combat troops available.

Whereas a German infantry division of 10,000 men had only 543 motor vehicles and 218 motorcycles, plus 726 horse-drawn vehicles, the American infantry division, without any attached supporting elements in 1943, had 2,012 motor vehicles for 14,253 men, a vehicle for each seven men. The British were even more generous; the 1944 infantry division had 4,504 motor vehicles for 18,347 men, about one for each four men. These totals are incredible when one remembers that such infantry divisions were designed and trained to fight on foot. Only 13 of the American vehicles could be considered of combat value—the armored cars in the reconnaissance troop. All of the rest were behind the lines when the actual fighting began. Their only purpose was to carry men and supplies to the battle, not engage in it. Yet the field commanders had asked for more trucks, primarily to store a large quantity of supplies on wheels. Trucks were designed for moving, not storing, materials; supplies should have been stored in army dumps and moved to the division as needed. A plan to cut the number of vehicles from 20 to 33 percent and service personnel by 13 percent was rejected by the field commanders.[11] A compromise produced the table of organization of July 15, 1943, which had 1,250 fewer men than the old 1942 division, but only a small reduction in vehicles.

So there were still too many vehicles. The American divisional vehicles could carry more than three thousand tons of supplies and equipment; the British vehicles could carry almost double that amount. When the division engaged in actions, these vehicles had no function other than to bring supplies from army depots, usually less than a few hours from the front. The daily requirement for a division began at about 450 tons, which meant that the Americans had in the neighborhood of six times the essential capacity, even if each truck made only one trip per day. Additional truck companies were available if a division moved too far in advance of its depot. During an advance, this large supply of vehicles made the Allied infantry divisions fully motorized in practice, but in combat most of the vehicles were idle.

To carry as organic equipment this enormous burden of vehicles that were used only occasionally was extremely wasteful. Each truck had to be shipped and supplied with gasoline from the United States, and each truck needed a driver, who had to be supplied with an average of thirty pounds of food, clothing, etc. per day. Each vehicle created a need for a comparable increase in the service facility to maintain it (fuel reserves, lubricants, spare parts, replacement vehicles, drivers, and repair crews). In the service company of the armored regiment, 174 enlisted men out of a total of 232 men were motor sergeants, drivers, or mechanics. They operated 133 vehicles plus two scout cars. Although these men provided maintenance for an armored regiment of 108 tanks and nearly 1,500 men, how often could work be found for all of the mechanics, let alone the drivers? They did not perform heavy repairs, only first-line maintenance. Behind them at the army level were an ordnance heavy auto maintenance company, a heavy maintenance company, a heavy maintenance company (tank), a medium auto maintenance company, and a medium maintenance company—five additional companies for each armored division in the field army and up to a thousand men, whose most frequent duty was to maintain vehicles for a division with less than 600 combat vehicles. The Germans managed with far less in the extremely unfavorable climate in North Africa.

The extent of the oversupply of vehicles is shown in the statistics for the landing in June 1944. The plan called for an assault phase to penetrate a few miles inland. The marines performed this task practically without vehicles. The

D-Day plan, however, called for 174,320 men and 20,018 vehicles. For each vehicle landed, one driver was required, meaning that at least 20,000 of the 174,000 men were not available for combat, but merely sat in their trucks because there was nowhere to go. During the first eleven days, 81,000 vehicles were landed, requiring a minimum of 81,000 drivers out of a total of 557,000 men. Inasmuch as larger vehicles also had assistant drivers and the vehicles needed supporting maintenance units, probably 150,000 of the men drove and cared for vehicles, while 400,000 did the fighting and other service work. There was a vehicle for every seven men, and yet the distance from the beach to the front line was only twenty miles, a round trip of two hours or less. The mystery of those early days on the beach was where did they put all the trucks?

On the assumption that at some time those vehicles were used to carry some form of supply, the next question is, was it all necessary? Though it was reassuring to have a full larder at all times, each ton of materials had to be carried across the ocean, placed in depots, sorted, protected from the weather and theft, inventoried, and maintained. All of this work required men who would otherwise have been available to fight. Good management was often completely ignored. An example was the buildup of small arms ammunition in North Africa in early 1943. Following preinvasion schedules for the delivery of ammunition based on World War I trench warfare experience, the army poured ammunition into North Africa. Millions of rounds accumulated on the docks far beyond the needs of the troops, but no one would take the initiative to halt the flow. Meanwhile, there was a dire shortage of small arms ammunition in the United States for divisions in training.

The lack of realistic demands on the part of the field commanders is revealed in a detailed examination of the supply doctrine of the United States Army at the planned supply levels, the levels requested by the commanders, and the actual consumption. The army divided supplies into five classes. Class I was food. Class II included clothing and personal equipment, general supplies, replacement vehicles, and miscellaneous equipment. Class III was gasoline, oil, and lubricants. Class IV included engineer construction material, quartermaster, and motor maintenance items. Class V was ammunition. Over the years, complete tables were worked out to determine the average amount of each item needed by every kind of unit.

The unit tables were combined to determine the daily allotment for each division and its supporting troops. This exact figure would change from day to day, as units moved from one command to another. To simplify planning, a figure was derived by adding up the total supply needs of the theater of operations and dividing it by the number of divisions in the theater. Supplies were then allocated by "division slice," which represented the total number of men in the theater divided by the number of divisions. Supplies were usually assigned by the theater supply system to field armies according to the number of divisions in the army, each division representing a division slice.

The estimate on which the D-Day supply situation was based was 541 tons per division slice during normal combat, 426 tons when regrouping, and 462 tons when engaged in rapid pursuit of the enemy. Rations remained static because the need for food did not change. Equipment replacement and service supply were also assumed to remain about the same in all three situations, but gasoline consumption increased to 40 percent of the total during pursuit. Ammunition consumption dropped sharply during regrouping and pursuit. As shown in Table 11, these estimates were quite accurate when compared to actual experience. September 1944 was a period of combat; April 1945 was generally a period of rapid pursuit; and February 1945 was a period of combat and regrouping. These computations were made to arrive at some reasonable figure for estimating the supply needs of a combat force. The 450 to 550 tons per division slice was ample, even with somewhat lavish expenditures in certain lines. For example, the Ninth Army expended more than 50 percent more tonnage for rations than the other American armies, indicating the diversion of large stocks of food to the civilian population. The Seventh Army used 70 percent more ammunition, indicating that they were supplying the French First Army with ammunition and artillery support. The total figure of 550 tons per division was sufficient to include these extras.

Nevertheless, in September 1944, General Omar Bradley was demanding 650 tons per division slice and, when he received only 550 tons, complained that the supply services had failed. For that reason, divisions were not permitted to come forward to take part in the battle at the crucial point, and attempts (not always successful) were made to limit the amount of gasoline that Patton's Third Army was permitted to draw from the depots. Patton wisely ignored the rules, instructing his troops to take as much as they could get, and proceeded to charge across France.

The British experience in North Africa indicated that it was possible to fight even in that inhospitable climate with less equipment. In January 1941, the British Middle East forces were consuming 350 tons per division slice in battle, and 10 percent of that tonnage came from local sources. The division slice was at 35,000 men, not much less than the American total of 40,000 men. Consumption was about twenty pounds per man for the British compared to thirty pounds for the American.[12]

The Germans made do with much less. Whereas the American foot soldier consumed an average of thirty pounds of supplies of all kinds per day, the German soldier generally used about fifteen pounds during limited combat, even though the staff manual allocated as much as fifty pounds per day while on the offensive.[13] During the retreat in August 1944, the German army in the West requested 2,250 tons of supplies per day: 1,000 tons of ammunition, 1,000 tons of fuel, and 250 tons of food (enough for only two and a half American division slices) to supply about twenty weak divisions, probably fewer than 200,000 men. Actual receipts were about 400 tons, which meant only about four pounds per man. Divisions were probably living on reserve stocks and supplies acquired outside of normal channels. In a more stable situation in April 1943, the 134th

Table 11. **Division Slice Needs per Day, European Theater**
(in tons)

	Normal combat	Reorganizing	Pursuit	Sept. 1944	Feb. 1945	April 1945
I Rations	100	100	100	78	81½	80
II Replacement clothing, vehicles	117	117	117	75	93	90
IV Service unit material				110		
III Gas and oil	144	144	180	144	124	180
V Ammunition	180	65	65	153	124	100
Total	541	426	462	560	422	450

German Infantry Division on the Russian front had a daily requirement of 27 tons of rations and munitions for 15,000 Germans and 8,000 Russian Hiwis. In addition, the 5,600 horses required over 50 tons of hay and fodder each day. The total daily requirement was 77 tons for 23,000 men compared to 541 tons for 40,000 Americans.[14] The Germans could fight with much less food, fuel, and artillery ammunition per man, but were provided with larger amounts of small arms ammunition that was often the final deciding factor.

The American soldier received almost twice the weight of food given to the German soldier. The American was allotted six and a quarter pounds per day, including packing and containers. The German combat soldier was allotted only three and a third pounds per day, including the packaging. Both armies sought to provide the men with hot meals whenever possible. Even in combat, from 80 to 90 percent of the American army was served hot meals. The Germans had little to compare with the canned "C" ration of the Americans and relied heavily on sausage and bread with hot soup for their basic ration. According to the ration tables, the American allotment per division slice would have been 120 tons for 40,000 men, yet actual consumption was about 80 tons or only four pounds per man, nearer to the more realistic German figure. The planners continued to use 100 tons, which resulted in enormous reserves and wasted shipping space.

In contrast, the American supply tables were less generous than the German tables in providing small arms ammunition. In both the German and American armies, the practice was generally to supply a division with a reserve supply of two "units of fire," the amount of ammunition needed for about a week or more of combat. One of the units of fire traveled with the weapon and the second was carried in the supply column of the division. The German unit of fire per weapon was usually greater, and the number of automatic weapons in the division was higher. For example, the Germans used many more light machine guns in the division and carried 3,450 rounds with the troops and 2,500 at the division level for each machine gun. The American machine gun had a slower rate of fire and was assigned only 2,000 rounds for both units of fire. Only 750 rounds were allotted to the Browning automatic rifle, which supposedly took the role of the light machine gun in the squad. A German infantry platoon carried over 10,000 rounds for the three light machine guns, 2,100 rounds for the twenty-one rifles, and 2,000 rounds for the three machine pistols, a total of 14,000 rounds of ammunition for the combat weapons in a platoon. In comparison, the American platoon had only 2,250 rounds for the three Browning automatic rifles and 3,400 for the thirty-three M1 rifles in the rifle squads, a total of 5,650. In other words, the German platoon, with fewer men, was expected to fire more than two and a half times the number of bullets. In the rifle company, the Americans had an added 4,000 rounds for two light machine guns, while the Germans had four additional light machine guns at the company level with 13,800 rounds. For the total company, the comparison of rifle and machine gun ammunition for the combat personnel was 56,000 for the Germans to 21,000 for the Americans—a clear indication of the German philosophy of spraying the battlefield with large quantities of small ammunition in comparison to the American concern for aimed fire.[15]

The British ammunition scale proposed on January 13, 1943, for the infantry battalion provided for 50 rounds of ammunition carried by each of 517 riflemen, plus a reserve of 52,000 rounds in the battalion; 160 rounds for each of 170 men with Sten guns with a battalion reserve of 16,320 rounds; and 1,000 rounds with each of 56 men carrying Bren guns and a further 28,000 in the battalion reserve, for a total of 205,100 rounds of small arms ammunition in the battalion. The British total was probably very close to the German total, indicating a similar philosophy of fire.[16]

For artillery ammunition, the Americans and Germans allotted about the same number of 105mm howitzer shells and 150mm howitzer shells to their divisions, but the Americans had far greater reserves. The Germans usually had ample supplies of small arms ammunition, but were chronically short of artillery ammunition. Nevertheless, in certain circumstances, the Germans were able to use artillery at a level comparable to the American army's use. During a breakthrough on the Russian front, the five artillery battalions assigned to the 134th German Infantry Division fired 193 tons of shells on July 16, 1943, and 93.5 tons of shells on July 25, 1943.[17] The Americans always had a bountiful supply of ammunition and were able to provide divisions in combat with 100 to 180 tons per day, regardless of the planner's allotment. In 1943, the Americans had stockpiled in England 150,000 rounds of 105mm howitzer shells for each division, about a four-month supply.[18] During the heavy battles in Normandy in July 1944, the average 105mm howitzer fired only 41 rounds per day or 1,271 rounds per month. With thirty-six howitzers in the division, the total use per division was only 46,000 per month, slightly over the average of 37,000 rounds per month supplied to the divisions under the tables. During the fluid warfare in August, usage dropped to 29,000, below the combat allotment, but more than the amount estimated for a division in pursuit.

In general, the amounts of artillery ammunition provided were ample, regardless of the tables. Even with the American tendency to be lavish in the use of shells, the only shortages resulted from failure to anticipate needs for certain special situations, and these were usually remedied within a short time. Each artillery battalion had enough trucks to resupply it from army depots that were seldom more than hours away.

In these two select classes of supply, rations and munitions, the tables provided ample supply. Both the Germans and British considered the Americans to be incredibly wasteful in their use of both of these commodities, and yet consumption did not keep up with the quantities provided. Therefore, rather than considering the plans as minimal, as the supply officers claimed, we can, in fact, say that they were excessive. A delivery of 450 tons per division was ample over the long run. Shortages of even 20 percent would not have impaired the function of most divisions on most days, and intelligent allotment of supplies would have prevented the problems that did occur.

Still the planners produced enormous requirements for supplies, vehicles, and service personnel. During the first eleven days after D-Day, a total of 557,000 men and 183,000 tons of supplies were landed. Consumption was about thirty pounds per man per day, but nearly sixty pounds per man per day were delivered. And yet the supplies delivered were only 73 percent of the planned schedule that the supply officers had said was the minimum. By the end of the twelfth day, there was a reserve stock of 116,000 tons of supplies for eighteen divisions, about a fifteen-day supply! This excessive buildup of supplies took place during a period when delivery of a few extra divisions would have greatly simplified the problems of the field commanders. Every ton of supplies and every vehicle meant that fewer combat troops could be delivered, yet less than 60 percent of the supplies were actually being used.

The British had a seven-day reserve of rations and extra gasoline to drive every vehicle 150 miles, that is, all the way to Paris and beyond. Despite a storm in the channel, reserves continued to grow. The plan, on June 30, was at 80 percent completion—289,000 tons of supplies had been delivered, an average of 12,000 tons per day. Of course, the deliveries included the cargo for the arriving units, but this was a small portion as the troops and vehicles were counted separately, and most of the first ten days' supply was carried on the vehicles of the landing units. By July 17, the Americans had a fourteen-day reserve of all supplies; they had delivered supplies for sixty-five days within forty-one days. The reason given for such gross overplanning for supplies was that the advances had been slower than expected and that demolitions had been fewer, requiring smaller amounts of engineer supplies than anticipated. The other side of the coin was that if the service element had been cut down, there could have been more combat troops and, with a rapid advance, even fewer demolitions to repair.

General Marshall was aware of the lavish supply tables, but he made the point that American troops were fighting far from home without the incentive of defending their homes and that Americans were more accustomed to a better life than other troops. Therefore Marshall was insistent that Americans have supplies of items considered as luxuries by other armies.[19] When Churchill asked about numbers of noncombatants, the British staff answer was that their troops required a higher standard of comfort and welfare than the Germans.[20]

The excessive demands for vehicles made by the field commanders was an issue on which Marshall and Churchill agreed. Along with General McNair, Churchill was harshly critical of the rapid growth of the number of service units. Service troops were required to provide the vehicles, equipment, and supplies to make it possible for the combat troops to move and fight, but how much was enough? Trucks and supplies do not win battles, nor do mechanics and stock clerks. In North Africa, 40 percent of the troops were in service units, and at one time during the planning for Normandy, the plan called for 51 percent of the men to be in service units. All other armies worked on a much leaner base, ranging from practically none in the Russian army to very few in the French army, where service units were considered nonmilitary.

On both sides, at the top echelon, there was a continuing, though unsuccessful, campaign to control the size of the service establishment and the allocation of noncombat materials. Only in the final months of the war was Hitler able to make decisive cuts in what the Germans called the "Etape," the rear area units.

In the United States, the growth of service units could not be stopped. On December 31, 1941, a survey revealed that service units (including all engineers, some of whom were technically combat support units) made up 26 percent of the army of 1.65 million men. Combat troops made up 52 percent and the air force 16 percent. In the spring of 1942, the War Department made another survey of the army and came to the conclusion that it had insufficient service troops to support a force in Europe according to experience in World War I. Only 11.8 percent of the army consisted of service troops (exclusive of combat engineers), whereas at the end of World War I, 34 percent of the 2 million men in France were nondivisional service troops, exclusive of the service troops assigned to combat units. Primarily on this basis, a decision was made to radically increase the percentage of service personnel to 35 percent.

After June 30, 1942, so many men were used to form new service units that there were not enough recruits to fill the new armored and infantry divisions. For example, the activation of the Ninety-seventh Division was deferred beyond its planned December 1942 date, and the Second Cavalry Division was partially deactivated to provide men for the Ninth Armored Division.[21] Though some divisions were formed on paper, no men were assigned to fill them. Therefore, these divisions remained at cadre strength for the last three months of 1942. Meanwhile, the service units kept coming on. During 1942, only 1.07 million men were added to the combat arms, while 1.42 million men went to service units.

General McNair objected strongly to this misuse of manpower. On September 30, 1942, he wrote, "From the general information at hand, it appears that over-all production of services to combat forces is grossly excessive; and some definite measures to control the dissipation of manpower to these non-combatant functions must be instituted at once."[22] But McNair did not have the power to stop the increase, and, rather than going down, the service element continued to increase. By the end of 1942, the service units constituted 34.4 percent of the 5.4 million men in the army and air force. The combat arms dropped to only 36 percent, while the air force increased to 23.5 percent.[23]

At the beginning of 1943, a hard look was taken at the future of the army. The old plan had been to mobilize 37 additional divisions in 1943, bringing the total to 110. To do this, however, the number of service troops needed to be curtailed sharply. The total manpower available for the Army Ground Forces and the Service of Supply was estimated at about 5.5 million men. Unless the service element was revised downward, the army could not grow beyond 110 divisions; in other words, we would have reached the peak at the end of 1943. Regardless of these hard facts, the number of nondivisional combat units and service units continued to increase. The plan for the end of 1943 called for only slightly over 1 million men in divisions, 1.3 million in nondivisional combat units, 1.2 million in service units, and about 1.3 million in various overhead and other nonunit assignments.[24] In fact, the army never grew beyond ninety divisions; only seventeen new divisions were activated during 1943 because of the demands for other purposes.

McNair was not alone in his concern about the growth of the service element. Churchill was especially adamant about the growth of the "administrative tail," as he called it, in the British army. This growth was indicated by the increasing number of men in the division slice, the total number of men divided by the number of divisions. In December 1940, as the available pool of manpower began to run dry in Britain, Churchill began his struggle to hold down the number of men assigned to service units. In a memo on December 9, 1940, he compared the German army division slice of only 21,000 to the 35,000 men in the British division slice and the growing demand for service units in the British army.[25]

The secretary of war replied to his questions in January, basing the defense primarily on the greater British needs for supplies and vehicles because they were fighting away from home, because there were heavy demands for construction in North Africa where few civilian facilities existed, and because of the climate that caused a greater need for medical facilities. Even so, there were only 212,000 nondivisional troops for seventeen divisions in the Middle East. The reason for the high percentage of British troops in nonfighting roles was that twelve of the seventeen divisions were non-British, whereas very few of the service units were non-British.

In contrast, the Germans had a larger division slice than the figures Churchill was using. On August 1, 1940, the Germans had 6 million men in 205 divisions, for a division slice of nearly 30,000, and that did not include the SS, the Nazi Motor Corps (training drivers for the army), the RAD (German Labor Service, made up of young men), and other service organizations.[26]

A year later Churchill quoted official figures showing 6.5 million Germans in 320 divisions for a slice of 20,000 compared to 41,000 for the British.[27] Ismay's reply pointed out that there were closer to 7 million Germans, producing a slice of 28,000, which did not include antiaircraft units, the SS, the RAD, the Todt Organization, and the Nazi Motor Corps.[28] In February and March 1943, another exchange of memos related to the ability of the Germans to produce more divisions with fewer men, this time based on a German report of February 10, 1943, indicating that the German slice for units in theaters was 20,000 or less.

In October 1943, Churchill was again on the subject. He began with a request for the ration strength of all forces in Italy. Brooke replied on October 27, 1943, that the German division slice in Italy was about 20,000, the British 42,000, and the American 40,000. The Russians were estimated at 15,000 men per division.[29] In a long memo on November 1, Churchill complained of the lack of a common yardstick by which to measure one army against another because divisions varied greatly. He asked whether the British actually got full value from their manpower in the larger divisions. He cited the example of the Fifth British Division that had just been sent to Italy. It had an assignment of 18,480 men, but Churchill wished to know what was the composition of the other 23,000-plus men who made up the division slice of 42,000 in Italy: "What proportion of these 23,000 are combatant troops in the sense of taking their places in the fighting line at some time or other?" He continued:

> My impression is that the Germans get about 12,000 men who actually fight out of divisions of 20,000 gross, and we get about 15,000 or 16,000 out of divisions of 42,000. If so the result is not very encouraging, considering that the Germans fight at least as well as we do and move over great distances with much rapidity. On the other hand, the British corps and army commanders have larger proportions of artillery, engineers, signals, etc., in their hands than the Germans, and can therefore support their divisions more powerfully as circumstances require.

In concluding he raised the same question raised by this chapter: "I take a grave view of the increasing sedentary and non-combatant tail which we are acquiring. For an operation like 'Overlord,' where every man has to have his place in the boat and be fed over the beaches, the most thorough analysis must be made of the rearward services, especially in the opening phases."[30]

Needless to say, Churchill did not win his battle. The British and American supply officers were in agreement that their soldiers would not walk into battle unwashed and fed on rice like the Japanese or on sausage and soup like the Germans. Even "C" rations were considered suitable only in emergencies. It was believed that Allied soldiers required a much higher standard of support. They would ride to battle freshly showered and fed on civilian-quality food. One questions how much of this comfort reached the rifleman and how much remained with the service elements who were supposed to provide these comforts to the combat troops, but more often found themselves supporting one another. The other factor was that the Germans could use civilian resources to provide such services as repair of heavy damage to tanks, whereas the Allies had to bring this capability with them.[31]

A close look at some of the service units brings into question the quality of control that was being exerted over the American army. An example of the misuse of service units is the excessive number of medical personnel assigned to support a division. Practically all battle casualties occur in the infantry regiments. For the 9,354 infantrymen in the three regiments in an infantry division, there were assigned 4,541 medical personnel. The loss by a division of 2,000 wounded and 2,000 sick in a month was considered heavy, yet with over 4,500 persons in the medical organization for each division working six days a week (about 112,000 man days per month), there would be over 28 man days per casualty per month.

In Sicily, in July 1943, the Third U.S. Infantry Division suffered 1,925 killed, wounded, and missing, plus 2,983 losses not related to battle—sickness, accidents, transfers, and all other causes. Of the total of 4,908 lost, about 4,000 came under the care of the medical units. In Italy, the Third Division lost 8,590 men in fifty-nine days. Of these, 2,213 returned from hospitals within the fifty-nine-day period. Again, the medical units were called on to treat fewer than 4,000 men per month, about 30 man days per casualty.[32]

During the ten months from July 1944 to May 1945, the Sixth U.S. Armored Division evacuated 10,325 patients, both battle and nonbattle casualties, including German prisoners. In addition, the division medical battalion returned many men to duty after short periods of treatment. The average number of seriously wounded and sick, however, was only 1,325 per month, far less than experienced by the Third Infantry Division in Italy. Yet the division slice contained 4,500 medical personnel to treat slightly over 1,300 serious casualties per month, nearly 109 man days per casualty.[33]

Although the comparison is not completely adequate, a metropolitan hospital in 1975 employed 2,120 persons in all capacities, working five-day weeks (about 44,000 man days per month) to treat 24,824 patients, who spent an average of ten days each in the hospital, plus 43,000 patients who visited the emergency room and nearly 17,000 out-patients. Although not all of the doctors are included in the total personnel, the ratio (without including the 60,000 nonhospitalized patients who would have been included in the military figures) is about 22 man days per serious patient.[34]

A more pertinent comparison was the assignment of German medical personnel. On the Russian front, where the ratio of German losses was certainly higher than the losses the Americans expected, the Germans provided about 400 medical personnel for each division with about 7,500 infantrymen. But, because the seriously wounded were evacuated to hospitals in Germany, this figure is misleading.[35] Despite that qualification, the number of American medical personnel per division (4,500) seems excessive in comparison.

In another area of service, the American quartermaster units reached a total of 3,800 companies and platoons by the end of the war. In addition to units formed by the Army Air Force and the Army Ground Forces, the quartermaster general formed over 150 laundry units, 237 service companies, 40 salvage-repair companies, and 24 fumigation and bath companies. It would seem that the need for these units was exceptional and that for the most part they offered services to noncombatant units that might well have performed these services for themselves. Infantry units seldom had the services of a laundry unit or a bath company.

Every soldier assigned to a service unit was one less soldier available for combat. The increasing number of men in the service units in the American and British armies was reflected in the growth of the division slice. Table 12 compares the slices of the American, British, and German divisions, dividing the troops into service and combat categories. Although statistics drawn from different sources cannot be compared with absolute accuracy, the table does reveal the major point—that whereas 67 percent of the German troops were combat

Table 12. Total Number of Troops per Division

Branch of service	United States			Britain	Germany		
	Nondivisional troops	Table of organization divisional troops	Total divisional slice	Total divisional slice	Nondivisional troops	Table of organization divisional troops	Total divisional slice
Antiaircraft	5,150		5,150	2,460	70		70
Armor and mechanized cavalry	840	155	995				
Coast artillery	1,059		1,059				
Field artillery	1,404	2,160	3,564	7,380	802	2,497	3,299
Infantry	1,733	9,354	11,087	5,740	229	7,594	7,823
Engineers		647	647	5,330	937	620	1,557
Total Combat	10,186	12,316	22,502	20,910	2,038	10,711	12,749
Total Service	18,900	2,000	20,900	20,090	2,755	3,516	6,271
Total	29,086	14,316	43,402	41,000	4,893	14,227	19,020

SOURCE: *Kriegstagebuch*, 3:1569; Mueller-Hillebrand, *Das Heer*, 3:217; Keilig, *Das Deutsche Heer*, 1:101, V, pp. 60–66 and 2:204, 1943, I; Greenfield et al., *Organization*, p. 202; Winston S. Churchill, *The Hinge of Fate* (Boston: Houghton Mifflin, 1950), p. 921.

soldiers, only 52 percent of the Americans and 51 percent of the British were combat soldiers.

In North Africa, the British apparently had a higher percentage of combat troops. On July 20, 1943, in response to a query from Churchill, Allied forces headquarters provided the following breakdown of British troops in North Africa as of July 7, 1943:

Combat troops		174,561 58%
Service troops in divisions	16,588	
Service troops, nondivisional	109,662	
Total service troops		126,250 42%
Total troops		300,811

In addition, 50,197 nonmilitary laborers were employed. If the nonmilitary personnel were included as service troops, the combat percentage would drop to slightly under 50 percent. In mobile warfare, the Allies could not depend on finding local labor and would have to provide service units.[36]

The major difference between the American and the German division slice was in the nondivisional troops, most of whom were service troops. The Germans considered most of their engineers combat troops, whereas the Americans split them between the combat and service troops. If the engineers were reclassified on the American chart, the percentage of combat troops in the total division slice would have been nearer to the 67 percent combat in the German total. The American problem was dispersion of combat troops into support roles such as engineers, antiaircraft, and coast artillery, which, as Churchill pointed out, gave the division more power, but, on the other hand, supporting troops such as the antiaircraft troops were not always needed. In the German armed services, the navy manned much of the coast artillery, and the air force crewed practically all of the antiaircraft guns, so these totals were not accurately reflected in the German figures. Table 13 indicates how a revised chart might be developed.

The Germans extracted an even better ratio of combat troops under this for-

Table 13. **Revised Division Slice**

Branch of service	United States	Germany	Great Britain
Armor	995	70	2,460
Field Artillery	3,564	3,299	7,380
Infantry	11,087	7,823	5,740
Total combat	15,646	11,192	15,580
Engineers	647	1,557	5,330
Other services (incl. some engrs.)	20,900	6,271	20,090
Total service	21,547	7,828	25,420
Total Divisional Slice	37,193	19,020	41,000
Combat Percent Excluding Engrs.	42	59	38

mula. They created 311 divisions at reduced strength from 6.91 million men, but still put at least 2 million infantrymen on the line. The Americans, on the other hand, obtained only 90 divisions from 4.8 million men in the Ground Forces and Services of Supply and put about 1 million on the line. Could any of the obvious advantages of the service structure have compensated for the reduction in fighting value to that extent?

The lavish scale of service units was illustrated by the American Seventh Army, which had the smallest service component in Europe in 1944. The service element of the Seventh Army was able to support its own troops and help the French First Army, as well as provide equipment and arms for new French divisions being formed from the resistance groups in France. The service element of the American Seventh Army was ample enough to support two armies, while equipping several new divisions, and still provide supplies and replacements of all kinds. The service units in the other American armies were much larger and did not have the extra burdens.

Field commanders had an inborn fear of running short. Few would admit that they could not benefit from additional quantities of some resource. The result was a tendency to inflate all requisitions. If a signal company were needed, a signal battalion was demanded; if three hundred trucks could carry 750 tons to supply a division for a day, a thousand trucks were requested, even though the depot was only a few hours away; if 450 tons a day were needed, 650 tons were demanded.

As much as one can sympathize with the field commander for his extravagance, the problem was compounded by the second echelon which automatically placed another percentage on the top of the original request to cover themselves in the event of any unforeseen circumstances. The result was a buildup of inventory that, when carried to excess, was an indication of poor management. In 1943, ample supplies of practically everything were available in depots, at ports, on ships, in reserve stocks, and in the hands of the units, but because there were always unfilled requisitions somewhere, the impression of shortages was created. Supplies and service troops were definitely available in sufficient quantity for the invasion of France.

Rather than being short, as was claimed in 1943, the Allies already had a gross oversupply of all forms of nondivisional units, and the situation became more extravagant as the months passed. When manpower became tight in late 1944, the service units were tapped with no noticeable loss in efficiency. The one-year delay provided an extra margin that was quite unnecessary, and, considering the reduction in the number of divisions because combat troops were drawn into service functions, such a margin was an expensive luxury. Any argument that the invasion had to be postponed because of the lack of logistical support must be viewed in terms of the excessive demands of the planners.

12

INTELLIGENCE

An intangible yet essential necessity for a successful invasion was substantial knowledge of the enemy's forces and plans. Until 1975, opinion on the timing of the second front was strongly influenced by the British position that the invasion was delayed because intelligence was lacking. The revelation in 1975 that the British had broken the German codes as early as 1940 and had distributed details on enemy forces and plans to high-echelon commanders in a series of messages code-named ULTRA indicated that Allied intelligence was adequate to launch the invasion.

Only a few thousand of the ULTRA messages have been made public. Fred W. Winterbotham's account, *The Ultra Secret*,[1] is the most complete source of information regarding the British success in breaking the codes created by the German Enigma machine. The Enigma machine was a complex device that mechanically provided an infinite number of codes.

Information based on the deciphered German messages was distributed to a few high-ranking officers. The messages were classified as ULTRA, being more secret than the British MOST SECRET classification. In 1977, the British government began releasing some of the ULTRA files for use by scholars. The files released by March 1978 do not cover the period most pertinent to this study, but there is no reason to assume that the coverage for the time period (1944) and the area (the Mediterranean theater) was more complete than for other times and places.[2] The data made available in 1944 to the British commander in Italy included the day-by-day location of German battalions, frequent lists of available munitions stocks, and intelligence summaries prepared by the Germans so that leaks in Allied codes could be sealed.

The information was made available by a British cryptographic machine that was able to break in a short time the multiple codes created by the German Enigma machine. The Enigma machine was a series of rotating drums, remotely similar to a slot machine. To use the machine, the operator set the drums in relationship to one another according to a key. The message was fed in with one electric typewriter, and the encoded message was printed out on a second typewriter. The receiver of the coded message would feed it into the machine after the drums had been set in the same relationship or key that had been used when the message was encoded. The machine would then type out a clear message on the second typewriter. Any code can be broken eventually if enough messages are available. The advantage of the Enigma was that the code could be changed frequently simply by using a new key, that is, a different setting of drums. A code book might contain separate keys for the time of the day, the day of the month, and the month, so that five messages from the same source could be transmitted in five different codes, because they would have been sent at different times. Therefore, to decipher messages, the British needed not only an Enigma machine, but also a current list of the keys being used.[3]

The need for a current list of combinations ended when an Englishman, Alan Turing, invented a machine that broke the codes by rapidly trying out one key after another until the message made sense.[4] The Turing Engine first deciphered an Enigma message by chance in June or July 1939, after the Polish secret service had made an Enigma machine available to the British. Three Enigma machines, each with a complete set of current keys, were captured—the first in April 1940 from a plane shot down off Norway, the second in May 1940 in France from a German signal unit, and the third in May 1941 from a U-boat. Each set of captured keys made it possible to further improve the Turing Engine. By April 1940, the Turing Engine was decoding many Germany messages.[5] This information, for example, gave the RAF advance knowledge of the exact composition of each raid during the Battle of Britain.[6]

An elaborate security system was necessary to prevent the Germans from learning that their codes were being broken. Special liaison units were created to transmit the data sent by only the most secure British codes to a limited number of commanders. The interpretation of the original decoded message was entrusted to a select group of men in London who transmitted only parts of the enormous amount of intelligence received.[7] No recipient was permitted to divulge the source of his information.

By early 1942, there were many Turing Engines in operation, and, by 1943, the British were decoding from two to four thousand messages every day.[8] From these messages, early in 1942, the British had learned the state of readiness of each German unit, its strength, its equipment, and the amount of supplies available for its use from reports made periodically by every German division to the high command.

The limitation of the system, according to Winterbotham, was that the British could decode only the messages that were sent by radio. He meant that the ULTRA intercepts could obtain only certain messages—anything sent by telephone or telegraph wires would not have been available. To explain why some types of information that typically were sent by teletypewriter over telephone and telegraph lines were also known to the British, Winterbotham claimed that such information had been sent by radio to ease the heavy burden on the telephone and telegraph lines.[9]

The claim that the German telephone and telegraph lines were overburdened is not valid. The fact that the British acknowledged receipt of only the relatively few messages sent by radio is a crucial point because any information they did not wish to reveal could be held back with the excuse that messages relative to a particular event had not been sent by radio. Such was the claim in regard to Dieppe and Kasserine.

There is some reason to doubt Winterbotham's explanation and to believe that, instead, the British possessed far more information than was released to their own forces, as well as to the Americans. The explanation that the Germans sent radio messages to relieve the telephone lines is not credible when one considers the enormous capacity of European long distance lines for civilian use before 1939, compared to the limited number of radio frequencies available for long distance transmission. Alfred Jodl's diary of January 30, 1945, stated that messages for the high command of the armed forces and the high command of the army, as well as for the replacement army, received and transmitted in Berlin daily totaled 120,000 telephone calls and 33,000 teleprinter messages, but only 1,200 radio messages.[10] How could 1,200 radio messages relieve pressure on a system that was handling over 150,000 messages daily?

In 1939, the daily average number of telephone calls made in Germany was 7,457,000, and the number of telegrams sent was 46,254. In Berlin alone in 1938, there were over 574,000 telephones.[11] The 120,000 phone calls would have been an unnoticeable factor. The 33,000 teleprinter messages would have placed a strain on the telegraph system, but it was far easier to substitute the use of telephone lines to send these messages than to resort to the radio frequencies. The teleprinters themselves would still have to be used at both ends regardless of whether the message went over a telephone wire or by radio.

The efficiency of wire transmissions compared to radio over long distances can be demonstrated with one statistic. Because of the tremendous difficulty in laying and maintaining underwater telephone cables, only a few such cables have been put into operation between the United States and the rest of the world. Yet, in 1939, these few cables handled 25,000 messages daily, while the same number of messages were sent by the combined radio facilities of the United States.[12] The problem lies in the need to send messages by radio on separate frequencies. Over a long distance, no one else must use this frequency or the message will be garbled. For this reason, the Federal Communication Commission limits the number of radio transmitters having more than four watts of power (enough to reach only a few miles) and also restricts the frequencies on which licensed operators can transmit. In wartime the enemy was ready to jam radio messages or to intercept them, so the few frequencies that were available were subject to interference.

In contrast, a single telephone cable contained hundreds of wires, allowing dependable simultaneous transmission of as many messages as there were wires. Therefore, it is not reasonable to accept the British explanation that all of the information provided by ULTRA came from radio intercepts. Rather, one must assume that some came from telephone line tapping.

The German army used teletypewriters for the transmission of most orders and reports; the limited radio waves were used over short ranges by mobile units or where telephone lines were lacking, for example, across the Mediterranean. The telephone lines were the best source of the routine information that the British were receiving—such as unit reports on numbers of men, as well as orders regarding operations. The British certainly took a great deal of interest in telephone lines in 1943. A mimeographed table dated December 12, 1942, was given to the OSS by the British in March 1943, listing about seven hundred underground telephone cables in unoccupied France in use by the Germans, classified as to whether they were used by the army, navy, or for railroad operations.[13] Between June and September 1943, the OSS was provided by the British with six more detailed reports concerning telephone lines in France.[14] It would appear that the British were enlisting the aid of the OSS in their tapping enterprise and that the information found its way into the general file. Notations at the end of intelligence reports indicated that the information was delivered by way of wireless or by "bag" to London, which points to the fact that some high-grade intelligence came out of France. A report dated May 25, 1943, noted as being from "Polish Intelligence" (the source given for much of the high-quality information), contains photostats of reports in French of monitored telephone conversations between Germans in France. This information was taken to London by bag.[15] One must assume that at least part of the information being decoded by ULTRA came from intercepted teletypewriter messages from France and that, as a result, the British probably had absolutely complete information regarding German troops and plans in the West. The extent of this information can be measured by the accuracy of the intelligence reports provided to Americans.

The degree of accuracy of the intelligence reports given to the OSS can be tested by comparing them to the official German unit lists. On September 1, 1942, a report supposedly from "Polish Intelligence" reporting information from the Swiss General Staff, outlined the number of German divisions in France as five Landesschutzen divisions (actually there were six); six Landwehr divisions (probably correct; there were ten by October 1942); three to four divisions of crack troops from the East to rebuild (actually there were four); fifteen divisions of the Thirteenth Wave (actually there were seven of the Thirteenth Wave, four of the Fourteenth Wave, and two of the Twentieth Wave); three panzer divisions (correct); and two SS divisions (correct).[16] The references in parentheses refer to total divisions in the West, less the three divisions in the Netherlands listed on the German order of battle of August 12, 1942.[17] The reserve divisions, referred to as Landwehr, were in the process of being formed in August through October, and only two were listed in the order of battle of August 12, although ten were formed by the end of October. Therefore, the information is quite accurate.

Another report, dated November 8, 1942, was even more explicit in actually identifying each unit.[18] Table 14 compares the report to the German order of battle. The source of the information on this chart was again "Polish Intelligence." The degree of accuracy is almost perfect. The intelligence report did not pick up divisions that had just been formed in the preceding few weeks and missed two divisions being reformed. There is a little jumble in corps assign-

Table 14. **German Dispositions Reflected in Allied Intelligence Compared with Actual Dispositions**

Allied Intelligence November 8, 1942	German Order of Battle November 15, 1942

Army Group West Reserve
  6 Pz, 7 Pz, 10 Pz, 26 Pz, 27 Pz
	Army Group West Reserve
	  6 Pz, 7 Pz, 10 Pz, 26 Pz, 27 Pz

SS Corps: 1 SS, 2 SS	I SS Corps: 1 SS, 2 SS
? SS Division	3 SS
Goering Brigade	Goering Division
Air Force Rifle Division	
Division "West" in Paris	325 Security Division in Paris 39**, 161*** (arrived Nov. 1942)
1st Army	1st Army
LXX Corps: 715, 708, 15, 327	LXXX: 715, 708, 15, 327, 344**
7th Army	7th Army
XXV: 333, 17, 335, 709, 337	XXV: 333, 17, 709, 337, 346**, 343**
LXXXIV: 319, 320, 716	LXXXIV: 319, 320, 716
15th Army	15th Army: 38**
LXXI: 711, 332, 302	LXXXI: 711, 332, 302, 348**
LXXXVIII: 321, 106, 304, 306	LXXXII: 321, 106, 304, 306
Belgium: 712, 23	LXXXIX: 712, 65**
Low Countries: three divisions	LXXXVIII: 167***, 719, 347**
	LXXXIII: 335
	Denmark: 23

SOURCE: OSS Reports, File 23408; *Kriegstagebuch,* 2:1390.
**Division newly formed in October 1942.
***Rebuilding division not reported in Allied intelligence.

ments, and the three divisions in the Low Countries were not identified. The Goering Brigade was technically a division in November, but another report described this development in detail. The Air Force Rifle Division does not show up on the German list; the Air Force Seventh Flieger Division left France on September 4. The summary of the report gives a total of forty-one divisions which is identical to the actual number. Nine days later, another report gave an accurate statement on the number and state of equipment of the five panzer divisions.[19]

On November 26, 1942, "Polish Intelligence" reported actual sighting of rail convoys. The information was given and analyzed; every error was picked out and corrected, even to the point of correcting the designation "security division" to occupation division for the 712th, 713th and 716th Divisions, as well as to stating that the 620th and 231st Divisions did not exist.[20] Another report on November 18, 1942, noted the existence of a Fifteenth Infantry Regiment in France and questioned that fact because this regiment was part of a division on the Eastern front. This regiment, actually 15 (B) Infantry Regiment, was created in October 1942 and assigned to the 189th Reserve Division in France, one of the few instances where the Germans assigned duplicate numbers to units. One almost detects the British intelligence people scolding the Germans for this carelessness.[21] A report of December 1, 1942 ("emanating from good and well-proved sources"), reviewed the dispositions in France, corrected a minor error in the November 8 report, and described the movement of divisions to the south following TORCH.[22] These samples of information provided to the OSS indicate that the British had a very exact knowledge of the German forces in France during 1942.

Winterbotham understated the case when he said that ULTRA gave only sketchy details on the "60 odd" German divisions in the West. His information was far more accurate than he had revealed. In actual fact, the British had a near perfect knowledge of manpower, equipment, and other shortages as well as the difficulties of using the Poles and Russians in German units. "We [the British] learned, too, that the actual strength of the new divisions did not amount to more than 50% of the establishment total."[23]

Despite the accuracy and availability of the information, very little of it appears in the War Office files. Most of the intelligence files are still closed (1978), but one review by Military Intelligence 14 dated March 23, 1943, was attached to a document in the War Office files. Comparing this sketch map showing the location of German divisions in France to the actual German dispositions reveals some curious discrepancies. The British consistently claimed there were forty divisions in France at the time, but the sketch shows only thirty-three, including four for which the identification was not known. There were errors on the sketch that were correct on the November 1942 analysis described above. The 715th Division was incorrectly numbered 718th; the Eighty-first, Eighty-second, and Eighty-ninth Corps were incorrectly shown as Thirty-second (?), Thirty-sixth, and Eighty-third; and the 526th Division (a headquarters for the training units left in Germany when the 156th Reserve Division was created and sent to Belgium) is shown in Belgium along with the 156th Reserve Division. In only one instance was a division that had been sent to Russia still recorded as being in the West. Why MI 14 was using comparatively inaccurate information when far better material had been supplied to the OSS is a mystery. Perhaps MI 14 introduced the inaccuracies that did not distort the general conclusions to provide a cover for ULTRA, realizing the review would receive wide distribution.[24] The British certainly had enough knowledge of the German forces to conclude that an invasion was quite possible in 1943.

The Russians also had good information through the agent "Lucy" in Switzerland, who received his information directly from sources in the German General Staff.[25] However, neither Stalin nor Churchill would reveal the extent of their information, and this led to a bitter exchange in August 1942. In Churchill's words, "He [Stalin] then said that there was not a single German division in France of any value, a statement which I contested. There were in France twenty-five German divisions, nine of which were of the first line. He shook his head."[26] All of the important data from ULTRA were shown to Churchill, and what he told Stalin was not true. Actually, there were thirty-three German divisions in the West in August. None were of the first line. The Tenth Panzer was the only quality unit; ten divisions of the Thirteenth and Fourteenth Wave were beginning to receive artillery and vehicles. Churchill had distorted the facts for his own ends.

Not only the Russians, but also the Germans, had an effective decoding and information operation. Any code used over a long period of time was subject to being broken by the patient work of the cryptographer. The British Turing Engine simply speeded up the procedure and needed fewer messages to work with. The British were aware that the Germans were working to break their codes. On May 28, 1942, the British received a list of radio interception units, and their frequencies being used in France complete with comments respecting their working order.[27] For long periods, the Germans decoded messages sent by the Royal Navy because of the volume sent by radio and the fact that the ships were at sea and could not all receive new code books simultaneously. With a great deal of material to work with, all in the same code, the task of deciphering was much simpler. To change codes, the British had to wait until all units had the new books, because sending the same message in the old code, that had been broken, and in the new code would immediately compromise the new code. ULTRA messages were sent using code books in which the code was used only once and then discarded, which made it almost impossible to break, but this required far too many code books for practical routine operations.[28]

The Germans also penetrated the scrambler telephone that Roosevelt and Churchill uséd. The scrambler telephone was invented in 1939 and was first used by Roosevelt in September. By March 1, 1942, the Germans had discovered a method of unscrambling the conversations and were tapping the transatlantic telephone cable. On March 6, 1942, Hitler was informed that all telephone traffic between Britain and the United States was being deciphered. This fact was made known to only a few people; one copy was sent to Heinrich Himmler, only, who in turn passed select passages on to others. The army, navy, and air force intelligence services were not included, nor was the Abwehr, the German counterintelligence service. The decoded telephone conversations were referred to in documents as "sichere quelle," an unimpeachable source. Included in the intercepts was a conversation between Roosevelt and Churchill on May 5, 1944, alerting Hitler to the immediate coming of the second front.[29] Hitler probably learned more than has been revealed, which accounts for his "intuition" about Normandy in the spring of 1944.

On July 29, 1943, the High Command War Diary noted that the conversation between Roosevelt and Churchill regarding the Italian surrender had been intercepted and decoded.[30] Earlier, however, on July 23, 1943, all German troops and equipment convoys to Italy had been stopped, except for coal trains, indicating that the Germans had earlier knowledge. Because this information came to the attention of the Allies, they, in turn, must have suspected that the Germans knew something was afoot.[31]

The Germans had other sources of information as well. Rear Admiral Wilhelm

Franz Canaris was able to supply Hitler with a detailed summary of all matters discussed at ARCADIA, complete with the plans for the attack on North Africa, along with possible future plans for the Mediterranean in 1943 and plans for the buildup of American forces in the United Kingdom.[32] Rommel was provided with complete details of British forces in North Africa from September 1941 through August 1942 by way of an American military attaché, Colonel Frank B. Fellers, who sent reports to Washington in a code that the Germans had penetrated.[33] In May 1943, the Spanish military attaché in Washington provided a transcript of the minutes of the TRIDENT Conference.[34] Therefore, the Germans were also provided with a great deal of information on the Allied forces.

In no previous war had commanders been provided with such detail on their opponents. The Allied leaders had sufficient knowledge to make good decisions. On the other hand, the Allied forces were so formidable that any information learned by the Germans only served to undermine the morale of the German generals or led them to disbelieve the information, as they often did.

The supposed lack of intelligence played a major role in two battles that affected the timing of the second front—Dieppe, used as evidence that the German defenses were too strong in 1942, and Kasserine, interpreted as proof that the Americans were too poorly trained in 1943. These two defeats resulted, in part, from a supposed lack of knowledge of enemy forces and intentions. Reportedly, we did not know how strong the defenses were in Dieppe itself, and we did not expect the Germans to attack at Faid. In neither battle, however, was lack of intelligence the culprit. The losses resulted from poor handling of the available forces rather than from unawareness of German plans and resources.

As we have seen in the earlier chapters, Churchill and Brooke were reluctant to invade in 1942. To aid and abet the Russians, however, the British did mount a major propaganda campaign to convince the Germans that the invasion would be launched during the summer of 1942. London Controlling Section, charged with deception, began an intensive campaign, through diplomatic circles, in early 1942 to convince the Germans that the invasion was coming. Commando raids were staged to reinforce the idea.[35] On March 9, 1942, Roosevelt urged the British to consider the second front. On the same day, the British Joint Chiefs of Staff opposed a major invasion "mainly because nothing was known of German defenses and resources were too meagre to be staked on gambles."[36] Although the extent of the secrets revealed by ULTRA for this period is unknown, there is little doubt that the British had a good idea of the German forces and defenses in March 1942, but chose to underestimate the comparative ability of both their own troops and those of the Americans and to overestimate the defenses.

Still, something had to be done to pacify the Americans and the Russians. Mountbatten suggested a raid on Cherbourg that would threaten the Germans and draw their planes into an air battle with the RAF. After some discussion, the target was changed to Dieppe on April 4. The reasons given for launching a major raid were to provide a rehearsal for SLEDGEHAMMER and to draw German troops and planes from the East. During April and May, planning proceeded, and on May 18, the Second Canadian Division moved to the Isle of Wight for special training.[37] By June, plans began to fall apart. Churchill continued to support RUTTER, code name for the operation, because it would give substance to the rumors threatening a second front.[38] By continuing the rumor campaign, however, the British were alerting the Germans to defend the very coast around Dieppe where the planners were expecting to surprise the defenders.

The Royal Navy and the RAF were lukewarm on the operation and refused to give their full support.[39] No ship larger than a destroyer nor any significant number of bombers were to be involved. Instead of smashing the enemy defenses with naval and air bombardment, the army hoped to surprise the defenders, while at the same time the London Controlling Section was doing its best to warn the Germans that the British were coming.[40]

On June 17, 1942, Churchill went to Washington to oppose SLEDGEHAM-MER, but he could not shake the American will to attack. On his return, the British Joint Chiefs of Staff, in a meeting held on July 2, refused to participate, but how could they convince the Americans? The Dieppe raid was planned for July 4; but, complete naval and air support were withheld for technical reasons, and a frontal assault against the defenses was to be used, rather than the strong flanking attacks advocated by the planners. Though Brooke and Mountbatten both told Churchill, on June 29, that success was doubtful, Brooke advised Churchill to allow the attack in order to gain knowledge for the future invasion. Fortunately, on July 4, the operation was called off because the commander of the airborne troops said that the wind was not right and, therefore, the paratroops could not be dropped. On July 5, a further reason for cancellation was revealed: the Tenth Panzer Division was now at Amiens. The Tenth Panzer Division had moved to Amiens on June 4, and its location, nearly forty miles from Dieppe, had probably been known for some time. To further compromise the secrecy of the operation, the Germans discovered the troop convoy at anchor on July 7 and bombed three ships. The operation was then canceled.[41]

Now the interplay in the negotiations between Washington and London and the decisions regarding Dieppe became crucial. On July 8, Churchill cabled Roosevelt that SLEDGEHAMMER was impossible, and a crisis was created in Washington. On the same day, Mountbatten held a conference with planners of RUTTER, ending with a decision to try again, regardless of German knowledge of the previous plan. Meanwhile, Sir John Dill had warned Churchill of the bitterness in Washington, and on July 12, Churchill again urged Roosevelt to abandon SLEDGEHAMMER in favor of the attack on North Africa. On that same evening, with Churchill's approval, the raid on Dieppe was officially reopened. While the Canadians were being assembled for the raid, the British deception services continued to pour out rumors that the invasion would be launched on the Calais coast, and no effort was made to conceal or confuse the Germans concerning the shipping being assembled.[42]

Did the Germans really expect an attack? In July, Hitler personally ordered troops from the eastern front to the West to defend against an invasion. On July

9, Hitler ordered the SS Das Reich Division, the SS Adolf Hitler Division, the Goering Brigade, and the Seventh Parachute Division to the West and ordered three Walkure II (emergency) divisions (Thirty-eighth, Thirty-ninth, and Sixty-fifth) assembled by the replacement army and sent to the West. The Dieppe area was specifically mentioned as a danger area.[43]

Meanwhile, the Germans launched a counterdeception plan of their own, proclaiming that the Dieppe area was held by a much depleted division, the 110th Infantry Division, which was being rebuilt after hard service on the eastern front.[44] The British expected to find one battalion of the 110th Infantry Division plus other units totaling 1,700 men in Dieppe. They did not expect the battalion to be at full strength because it had recently come from Russia, but it had "a good fighting record."[45] In fact, the area near the port had been held by the 302d Infantry Division since May 1941. This division had provided the cadre for the new 668th Infantry Regiment of the 370th Infantry Division in March 1942 and, as a result, had received large numbers of replacements. More than 2,400 new men had been added to the division in late July 1942, many of whom were from Polish districts. The fact that the 571st Infantry Regiment, which held Dieppe itself, was 20 percent Polish affected efficiency, because many of the Poles spoke only a few words of German.[46] On the whole, the troops encountered were fewer in number and of poorer quality then the British expected. The disaster resulted not from better German forces, but from lack of heavy naval gunfire to silence machine-gun posts in the cliffs.[47]

The Germans were expecting an attack but did not have the specific time and place.[48] The German naval cryptanalytical bureau had broken the Royal Navy code at Portsmouth and learned of the large-scale naval movements.[49] On June 25, 1942, the German Fifteenth Army reported an increase in landing craft in the Portsmouth area. The report noted that between June 1 and 22 the number had increased from 1,146 to 2,802 and described the number of each type. On July 28, the Fifteenth Army reported that air reconnaisance had seen a convoy of ships off the Isle of Wight.[50] The Germans were definitely on the alert.[51] A German prisoner taken at Dieppe told the British his unit had been on high alert during June 30 to July 25 and again after August 1, but this was normal during favorable periods of tide and weather. There were no special precautions, however, in the first week of July nor from August 18 on.[52] To make matters worse, on the way to Dieppe, the convoy accidentally encountered some German ships that gave the defenders a forty-five-minute warning of the actual time of the attack.[53]

According to Mountbatten in a memo to Churchill, the British did achieve tactical surprise even though strategical surprise was not possible because of rumors of a second front. Did the British know that the Germans were alerted? One has to accept Mountbatten's personal note to Churchill that tactical surprise was achieved.[54]

Dieppe is not covered in Winterbotham's book nor in the OSS reports or the ULTRA files that have been opened. Winterbotham did comment, however, that after meeting Mountbatten in Asia, "I had last seen him . . . at a staff meeting in London before the unhappy Dieppe raid of 1942. He was then commanding the experimental combined force which undertook that operation." If Winterbotham had been at a staff meeting just before the raid, his only purpose in attending would have been to transmit ULTRA data to the group.[55] There was apparent dissension within the ranks regarding the role of the intelligence services in the Dieppe operation. Colonel Oliver Stanley, chief of the London Controlling Section, was so upset by the deception plans regarding Dieppe that he resigned and, after the raid, was replaced by Colonel John Bevan.[56]

Regardless of secrecy, or its lack, the Canadians landed at 6:00 A.M. on August 19. The Germans alerted the Tenth Panzer Division and the Adolf Hitler SS Division.[57] An advanced element of the Tenth Panzer Division reached the village of Hautot, three miles from Dieppe, by 4:30 P.M. and took no part in the defense. Traveling less than forty miles in ten hours was not a great performance by the Tenth Panzer Division.[58] Fortunately for the Germans, the Allied force never got off the beaches, and of the 6,086 men engaged, 3,623 were killed, wounded, or captured.[59] The mistakes that led to these heavy casualties were the product of a complex and inflexible plan that could not be changed to fit such conditions as the failure of the attacks on the east flank to silence numerous machine guns in the cliffs overlooking the beach. The primary fault was the concentration of effort in the frontal assault on a defended locality.[60]

After tempers had cooled and reports were filed, Churchill on December 21, 1942, demanded answers concerning the attack. "Although for many reasons we have made Dieppe look as good as possible, now I must be informed on the plans. . . . Who made them? Who approved them?" Churchill wanted to know who advised the frontal assault. The tone of the memo to General Ismay reflected Churchill's concern and his desire to find the party responsible for the failure. Ismay's reply puts the burden on Montgomery, who in May 1942 as commander of the Southeast Command had been given the responsibility by the commander in chief of the Home Forces. Numerous plans had been offered by the Combined Operations Headquarters, but Montgomery was responsible for approving them. The General Staff "was not especially informed" of the operation.[61]

By the date of the attack on Dieppe, Montgomery was in North Africa, and by December 1942, after El Alamein, he was Britain's hero. Churchill's search for the responsible person ended.

The experience did lead to better planning in the future, using better landing craft, improved security measures, heavy naval support, and more air support. But most of the "lessons learned" had been learned at Gallipoli during World War I. The mistakes were made in spite of the advice of the planners, who specifically requested more information about the cliffs, who wanted more air support, who wanted a heavier naval bombardment, and who opposed the frontal assault.

In the final version of the plan, the question of the machine-gun posts in the cliffs to the east was mentioned twice, in Appendix A, 3, e, VI: "It has not been possible to deny or confirm the existence of M. G. posts in the low cliffs to the East of the entrance to the harbour," and again in Appendix D in which the Royal Regiment of Canada was to clear machine-gun posts in the east headland.[62]

In J. H. Roberts' report of the operation, the Royal Regiment of Canada could not establish a bridgehead on Blue Beach and could not scale the cliff to knock out the machine guns on the east headland, nor could the destroyers or gunboats provide sufficient fire.[63] The naval commander, Captain J. H. Hallett, reported that there was no reason why a battleship could not have been used for the first few hours. If there had been one, it "could probably have turned the tide of battle ashore in our favor."[64] The heavy fifteen-inch guns would have blasted the machine-gun posts quickly. The continued fire of the machine guns caused the heavy casualties during the departure.

The other problem that led to the disaster was the inability of the tanks to get off the beach to help the infantry. The planners were aware of the tank obstacles on Red and White beaches.[65] To cope with the obstacles, engineer demolition parties were in the first boats to land, but the machine guns from the cliffs killed and wounded many of the engineers, and the explosives were set fire in the boats. The tank obstacles were never removed, and the tanks were stranded on the beach.

A review of the planning leading up to the raid reveals that the lessons learned had been discussed at length before the raid. Churchill was not at all impressed with the reports following Dieppe. The recommendations that generally asked for more of everything sounded fine, but if applied to all movement, according to Churchill, "the only result will be to render operations of this character utterly impossible. The maxim 'Nothing avails but perfection' may be spelt short, 'Paralysis'."[66] In this short sentence written on December 6, 1942, Churchill summed up the policy of the British for the next eighteen months. Dieppe even failed to perform the mission of drawing German troops to France from the eastern front. Just before the raid, Hitler was sending divisions to the West. In the light of the disaster, the Germans felt that no further attempt would be made for some time and were unconcerned about stripping trained divisions from the West in late 1942 and early 1943 to resist the Russian onslaught in the East. The trained divisions were replaced with newly formed units and "reserve divisions" consisting of replacement training battalions.[67]

In contrast to the incompetence shown in the Dieppe raid, only a few months later the British were able to stage a near perfect performance in an area of their choosing. The TORCH operation was far larger, yet the security was perfect even though the Germans had been alerted to the general plan. The German code breakers had been deceived, and ULTRA gave full information on German plans. Furthermore, to provide a sea free of U-boats, information was provided to the Germans concerning a convoy of empty ships returning from Africa. The

Germans responded by diverting all U-boats in the South Atlantic to pointlessly attack this prey, leaving the way clear for the troop ships.[68]

In view of the evidence of complete information of German plans and resources and the demonstrated ability to manipulate that information for their own purposes, the proposition that the Allies were unaware of German weakness in the West is not credible.[69] The Allies had full knowledge of the strength of the German army and knew that it could be overwhelmed by Allied forces in 1943.

13

COMBAT EXPERIENCE

The British claimed in 1942 and in early 1943 that the American troops lacked combat experience and therefore were not capable of facing the German army. The invasion of North Africa was urged by the British as a means for Americans to gain combat experience, after which they could return to invade France.

The high hopes of a speedy conquest of North Africa were dashed by the quick German reaction and seizure of Tunisia. Allied attempts to extend their lines around the southern flank led to the battles around Faid and Kasserine. The defeat at Kasserine, or more specifically at Sidi Bou Zid and then Kasserine, had a definite impact on the decision as to when to launch the second front. Because of the setbacks between February 14 and 22, 1943, the ability of American troops was believed to be inferior. General Alexander, appointed army group commander in North Africa on February 19, noted in his memoirs that the Americans performed badly at Kasserine, and, therefore, it was necessary to set them up for an easy victory to restore their morale.[1] He even denied them credit for finally halting the Germans. Alexander claimed that his orders to Montgomery to speed up the operations against the Axis forces on the Mareth line resulted in Rommel turning his forces to meet this threat and thereby saved the Americans on February 22.[2] Contemporary German records do not bear out that statement. Instead, Rommel admitted that the American resistance was too strong, and he withdrew. Some of the German forces were sent north of Pont du Fahs for a broad front attack under the Fifth Panzer Army, while others were regrouped over a period of twelve days before launching an attack against the weak forward elements of the Eighth Army.[3]

The unfortunate result of Kasserine was the impression left in the mind of Alexander (and other British officers) that the Americans could not fight. George F. Howe writes, "General Alexander's unfavorable estimate was destined to linger, encouraging him to depend more heavily upon British units than later circumstances warranted."[4]

Because it played such an important role in later decision making, this action deserves careful study. The Americans did not perform brilliantly in their initial encounter with first-line German units. Lieutenant General Lloyd R. Fredendall, commander of the United States II Corps, was the major culprit. Had he been a more forceful and talented commander, he might have prevented some of the losses created by the initial dispositions. Nevertheless, the commander of the

First British Army, Sir Kenneth Anderson, who was Fredendall's superior, took an active part in the battle and, as a recipient of the ULTRA intelligence reports, had far more information about German plans and dispositions than was made available to Fredendall. Though Anderson was not relieved during the campaign, he never again commanded a force in combat.[5]

Most of the defeats that occurred during the period of February 14 through February 22 were the result of placing in the path of the Germans vastly inferior American forces with orders either to hold positions or to attack, which led to their destruction. These sacrifices would have been excusable if there had been no knowledge of German plans, but such was not the case. The discussion revolves around two points—how much did Anderson know about German plans and how well did the American troops behave in view of the way they were utilized?

Winterbotham expressed regret that ULTRA did not provide a warning of the attack on Kasserine. He had always worried that commanders would place too much reliance on the reports, that is, if ULTRA did not mention an attack, then there would be no attack. The reason he gave for the lack of mention in ULTRA was that Rommel had prepared the attack in secret without informing other commanders. At the same time, however, Rommel was very obliging in providing Kesselring full information by radio about Axis forces on the Mareth line and details about his plan to attack at Medenine on March 6. With this information, intercepted by ULTRA, Montgomery was able to defeat Rommel decisively.[6]

In fact, ULTRA did provide the British with ample warning of Rommel's plan to turn his forces north. On December 16, 1942, Rommel wrote an appreciation of the position in North Africa. He saw three courses: first, to stop the Eighth Army—no point; second, to delay the Eighth Army with a small force and send most of his troops to Tunis—this move would be under heavy air attack; or third, to attack the line of communication by way of Gabes, Gafsa, Tebessa, and then to Bone. This would cut off the Allies and force them to surrender. Captured American supplies would help the logistical problem.

This memo was intercepted and distributed among British and American officers, including the II Corps. Written on the memo was an unsigned comment that Rommel did not have sufficient transport, but he "has surprised us before & may do so again." The commentator expressed fear that French troops had insufficient weapons to stop such an attack.[7]

ULTRA was functioning well in early 1943. The daily intelligence summary issued by Allied Forces Headquarters contained "sidelined" information that was not to be passed on except by permission. The intelligence presented could come only from intercepted messages; for example, the details of the tank strength of the Fifteenth Panzer Division on January 19 were passed on the same day, giving types and running condition. No other source could provide information so quickly. General Lucas K. Truscott reported reading "radio intercepts" regarding German plans before the battle.[8] On January 29, 1943, a detailed résumé of the German army was issued by Allied Forces Headquarters in North

Africa that included the German order of battle as of January 20, 1943, as reported by British intelligence sources that described the type and location of all German divisions.[9] Hitler's order of February 4, 1943, regarding the creation of new divisions and the revision of the table of organization of the infantry divisions, was passed on to the Americans in a report on March 26, 1943.[10] Both pieces of information indicate that ULTRA was functioning during that period. ULTRA was made available to Eisenhower and his immediate staff; to the commander of the U.S. Twelfth Air Force; to Anderson, commanding the British First Army; and to the British air commander. They, in turn, could pass some of the content to lower echelons, and one avenue was the "Daily Report."[11] Eisenhower and his deputy, General Mark Wayne Clark, were not too interested in ULTRA, which was handled by the chief of intelligence for the Allied Headquarters, British Brigadier E. T. Mockler-Ferryman. After Kasserine, presumably because of his mishandling of the intelligence regarding Kasserine, described as "his excessive reliance on one type of information," he was replaced by another British officer, Brigadier Kenneth W. D. Strong.[12] Later, Eisenhower singled out Strong as an outstanding staff member in North Africa and ignored the presence of Mockler-Ferryman.[13] One has the feeling that Mockler-Ferryman was made the scapegoat in the affair.[14]

The initial attack was launched by a battle group under General Heinz Ziegler, chief of staff under General Hans-Jürgen von Arnim, commander of the German Fifth Panzer Army, who was equal in position to Rommel, the commander of the German-Italian Panzer Africa Force. Both were directly subordinate in theory to the Italian Comando Supremo, but in fact were commanded by Kesselring, whose technical post was adviser to Comando Supremo. Winterbotham stated that ULTRA was reading signals between Rommel and Kesselring in February 1943.[15] For that reason, the British must have been aware of most of the planning outlined below.

Planning for the attack began on January 28, when Comando Supremo authorized von Arnim to probe the Eastern Dorsale in Tunisia, including the passes at Pichon, Fondouk, Faid, and El Guettar.[16] This action was basically defensive in nature and was accurately reported in the daily summary of the Plans and Operation Division of February 13 in Washington, which based its information on a British report of February 3. They reached the following conclusions:

1. We agree local Axis offensive operations must be expected to widen bridgehead. This likely to be defensive in character until Axis have built up forces to state when larger operations may be possible.
2. Consider only 2 armies likely in Tunisia.
   A. Von Arnim in area from Bizerta to SFAX.
   B. Rommels South from SFAX to Mareth line.
3. Consider 15 Panzer Division will have to be maintained in Mareth area. Most unlikely Rommel will denude himself of all tanks. This division will not therefore be available for operations westwards. Consider proportion at least of 10 Panzer Division must be retained in area of our 6th Armoured Division. Part of

10 Panzer Division may however well be used to clear up Ousseltia Pichon area. Operation at present likely to be confined to:

A. Attempt to clear up Ousseltia area.

B. Maintenance of present Faid position until 21 Panzer Division has been strengthened.

C. Attack on GAFSA by forces which are predominantly Italian including some 40 tanks. Probably Centauro Division believed to be in GABES area will take part.

4. Reinforcements for Rommel known to have arrived Tunis lately. These may include one or more Marsch battalions. Consider Ariete Division will not be reformed but that elements now in GABES area will be absorbed by Centauro.

5. Any exploitation of successful Axis attacks beyond general lines Gafsa, Sbeitla Pichon unlikely owing to strength of forces and supply position. Axis cannot risk at this moment to embark on operation which might mean heavy losses of men and equipment. A slight increase in enemy activity reported south and east of FAID actually referred to GAFSA instead.[17]

This same information was cabled directly to Eisenhower by Marshall on the afternoon of February 12, 1943.[18] On February 4, however, General Truscott, who apparently was reading the ULTRA intercepts at the Advanced Headquarters at Constantine, cabled Eisenhower regarding the substance of von Arnim's February 3 plan, that is, the attack at Ousseltia and Pichon.[19]

On February 2, the chief of the Imperial General Staff (CIGS) summary reported considerable motor transport movement in Pont du Fahs moving northeast away from Faid.[20] This movement reflected Axis planning on February 3, but on February 4, Rommel suggested a change in a message to Kesselring, proposing that elements of the Afrika Korps attack Gafsa through the pass at El Guettar, while forces from the Fifth Panzer Army strike at Sbeitla through the Faid pass.[21]

On February 4, Military Intelligence GHQ Middle East Forces (GHQ MEF) reported elements of the Twenty-first Panzer Division in the Faid area.[22] On February 5, the G-2 of Allied Forces HQ (Mockler-Ferryman) reported the Fifth Company of Eighth Panzer Regiment in Sened and other elements of the Fifteenth Panzer Division in Gabes. This was evidence that most of the mobile troops from the Afrika Korps had now turned north. Mockler-Ferryman refused to believe the reports, cautioning that the information should be treated with reserve.[23] The next day brought confirmation. GHQ MEF reported that the Twenty-first Panzer Division was now under the command of the Fifth Panzer Army in Tunisia and the Fifteenth Panzer Division was fifty-two kilometers northwest of Gabes on February 1.[24]

On February 5, General Vittorio Ambrosio (the Italian commander in chief) told both von Arnim and Rommel of the favorable opportunity at El Guettar, but neither German general wished to surrender armored forces to attack in that area. Kesselring supported the idea, however, and, on February 8, he issued orders for an attack through Gafsa with units of the Afrika Korps and, in the north, with elements of the Fifth Panzer Army.[25] On the following day, Kesselring flew to Tunisia to work out the details. The Tenth and Twenty-first Panzer Divisions of the Fifth Panzer Army were to attack Sidi Bou Zid between February 12 and 14, after which the Twenty-first Panzer Division was to aid Rommel in the second phase, an attack on the southern flank through Tebessa to destroy Allied supply lines. Von Arnim objected to the second phase and suggested, rather, a limited attack toward Pichon as the second phase.[26] The decision was not clear. Von Arnim, on February 8, issued a very detailed operational order to the Tenth Panzer Division designating the troops to take part and outlining their role in the attack on Sidi Bou Zid. The day of the attack was to be given later as "A tag."[27]

On February 10, Kesselring informed the German Armed Forces High Command of the plan, specifically mentioning the intent to surround the forces at Sidi Bou Zid, followed by an attack on Gafsa by the Afrika Korps with the aid of units from the Fifth Panzer Army.[28] On February 11, the plan was approved by Comando Supremo.[29] On the same day, the Tenth Panzer Division received a radio message designating February 14 as "A tag." On February 12, a message from the Twenty-first Panzer Division to the Tenth Panzer Division gave a complete order of battle of all the American troops around Sidi Bou Zid and Kasserine and detailed mimeographed orders designating the various battle groups and the plan for their employment.[30] The plan was certainly not a carefully guarded secret known only to Rommel.

How much did the Allies know and how much was passed on to the battlefield leaders? The Washington daily summary provided no information from the British subsequent to the February 3 report. The troops at Sidi Bou Zid, however, were expecting a small-scale attack on the morning of February 14. Truscott reported: "During the second week in February, intercepted radio messages indicated that the Germans were planning another attack on the Tunisian front in greater strength than their previous ones." Although the British First Army intelligence officers interpreted the information to indicate an attack around Fondouk, Truscott wrote: "So far as I could see from my access to this same intelligence, there was nothing to substantiate this alarm over the possibility of a German attack from the Fondouk area toward Maktar. I had no grounds for doubting this source of intelligence, which heretofore had been almost infallible, but there were no other factors in the situation as we knew it to support this conclusion of the intelligence sections."[31]

Truscott clearly stated that he had seen no ULTRA to reverse von Armin's February 3 plan for an attack around Fondouk. Truscott did see the steady stream of reports sent by First Army Headquarters to Eisenhower based on patrols, air reconnaissance, and French agents between February 5 and 11, all indicating movement of Germans to the Faid area and of Rommel's forces north for the attack on Gafsa. Eisenhower marked his copy of the cable log with notes on February 8 and 12, indicating his concern about German troop movements toward Faid. The CIGS summaries for February 6 through 14 provided seven items relating the concentration of Germans around Faid and Gafsa.[32] The February

3 report had noted that the Germans would remain on the defensive at Faid "until 21 Panzer Division has been strengthened." That requirement was met on February 10, according to the First Army War Diary Intelligence Summary 29 that reported the rebuilding of the Twenty-first Panzer Division to two tank battalions, three infantry battalions, and strong antitank, reconnaissance, and antiaircraft battalions.[33] The final element to move into place was the Tenth Panzer Division. The daily intelligence summary of GHQ MEF provided ULTRA information on the movement of the Tenth Panzer southward toward Faid on February 9. The same source reported the move of Panzer Grenadier Regiment Afrika and a tank battalion of the Fifteenth Panzer Division toward Gabes on February 12.[34] Major elements of all three German panzer divisions in North Africa were now concentrating opposite the American II Corps.

Eisenhower was alarmed by the reconnaissance reports, as is indicated by his annotations on the Cable Log. There was conflicting information in the cable from Marshall on February 12, containing details of the von Arnim plan that had been discarded on the eighth. The ULTRA reports and traditional sources of information clearly pointed to Faid and Gafsa.

On February 13, Eisenhower went to Fredendall's headquarters to review defensive preparations. Anderson's headquarters had warned all units that the Germans would attack on the fourteenth.[35] The II Corps intelligence officer thought that the attack would come in strength at Gafsa and perhaps at Faid, based on local reconnaissance, air reconnaissance, and prisoner of war interrogation. Anderson arrived at II Corps Headquarters late in the evening of February 13 and immediately tried to convince the II Corps intelligence officer that, despite his information, the attack would come farther north. The conference had barely ended when Anderson received a telephone call offering "additional confirmation that the enemy was about to attack in the north." General Louis-Marie Koeltz, commanding the French XIX Corps north of the Americans, also received a call late in the afternoon of February 13 that an attack in his sector, which included Pichon, "was firmly expected." In the late evening of February 13, Anderson called Eisenhower at Sbeitla to inform him that the Germans would attack the next morning in the north and that the attack in the south would be only a diversionary one.[36] All of this confusion may have been the result of an elaborate hoax perpetrated by the Germans purposely to confuse the Allies, but no proof has appeared.

Eisenhower was convinced by Anderson's interpretation. Even after being informed of the attack at Sidi Bou Zid on the morning of the fourteenth, he was so certain that it was a diversion and of little importance that he went sightseeing with General Truscott.[37]

Regardless of the attack and unit identifications, Mockler-Ferryman was convinced that it was a diversion. In the intelligence report of February 15, enemy intentions were assumed to be the capture of Pichon with flanking support from Faid. The Sidi Bou Zid and Gafsa attacks were being made "in order to distract Allied reinforcements."[38]

The false interpretation of intercepted information was used to overrule local intelligence. Wintherbotham placed the blame for the surprise on the fact that ULTRA did not mention it, and, therefore, little effort was made to gather intelligence in the traditional manner by air, patrols, interrogation, and observation. Truscott also stated that insufficient local reconnaissance was made. In fact, all of the traditional intelligence was gathered by II Corps but was overruled by Anderson. On February 13, Colonel P. M. Robinette, who commanded Combat Command B of the First Armored Division, awaiting the attack Anderson had forecast, stated that "the only evidence [of an attack in the Pichon area] he [Robinette] could see was a growing nervousness among the staff members of higher headquarters," while the II Corps intelligence officer had considerable evidence of enemy activity at Faid and El Guettar.[39]

This confused intelligence picture had an adverse impact on the dispositions ordered by Anderson. Combat Command B with over 100 tanks was held north behind Pichon, where the attack did not come. Combat Command A with fewer than 50 medium tanks was in the village of Sidi Bou Zid directly in the face of Combat Group Ziegler with over 150 German tanks including four Tiger heavy tanks. Combat Command C was in between with about 50 more medium tanks.[40] On the first day of the attack, February 14, Combat Command A was overwhelmed by the much larger German force, losing 44 tanks and other equipment, and was driven back, leaving the 168th Regimental Combat Team stranded on the hills overlooking Faid pass. On February 15, Combat Command C was ordered to attack with only one tank battalion in an attempt to save the infantry. Anderson refused to release Combat Command B or a British tank battalion that remained in reserve awaiting the attack at Pichon.[41] The weak American force was routed by the far more powerful German forces. Another 48 tanks were lost, and the Americans were driven back. The infantry was ordered to infiltrate back during the next two nights after destroying their heavy weapons and supplies.[42]

The remnants of Combat Commands A and C were still holding a line about fifteen miles behind their starting position on February 15 when Anderson gave orders for a general withdrawal along the entire southern part of the Tunisian front to take place on February 16. Anderson finally released Combat Command B to take part in the battle, and it played the major role in the withdrawal. The entire First Armored Division was ordered to a reserve position south of Tebessa, and it did not return to the battle until Combat Command B was finally called in again on February 21 against Rommel's forces. The division lost 112 medium tanks and 5 light tanks, 31 self-propelled weapons, and 80 half-tracks in the four days from February 14 to 17. The First Armored Division still had about 80 medium tanks and 80 light tanks, while the British had about 180 tanks.[43]

The Americans had fought bravely against heavy odds. The only panic occurred among some troops in the rear near Sbeitla on the night of February 16, but the front line held the Germans until ordered to withdraw the following day. After the battle, the men of the First Armored Division merely wanted new tanks, because they believed that they could defeat the Germans.[44] Most of the prisoners taken were from the 168th Regimental Combat Team, which had fought well until it ran out of rations and ammunition and was ordered to break out of the encirclement. Although some succeeded, 1,400 were captured while trying to escape.[45]

The second major blow came at Kasserine Pass itself by troops of the Afrika Korps led by Rommel. The pass was held on February 18 by a battalion of engineers and the I Battalion, Twenty-sixth Infantry. The engineers were not well-trained infantry and were not equipped with infantry heavy weapons. Though many of the engineers panicked during the afternoon of February 18 and fled, some had returned to the front line on the nineteenth. The III Battalion, Thirty-ninth Infantry, also arrived on the nineteenth with a company of Grant tanks.

Rommel attacked on the nineteenth. Permission to launch this particular attack was the subject of several radio messages between Rommel and Kesselring, and the attack was expected.[46] The Germans used the I Battalion, Eighth Panzer Regiment, Thirty-third Reconnaissance Battalion, and two battalions of the Panzer Grenadier Regiment Afrika in the attack, all first-rate, experienced troops. The Americans held well and lost only one hundred prisoners of war to the Germans.

On the twentieth, the Germans attacked again, reinforced by an Italian tank battalion and an infantry battalion, but with little success until Rommel arrived during the afternoon and threw in two more infantry battalions. By 4:30 P.M., Rommel was putting in every unit available, including elements of the Tenth Panzer Division just arriving. By nightfall, the Americans, aided by a small British detachment, had been driven back about three miles.[47] During the course of the day, the III Battalion of the Sixth Armored Infantry had been used to hold a hill north of the pass, and the half-tracks used to transport the battalion were parked at the rear of the hill. When the Germans broke through, the troops escaped, but many of the half-tracks and trucks were captured by the Germans when the drivers fled. It was this group of vehicles that Rommel stopped to examine on the twentieth and commented on in his diary. The quotation from his diary has been used out of context as proof that the Americans abandoned large amounts of equipment. Only thirty half-tracks were captured at Kasserine, and Rommel's comment was directed at the quantity and quality of American equipment issued to their troops, rather than to the quantity captured by the Germans.[48]

On the night of February 20, Rommel was discouraged. To fight through Kasserine Pass had taken two days and required every available unit. Meanwhile, the Allies brought up elements of the British Twenty-sixth Armored Brigade and Combat Command B from the First Armored Division. During the next two days, Rommel made very little headway against growing American and British forces. His only real success was against the British Twenty-sixth Armored Brigade when tanks of the Tenth Panzer Division managed to penetrate the British lines at dusk on February 21, taking 571 prisoners.[49]

Kesselring visited Rommel on the afternoon of February 22, when both agreed to abandon the attack because the Allies had moved in too many reserves. The Germans withdrew the next day, followed very slowly by the Allies.[50]

There is no doubt that the American II Corps was severely bruised between February 14 and 22. Of the 30,000 men engaged, 300 were killed, 3,000 wounded, and 3,000 captured. The corps lost 183 tanks, 194 half-tracks, 208 guns, and 512 trucks. The Germans lost only 201 killed, 536 wounded, and 252 captured. They also lost 20 tanks and 67 other vehicles.[51] The great disparity in tank losses resulted from the fact that the Germans held the field immediately after all of the major tank battles and therefore could salvage tanks with minor damage, whereas the Allied tanks with minor damage were either destroyed by their crews or captured.

The tank losses fell on the II and III Battalions of the First Armored Regiment that were hit hard on successive days at Sidi Bou Zid. Most of the prisoners were members of the 168th Infantry Regiment that was surrounded on the hills east of that village. The rest of the corps remained in fighting trim, and because of their strong resistance, Rommel was finally forced to give up the attack and withdraw.[52] Tank replacements were available, and American infantry replacements arrived at the rate of eight hundred per day, which resulted in the rapid reconstitution of the units.

During this period, the II Corps was faced with the major part of the Axis armored forces in Tunisia; only half of the Tenth Panzer Division was held back by von Arnim; and some elements of the Afrika Korps were left by Rommel on the Mareth line. What amounted to the First U.S. Armored Division, reinforced with some infantry battalions from the First and Thirty-fourth Infantry Divisions and the British Twenty-sixth Armored Brigade, stopped the equivalent of two German panzer divisions. The major American losses occurred during the first two days as a result of the faulty disposition of troops, enabling the Germans to deal with the tank battalions one at a time, facing each one with overwhelming odds.[53] One must keep in mind that the Americans were fighting some of the most experienced tank units in the German army which were equipped with the latest tanks on a scale superior to divisions on the Russian front. Even after a severe drubbing during the first two days, the Americans did not run, but withdrew skillfully, perhaps the most difficult task for a unit to perform. Rommel's military biographer writes: "The American military image has suffered unfairly as a result of Kasserine. During the battle there was much incompetence, folly and fear: but all these deficiencies had been earlier displayed by 8 Army, and to the historian what is now significant is that, in spite of them, the line held."[54] Kasserine supposedly proved that American troops were not trained well enough to fight the Germans in France in 1943, but the decision to go on to Sicily and probably to Italy had been made at Casablanca a month before.

Although the actual state of Allied knowledge and, more specifically, British knowledge of German forces and plans has not been revealed, sufficient evidence has been released to at least question the use of that intelligence and consequent manipulation of the Allied forces. Despite a certain amount of suspicion by the troops that they had not been given a fair chance at Kasserine, the morale of the Americans remained at a high level. They believed that they could defeat the Germans if provided with equal odds. A fair appraisal of the battle would lead to the same conclusion.

The impact of the battle on the delay of the second front was unfortunate. The effect was to justify the position that the Allies were not ready to tackle the unknown power of the Germans. In actual fact, the reverse was true. The Americans at Kasserine had demonstrated their ability to resist a concentrated German attack immediately after a withdrawal and before they had time to prepare defensive positions. A close look at Kasserine reveals many examples of American military skill and flexibility, such as the use of the Ninth Division artillery. When the fighting abated, the Germans surrendered the field of battle to the Americans. In most battles, he who possesses the field of battle at the end is declared the victor.

14

THE ALLIED ORDER OF BATTLE

Did the Allies have enough divisions to invade France in 1943? As has been indicated before, adequacy was always a matter of comparison. The strength of the German army in the West increased sharply from June 1943 to June 1944. There was no comparable increase in the strength of the Western Allies during the same period. If the number of divisions available to the Allies in June 1944 was considered adequate to attack the greater number of German divisions in France in 1944, then a similar number available to the Allies in 1943 should have been sufficient to face a smaller number of German divisions. Because the major contribution to the land battle would be made by the Americans, the crucial point was the time when sufficient American divisions would be ready. How many were required and how much training would they need?

Only sixty American divisions were delivered to Europe during World War II. Of these, only forty-five had entered combat by the end of 1944; eleven more entered action during the following three months. During April and May 1945, three more divisions saw combat; the last division arrived but did not see any fighting. If the sixty divisions had been trained and delivered by December 1943, this force would have been sufficient to launch a second front in 1943.

The plan for opening the second front called for only thirty-nine American divisions in the first nine months. Two divisions were to land on D-Day, plus two airborne divisions. Only three American divisions were to be attacking, and six divisions were to be holding defensive positions two months after D-Day. Six months after D-Day the plan called for twenty-four American divisions attacking and six defending. Nine months after D-Day there would have been six on the defensive and thirty-three on the offensive.[1] This plan was generally followed in 1944. Divisions needed a little more than one year's training. Therefore, the availability of ten assault divisions with two years of training and thirty divisions with one or more years of training for follow-up would have been in excess of the need of the plan.

This goal was by no means unattainable by April 1943. In January 1942, when Eisenhower prepared the ROUNDUP plan, forerunner of OVERLORD, the American army consisted of thirty-six divisions, of which fourteen infantry, two armored, and one cavalry were considered combat ready.[2] By February 1, 1942, three more infantry divisions completed their training, followed a month later by eight more infantry and another cavalry division. By April 1942, there were twenty-nine trained divisions, and thirteen were fully equipped with a combat supply of ammunition ready for shipment overseas.[3] By the end of 1942, there were seventeen divisions overseas, eight of them in Europe and Africa. Nine divisions were sent to the Pacific. During 1942, twenty-seven infantry, nine armored, and two airborne divisions were added to the thirty-seven divisions existing in December 1941, though two were lost.[4] On January 1, 1943, there were seventy-three divisions, of which thirty-five had more than a year's training.

So many divisions were available in early 1943 that the army slowed its rate of growth after the decision to launch TORCH postponed the major invasion. On October 25, 1942, a War Department memo directed the reduction of the expansion of the ground army because the early employment of a mass army was not practicable and future growth was not to be directed primarily at an invasion of Europe, "which may prove impracticable of accomplishment."[5]

During 1943, the training of armored divisions, tank battalions, tank destroyer battalions, and heavy artillery battalions was postponed. The three divisions that were to be activated in May, June, and August of 1943 were deferred to the end of 1943. Ten further divisions were deferred until 1944. Only seventeen new divisions were created during 1943, compared to thirty-seven in 1942. The decision was made in part because no divisions were going overseas as previously planned, therefore there was no housing for new divisions in the United States.[6]

The shortage of equipment, especially weapons and ammunition, which delayed training in 1941, was ended by early 1942. By March 1943, the Army Ground Forces planned to provide nondivisional units with 100 percent of their equipment within four months after they were formed and infantry divisions within six months. Ammunition was to be provided in sufficient quantities to allow every soldier to fire his weapons well enough to qualify him in their use.[7]

Rather than a shortage of trained units and equipment in 1943, the problem was a surplus. Faced with strategic decisions to delay the invasion of France, the War Department could not ship the troops overseas, and the fully trained units were clogging the camps. General McNair, chief of the Army Ground Forces, finally suggested that the rate of induction of new men into the army be reduced and that divisions be created only as needed by overseas theaters, that is, as a division was shipped, it would be replaced by a new one. McNair also requested that a pool of trained infantry replacements of 1.5 million men be created to provide replacements when losses began. The War Department reacted by cutting back on the number of divisions, but instead of creating a reserve of replacements, diverted the men into other branches of the armed services. By June 1943, the demand from overseas was not for more divisions, but for an adequate stream of infantry replacements, which were required in far larger numbers than had been anticipated.[8]

Across the board, there was a general attitude of placing the infantry divisions on a very low priority—behind the air force, which had the pick of the more skilled and intelligent men drafted; behind the French, who were receiving equipment that could have been used to form ten new American divisions; behind the Army Special Training Program that took the cream of the men available and sent them back to college to resume their studies. The infantry was at the bottom of the pile, receiving the least educated and poorest physical specimens. The navy, too, wanted prime manpower for manning its ships and creating marine divisions. The navy had first choice through the enlistment procedure, and the air force picked over the rest, both through original enlistment and also by offering drafted men the opportunity to volunteer for a better life in the air force. Of the nine million men in the armed forces in 1943, the army had only four and a half million to fight the major battles; the air force two and a half million, and the navy nearly two million. The ground forces were at a further disadvantage. They did not receive the promised quotas of even the poor quality men. By June 1943, shortages began to occur despite the delay of the schedule of unit activation.[9]

Cutbacks were made in the plans for nondivisional battalions in November 1942. The total number of combat support battalions, excluding engineers, planned for the army by the end of 1943 was reduced to 1,361. By June 30, 1943, 1,093 of these battalions had been activated. At that point, further activation practically stopped, and some of the antiaircraft and tank destroyer battalions were deactivated. From July 1943 until May 1945, only about 20 tank battalions and 100 field artillery battalions were added.

Type of battalion	Active Dec. 31, 1942	Plan of Nov. 24, 1942 for Dec. 31, 1943	Active June 30, 1943
Field artillery	142	240	212
Tank	26	38	41
Tank destroyer	80	144	106
Antiaircraft	391	781	547
Infantry	153	158	187
Total	792	1,361	1,093

By May 1945, fewer independent combat battalions (901) were in existence than in June 1943. Nondivisonal combat troops dropped from 689,000 on June 30, 1943, to only 670,000 on March 31, 1945. Divisional troops increased slightly from 1,060,000 on June 31, 1943, to 1,125,000 on March 31, 1945.[10] The army reached its peak by June 1943 and remained stable throughout the rest of the war, merely replacing losses that occurred either through new draftees or transfers from other branches. Waiting until 1944 did not make more men available for the invasion.

On June 30, 1943, there were sixty-three infantry, two cavalry, fifteen armored, and four airborne divisions, a total of eighty-four. Only six more divisions were formed during the next two years of war, and one was disassembled.[11] By April 1943, most of the forty-seven divisions formed before June 30, 1942, were trained, most of them having had a full year to organize.

A substantial American army was ready by April 1943, and additional units were completing their training at a rapid pace. The question is, what happened to the divisions? When the invasion was launched in June 1944, there were only twenty United States divisions in England. A careful examination of the dissipation of these units is very pertinent at this point. Table 15 details the story month by month, and Table 16 lists the divisions formed before December 1941. General Marshall reacted strongly to the British refusal to comply with the plan to invade Europe in 1943. When it became obvious to him during the discussions in the summer of 1942 that the British would not go along, a dramatic shift in troop assignments took place. Nor should one underestimate the personal influence of General Douglas MacArthur in this shift of policy. One often forgets that MacArthur had been Chief of Staff and a four-star general in the 1930s when Marshall was a colonel. Throughout the war, relations between the two were strained. MacArthur had no intention of having his theater in the southwest Pacific relegated to a minor sideshow despite the overall strategy of the Joint Chiefs of Staff. He had great personal magnetism and a devoted and skilled group of publicists on his staff.

The impact of American public opinion was continual and heavy. Newspapers such as the Chicago *Tribune*, which had formerly advocated isolationism, gave the Pacific war first place. America was still isolation-minded in 1941. Only the Japanese attack brought America openly into the war on Britain's side. In 1940, Roosevelt had said that American boys would not be sent into any foreign war. Military and political decisions on the distribution of troops could not ignore the public demand for revenge for the humiliation of Pearl Harbor and the rescue of the men at Bataan and Corregidor, who fought on until May 6, 1942, only six months before the invasion of North Africa was launched. How Eisenhower, who had served with the Philippine army, could calmly make plans in early 1942 to place the European theater first and divert forces across the Atlantic, while his friends were still fighting for their lives on Bataan, is a great credit to his professionalism and ability to face the hard cold fact that those men were lost and nothing could be done to save them.

The other factor influencing the dissipation of our forces was the overriding concern of the navy for Pacific involvement. The navy under Admiral King saw the Pacific as its own personal war and fought bitterly to obtain the resources to speedily defeat Japan. If this entailed the diversion of landing craft and amphibious tractors from the Atlantic, the army would simply have to accept it. King also demanded a share of the army divisions to provide garrisons for the islands and to support the marines in their task of taking Japanese-held islands.

Marshall was thus faced by three strong forces, all with powerful influence on the president—MacArthur, public opinion, and the navy—all competing for the divisions being trained for the war in Europe. Can he be blamed for being influ-

Table 15. **Formation and Overseas Movement of United States Divisions**

Date	Divisions formed	Cumulative total	Pacific	Cumulative total
1941 Dec.	see Table 16	39	Phil, 24, 25	3
1942 Jan.	Americal	40	Americal	4
Feb.	6A	41		
Mar.	77, 90, 7A, 82	45	27, 41	6
Apr.	8A	46	32	7
May	85, 93, (Phil)	47	37, (Phil)	7
Jun.	76, 79, 81	50	1 Mar	8
Jul.	80, 88, 89, 95, 9A, 10A, (2 Cav)	55	2 Mar	9
Aug.	78, 83, 91, 96, 11A, 101A/B	61	40	10
Sep.	94, 98, 102, 104, 12A, 3 Mar	67		
Oct.	84, 92, 13A	70	43	11
Nov.	99, 100, 103, 14A	74		
Dec.	86, 87	76		
1943 Jan.				
Feb.	97, 2 Cav, 11A/B	79		
Mar.	106, 20A	81		
Apr.	66, 75, 17A/B	84	7, 3 Mar	13
May	69	85		
Jun.	63, 70	87	33, 1 Cav	15
Jul.	10, 42, 71, 16A	91	6	16
Aug.	65, 13A/B, 4 Mar	94		
Sep.			4 Mar	17
Nov.				
Dec.			38	18
1944 Jan.	5 Mar?	95	93	19
Feb.			31	20
Mar.	(2 Cav)	94	77	21
Apr.			98, 11A/B	23
May				
Jun.			81	24
Jul.			96	25
Aug.	6 Mar	95		
Sep.			5 Mar	26
Oct.			6 Mar	27
Nov.				
Dec.				
1945 Jan.				
Feb.			86	28
Total		95		28

( ) indicates a division that was captured, disbanded, or moved from one theater to another.

Mediterranean	Cumulative total	Britain and France	Cumulative total
		1 Mar	1
		34	2
		5 (1 Mar)	
		1A	3
		1	4
		29	5
, 3, 34, 1A	4	(1, 34, 1A)	2
, 2A	6		
6, 82A/B	8		
5	9		
		101A/B	3
		2, 28, 3A	6
8 (1, 9, 2A)	7	1, 8, 9, 2A	10
5 (82A/B)	7	82A/B, 4A	12
		4, 30	14
Cav	8	5A, 6A	16
2 Cav)	7	79, 83, 90, 91	20
		35, 7A	22
		80	23
		94, 95	25
3, 36, 45)	4	3, 26, 36, 44, 45, 104, 9A, 17A/B	33
2	5	84, 99, 100, 102, 103, 10A, 11A, 12A	41
		75, 78, 87, 106, 8A, 14A	47
		42, 63, 66, 69, 70, 76	53
0Mtn	6	65	54
		71, 89, 13A, 16A, 20A, 13A/B	60
		97	61
	6		61

Table 16. **United States Divisions Formed before December 1941**

Division	Date of formation	Division	Date of Formation
1	May 1917	35	Dec. 1940
2	Sep. 1917	36	Nov. 1940
3	Nov. 1917	37	Oct. 1940
4	Jun. 1940	38	Jan. 1941
5	Oct. 1939	40	Mar. 1941
6	Oct. 1939	41	Sep. 1940
7	July 1940	43	Feb. 1941
8	July 1940	44	Sep. 1940
9	Aug. 1940	45	Sep. 1940
24	Feb. 1921	1 Cav	Sep. 1921
25	Oct. 1941	2 Cav	Apr. 1941
26	Jan. 1941	1 Armd	July 1940
27	Oct. 1940	2 Armd	July 1940
28	Feb. 1941	3 Armd	Apr. 1941
29	Feb. 1941	4 Armd	Apr. 1941
30	Sep. 1940	5 Armd	Oct. 1941
31	Nov. 1940	1 Marine	pre- 1941
32	Oct. 1940	2 Marine	Feb. 1941
33	Mar. 1941	Phil.	pre- 1941
34	Feb. 1941		

enced by these pressures when the British, for whose aid these forces were designed, were reluctant to use them?

When the war broke out, three divisions were already in the Pacific, the Philippine Division on Luzon and the Twenty-fourth and Twenty-fifth in Hawaii. In January 1942, Task Force 6814, which became the Americal Division, was sent to New Caledonia, under the pressure of maintaining our lines of communication with Australia. To stabilize our position in the Pacific, the Twenty-seventh Division went to Hawaii in March, followed by the Forty-first and Thirty-second Divisions to Australia in March and April. In addition, many smaller units were sent to occupy the islands and bases from one end of the Pacific to the other. In May, the Thirty-seventh Division was sent to the Fiji Islands, and in June, the First Marine Division went to the South Pacific. The defensive posture of the Pacific was considered fairly secure with three divisions in Hawaii, one at New Caledonia, one at Fiji, one in New Zealand, and two in Australia, along with the Australian army. In May, an attempt by the Japanese to take Port Moresby was thwarted at the Battle of Coral Sea, and the Battle of Midway, on June 4, 1942, secured American naval supremacy in the mid-Pacific.

With the Pacific stabilized, Marshall should have been pouring divisions across the Atlantic in midsummer. Instead, there was limited activity. The Thirty-fourth Division went to Northern Ireland in January 1942, and the Fifth replaced the First Marines in Iceland in March and April. The First Armored

Divisions went to Britain on May 11, followed by the First Infantry Division on August 7, and then the tide turned when the decision was made to divert our energies into the North African venture. Instead of continuing the buildup in England, Marshall sent the troops the other way. The Fortieth Division was added to three others already in Hawaii in August, and the Forty-third was sent to New Zealand in October.[12] The Twenty-ninth, which sailed on October 5, was the only American division to go to the British Isles for the remainder of the year. The Third Division, the Second Armored, and the Ninth Infantry Division went directly to North Africa in October and December. By the end of 1942, there were six American divisions in Africa (First, Third, Ninth, Thirty-fourth, First Armored, and Second Armored), the Fifth in Iceland, and the Twenty-ninth in Ireland. There were nine army divisions in the Pacific (Twenty-fourth, Twenty-fifth, Twenty-seventh, Thirty-second, Thirty-seventh, Fortieth, Forty-first, Forty-third, and Americal) plus two marine divisions (First and Second). This distribution of forces clearly indicated that all hope for a second front in 1943 had been abandoned in July 1942. This was a policy decision not dictated by need for the troops in the Pacific; very little use was made of the troops sent to the Pacific until 1944. Of the eleven divisions available in the Pacific in 1942, the Thirty-second was heavily engaged in New Guinea attacking Buna on the north coast of New Guinea, joined later by the Forty-first. The Americal and the Twenty-fifth Divisions saw action, along with the First and Second Marines, at Guadalcanal beginning in October 1942. The remaining five divisions (Twenty-fourth, Twenty-seventh, Thirty-seventh, Fortieth, and Forty-third) took very little part in the war until 1944. Despite their long months overseas, they had short periods of combat. The total casualties suffered by these five divisions ranged from three to seven thousand compared to twenty-one thousand suffered by the First Division, seventeen thousand by the Second, and twenty-six thousand by the Third in Europe.

The Australians had taken over most of the fighting in New Guinea in 1943. The Forty-third was clearing up Guadalcanal after the Japanese left in January, and elements took the small Russell Islands without a fight in February. In June, the Forty-third and Thirty-seventh, later reinforced by the Twenty-fifth Division, invaded New Georgia, held by about ten thousand Japanese, and cleared it by August. By October, the Central Solomons were cleared with losses of only a thousand Americans killed (about the same number killed within a few days at Tarawa)—rather light losses for six months of fighting by three divisions.

Though most of the troops already in the Pacific were marking time, shipments there jumped from twelve thousand in August 1942 to twenty-two thousand in September and twenty-nine thousand in October, and then dropped to an average of about eighteen thousand per month until April 1943. Seven additional divisions were sent during 1943. The Seventh Division was used to clear out Kiska and Attu and then sent to Hawaii. In April 1943, the Third Marine Division arrived in the Pacific. In June and July, the Thirty-third, First Cavalry, and Sixth Divisions were sent to MacArthur. In September, the Fourth Marine Division was ready, and in December the Thirty-eighth went to the Pacific. A total of eighteen divisions were in the Pacific in December 1943, yet very little action took place.

The first major attack conducted in the Pacific by American troops in 1943 was the attack on Bougainville on October 27, 1943, by the Third Marines and the Thirty-seventh Division against forty thousand Japanese. In December, the First Marines and the Thirty-second Division attacked New Britain against fifteen thousand Japanese. There were other regimental-size actions by United States troops, but nothing really happened until the end of October. Yet seventeen divisions were there by then—four marine divisions, four regular army divisions, and nine National Guard divisions or divisions with National Guard units.

Shipment of these divisions to the Pacific was costly. Because of the distances involved and the lack of unloading facilities, double the amount of shipping was needed to transfer a division to the Pacific than to Europe. Far more supplies were needed to maintain them because good bases were not available. With the shipping diverted to send nine unneeded divisions (Fortieth, Forty-third, Seventh, Third Marine, Thirty-third, First Cavalry, Sixth, Fourth Marine, and Thirty-eighth) to the Pacific, those sent from the time the Japanese went on the defensive in July 1942 until the end of 1943, probably eighteeen divisions could have been sent to England, at least fourteen of them by July 1943. Of the nine divisions considered unneeded, only two (Forty-third and Third Marines) were used during 1943, so that operations in the Pacific probably could have proceeded at the same level without them.

The number of divisions sent to Europe was limited only by the decisions of the president and the War Department. There was no shortage of troop carriers. Ships were available for more men than were actually sent. The amount of cargo space was also growing. The average shipment of cargo from army ports grew steadily from January 1942 to March 1943. The average for the last six months of 1942 was over 500,000 tons per month. In the first quarter of 1943, the average amount sent to Europe had increased to over 810,000 tons per month.[13] After BOLERO (the buildup of American forces in Britain) was abandoned in July 1942, surplus shipping was available in New York City, according to Lieutenant General Frederick E. Morgan. This was verified by the actual shipping charts.

In August 1942, 102,000 men were shipped to England and 19,000 elsewhere. In October, 100,000 were shipped but of these 33,000 went to North Africa and only 16,000 to England. Large numbers continued to go to North Africa, while a low point of only 680 men were shipped to England in March 1943. On March 27, 1943, the Joint Chiefs of Staff radically altered the 1943 plan for troop movement at the expense of the buildup for the invasion. In the last nine months of 1943, the revised plan called for shipment of 800,000 men to England, instead of 900,000 in the earlier plan; nearly 300,000 to the Pacific instead of 62,000; and 150,000 to North Africa instead of 116,000. These changes reflected more diversion from the major point of decision, but at least the troops began to move. The rate of shipment to all destinations jumped in one month from 73,000 in

March 1943 to 155,000 in April and continued to increase until the final quarter of 1943, when nearly 600,000 men were shipped in three months. During the last three quarters, North Africa received 300,000 (more than double the approved plan); the Pacific received its planned 300,000, and England received only 700,000 (100,000 short).[14]

Regardless of the massive diversion of American troops to the Pacific, there were still considerable numbers available in Europe for the invasion force in 1943. In addition to the eight divisions shipped by December 1942, five more were sent to the Mediterranean (Thirty-sixth, Forty-fifth, Eighty-second Airborne, Eighty-eighth, and Eighty-fifth); four were shipped back from the Mediterranean to England (First, Ninth, Second Armored, Eighty-second Airborne). Six divisions were sent directly to Britain (101st Airborne, Second, Twenty-eighth, Third Armored, Eighth, Fourth Armored). A glance at Table 15 reveals an erratic pattern of shipment, indicating that troop movements took place by choice, not by the availability of shipping. For example, no divisions were shipped between January and March 1943, yet four were shipped in April, then one in May, two in June, one in July, one in August, and four in September. The United States could have provided with ease sixteen divisions for a landing in April 1943 by diverting four of the Pacific-bound divisions (Seventh, Thirty-third, First Cavalry, and Sixth) and by speeding up the shipment of the Forty-fifth and 101st Airborne.

To the American divisions could have been added in 1943 a much larger British contingent than was available in 1944. Determining the size of the British army and its fighting capability is almost as complex as defining German capabilities. The quality and fitness of British divisions varied. At the bottom of the scale were the county divisions that had been formed in 1940 from Home Guard and other units to provide a static coastal defense force. During 1942, these divisions were being phased out, although the Home Guard continued to provide a semblance of coast watchers for a much reduced threat of German raids. Next came the lower-establishment divisions that were also used for coastal defense with fewer service troops. Some of the lower-establishment divisions were reinforced to first-line units later on; others became training divisions.

Disregarding the defensive forces, the British Home Forces were formidable in 1942 and 1943. In January 1942, there were thirty-nine divisions in the United Kingdom, seven armored, fifteen active infantry, nine lower establishment, one airborne, one marine, three Canadian infantry, two Canadian armored, and one Polish armored. In addition to the 2,250,000 men in the army, there were 1,500,000 in the Home Guard. Of the thirty-two British army divisions, Brooke stated that one-third were performing beach defense and were without motor transport. Of these, nine were lower-establishment divisions. The other twenty-three (seven armored, one airborne, and fifteen infantry) had their motor transport. Of all these divisions, most of which had been organized for a year or more, Brooke considered that only six were equipped to fight the Germans and that only two were able to proceed immediately overseas. Yet seven divisions plus the newly formed Seventy-eighth Division were sent overseas during the next twelve months.[15] One questions the criteria that Brooke was using.

Equipment was not a major problem. The shipment of 2,250 tanks and 1,800 Bren gun carriers to the Russians by June 1942 slowed the formation of the armored divisions, and the shipment of forty to fifty thousand replacements and reinforcements overseas each month was a drain on manpower.[16] But during 1942, the only major shortages in equipment were in weapons that had recently been added to the tables of equipment, the 40mm antiaircraft guns and the six-pounder antitank guns. All shortages were to be made up by January 1943. Even the Home Guard was being given Sten guns and increased supplies of ammunition for their American rifles.[17] By the end of 1942, the tank shortage was remedied by American sources. The shipment of men overseas included probably only about ten thousand replacements; the rest were new units being sent away from the British Isles—a further dispersal of the troops that should have been gathering for the cross-channel attack.

In fact, Brooke was shipping more units than were required and fewer replacements. A rifleman could be trained in six months, but it took about a year to form a division. Yet, much to Churchill's dismay, the Forty-fourth Infantry Division and the Eighth Armored Division were sent to North Africa in 1942 only to be broken up in January 1943 to provide replacements. After years of training, these divisions were dismantled, having done very little fighting.[18] The formation of British divisions and the manner in which they were scattered in 1942 are detailed in Tables 17 and 18.

By May 1942, the War Office projected the British contribution to a second front in April 1943 as follows: ten British infantry divisions, each with an attached tank brigade; eight British armored divisions; two Canadian armored divisions; three Canadian infantry divisions; one Polish armored division; one Allied infantry division (Czech, Belgian, Dutch, and Norwegian); and one or two British airborne divisions; for a total of twenty-six or twenty-seven divisions (fourteen infantry, eleven armored, one or two airborne). The War Office believed that sufficient service units could be provided by the spring of 1943 through the conversion of infantry units that would eliminate two British infantry divisions. A total of 939,000 men would be required for the invasion force, 775,000 British, 134,000 Canadian, and 30,000 other Allies. The British already had 848,000 soldiers in the Home Defense Field Army in May 1942.[19]

A month later, a plan to reorganize the field force in the United Kingdom included the reduction of the armored division to one armored brigade and one infantry brigade, while the new infantry divisions were to have two infantry brigades and one tank brigade. At the end of the reorganization, the field force would have the eight armored divisions and ten infantry divisions planned for the April 1943 invasion force.[20]

The invasion force was organized in July 1942 as follows: British First Army: V Corps (Fourth and Seventy-eighth Divisions), XII Corps (First, Forty-third, and Forty-sixth Divisions), IX Corps (Sixth Armored and Ninth Armored Divisions); British Second Army: II Corps (Third and Fifty-third Divisions), I Corps (Eleventh Armored and Guard Armored Divisions); Canadian army: I Canadian Corps (First, Second, and Third Canadian Divisions), II Canadian Corps (Fourth and Fifth Canadian Armored Divisions); Headquarters Reserve: Forty-second Armored, Seventy-ninth Armored, First Airborne, Fifty-second Divisions, and two airborne brigades; reserve in the United Kingdom: Eightieth Armored Division and three armored brigades, plus the Sixty-first, Forty-ninth, and Fifty-ninth Divisions; lower-establishment divisions (Fifteenth, Thirty-eighth, Forty-fifth, Forty-seventh, Forty-eighth, Fifty-fourth, Fifty-fifth, Seventy-sixth, and Seventy-seventh). The armored divisions were to be equipped with Cromwells and Crusaders with a reserve of 105 percent, that is, for each tank assigned to a unit, there would be an additional tank in reserve to replace losses. The tank brigades would have Churchills, but no Churchill reserves would be available by April 1943.

Brooke believed that there were sufficient armored, infantry, artillery, and engineer units available in July 1942 to carry out the plan, but that some service units still had to be formed.[21]

After the decision was made to send the First British Army to North Africa on July 24, the size of the potential attacking force was reduced. In late July, however, Lord Cherwell informed Churchill that the British expeditionary force for April 1943 could contain seven infantry divisions, five armored divisions, one airborne division, two armored brigades, four tank brigades, and four separate infantry brigades. In addition, nine lower-establishment divisions would remain in Britain.[22]

In August 1942, the forces actually in the United Kingdom were in excess of the planned invasion force in some respects. There were five additional infantry divisions, an extra armored brigade, and eight extra infantry brigades. Not included in the July plan, but available in Britain in August 1942, were five Canadian divisions, the Polish armored division, four Allied brigades, and two American divisions. A total of thirty-four divisions and twenty-five brigades were available, most if not all very close to or over authorized strength with a year or more of training.[23]

The dispersal of the British forces picked up momentum after August. During 1943, additional British divisions were sent to North Africa, Sicily, and Italy, even though in December 1942 the British already had twenty-three of their own or their Allies in the Mediterranean area, far more than were needed to hold North Africa.

According to Churchill, on April 30, 1943, the British had thirty-eight British and Allied divisions overseas and twenty-seven in the British Isles (nineteen active, four home defense divisions, and four training divisions) that supplied replacements for both the army at home and overseas. Despite the fact that three British divisions and four American divisions were actually brought back in 1944, Churchill wrote to Stalin on March 11, 1943, that "there is no physical

Table 17. Movement of British and Allied Divisions

Date	Britain and France	Cumulative total	Mediterranean	Cumulative total	Pacific	Cumulative total	Africa
1942 Jan.	see Table 18	39	see Table 18	16	see Table 18	24	12Af
Feb.					(9 Ind, 11 Ind 8 Aus, 18)		
Mar.	(5)	38	(7 Aus)	15	26 Ind	21	
Apr.			(70)	14	5, 7 Aus	23	
May	78	39	(2 SA)	13	70	24	
Jun.	(2, 51)	37	51	14	2, 32 Ind A, 36 Ind. 43 Ind A	28	
Jul.	(8A, 44)	35	8A, 44	16	12 Ind	29	
Aug.			5	17	(5)	28	
Nov.	(6A, 56, 78)	32	6A, 56, 78, 2 FM 3Alg, 4 FMM	23			
1943 Jan.	(46) 80	32	46 (9 Aus, 8A, 44)	21	9 Aus, 2 Ind	30	11 EAf
Feb.			1 FI	22			
Mar.	(1, 4)	30	1, 4, 2 Ind, 3P, 5P, 12 Ind	28	(2 Ind, 12 Ind)	28	81 WAf
Apr.	(1A/B)	29	1A/B (5 Ind)	28	5 Ind	29	(12 Af)
May	6A/B	30	2 FA	29			

Jun.	(1 Can)	29	1 Can	30	11 EAf	30	(11 EAf)
Aug.					81 WAf	31	(81 WAf)
Sep.			1 FA, 5 FA, 9 FC	33	3 Ind	32	
Oct.	(42A, 5 Can A)	27	5 Can A	34	(70)	31	
Nov.	50	28	(50)	33			
Dec.	51, 1A/B (54)	29	(51, 1A/B)	31			
1944 Jan.	(RM) 7A	29	(7 A)	30			
Apr.	2 FA	30	(2 FA)	29			
Jun.			(10 A)	28			
Jul.	(9A)	29			82 WAf	32	(82 WAf)
Aug.	1 FI, 2 FM, 3Alg, 4 FMM, 9 FC, 1 FA, 2 FA	36	(1 FI, 2 FM, 3Alg, 4 FMM, 9 FC, 1 FA, 2 FA)	21			
Oct.	(59)	35	(5)	20			
1945 Mar.	5	36					
Total		36		20		32	0

( ) indicates a division was captured, disbanded or moved to another theater.

A—Armored	Aus—Australian	FA—French Armored
A/B—Airborne	Ind—Indian	FI—French Infantry
RM—Royal Marine	AF—African	FM—French Moroccan
Can—Canadian	SA—South African	FMM—French Moroccan Mountain
Can A—Canadian Armored	EAf—East African	FC—French Colonial
P—Polish	WAf—West African	Alg—Algerian

Table 18. Disposition of British and Allied Divisions

United Kingdom, January 1, 1942

Unit	Date	Destination or disposition
1st Airborne	Apr. 43	Mediterranean
Royal Marine	Jan. 44?	Disbanded to form landing craft crews
Guard Armored	Jun. 44	France
6th Armored	Nov. 42	Mediterranean
8th Armored	Jul. 42	Mediterranean
9th Armored	Jul. 44	Disbanded
11th Armored	Jun. 44	France
42d Armored	Oct. 43	Disbanded
79th Armored	Jun. 44	France
1st Infantry	Mar. 43	Mediterranean
2d Infantry	Jun. 42	India
3d Infantry	Jun. 44	France
4th Infantry	Mar. 43	Mediterranean
5th Infantry	Mar. 42	India
15th Infantry	Jun. 44	France
38th Infantry		lower establishment
43d Infantry	Jun. 44	France
44th Infantry	Jul. 42	Mediterranean, then disbanded
45th Infantry		lower establishment
46th Infantry	Jan. 43	Mediterranean
47th Infantry		lower establishment
48th Infantry		lower establishment
49th Infantry	Jun. 44	France
51st Infantry	Jun. 42	Mediterranean
52d Infantry	Oct. 44	France
53d Infantry	Jun. 44	France
54th Infantry	Dec. 43	Disbanded, was lower establishment
55th Infantry		lower establishment, May 44 raised to full division
56th Infantry	Nov. 42	Mediterranean
59th Infantry	Jun. 44	France, Oct. 44 disbanded
61st Infantry		
76th Infantry		lower establishment
77th Infantry		lower establishment

New Divisions after January 1942

Unit	Date	Destination or disposition
78th Infantry	May 42	formed, sent to Mediterranean Nov. 42
80th Infantry	Jan. 43	formed
6th Airborne	May 43	formed, Jun. 44 France

Allied Divisions

Unit	Date	Destination or disposition
1st Canadian Infantry	Jun. 43	Mediterranean
2d Canadian Infantry	Jul. 44	France

United Kingdom, January 1, 1942

Unit	Date	Destination or disposition
3d Canadian Infantry	Jun. 44	France
4th Canadian Armored	Aug. 44	France
5th Canadian Armored	Oct. 43	Mediterranean
1st Polish Armored	Aug. 44	France

Returned Divisions

50th Infantry	Nov. 43	from Mediterranean Jun. 44 France
51st Infantry	Dec. 43	from Mediterranean Jun. 44 France
7th Armored	Jan. 44	from Mediterranean Jun. 44 France
1st Airborne	Dec. 43	from Mediterranean Sep. 44 Holland
2d French Armored	Apr. 44	from Mediterranean Jun. 44 France

Mediterranean and Middle East, January 1942

1st Armored		
7th Armored	Jan. 44	Britain
10th Armored	Jun. 44	disbanded
50th Infantry	Nov. 43	Britain
70th Infantry	Apr. 42	India
1st South African		
2d South African	May 42	Captured
2d New Zealand		
7th Australian	Mar. 42	Pacific
9th Australian	Jan. 43	Pacific
4th Indian		
5th Indian	Apr. 43	India
6th Indian		
8th Indian		
10th Indian		
31st Indian Armored		
1st French Infantry	Aug. 44	to France

New Divisions after January 1942

8th Armored	Jul. 42	from Britain, disbanded Jan. 43
44th Infantry	Jul. 42	from Britain, disbanded Jan. 43
5th Infantry	Aug. 42	from Pacific to Germany Mar. 45
51st Infantry	Aug. 42	from Britain, Dec. 43 to Britain
6th Armored	Nov. 42	from Britain
56th Infantry	Nov. 42	from Britain
78th Infantry	Nov. 42	from Britain
2d French Moroccan	Nov. 42	from the Vichy French Army, Aug. 44 France
3d French Algerian	Nov. 42	from the Vichy French Army, Aug. 44 France
4th Fr. Moroccan Mountain	Nov. 42	from the Vichy French Army, Aug. 44 France
46th British Infantry	Jan. 43	from Britain

continued

Mediterranean and Middle East, New Divisions after January 1942 (*continued*)

Unit	Date	Destination or disposition
1st French Infantry	Feb. 43	formed from Free French Units, Aug. 44 France
1st British Infantry	Mar. 43	from Britain
4th British Infantry	Mar. 43	from Britain
2d Indian Infantry	Mar. 43	from India
12th Indian Infantry	Mar. 43	from India
3d Polish Infantry	Mar. 43	completed training
5th Polish Infantry	Mar. 43	completed training
1st British Airborne	Apr. 43	from Britain, Dec. 43 to Britain
2d French Armored	May 43	completed training, Apr. 44 to Britain
1st Canadian Infantry	Jul. 43	from Britain
1st French Armored	Sep. 43	completed training, Aug. 44 to France
5th French Armored	Sep. 43	completed training, Aug. 44 to France
9th French Colonial	Sep. 43	completed training, Aug. 44 to France
3d French Armored		lower establishment
7th Algerian		lower establishment
8th Algerian		lower establishment, Jan. 44 disbanded
10th Colonial		lower establishment, Jan. 44 disbanded
5th Canadian Armored	Nov. 43	from Britain

Pacific, January 1942

Unit	Date	Destination or disposition
(India)		
7th Indian		
14th Indian		
17th Indian		
19th Indian		
20th Indian		
23d Indian		
25th Indian		
34th Indian		
39th Indian/1st Burma		
(Malaya)		
8th Australian	Feb. 42	captured
18th British Infantry	Feb. 42	captured
9th Indian	Feb. 42	captured
11th Indian	Feb. 42	captured
(Australia)		
1st Aus. Armored		
1st Aus. Infantry	Jun. 44	becomes training division
1st Aus. Motorized	Sep. 42	becomes armored division
2d Aus. Infantry		
2d Aus. Motorized		
3d Aus. Infantry		

continued

(Table 18, continued)

Pacific, January 1942 *(continued)*		
Unit	Date	Destination or disposition
4th Aus. Infantry		
5th Aus. Infantry		
6th Aus. Infantry	Mar. 42	Ceylon
10th Aus. Infantry		
11th Aus. Infantry		
Divisions after January 1942		
(India)		
2d British Infantry	Jun. 42	from Britain
5th British Infantry	May 42	from Britain, Aug. 42 to Mediterranean
70th British Infantry	Apr. 42	from Mediterranean, Oct. 43 disbanded
26th Indian	Feb. 42	formed
32d Indian Armored	Jun. 42	formed
36th Indian	Jun. 42	formed
43d Indian Armored	Jun. 42	formed
2d Indian	Jan. 43	formed, Mar. 43 to Mediterranean
3d Indian	Sep. 43	formed
12th Indian	Jul. 42	formed ?, Mar. 43 to Mediterranean
(Australia)		
7th Australian Infantry	Mar. 42	from India
9th Australian Infantry	Feb. 43	from Mediterranean
Africa		
12th African	Nov. 40	formed, Apr. 43 disbanded
11th East African	Feb. 43	formed, Jun. 43 to India
81st West African	Mar. 43	formed, Aug. 43 to India
82d West African	Aug. 43	formed, Jul. 44 to India

possibility of moving it [the army in North Africa] back by sea to the British Islands.'' The British had the equivalent of twenty-six British and Allied (exclusive of the American) divisions in the Mediterranean area by the summer of 1943.[24] Only three were scheduled to return to England; the other twenty-three were relegated to garrison duty or embroiled in the Sicilian and Italian campaigns.

There was no insurmountable reason why the bulk of the troops in the Mediterranean could not have been returned to England to take part in the second front. With the troops already in Britain, a total of twenty-six divisions would have been ready. Britain's ability to provide replacements in 1943 for twenty-six divisions in a prolonged battle of attrition was not likely, but then again twelve months of battles such as the Sangro River and Monte Cassino in Italy would not have reduced the supply of British manpower to the low levels of 1944.

The French army was a force to be considered in any plans for an invasion of their homeland. In November 1942, along with the British and Americans, there were three French divisions fighting in Tunisia still using obsolete French small arms. Initially, Eisenhower had no confidence in the French troops, but by the end of November 1942, he thought that they could be relied on and urged that they be given better equipment, at which time the Allies began to supply them with American equipment.

In late 1942, the French had projected a plan to train and equip eight infantry divisions and two armored divisions at the rate of one per month after the Germans were driven from Tunisia. There were six Vichy French infantry divisions and two mechanized brigades in North Africa on which to base this organization. Eisenhower had less enthusiasm for this long-range plan than for the immediate improvement of the three divisions on the front.

In January 1943, the plan had been altered to include three armored divisions along with the eight infantry divisions and other minor units. The problem was obtaining the needed equipment. If supplies were sent to the French, American divisions training in the United States would be deprived. The total requirement was calculated at 325 shiploads. This was a maximum estimate based on the highest ration of support. Eleven American divisions, including men, supplies for sixty days, and all service and support units, would have taken only 332 ships!

A second look at the exaggerated requirements brought about a compromise. Only 150,000 tons of equipment were needed for two infantry divisions, two armored regiments, three tank destroyer battalions, three reconnaissance battalions, and twelve antiaircraft battalions. A special convoy, numbered UGS 6½, arrived in April 1943, with over seven thousand vehicles and equipment for the units according to standard American tables, including two units of fire, thirty-day replacements of major items, and a six-month supply of spare parts. The equipment went to the three divisions in action in Tunisia, the Second Moroccan Infantry Division, the Third Algerian Infantry Division, and the Fourth Moroccan Mountain Division. Rather than sending the equipment to North Africa, the Americans could have given the equipment already there to the French, moved the American II Corps (three infantry and one armored divisions) to Britain without equipment, and sent the new material to Britain.

The French divisions were very similar to American ones, with three infantry regiments, four field artillery battalions, a reconnaissance battalion, and an antiaircraft battalion. The major difference was that the French were not given M1 rifles, which were still in short supply. Instead, the French received the M1917 and M1903 rifles left over from World War I. The supply of M1917s ran short and were taken from the British Home Guard, who had received them in 1940. This was somewhat of a relief, as the American rifles looked similar to the British P14 rifle but took different ammunition. Each French rifle squad was given a Thompson submachine gun in place of the Browning automatic rifle. The net result was that the three French first-line divisions were reasonably well equipped by May 1943. The remainder of the French infantry divisions were using the older French rifles or captured German and Italian rifles. The British had organized the First Free French Motorized Division, which was still equipped along British lines in May 1943. The LeClerc Column that had come from Lake Chad in 1943 formed the French Second Armored Division. By September 1943, the French army had the First Infantry Division with British equipment, the Second Moroccan, Third Algerian, Fourth Moroccan Mountain, Ninth Colonial, First Armored, Second Armored, and Fifth Armored Divisions, all re-equipped with American weapons—a total of eight first-class divisions. In addition, the Eighth Algerian, Tenth Colonial, Seventh Algerian, and Third Armored were equipped with either older French weapons or captured weapons.

Had the British been willing to go on the defensive in the Mediterranean, six Indian divisions and the four poorly equipped French divisions would have provided ample security and tied down the Italian army and some German divisions. Roosevelt believed that three hundred thousand men would have been sufficient to maintain security in North Africa after the fighting ended in 1943.[25] They would have freed up to twenty-two British, French, Canadian, New Zealand, and Polish divisions for use in France. Though Italy would have remained in the war, her divisions had already been called home from many of their occupation duties. The complete failure of the Italians in North Africa does not indicate that the Germans would have entrusted them with any significant role, and some German divisions would have been held in the Mediterranean.

Therefore, the Allies could have gathered at least sixty divisions in early 1943—sixteen American, twenty-six British, eight French, three Polish, five Canadian, one New Zealand, and one Dutch-Belgian. Against these, the Germans would have mustered in May six trained mobile, nineteen static, and twenty reduced divisions with less than four months' training. In July, the Germans had thirteen mobile divisions. Of course, the Germans could have found a few more divisions in Norway, Denmark, the Balkans, and perhaps even in Russia, but matters were not going so well in the other theaters. At the same time, the United States would have been bringing in divisions from the vast pool in America. The Americans did deliver two or more divisions per month to the United Kingdom in 1944, while maintaining a flow of replacement and additional divisions to Italy and to the Pacific. The odds for a successful invasion would have been far better in 1943 than in 1944. The fact of clear Allied superiority in 1943 is unalterable. Even if the number of available Germans had been doubled and their divisions had been equal to the Allies (which was not the case), the odds were still in favor of the Allies. Even if the German buildup had been much faster than it actually was by the end of the year, these forces would have been drawn from the South, and the Allies could have brought additional divisions from the South as well. Contrarily, in June 1944, there were only nineteen American and seventeen British, plus a French and a Polish division available for the invasion. The heavy commitment of British forces in Italy and the Middle East had reduced the potential considerably. From the force of British and Canadian divisions in England in January 1943, five British divisions were sent overseas (Forty-sixth, First, Fourth, First Airborne, Fifty-sixth); two Canadian divisions were sent to Italy (First Canadian and Fifth Canadian Armored); two British armored divisions (Forty-second Armored and Seventy-ninth Armored) were converted into landing craft crews (along with the British Marine Division) or equipped with special landing tanks; one infantry division was disbanded (Fifty-fourth); and two divisions were not considered for use in France (Ninth Armored and Sixty-first) because of lack of replacements. The only gain was the Sixth Airborne formed in May 1943. In June 1944, the Allies with thirty-eight divisions were able to sweep to the Rhine against twenty-seven mobile German divisions that were reinforced by other elements to make a total of about thirty-five divisions to resist the invasion. If the risk was acceptable at odds of thirty-eight to thirty-five in June 1944, why were the odds of sixty to six considered impossible in May 1943—or even sixty to nine in September 1943?

15

THE GERMAN ORDER OF BATTLE

While the Allies pondered the question of what to do with the tremendous forces at their disposal in 1943, Germany's strength was at a low ebb. A series of military catastrophies began in September 1942 that left the German army at one of its weakest stages by the spring of 1943. In Russia, North Africa, and the Balkans and in the air, Germany suffered one defeat after another. Strenuous efforts to compensate for these losses of men and equipment resulted in only marginal success until late in 1943 and in 1944.

German military preponderance in Europe extended from September 1939 to December 1941, when the Russians launched their winter offensive. The reduction in power began in the West after the conquest of France in 1940. German divisions were scattered among the towns of France, refitting and resting. Some eighteen divisions were furloughed; the men were discharged and sent home as being unnecessary for the conquest of Great Britain. Rather than infantry, the Germans needed control of the skies over southern England as an essential prerequisite to invade Britain. Without a sufficient navy, the Germans had to rely on air power to clear the channel of the Royal Navy. When the Luftwaffe failed to gain control of the air, Hitler abandoned the cross-channel attack and, in late 1940, announced his decision to attack Russia. All first-class divisions were gradually drained away to the East. A weak defensive force was left on the coast. In November 1940, nineteen divisions were formed to occupy France and guard the Atlantic Coast. Lacking mobility and working with captured equipment, these substandard units were considered sufficient to protect the shore against any immediate British threat, while Hitler turned his attention to the East.

By June 1941, only thirty-nine divisions were left in the West. Chart 1 makes more graphic the movements of all German divisions assigned to the West during the period June 1941 to June 1944. Divisions assigned to the West were either newly formed or being rebuilt so that few had any combat value until four months after they arrived. A more conservative approach would be to consider divisions combat ready after the eight months that the German author Burkhart Mueller-Hillebrand considered necessary to work up a division or the twelve months that General McNair considered necessary to create American units from untrained recruits.[1]

The groups are described more fully later in this chapter. Group C consisted of sixteen infantry divisions and one panzer division stationed in France in June

CHART 1. German Divisions in the West, June 1941–June 1944

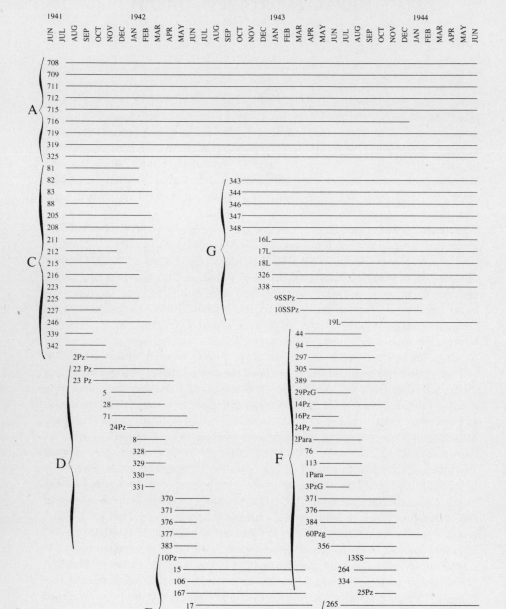

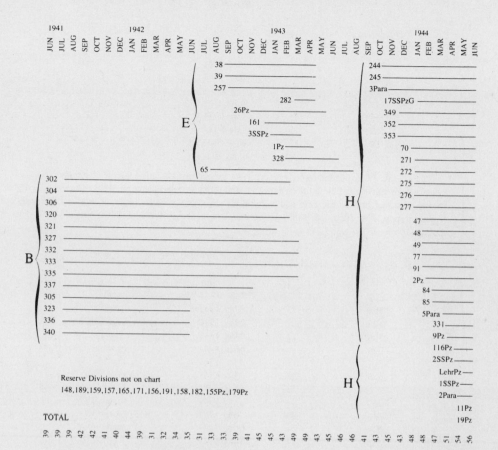

Reserve Divisions not on chart
148,189,159,157,165,171,156,191,158,182,155Pz,179Pz

TOTAL

All of the German divisions that served in the West from June 1941 until June 1944, can be divided into eight groups depending on the time they were present. In essence, Groups A, B, and C were present in June 1941. Group D began to arrive in September 1941 and left by July 1942. Group C left by February 1942. Group E began to arrive April 1942, and most units were gone by April 1943 along with Group B. Group F arrived in February 1943 and left by October 1943. Group G began to arrive in October 1942 and Group H in June 1943. Groups A, G, and H were still in France in June 1944, with a few exceptions.

Each division and its condition are described below. German infantry divisions were established in "waves" of varying numbers of divisions organized with the same table of organization and composition. Static or occupation divisions were not formed in waves in some instances. Other divisions for which no wave is indicated were generally being refitted according to full organization tables. I have attempted to simplify an exceedingly complex series of events, and minor inaccuracies are certain to exist, although the general outlines are correct.

EXPLANATION OF GERMAN DIVISIONAL GROUPS
(See Chart 1)
GROUP A

Division	Wave	Arrived	Departed
708	15	June 1941	
709	15	June 1941	
711	15	June 1941	
712	15	July 1941	
715	15	July 1941	January 1944
716	15	July 1941	
719	15	July 1941	
319	13	May 1941	
325	None	June 1941	

The Fifteenth Wave began forming in April 1941 for occupation duties. The divisions had only two infantry regiments, one field artillery battalion, and a reduced-service component. There were only twelve machine guns in the rifle company. Both arms and vehicles were French or other non-German types. The 325th Division was formed from security units in Paris. See Group B for description of the Thirteenth Wave.

GROUP B

Division	Wave	Arrived	Departed
302	13	May 1941	February 1943
304	13	May 1941	January 1943
305	13	May 1941	June 1942
306	13	May 1941	January 1943
320	13	May 1941	February 1943
321	13	May 1941	January 1943
323	13	May 1941	June 1942
327	13	May 1941	March 1943
332	14	June 1941	March 1943
333	14	June 1941	March 1943
335	14	June 1941	March 1943
336	14	May 1941	June 1942
337	14	June 1941	November 1942
340	14	June 1941	June 1942

The Thirteenth Wave was formed in November 1940 for occupation duties. The divisions had three infantry regiments but only three light field artillery battalions with Czech guns. The reconnaissance battalion was missing. Captured weapons and vehicles were used, and the division lacked mobility. The men were from twenty-four to thirty-five years of age. During the summer of 1942, the divisions were equipped with German weapons for combat duty in the East.

The Fourteenth Wave was formed in November 1940 for occupation duty. French weapons and vehicles were used except the field artillery was World War I German types. Later the units received German equipment and were used for combat in the East.

GROUP C

Division	Wave	Arrived	Departed
81	6	March 1941	January 1942
82	6	March 1941	January 1942
83	6	March 1941	February 1942
88	6	March 1941	January 1942
205	3	March 1941	February 1942
208	3	June 1940	February 1942
211	3	June 1940	February 1942
212	3	March 1941	November 1941
215	3	June 1940	December 1941
216	3	June 1940	January 1942
223	3	June 1940	November 1941
225	3	June 1940	January 1942
227	3	June 1940	October 1941
246	3	March 1941	February 1942
339	14	June 1941	September 1941
342	14	June 1941	October 1941
2d Pz		September 1941	October 1941

The Sixth Wave was formed in December 1939 and equipped with Czech arms and vehicles, although it was short of the latter. In June 1941, the divisions received French vehicles and World War I German field artillery. From June 1940 to January 1941, the men were furloughed. They were assembled and sent to the East with modern weapons.

The Third Wave was formed in August 1939 for occupation duty. Most of the men were older reservists. Some were furloughed from July 1940 to February 1941. The units had captured weapons and vehicles. In 1941, the units received German equipment and were placed in combat.

See Group B for a description of the Fourteenth Wave.

The Second Panzer was being refitted.

GROUP D

Division	Wave	Arrived	Departed
5		November 1941	February 1942
8		January 1942	March 1942
28		November 1941	March 1942
71		November 1941	May 1942
328	17	January 1942	March 1942
329	17	January 1942	March 1942
330	17	January 1942	February 1942
331	17	January 1942	February 1942
370	19	April 1942	July 1942
371	19	April 1942	July 1942
376	19	April 1942	June 1942
377	19	April 1942	June 1942
383	18	April 1942	June 1942
22 Pz		September 1941	March 1942
23 Pz		September 1941	April 1942
24 Pz		December 1941	June 1942

234

The Seventeenth Wave was formed in December 1941. The units were called Walkure divisions and were formed from units of the replacement army, training personnel, recuperating wounded, and twenty-year-old recruits. Although assigned to combat, the divisions were still using French artillery in 1943.

The Eighteenth Wave was formed in April 1942 from the replacement army with new recruits, former students, and others previously exempted from military service. The divisions used civilian vehicles. They were in combat in 1942. These divisions were called "Rheingold."

The Nineteenth Wave was formed in the West in March 1942 by taking fit men from occupation divisions in the West and forming them into combat divisions. The divisions were ready between May 15, 1942, and June 1, 1942, and were sent to the Russian front.

The Fifth, Eighth, and Seventy-first were from the eastern front and being refitted. The Twenty-second, Twenty-third Panzer Divisions were being newly organized.

GROUP E

Division	Wave	Arrived	Departed
15		May 1942	March 1943
17		June 1942	April 1943
23		July 1942	February 1943
38	20	August 1942	April 1943
39	20	August 1942	April 1943
65	20	August 1942	August 1943
106		May 1942	March 1943
161		November 1942	May 1943
167		May 1942	March 1943
257		August 1942	April 1943
282		September 1942	May 1943
328		January 1943	June 1943
1 Pz		January 1943	June 1943
6 Pz		July 1942	December 1942
7 Pz		June 1942	January 1943
10 Pz		April 1942	December 1942
26 Pz		October 1942	August 1943
1 SS Pz		July 1942	February 1943
2 SS Pz		July 1942	February 1943
3 SS Pz		November 1942	March 1943

The Twentieth Wave was formed in July 1942 as Walkure II from companies in the replacement battalions mobilizing them for combat in the East. The divisions were hastily assembled but held in the West for months before being sent to the Russian front.

The Twenty-third, 282d, and Twenty-sixth Panzers were new divisions. All of the other divisions were units refitting after fighting on the eastern front.

GROUP F

Divison	Arrived	Departed
44	March 1943	August 1943
76	April 1943	August 1943
94	March 1943	September 1943
113	April 1943	August 1943
264	July 1943	November 1943

297	March 1943	September 1943
305	March 1943	August 1943
334	July 1943	November 1943
356	May 1943	November 1943
371	March 1943	November 1943
376	March 1943	November 1943
384	March 1943	November 1943
389	March 1943	October 1943
3 Pz G	March 1943	July 1943
29 Pz G	March 1943	July 1943
60 Pz G	March 1943	January 1944
1 Para	April 1943	August 1943
2 Para	March 1943	August 1943
14 Pz	March 1943	October 1943
16 Pz	March 1943	June 1943
24 Pz	March 1943	August 1943
25 Pz	September 1943	November 1943
13 SS	August 1943	February 1944

The 264th was a new static division. The 356th and Second Parachute were new divisions. The Thirteenth SS was being formed from Moslem recruits from Bosnia. The First Parachute and Twenty-fifth Panzer were refitting after Russian service. The 334th was being reformed from remnants after the division surrendered in Tunisia. All of the rest were being reformed from remnants after the division surrendered at Stalingrad.

GROUP G

Division	Arrived
326	December 1942
338	End of 1942
343	Fall of 1942
344	Fall of 1942
346	October 1942
347	November 1942
348	October 1942
16 GAF	March 1943
17 GAF	January 1943
18 GAF	January 1943
19 GAF	June 1943
9 SS PG	January 1943
10 SS PG	January 1943

The Ninth and Tenth SS PG were new divisions formed from recruits. All of the rest were occupation divisions. The German air force divisions were assembled from air force men with no cadres of army personnel and had poor morale. The rest were "Kriemhilde" divisions formed beginning in October 1942 by taking trained men hastily from the replacement army. These divisions had little battle knowledge.

Division	Wave	Arrived	Type
47		January 1944	Static
48		January 1944	Static
49		January 1944	Static
70		December 1943	Static
77	25	January 1944	
84	25	February 1944	
85	25	February 1944	
91	25	January 1944	
242		September 1943	Static
243		September 1943	Static
244		October 1943	Static
245		October 1943	Static
265		June 1943	Static
266		June 1943	Static
271	22	December 1943	
272	22	December 1943	
275	22	December 1943	
276	22	December 1943	
277	22	December 1943	
331		April 1944	Refit
349	21	November 1943	
352	21	November 1943	
353	21	November 1943	
Lehr Pz		May 1944	
2 Pz		January 1944	
9 Pz		April 1944	
11 Pz		June 1944	
19 Pz		June 1944	
21 Pz		July 1943	
116 Pz		April 1944	
1SS Pz		May 1944	
2SS Pz		April 1944	
12 SS Pz		August 1943	
17 SS Pz Gren		November 1943	
2 Para		May 1944	
3 Para		October 1943	
5 Para		February 1944	

The static divisions were formed from remnants of worn-out divisions, from reserve divisions, and from elements of the replacement army.

The Twenty-first Wave was formed in late 1943 as "New Type" divisions of 1943, each division taking the place of a worn-out division and drawing elements from divisions burned out in Russia and reduced to regimental size. The Twenty-first Wave was well equipped with artillery, machine guns, and twenty-four self-propelled guns. The men came from the replacement army and ranged from twenty to forty-two years of age.

The Twenty-second Wave was similar to the Twenty-first Wave.

The Twenty-fifth Wave was formed from the reinforced infantry regiments formed in late 1943 to defend the West. These regiments came from elements of the replacement army. The divisions were combat ready by May 15, 1944 and organized as Type 1944 infantry divisions.

The 331st and the Parachute and Panzer Divisions were all refitting after service elsewhere or were new formations.

1941 and sent to the East (with the exception of the 342d which went to the Balkans) between October 1941 and February 1942. All of the infantry divisions were originally equipped with captured vehicles and captured weapons, but some were made up of young men who were able to endure Russian fighting. Group B consisted of fourteen divisions in France in June 1941 that left between June 1942 and March 1943. All were originally formed as occupation divisions and equipped with captured vehicles and weapons, but young men filled the ranks. By February 1942, they were refitted for combat duty. The core of the defense of the coastline fell on the nine occupation divisions grouped under A (all made up of older men with little transportation and few weapons, fixed to their coastal defense positions) plus Group D, newly formed divisions and the first group of burned-out units that returned from Russia for refitting.

By February 1942, with the departure of Group C, the defenses were slim, though the arrival of eleven of the sixteen divisions of Group D between September 1941 and January 1942 replaced them in part. Group D consisted of three new panzer divisions being formed (Twenty-second, Twenty-third, and Twenty-fourth) and four burned-out infantry divisions from the East being reformed on a smaller table of organization (Fifth, Eighth, Twenty-eighth, and Seventy-first). An additional four divisions were Walkure units (328th, 329th, 330th, and 331st) formed from the replacement army, taking instructor personnel and newly trained recruits and forming them into units. The other five divisions of Group D (370th, 371st, 376th, 377th, and 383d) were formed by taking men from other units assigned to the West to form divisions of trained men and replacing them with recruits. All sixteen divisions of Group D were sent to the East by July 1942 to take part in the summer offensive. Therefore, from March to June 1942, the only mobile combat-ready divisions in France were two or three divisions of Group D and fourteen divisions of Group B, many of which had been stripped to provide men for the new units. The number of combat-fit divisions had dropped to ten in July and eleven in August 1942. The Germans, however, still had strategic reserves in the East, despite the losses suffered in the Russian offensive during the winter of 1941–1942, and these reserves theoretically could have been sent West while the divisions in France fought a rear-guard action. After the Germans committed themselves to the summer offensive in southern Russia in July 1942, troops could not have been withdrawn easily.

The twenty divisions in Group E were either worn out and being rebuilt or were new formations. By September 1942, the date of the first plan to attack France, four from Group E were combat ready along with ten from Group B, totaling only fourteen, not enough to stop an Allied invasion, even at that early date.

Realizing the dangerous turn of events, on September 12, 1942, Hitler ordered drastic measures to replace the losses that occurred during the early part of the summer campaign. He ordered greater use of Russian volunteers in the supply service to free Germans for combat duties. The number of service troops was reduced. On October 29, 1942, a 10 percent cut was made across the board in total manpower assigned to service units. This included supply, rations, medical, transport, ordnance, postal, military police, and technical troops. Other service units were reorganized; for example, the transport column was reduced in the infantry division by about one-third, reducing the amount of munitions and supplies that could be carried.[2] The most serious cuts were made in the actual combat strength of the infantry division. Divisions were reduced from nine infantry battalions to seven. The normal fighting strength of the infantry company was reduced from 180 men to 80.[3]

To provide replacements for losses, wounded were to be returned to duty as soon as possible, and eighteen-year-old boys, who had just been drafted, were used for filling divisions in France. The air force, the SS, and the navy were called upon to make greater efforts to assist the army. The air force had nearly two million men, but Goering protested a plan to use some of them in the army. As a result, the air force created twenty new field divisions that were to fight as infantry alongside the army, but still under Goering's command.[4]

The new Luftwaffe field divisions were built around airfield defense regiments and antiaircraft battalions. The army was to supply the additional equipment needed for combat, but all leadership from generals to noncoms was to come from the Luftwaffe, which had little knowledge of land warfare. The new divisions lacked the equipment and specialists needed to make a division functional, whereas army divisions with equipment and specialists lacked riflemen. The Luftwaffe divisions proved unsuccessful in battle, despite the high caliber of the young men. Only after the Luftwaffe divisions were incorporated into the army and received trained leaders did they perform up to standard.[5]

Himmler also received permission to increase the SS. From 230,000 men in December 1942, the SS was increased to 433,000 in July 1943. The new SS divisions were formed with army cadre, and for the first time conscripts were taken into the SS instead of volunteers. Foreign volunteers were also accepted in increasing numbers.[6]

The full extent of the difficulties had not yet become apparent. Hitler still expected to capture Stalingrad, the oil wells in the Caucasus, and Alexandria in Egypt. Hitler was already planning the campaigns of 1943 and, on November 1, 1942, ordered the formation of forty-two fresh divisions to be ready by the spring of 1943. Twenty infantry divisions were to come from rebuilding battle-worn units from the eastern front. Seven panzer and motorized divisions were to be rebuilt in the West, while fifteen fresh infantry divisions were to be obtained from the armies in the West. These forty-two divisions were to spearhead the attack that would finish Russia in 1943.

To replace the units transferred from the West, Hitler ordered the creation of five new occupation divisions to be filled with limited-service men and three new infantry divisions from men in other divisions in the West, whose places would be taken by the new eighteen-year-old draftees in 1943.[7] The plan was implemented. In France, five new occupation divisions were formed, along with the three new infantry divisions, and ten infantry divisions were sent to Russia by March 1943.

In December 1942, the Germans had twenty-three combat-ready mobile divisions in France, plus nine static divisions and thirteen other divisions being formed. At the Casablanca Conference, General Brooke described this force as forty-four divisions, very close to the actual number (forty-five), without defining their state of readiness. Had the Allies launched the attack on France in September 1942 and tied the Germans to the West, making it impossible to move most of the combat divisions to Russia in early 1943, the Russians would have been able to make much greater gains in the Ukraine. As it was, ten infantry divisions from France were used to stop the Russian offensive along with five panzer divisions that had been rebuilt in the West. Of the seven panzer divisions that were to have been prepared for the 1943 campaign, five went to Russia, the Twenty-sixth Panzer did not complete its training, and the Tenth Panzer was sent to Tunisia to help out there. Because of the intensity of the Russian pressure, the plan to rebuild twenty divisions there was abandoned, and only two divisions were rebuilt in the East.[8]

The original plan to build a reserve for 1943 had collapsed. Out of the thirty panzer divisions in the German army in November 1942, eight had been lost by May 1943, five in Russia and three in North Africa. Three panzer divisions were lost at Stalingrad, along with fourteen infantry divisions and three motorized divisions. Two more panzer divisions were lost in the battles fought during the winter in the Ukraine, as well as two infantry divisions and two Luftwaffe field divisions. Tunisia cost three panzer divisions, a motorized division, and two infantry divisions. A total of thirty-two divisions was lost.[9]

On February 4, 1943, Hitler issued a new plan for rebuilding the army. Divisions in the East were to be provided with additional men and equipment in preparation for the summer offensive in 1943. Twenty-six old divisions were to be refitted and five new ones created in the West.[10] Sixteen divisions lost at Stalingrad were to be reestablished with the old divisional numbers.[11] The program in France resulted in the creation of eight new occupation divisions, two new infantry divisions, two new parachute divisions, and two new SS divisions and the rebuilding of the sixteen divisions lost at Stalingrad.

The eight occupation divisions (343d, 344th, 346th, 347th, 348th, Sixteenth Air Force, Seventeenth Air Force, and Eighteenth Air Force) were created for the most part from cadres provided by the units leaving for Russia. In effect, the divisions being shipped out sloughed off their older men to create the fortress infantry regiments that made up the five army divisions. For example, the 346th Division was formed from cadres from the 257th, 319th, 320th, 304th, and 332d Divisions with fillers from Wehrkreise VI and IX. It had only five fortress infantry battalions and two artillery battalions, plus engineers, signals, and service. The total strength of this division was probably about five thousand men.[12] The three air force divisions were formed in Germany from airfield protection units and antiaircraft gunners and had minimum service elements.

The two new infantry divisions (326th and 338th) were formed from alarm units from the replacement army as "Kriemhilde" divisions. In May 1943, these units had exchanged all of their younger men for oldsters and were formally reclassified as occupation divisions, and their infantry regiments received the fortress designation.[13]

The two new parachute divisions were produced by dividing the Seventh Flieger Division that had been burned out on the eastern front and by adding various air force elements and new recruits. The two new SS divisions were made up of young draftees; a long time was needed to work them up into fighting units because of the youth of the draftees and lack of a good cadre.

The sixteen Stalingrad divisions are more complex to describe. The tattered fragments of these divisions, seldom more than a thousand men, began to filter into France in March 1943. The men were the rear service elements, men who had not been in Stalingrad because of wounds or furloughs, and wounded who had been flown out of the pocket and had recovered. On February 11, 1943, the order had been given that six of the divisions were to be completely rebuilt by April 1, four more by April 15, and the remainder by September 1. The divisions without troops were to receive six new infantry battalions and nine artillery batteries.[14]

Matters did not go too well with the Stalingrad divisions because of the competition for weapons from the units being refitted for participation in the battle for Kursk. On March 13, the commander of the West complained that the rebuilding of the Stalingrad divisions was going slowly because preference was being given to the East for rifles, machine guns, antitank guns, and artillery. The Fourteenth, Sixteenth, and Twenty-fourth Panzer and the Sixtieth Motorized had received no German weapons, whereas the Third Motorized and Twenty-ninth Motorized were missing 25 percent or more of their weapons. Without arms these units could not be expected to take part in the defense of France.[15]

On March 23, the high command informed the western commander that by the middle of April, all units would receive 25 percent of their German weapons, and the remainder would soon follow. In the interim, twenty-five thousand French rifles and four thousand French light machine guns were offered to permit training to continue and to improve the defensive capability.[16]

By mid-April, some of the Stalingrad divisions had full complements of men, as shown on Table 19. Those with the most men had benefited from the inclusion during April of existing units, most of which had been formed in October and November of 1942. With up to six months' experience, these soldiers were approaching combat readiness. However, if the quality of the tanks in the armored formations was any indication of the equipment, it must have been rather poor. French rifles and light machine guns in the hands of retrained Luftwaffe men did not make first-class divisions.

Yet the demands for units had to be met. On February 17, the Seventy-sixth, Ninety-fourth, and 305th divisions were alerted to provide battle groups to replace the Seventeenth, Thirty-eight, Thirty-ninth, 106th, 161st, 182d, and 257th Divisions, which were being sent to the East. The Forty-fourth and 113th were also required to take on reserve assignments when the departing divisions left in late March.[17]

Table 19. **Refitting the Stalingrad Infantry and Panzer Divisions**

Division	Units added	Number of men, Mid-April 1943*	Number of Tanks Mid-April 1943
44	887th and 888th Infantry Regiments	16,035	
76	876th and 877th Infantry Regiments, NCO schools, WK II and III 2,000 Luftwaffe men	15,181	
94	875th and 878th Infantry Regiments, NCO schools, 2,000 Luftwaffe men	15,511	
113	881st, 882nd, and 884th Infantry Regiments, NCO schools	16,112	
297		5,181 (only 3 battalions and 1 artillery battalion)	
305	879th and 880th Infantry Regiments	14,402	
371		5,624	
376		3,763	
384		4,807	
389		3,954	
3 Pz Gren	386th Motorized Infantry Division	15,000 ?	61
29 Pz Gren	345th Motorized Infantry Division	15,000 ?	65
60 Pz Gren	271st Infantry Regiment	4,955	28
14 Pz		7,008	35
16 Pz	890th Motorized Infantry Regiment 4,000 men from the old division	10,080	18
24 Pz	elements of 890th and 891st Motorized Infantry Regiments	15,380	29

SOURCE: Wolf Keilig, *Das Deutsche Heer, 1939–1945*, 3 vols. (Bad Nauheim; Podzun, 1965–1972), 2:101 44 Division; *Kriegstagebuch*, 3:130, 265–335. Tessin, *Verbande und Truppen*, passim.
*Includes men in hospitals and detached on special service.

The departing experienced divisions had formed the backup behind the new divisions and the reserve (training) divisions that were being used for coastal defense for lack of any other. Then even that reserve was being withdrawn. A great risk existed in early April until the replacement divisions were better trained or at least filled with men. The Forty-fourth Division picked up ten thousand men on April 5; the Seventy-sixth about thirty-five hundred between April 6 and 12; the 113th about three thousand in the first week of April; the 305th about ten thousand on April 5; and the Twenty-fourth Panzer about seventy-five hundred on April 13. These divisions were certainly in a very unstable state in April.[18] The high command informed the western commander that not even recruits would be available to fill the 384th; and at the same time he was ordered to halt the use of the reserve divisions for coastal defense because it interfered with their training.[19]

Other units were used to flesh out the defensive posture including the 100th Panzer Regiment, the Thirtieth Mechanized Brigade, the West Mechanized Brigade, and elements of the Hermann Goering Division.[20] To make them sound more formidable, small groups were given grandiose names. The mechanized brigades actually were two to four training battalions of cavalry and mechanized troops. These units would have had little impact on a battle.

The great fear of the Germans in the spring of 1943 was an Allied descent on Brittany, where the U-boats were based. The forces assigned to Brittany were very weak, and none of the U-boat bases had adequate defenses from land attack.[21] To attempt to create a semblance of defense, the western commander on February 5, 1943, set out to establish a reserve of six to eight mobile divisions. It was to be built around the First Panzer, Twenty-sixth Panzer, 326th, 338th, 343d, 344th, 346th, 347th, and 348th Infantry Divisions. The infantry units were all new occupation divisions formed in October 1942 with limited mobility and older men. Priority was given to the Ninth and Tenth SS Divisions and the Twenty-fourth Panzer Division to have them ready by June 1. The target for April 1 was four fully equipped and combat-ready mobile divisions.[22]

Therefore, while the planners of the North African invasion talked fearfully of the powerful force of forty or more German divisions in the West, which would quickly grind up the twenty-one divisions that the Allies might land on the channel coast, all that was left by April 1943 were nineteen occupation divisions, the twenty-three Stalingrad divisions, and other forming divisions having a minimum of training, ten training divisions, the Twenty-sixth Panzer, Sixty-fifth, and 328th. The Germans left France exposed to concentrate on Russia. For the locations of the various elements of the German army at this time, see Table 20.

The German military program in 1943 was directed toward the East. The plan was to concentrate a strong force to cut off the Russian salient at Kursk with the hope of breaking through for another big gain. While the Germans prepared, the Russians also poured troops, guns, planes, and tanks into the Kursk area, readying for the most crucial battle of the war. If the Germans could be met head-on during the summer months by the Russians and decisively defeated, German initiative on the Russian front would end; henceforth, the Russians would call the tune.

In fact, most of the German army was on the Russian front. On July 1, 1943, of 3,142 tanks available to the Germans, 2,269 were in the East, along with 997 of the 1,422 assault guns and 500 of the 600 tanks considered obsolete. Out of the total of 276 divisions in the German army, 186 were on the Russian front along with seven of the twelve SS divisions.

All of the best divisions were centered on Kursk, about fifty, including sixteen panzer or motorized.[23] All of the new Panther tanks and the Tigers were also sent to Kursk. As the German concentration increased, they were tied to the area by the growing might of the Russians. Even if the Germans did not launch an attack, they still had to keep their forces there because it was feared that the Russians might use their immense buildup to launch an attack of their own.

After the German defeat at Kursk in early July, the Russians made probing attacks in the South to draw off the German reserves. Then, on August 3, 1943, the Russians launched a major offensive in the center, driving seventy miles in five days, followed by another attack in the South on August 13. The Russians advanced steadily during August and September and crossed the Dnieper River by the end of September.[24] There were no surplus German divisions in Russia to reinforce the West in the event of an invasion.

Were there divisions available in theaters other than the Russian front, that could be moved into France? There were ninety divisions in other theaters. Surely some of them were available. In the northern part of Finland near Pet-samo, the German Twentieth Army had been stalemated since the early days of the war. Despite the growth of the Russian forces opposing this army, its strength remained about the same. By 1943, it had seven divisions, three mountain (Second, Sixth, and Seventh), two infantry (163d and 169th), the SS Division North, and 210th Coastal Defense Division, and six regiments.[25] These forces could not be weakened because of the danger to the nickel mines located there. Germany's supply of this essential metal would be substantially reduced if the Russians drove the Germans out of this area. The Germans therefore formed a defensive system that held month after month. The climate was so severe that any effort to launch an attack would require more supplies than could be provided over the trails. Even moving troops in and out was a severe test of endurance. The best the Germans could do was to hold onto the shelters that had been dug out of the rocky soil and hope that Ivan would do the same.

The position in Norway was also static. The garrison had been increased on paper from eight divisions in June 1941 to twelve in April 1943, mostly by combining the coastal defense battalions and coast artillery batteries into occupa-tion divisions (230th, 270th, and 280th). These were divisions in name only. The 280th consisted of a headquarters, four fortress battalions, a signal company, and attached coast artillery.[26]

There were two divisions each at the major strategic ports, Narvik (199th and 702d), the terminus of the rail line that brought Swedish iron ore to the Atlantic

Table 20. German Order of Battle, April 1943

Army	Corps	Division	Location	Type
	88	347	Ijmuiden	Occupation
		16 LW	Netherlands	Occupation
		719	Dordrecht	Occupation
15	Reserve	24 Pz	N. France	Reforming
		26 Pz	France	Forming
		384	France	Reforming
		305	France	Reforming
		44	Belgium	Reforming
15	89	712	Flushing	Occupation
		65	Flushing	Mobile
		165	Schelde	Reserve, training
	82	18 LW	Dunkirk	Occupation
		161	Channel Coast	Mobile (in transit to Russia)
		282	N. France	Newly formed March 1943
		156	Calais	Reserve, training
		171	Epinal Belgium	Reserve, training
		191	N. France	Reserve, training
	81	17 LW	Le Havre	Occupation
		711	Rouen	Occupation
		348	Dieppe	Occupation
7	Reserve	16 Pz	N. France	Reforming
		389	Brittany	Reforming
		113	Brittany	Reforming
		371	Brittany	Reforming
		76	Brittany	Reforming
		7 Flieger	N. France	Rebuilding (becomes 1 Para May 1943)
		2 Para	Normandy	Forming
		1 Pz	Normandy	Reforming, nearly ready
	84	319	Channel Islands	Occupation

Army	Corps	Division	Location	Status
		716	Caen	Occupation
		709	Normandy	Occupation
	25	94	N. France	Reforming
	87	346	N. France	Occupation
		343	Brittany	Occupation
1	Reserve	14 Pz	W. France	Reforming
		297	Bordeaux	Reforming
		3 Mot	Pyrenees	Reforming
	80	158	La Rochelle	Reserve, training
		708	Royan	Occupation
	86	715	Atlantic Coast	Occupation
		344	Bordeaux	Occupation
Felber	83	328	Marseilles	Mobile
		338	Rhone Delta	Occupation
		326	Narbonne	Occupation
		60 Mot	S. France	Reforming
Group D	Reserve	29 PG	France	Reforming
		9 SS	Reims	Forming
		10 SS	S. France	Forming
		376	Netherlands	Reforming
		325	Paris	Security
			Reserve Divisions	
		148	Toulouse	Training
		157	Besancon	Training
		159	Central France	Training
		182	Nancy	Training
		189	Besancon	Training
			In transit to other theaters	
		17		
		38		
		39		
		257		

for shipment to Germany, and Trondheim (Fourteenth Luftwaffe and 181st), a major fishing port jutting out to the West. Both of these ports had been attacked by the British with strong forces in 1940 and required protection. With the command of the sea, the British could move troops in faster than could the Germans, who had poor road and rail connections. The Germans no longer had complete control of the air, as in 1940, to drive off the British should they attack there again.

The 710th Division was stationed in Oslo, the political and economic center of the country. In southern Norway were the 269th Division east of Lillehammer and the 214th west of Oslo. The Twenty-fifth Panzer and the 196th Divisions formed a reserve to keep Sweden in check.[27] A reading of Churchill's repeated suggestions for a descent on Norway during 1942 and 1943, gives a better understanding of Hitler's concern for Norway. Commando raids kept the garrison active, and there was a continual effort to keep open a road along the coast to Narvik and beyond to Finland.

Most of the infantry divisions in Norway were required to provide regiments, battalions and cadres for the new occupation divisions in 1943. The Twenty-fifth Panzer Division formed in February 1942 had only one tank battalion (mostly Panzer IIs and French Somuas), three infantry battalions, and one artillery battalion until June 15, 1943, when it was reinforced by training battalions and units from other divisions.[28] Beginning in September 1943, there was a steady exodus of forces from Norway, being replaced by newly formed occupation divisions with older men. Before departure from Norway, the divisions had to be built up with young recruits, and the older men were transferred out before the divisions were considered fit, even for fighting partisans in Yugoslavia.

When the Twenty-fifth Panzer Division was shipped to France in August 1943, it was replaced by a new division, Panzer Division Norway, which in reality was only a brigade consisting of three motorized infantry battalions, a tank battalion with thirty-six old French tanks, an antitank battalion, and one artillery battalion.[29] Consequently, the Norwegian divisions would not have been a rich source of reinforcement for the invasion coast in 1943.

Neither did the Balkan theater have much to offer to the West in 1943. As the Russian position grew stronger, the partisans were able to attract more recruits. Air drops of supplies from the British, as well as small boat landings, brought in equipment for Tito's men, but most of the weapons had been captured from the Germans, the Italians, and other forces fighting for the Germans. The net result was that more German troops were needed in the Balkans rather than a surplus being available for other areas. In April 1943, Crete was held by the Crete Fortress Brigade and was being reinforced by the Eleventh Luftwaffe Division and the Twenty-second Infantry Division. Greece and Serbia were occupied by the 704th Infantry Division and three Bulgarian divisions. In Croatia, fighting Tito, were the 714th, 717th, and 718th Infantry Divisions and the 187th Reserve, Seventh SS Cavalry, and two Croat divisions (369th and 373d). Eight Italian divisions completed the garrison in Albania and Greece. In April, the four static infantry divisions were reorganized into rifle divisions (104th, 114th, 117th, and 118th).

The Balkans were being reinforced. In May, the First Mountain Division arrived from Russia, followed in June 1943 by two additional divisions from France. The First Panzer Division went to Greece, and the 297th Infantry Division went to Montenegro on the Adriatic Coast. By August, the 100th Rifle Division, a rebuilt Stalingrad unit, was considered able to fight and was added to the garrison. An additional reserve division (173d) was brought in, along with the Thirteenth SS Division that was completing its training, to bolster the forces in Croatia and Serbia. The headquarters of the Second Panzer Army was also sent from the Russian front to command the increasing forces.[30]

In general, the Balkans were proving to be an ever greater drain on German manpower. From a token force of five divisions in July 1942, the garrison grew to fifteen divisions on July 1, 1943, and twenty-five by June 1, 1944.[31] The partisans were holding down almost as many German divisions as the Allied armies in Italy. The position of this front at the rear of the line of communications of the Southern Army Group in Russia and near the northern entry into Italy made it essential that the area be kept under control. Consequently, the Germans could not afford to strip more than a few divisions from the Balkans to ward off an attack in France in 1943.

The situation in the South was not such that divisions could be drawn from that area either. In April 1943, the Germans were trying to build up their forces in Tunisia. After the surrender of the Axis forces in May, the Italian army certainly could not be counted on for first-line service even though the tales of the Italian lack of bravery were exaggerated. The issue was that Italian divisions even at full strength were far smaller than Allied or German units. The Type 42 Italian infantry divisions had only 7,000 men in its table of organization, and in actual combat this number often dropped to 3,000. The equipment of the Italian army was also far from being first class. The infantry battalion had only 450 men with twenty-seven machine guns. An infantry regiment had only ten 47mm antitank guns, eight 81mm mortars, and thirty-six 45mm mortars, in addition to machine guns and rifles. The entire division had only 248 automatic weapons.[32] This was not enough equipment to allow the troops to engage in combat against units of 18,000 men or more with fifty tanks and fifty tank destroyers attached.

In May 1943, the Italian army consisted of over three million men in more than ninety divisions, but many of these were coastal divisions with older men and little training, as well as units in the process of reforming after heavy losses in Russia. Thirty Italian divisions were on occupation duty in the Balkans; four were in France; two were on Corsica; four were on Sardinia; and ten were on Sicily. The remainder were in Italy itself, including eight divisions of the Eighth Army, which had been withdrawn from Russia, and many coastal divisions.[33] The Italians would have been hard pressed to defend themselves, even if the Allied forces had been reduced to a minimum in the Mediterranean, because they were pinned to their coastal defense and had few reserve units left to meet an invasion. In the event of an invasion in France, no help would be found among the Italians.

There was no German garrison in Italy in April 1943. As a matter of fact, in May 1943, the following units surrendered in Tunisia: six divisions (Tenth Panzer, Fifteenth Panzer, Twenty-first Panzer, Ninetieth Motorized, 164th, and 334th), plus elements of the 999th and Hermann Goering Divisions and the First Parachute Brigade. Only very small remnants of these units escaped; usually all that was left of the division was a unit that, for some reason, had not joined its parent formation and was still in Naples or some other port awaiting shipment. Replacements and returning wounded plus some base troops were also available. The major manpower sources were replacement battalions that were waiting in Sicily for transportation to Tunisia.[34]

During the summer of 1943, the Germans created a defensive force for Sicily and Italy primarily by drawing on forces in France. The divisions recreated in the South were of poor quality. The "Sicily" Division formed in May included eight infantry replacement battalions, a battalion of artillery from the Hermann Goering Division, an army artillery battalion, and two newly formed artillery battalions. The Naples Antiaircraft Battalion and the 215th Tank Battalion from army troops were added. On July 1, 1943, the few hundred survivors of the old Fifteenth Panzer Division were assigned, and the division was retitled the Fifteenth Panzer Grenadier Division.[35]

The "Sardinia" Division was organized for the defense of that island. On July 7, it was redesignated the Ninetieth Panzer Grenadier Division. On Corsica, the Sturmbrigade Reichsfuhrer SS was upgraded to the Sixteenth SS Panzer Grenadier Division in September, and on Sicily, the Hermann Goering Division reformed the regiment that had been lost in Tunisia.[36] German resources in the South were very slim in the summer of 1943.

Its heavy losses and expanding responsibilities placed the German army in a crisis situation in 1943. Between June 1941 and June 1943, the Germans suffered nearly four million killed and wounded; 1,985,000 of these casualties had occurred between July 1, 1942, and June 30, 1943. By the end of March 1943, the German army was short 830,000 men in its table of organization. Stringent methods were used to overcome this deficit: combat-fit men were combed out of service units; divisions were reduced in size; air force men were used as infantry; occupational deferments were tightened; and even Russians were employed as soldiers.

The quality of the German infantry declined. Men who had been grooms for horses, supply clerks, and teamsters did not make the best infantrymen. Teenagers in the Labor Service were assigned to man antiaircraft guns. Recruits with a few months' training were used to fill the divisions in the West or formed into reserve divisions for occupation duty. From June 1941 until June 1943, the replacement army provided 3,270,000 recruits and 1,100,000 trained men for new units, the latter mostly men who had been wounded and were being returned to duty.

The program met with some success. Between April 1 and June 30, 1943, nearly 350,000 men were added to the army against only 134,000 losses. By July 1, 1943, the total number of men in the army had increased to 4,484,000 from less than 4,000,000 a year before.[37] But the impact of the losses was great; there had been almost a 100 percent turnover in the army in two years. The average German soldier had only two years of experience. The British army had a far smaller turnover, and the average soldier probably had three years of experience. Even the American soldier had two years of training by the end of 1943.[38] The result of this high turnover was a German army quite inferior to the highly competent force that battered its way across Russia in 1941. Germany's divisions in 1943 were filled with inferior men and lacked offensive power.[39]

In her desperate need for manpower, Germany turned to the prisoner of war camps. As early as 1941, Russian volunteers called Hiwis, for Hilfswelligen (volunteer helpers), were assigned to the service elements of the German army, replacing Germans for combat duties. Although they were not armed in the beginning, they were later given rifles to defend themselves from the partisans.[40] On October 29, 1942, the high command officially ordered the Hiwis to be used as laborers, wagon drivers, assistant truck drivers, blacksmiths, shoemakers, horseshoers, and in other jobs not requiring highly skilled specialists.

Hiwis were not to be used in combat by the divisions and units to which they were assigned. The preferred ethnic groups were the Russian Turks, Don Cossacks, and Cossacks from the Terek and the Kuban. The field commanders were alerted to the possibility that even these dissident Soviets might commit espionage and sabotage.[41]

An example of the impact of the use of Russians was the experience of the 134th German Infantry Division. In January 1943, combat-fit Germans were combed out of the artillery regiment and supply units and replaced with Hiwis. A special school was established to retrain the Germans as infantrymen. By March 1943, additional Hiwis were formed into the 134th Ost Battalion, and two platoons of Hiwis were attached to the 134th Pioneer Battalion. By April 1943, 2,300 Hiwis were assigned to the 134th division and a further 5,600 prisoners of war were attached for labor details.[42]

Behind the front line, a specified number of Hiwis were employed in a long list of rear area units. Each vehicle transport company was to have 38, a heavy motorized bakery company 71, a butchery company 42, an army horse hospital 114, a veterinary company 76, and a horse depot 130.[43] The 1942 table of organization of the infantry division had called for 700 Hiwis; the new table of September 1943 increased the number to 2,005, about one-seventh of the total men in the division.[44]

The Hiwis were used most often to care for and drive the ever present horses in German units. The basic unit for providing supplies to the infantry was the horse-drawn vehicle squadron, which could transport sixty tons in Panje wagons, small Russian carts. On August 25, 1943, the table of organization of these units included 2 officers, 27 German noncoms, 71 German privates, and 159 Hiwis.

The unit had 381 horses and 176 wagons. All of the Hiwis were armed with rifles for security.[45]

The Germans made provision to use as many Hiwis as were available after 1943. The problem after the Germans started losing battles was to get the Russians to volunteer. Conditions in the prisoner of war cages were so terrible that, for many, it was worth the chance. When men were dying all around, the opportunity for better food and treatment in exchange for caring for some horses did not appear as difficult a choice as it would appear after the war. In the West, over seven thousand black French colonial prisoners of war were used as Hiwis by the divisions in France. In the south of France and Italy, former Italian soldiers performed these roles.[46]

During the summer of 1942, the Germans also began to recruit Russian prisoners for combat roles. Why these men were willing to don the uniform of the enemy can best be understood by the experience of an Armenian who deserted from the 812th Armenian Battalion in 1944. He had been captured in November 1941 and put in a prisoner of war cage. There followed a fifteen-day march to the rear with very little food and brutal treatment. Those who left the line of march for any reason were shot. In a prison camp near Minsk, the survivors were placed in barracks where men died every night from lack of food, heavy labor, and brutal treatment.

Early in 1942, the barracks and food improved. For six weeks the prisoners were given training to bring them back into good physical condition, and, in May, our prisoner was among a large group sent to Poland, where they were formed into four Armenian battalions each of about a thousand men. They were given some German heavy weapons and captured Russian rifles and machine guns. Clothed in German uniforms, they began training. The companies were commanded by Germans, but the platoon leaders were Russians. Early in 1943, two of the Armenian battalions were sent to the West and two to the East.[47]

At the beginning of 1943, 176 battalions of Russians had been formed to provide occupation troops in the West, in Italy, in the Balkans, and in Russia. More than fifty-two thousand Russians were recruited into larger combat units, including the Pannwitz Cossack Corps of two divisions. During the summer of 1943, two new divisions were formed, the 162d Infantry Division, with German cadre, which was sent into combat against the British in Italy, and the First Cossack Division that fought against the partisans in Yugoslavia. A Russian general, Andrei Andreyevich Vlasov, began forming the Russian Liberation Army in June 1943, which eventually included two additional divisions.[48]

As the Germans began to lose battles on the eastern front after July 1943, the Russians began to desert back to the communists. Therefore, the Ost troops were sent West to make desertion more difficult. A pernicious system was introduced of taking individual battalions from German divisions in the West and sending them to Russia. The battalions were replaced by battalions of Ost troops at a two-to-one ratio. During the summer of 1943, ten battalions of Ost troops had been sent in without weapons. Rundstedt provided them with French rifles and machine guns.[49]

In September, a further 15,800 Ost troops were sent, and during November and December, another 25,000 were exchanged for German troops in the West, Norway, and Denmark. By the end of October, thirty-four Ost battalions had arrived, with twenty-three more coming, in exchange for twenty German battalions. Rundstedt, however, was given specific instructions on the use of these troops; they were to be employed only as battalions supported by German units, even though that would have prevented the exchange of larger numbers of battalions. Discipline was to be maintained by the sharpest methods. An additional 40,000 Ost troops were sent to Norway, Denmark, and France in exchange for German troops in the last quarter of 1943.[50] Between September and November 1943, sixty Ost battalions were exchanged for thirty German infantry battalions drawn from German divisions in the West, and sent to the East where they were used to reinforce weak German units.[51] For example, on October 22, 1943, the II Battalion, 583d Infantry Regiment, 319th Division, which formed the garrison of the Channel Islands, was sent to Russia, where it became the II Battalion, 122d Infantry Regiment, 50th Infantry Division. In the place of this battalion, the 319th Division received, in April 1944, the 643d Ost Battalion and the 823d Georgian Battalion.[52]

By the end of 1943, the Germans had enrolled 370,000 Ost troops and were using 130,000 Hiwis in service units. Despite defeats, the Germans continued to find recruits in the prisoner of war camps. By June 1944, there were two hundred battalions of Ost troops, most of them in France and Italy. Most of the occupation divisions had one or more battalions of Ost troops attached, and there were a total of sixty battalions on coastal defense in the West. As might be expected, they did not prove to be very trustworthy when the invasion came.[53] Rundstedt, the commander of the West, considered the Russians "a menace and a nuisance to operations in France."[54] The foreigners did help to spread German manpower and permit its use in the most essential roles. Only with the help of her allies and foreign volunteers could Germany maintain over three hundred divisions in the field. Nevertheless, the Germans did not deceive themselves concerning the combat value of these troops.

Another source of men was the satellite armies. Although few non-Germans were used in the first campaign in 1941, the summer campaign of 1942 called for the use of two Rumanian armies, an Italian army, and a Hungarian army, in addition to the Finns in the North. The defeats of the winter of 1942–1943 lessened the enthusiasm of the satellites. By January 1943, Rumania had lost eighteen divisions and two hundred thousand men killed in Russia. On January 25, 1943, after Rumanian troops were accused by the Germans of fighting poorly, the Rumanian minister Mihai Antonescu formally requested that all of his troops be removed from the battlefront and that Rumanian units no longer be asked to take part in the war. Hitler was able to smooth relations, and the Rumanians continued to fight with the Germans. The Rumanians, however, were no longer reliable and finally betrayed the Germans to the Russians.[55]

Hungarian loyalty was also suspect. In a territorial dispute in 1941 between Hungary and Rumania, Hitler had given preference to the Rumanians, and this was not forgotten by the Hungarians. When the Second Hungarian Army was defeated by the Russians in January 1943, the Hungarians were temporarily withdrawn from the front. They later returned, but in November 1943, the Hungarian chief of staff requested that the three Hungarian corps be kept away from the active sectors.[56] Three light divisions and two security divisions continued to fight partisans in the rear areas.[57] When the Red Army reached their border in 1944, Hungarian units once again took an active part in front-line fighting.

Slovakian troops were also withdrawn from heavy combat areas. In the late summer of 1943, the Slovakian Motorized Division was attacked and routed in South Russia. The remaining troops were disarmed and sent to Rumania as a construction brigade. The Slovakian Security Division fought Russian partisans for a time, but by the end of 1943, this unit was also disarmed and sent to Italy as a construction brigade.[58]

The Italians, Germany's greatest ally, collapsed in 1943. After the defeat of the Eighth Italian Army in Russia in January 1943 and the surrender of the First Italian Army in Tunisia in May 1943, Mussolini requested that all of his troops be returned to Italy for defense. The major impact of their return was the loss of divisions in the Balkans, where the Italians had been providing an occupation force and fighting the Yugoslav partisans. After the surrender of Italy in September 1943, the only Italians fighting on the German side were about sixty thousand fascists being formed into four new divisions in Germany.[59]

In October 1943, the Spaniards demanded the return of the Spanish Blue Division that had been fighting for the Germans on the Russian front. The Spaniards provided no further active military cooperation. Sweden denied Germany further use of the rail route from the Baltic Sea to Norway. Turkey became less friendly and had to be threatened with a German motorized division. After remaining neutral for four years, Portugal permitted the Allies to use the Azores as a base for the submarine war.[60]

On the plus side for Germany, the Bulgarians, though not at war with Russia, provided three or four divisions for the occupation of Yugoslavia, while Croatia, a pro-German part of Yugoslavia, provided the manpower for three army divisions, based on German cadres, and a Croatian SS division. These divisions were used to combat the Serbian partisans.[61]

Even though the non-Germans were of little help on the fighting front, they were an essential part of the economic war, for they replaced the German workers who were drafted into the army. Germany was critically short of weapons in 1943. The increases in production that followed the appointment of Albert Speer as minister of armaments after the death of Dr. Fritz Todt in February 1942 were not fully realized until well into 1943. In 1942, 90 percent of the armament industry was still working on a one-shift basis, and much of Germany's industry was concerned with consumer goods to maintain the civilian standard of living.[62] Although the increases in munitions manufacture began in March 1942 and nearly doubled by the end of 1942, production was not keeping pace with losses on the battlefield and the needs of new units. The factors that kept production low were the need for reallocation of materials from civilian to war production and the shortage of labor.[63]

Labor was the important part of Germany's economic problem in 1942 and 1943. The army's need for men had upset the basic pattern of labor supply. During peacetime, Germany would normally lose six hundred thousand male workers annually through age or death, and these would be replaced by six hundred thousand young men. The changing composition of the German labor force as influenced by the war is shown below:[64]

Date	Men	Women	Foreigners	Total (in millions)
May 1939	24.5	14.6	0.3	39.4
May 1940	20.4	14.4	1.2	36.0
May 1942	16.9	14.4	4.2	35.5
May 1943	15.5	14.8	6.3	36.6

Despite Speer's urging that women be employed to the same extent as in Britain and America, Hitler rejected the proposal on the basis that factory work for large numbers of German women would harm them physically and morally, and the proposal was dropped. More than 1.4 million German women and over five hundred thousand Ukrainian women continued to be employed as domestic servants until the end of the war, while England reduced the number of female domestic servants to fewer than four hundred thousand by 1943.[65]

With no significant increase in the number of women in the work force, the Germans turned to foreign workers. In March 1942, a special office for labor allocation was created under Fritz Sauckel. The object of the office was not merely to assign workers to factories, but also to make large-scale importations of foreign workers into Germany.[66] By May 30, 1943, 6.3 million foreign workers and prisoners of war were employed in Germany. The German industrialists disliked the foreigners whom they feared as potential saboteurs or spies. In addition, the language handicap was troublesome, especially for Eastern workers.[67]

The conditions under which the labor was imported were brutal, and the work conditions were appalling. The result was that, rather than going to Germany, young men in Russia were joining the partisans. The atrocities committed by the SS in Russia also turned the people against the Germans and made labor recruitment more difficult.[68]

Rather than bring workers to Germany, Speer proposed using the industrial capacity of the occupied countries to assist the German war effort. Sauckel's efforts to conscript French workers caused many of them to flee from their homes, deserting their jobs in French factories that were turning out goods for Germany. During the summer of 1943, Speer began working with French, Belgian, and Dutch industrial leaders to convert them to the production of needed civilian items that would be sent to Germany, including shoes, clothing, cloth, and furniture. Speer's plan was to substitute these imported products for items previously made in Germany and use the productive capacity in Germany to turn out war materials: boots, uniforms, and military equipment.

In return for promises from Speer that French workers in factories so employed would not be deported to Germany, the French agreed to cooperate in September 1943. This arrangement was a great boon to the German war potential; in the end, ten thousand French factories had received protection from worker deportation in exchange for producing for Germany.[69] The same type of agreement was reached with Belgium, Holland, and Italy in late 1943. Buying products from the occupied countries was a far more efficient form of exploitation of foreign labor than bringing the workers to Germany.

Meanwhile, in Germany, more and more factories turned to war production. By the end of 1943, Germany was truly mobilized for war. Tables 21 and 22 show clearly the sharp increases in munitions manufacture.

The danger of all statistics is that they can be misinterpreted. Extracts can also be misleading. The Germans developed a production index to overcome part of this problem, as shown on Table 21. This index was based on monetary value of the products rather than on numbers and thus took into consideration not only numbers of units but also the growing complexity of the products manufactured; for example, a Tiger tank counted for more in 1944 than a Panzer I produced in 1940 because it was a far more powerful and expensive weapon, even though raw figures listed each as a single tank.

The average production index for 1941 stood at 98, but increased sharply after Speer took over, averaging 222 in 1943. A peak of 322 was reached in July 1944, but this leveled off to 227 by January 1945, indicating the effect of heavy Allied bombing after D-Day. For our purposes here, the major point is that German industry had not yet reached full production by 1943. Despite the bombing, weapons were being made in increasing numbers during the period from September 1942 until the end of 1944.

Shipbuilding and manufacturing of ammunition for existing weapons showed the greatest increases up to January 1943. Weapons production was below the

Table 21. **Monthly Index of German Production**
(Base Period January/February 1942 = 100)

	Total index	All weapons	Tanks	Aircraft
Annual average 1940	97	79	36	?
Annual average 1941	98	106	81	97
Annual average 1942	142	137	130	133
Annual average 1943	222	234	330	216
July 1944	322	384	589	321
January 1945	227	284	557	231

SOURCE: Mueller-Hillebrand, *Das Heer,* 3:182; *Kriegstagebuch,* 1:54E.

Table 22. Comparative Armaments Production

Country and year	Annual Production				Monthly average (thousands)		
	Tanks and assault guns	Light armd. vehicles	Field artillery	Aircraft	Rifles and SMG	Machine guns	Trucks
Germany							
1940	1,359	?	5,499	8,070	106	4.4	?
1941	2,875	2,200	7,082	11,000	102	7.7	?
1942	4,300	1,200	12,000	14,700	137	7.1	6.3
1943	9,200	2,600	26,904	25,200	209	14.1	6.4
1944	17,800	11,250	40,600	34,300	262	24.2	5.9
United States							
1940	286	0	1,143	3,129	4	.05	1.6
1941	4,052	86	9,197	15,860	24	1.5	15.0
1942	24,997	10,646	53,780	41,092	118	22.0	51.0
1943	29,497	6,182*	67,544	68,600	444	24.8	52.0
1944	17,565	?	33,558	69,956	320	21.2	50.0
Great Britain							
1940	1,399	6,070	3,164	15,049	6.7	2.5	7.5
1941	4,841	10,681	12,752	20,094	7	3.3	7.4
1942	8,611	19,317	41,134	23,672	169	5.7	7.9
1943	7,476	41,134	32,731	26,263	206	6.7	7.4
1944	2,474*	23,672*	13,494	26,461	101	4.4	6.7

SOURCE: Seaton, *Russo-German War*, p. 402; Keilig. *Das Deutsche Heer*, 3:206, 1944/45, p. 3; Robert W. Coakley and Richard M. Leighton, *Global Logistics and Strategy, 1943–1945* (Washington: Department of the Army, 1969), p. 832; William K. Hancock, ed., *Statistical Digest of the War* (London: H.M. Stationery Office, 1951), pp. 140, 143, 144, 148, 149, 152.
*Represents six months production only.

average increase at only 137 during 1942. During 1943, with the drive to rebuild the army, to increase the number of divisions, and to replace divisions lost on the eastern front, the production of weapons began to surge ahead. By January 1944, weapons production exceeded the average index by 30 points. This shift in emphasis of production was even more striking in tank manufacture. The index for tanks went from 154 in January 1943 to 438 by January 1944, nearly three times as much, at the expense of all other kinds of weapons and especially aircraft, which dropped to 132. Large numbers of tanks were not produced until April of 1943.[70]

The actual numbers of tanks and other weapons manufactured indicated the limited response that Germany made to the needs of the army before Hitler's declaration of complete mobilization for war in January 1943. To place the figures in perspective, the total produced in select groups of weapons is compared to similar production figures for the United States and Great Britain. In the manufacture of tanks and assault guns, field artillery, and aircraft, the annual production figures for Germany in 1942 were generally comparable to the figures for the United States in 1941, the year before Pearl Harbor. In other words, in the manufacture of major weapons, other than armored cars, Germany was producing in 1942, the year of her greatest victories, at the same rate as the United States in the year before she entered the war! By 1942, American production had reached an incredible level which the German figures of 1944 only began to approach. Even British tank production was double German production in 1942. By 1944, however, Germany caught up to the United States in tanks and guns. In manufacture of more routine weapons such as rifles and machine guns, German production was approximately the same as American production. British totals in these areas were roughly equal to German production as well, which placed the odds two to one against Germany without adding the Russian figures. Germany lost the production war in 1942, but through strenuous efforts began to gain ground in mid-1943. She managed to double her production in many categories in 1943, while American production leveled off in some areas and was even reduced in 1944. During 1942 and early 1943, Germany was barely replacing losses and building new units. After the middle of 1943, her factories concentrated on military products and provided sufficient weapons to equip a new army for the defense of the West.

Both in manpower and in weapons, Germany was at a low ebb in 1943. The Russian winter offensive of 1942–1943 shattered her army. The Battle of Kursk and the attacks from the South placed Germany on the defensive. Her allies grew less reliable, and her productive capacity was only slowly beginning to provide sufficient weapons. By the end of 1943, matters once again turned more to Germany's favor. Germany's war potential—troops and weapons—was far greater in the West in 1944 than in 1943. Allied delay of the invasion for a year gave the Germans an opportunity to create a strong defensive force in the West. This increase was not matched by a comparable improvement in the forces of the Western Allies. The idea that Germany was worn down by an additional year of war was false. The facts indicated the reverse was true.

16

RE-CREATING GERMANY'S ARMY IN THE WEST

While the Allied powers marked time and diverted their efforts to the Mediterranean and to the Pacific, the Germans created a new army in western Europe. The expansion of munitions production under the leadership of Albert Speer produced noticeable improvements in the quantity of weapons available toward the end of 1943. The production tables in chapter 15 clearly indicate the success of using non-German factories to produce civilian products, enabling German industry, with the help of foreign labor, to manufacture weapons to replace losses and equip new divisions.

The use of foreign labor released more men for the army, and additional manpower was dredged up from other sources. The total result was a dramatic increase in German power in late 1943; by 1944, the German war effort was in full swing. Despite losses in Russia and the defection of allies, Germany in 1944, was far more powerful in the West than she had been in early 1943. The year delay in the Allied attack on France meant that more German divisions and more tanks were waiting for the Allied landing craft to touch down in June 1944, not less.

The major achievement after July 1943 was finding men to use the weapons made available by Speer. The following chart shows the rapid growth in the number of foreign workers used to replace Germans entering the armed forces: (in millions)

Date	Men in Wehrmacht	Labor force	Men	Women	Foreigners
May 30, 1942	8.6	35.5	16.9	14.4	4.2
May 30, 1943	9.5	36.6	15.5	14.8	6.3
May 30, 1944	9.1	36.1	14.2	14.8	7.1

Despite 2.5 million permanent losses from May 30, 1942, to May 30, 1944, the armed forces were increased to 9.1 million men.[1]

To supplement German manpower, the army took in an additional 300,000 Hiwis during 1943 and planned to use more. By April 1, 1944, 77,861 Volksdeutsche of List III were in the army. Volksdeutsche were Germans living outside of the 1939 boundaries of Germany, primarily in the Polish Corridor. The Germans of military age were subject to conscription, but were classified according to their political attitude. List I were active Nazis. List II were passive Nazis who had preserved their allegiance to Germany. Men in Lists I and II obviously would make good soldiers and were not subject to special treatment.

List III were racial Germans who had absorbed Polish ways, but were considered susceptible to being converted to Nazi ideology. The men were given ten-year probationary citizenship and were drafted, but they were subject to special rules. They could not be promoted above the grade of *Gefreiter,* equal to an American private, first class.

In addition, there was a List IV, men hostile to Germany, who were not drafted into the army. As manpower needs grew, the army included in List III men antagonistic to Germany who deserted at the first opportunity in Italy and France. These men provided the replacements for the Polish divisions that fought in Italy and France.[2]

The SS took a step further and created six divisions, drawing their manpower from non-German sources. Most of the non-Germans were used in noncombat roles, in fighting partisans, or for occupation duty. Germans relieved from these duties were used to replace losses and create new divisions.

Despite the decline in quality, the Germany army had more divisions in June 1944 than in July 1943. An actual tally of the total divisions in the German army on July 1, 1943, is difficult to state in simple terms. The disposition of German divisions in July 1943 is given in Table 23. Often the deceptive measures of giving divisional numbers to noncombat units has succeeded in deceiving the historian. Inclusion of the forming, security, and reserve divisions also complicates the tally. The following lists are compiled from various sources, isolating the combat divisions from the totals.[3]

Divisions	July 1, 1943	July 1, 1944
Army	243	257
SS	11	21
Luftwaffe	22	6
Total	276	284

Despite the minor overall increase, the forces in the West were reinforced dramatically from thirty-three divisions in 1943 to fifty-four in 1944.[4]

The major source of additional men for the West was the Russian front. Losses in the East were not completely replaced; the men were used instead to build new divisions in the West. France had been a source of divisions for the East in the effort to stall the Russians until late 1943. The drives stopped only when the primitive Soviet supply system was outrun and had to await the repair of railroads to bring up supplies. Matters did not improve greatly for the Germans as the months passed; the commanders in the East begged for the few divisions left in the West.

The loss of troops on the Russian front was appalling. Between July 1943 and May 1944, the Germans lost forty-one divisions. The worst period was from July 1943 until December 1943. From July to October, the losses in the East were

Table 23. Disposition of German Divisions, July 1943*

Division	Russia	Norway Finland	Denmark	West	Italy	Balkans	Total	Home Army	Reforming
Infantry	127	13 2/3	1	24	0	1½	166½, 2/3		11
Panzer	21	1		1	1	1	25		3
Panzer Gren	5½			2/2	2½		7 4/2		5
Jager	5					4	9		
Mountain	3	4 2/3				2	9 2/3		
Total Army	161½	18 4/3	1	25 2/2	3½	8½	216, 5/2, 4/3		19
Luftwaffe	12	1 1/3	1	6	1	1	22 1/3		
SS	7	1		2	1	1	12		
Total German	180	20 5/3	2	33 2/2	5½	10½	250, 5/2, 5/3		19
Allied	16½					6	22½		
German noncombat divisions									
Security	10			1			11		
Field training	4						4		
Reserve				10		1	11	2	
Replacement								33	
Grand Total	210 2/2	20 5/3	2	44 2/2	5½	17½	298, 6/2, 5/3	35	19

SOURCE: Albert Seaton, *The Russo-German War, 1941–1945* (New York: Praeger, 1970), p. 353; Burkhart Mueller-Hillebrand, *Das Heer, 1933–1945*, 3 vols. (Frankfurt: Mittler & Sohn, 1965–1969), 3:122–25; *Kriegstagebuch*, 3:736.
*One-half represents a brigade, one-third represents a regiment.

911,000 killed, wounded, and captured, while only 421,000 replacements were provided. The total number of men on the eastern front dropped from 3,138,000 on July 1, 1943, before the attack on Kursk, to 2,619,000 by December 1, 1943.[5]

An example of the weakening of the Germans in the East is the decline of the Third Panzer Army. According to textbooks, a division at full strength could hold about ten miles, but by mid-July 1943, the weakened divisions of the Third Panzer Army were holding seventeen miles, with only about 3,000 combat soldiers per division, or one soldier for eighty yards. In May, the Third Panzer Army had 292,000 men, but by September, it was down to 230,000, and in October, it had only 200,000. Four very poor Luftwaffe field divisions held over fifty miles. When the Russians attacked on October 6, 1943, the Second Luftwaffe Division broke and ran, leaving a hole ten miles wide on the German front. The entire army had to pull back. By November, a great deal of territory had been lost but the army was holding on. It was short 200,000 men in its divisions, and the replacements that did come were of poor quality.[6]

Despite continued Russian pressure in early 1944 in the North and South, the Germans were able to maintain a stable front in the East while building in the West. The Germans lost 341,950 men in Russia from March 1944 to May 1944, while picking up 357,100 replacements. The combination of the spring thaw that made Russian roads impassable and the Russian desire to await the Allied attack before launching the next drive gave the Germans a respite in the East until June 1944.

The Germans were also able to stabilize the Mediterranean theater after July 1943. After the invasion of Sicily, the Germans began to make preparations for the long delaying action on the island and in Italy. By July, five additional divisions had arrived in Italy (Third Panzer Grenadier, Twenty-ninth Panzer Grenadier, Sixteenth Panzer, Twenty-sixth Panzer, and First Parachute), and a new SS division, the Sixteenth SS Panzer Grenadier, was forming on Corsica.[7] To make the Third Mountain and Fifth Mountain Divisions available from Russia, the 328th and 113th Infantry Divisions were sent to Russia from France. The 355th Infantry Division was formed in Germany to replace the two divisions taken from France.[8]

By the end of July 1943, a semblance of a defense had been provided for Italy. The delaying action in Sicily cost the Germans few casualties and comparatively little equipment. The next attack was expected in Sardinia, Corsica, Italy, or Greece, but there was little fear for the south of France until Sardinia and Corsica were occupied. The guesswork ended on July 25, when the Germans intercepted a telephone conversation between Churchill and Roosevelt which revealed that Italy would be invaded.[9]

The order was given to reinforce Italy. Seven divisions began to move there (Forty-fourth, 305th, Seventh-sixth, Twenty-fourth Panzer, Sixty-fifth, Ninety-fourth, and Second Parachute), while the 376th and 389th were moved to southern France to be on hand. The knowledge that the Allies would invade Italy meant that there was no further need to fear the invasion of France in 1943. With a sigh of relief, the high command, with Rundstedt's approval, continued to strip all of the mobile divisions with any combat readiness from the West.[10]

Between May and August, the Germans sent thirteen divisions into Italy, twelve from France and Belgium and one from Denmark (Seventy-first). Most of these units were still in the process of reforming, but they were the best available. The units sent to Italy were to prepare for the disarming of the Italian army and the defense against the Allied attack which they correctly guessed (or perhaps learned from another radio interception) would occur at Salerno.[11] The Germans were able to contain the Allied advance in Italy by a very skillful rear-guard action that ended in a stalemate at Cassino during the winter.

The Allied attempt to bypass Cassino with the amphibious attack on Anzio also ended in a stalement. The Germans had stabilized the Italian front by the spring of 1944 and lost little ground in the drive that gave Rome to the Americans in June 1944.

Hitler was also concerned about the Balkans. On July 25, 1943, the decision was made to raise the total number of German divisions to twelve, including two on Crete. Army Group E in Yugoslavia was to have two German rifle divisions, two German reserve divisions, two Croatian divisions, four Bulgarian divisions, and two Hungarian divisions to fight Tito and the partisans. Another army was to be formed from the Third Mountain, Fifth Mountain, a panzer grenadier, and two rifle divisions from Russia, plus a panzer division, the Gross Deutschland Division, the Bosnian SS division, and the Bulgarian panzer division. This was an enormous buildup and took into consideration the loss of the Italian troops that had formerly shared a major role in the occupation of the Balkans. Many of the divisions were to come from Russia.[12]

Denmark also had become a danger point, both as a link in the communication to Norway and as a potential landing site for the Allies. After transferring its recruits to the 179th Replacement Division, the 166th Replacement Division was sent to Denmark in January 1943.[13] The 233d Reserve Panzer Division was formed on August 10, 1943, from the advanced training elements of the 233d Replacement Panzer Division in Germany. The new reserve division was sent to Denmark in September 1943.[14] The Twentieth Luftwaffe Field Division, which was being formed in Germany, was sent to Denmark in July 1943 and was still in the process of formation in October 1943.[15] The only other unit in Denmark was the 416th Infantry Division formed in December 1941 with two regiments of Luftwaffe men and guard units, supported by only a single artillery battalion.[16] The total defensive force in Denmark was very weak in early 1943, but by October, there were three divisional formations that were capable of defending the coast and preventing parachute landings.

The major buildup occurred in France and the Low Countries. The July 25, 1943, plan for rebuilding the German forces called for twenty-five static divisions and one reserve division guarding the coast, six mobile infantry divisions in reserve behind the coast, six reserve divisions training in the countryside, three reserve divisions near the coast, and two motorized divisions in reserve. There was also a Bosnian SS division training in France. On July 1, 1943, the total of forty-four divisions in France given in the *Kriegstagebuch* summary included eleven reforming divisions. The July 7, 1943, Kriegsgliederung (order of battle) gave the actual fighting strength in the West as nine infantry divisions, two parachute divisions, and nineteen static divisions of nonmobile fortress troops. This force was stronger than it had been three months before; however, the needs of the Italian front weakened it again during the next four months.

According to the German General Gunther Blumentritt, during 1943, France was used as a convalescent home to reorganize divisions exhausted in the East. The continued exchange of divisions between the East and West was so detrimental to the coastal defense that special coastal defense divisions were formed and assigned permanently to sectors. In that way they had the opportunity to gain familiarity with the area and could defend the beaches with the most economical use of equipment and available manpower. Most of the officers and men were overage, and there were fewer weapons than in other divisions. A large proportion of the weapons were French, Polish, and Yugoslav and fired different kinds of ammunition. Most of the static divisions had only two infantry regiments and two field artillery battalions plus a medium artillery battalion. All the artillery was horse-drawn. Even these divisions were spread very thin, with only three divisions covering three hundred miles south of the Loire River.[17]

Another type of division used to occupy France was the reserve division. These units were simply paper organizations of advanced training battalions. Two reserve panzer divisions (155th and 179th), each reinforced with an artillery replacement battalion and an engineer company, were sent to France as the mobile reserve in early August 1943.[18] Young soldiers learning to drive obsolete and captured tanks were not really expected to form a mobile reserve because a major invasion was discounted after the Germans learned of the Allied plans to invade Italy. On September 10, the 182d and 189th Reserve Infantry Divisions were placed directly under the command of Rundstedt, the 182d being used to garrison the Paris area. Some of the reserve divisions were manning the coastal sectors along with the static divisions. Already in July, three reserve divisions were on coastal sectors, and more were proposed for this assignment, but they did not have the manpower or the training even for that limited duty. The reserve divisions had not even formed the combat groups, as ordered, because they lacked noncoms, vehicles, and trained soldiers. These divisions contained only a few alarm battalions formed for airlanding defense.[19]

Not only were men short, but the supply of weapons to the West was reduced in early 1943. Hitler ordered that no Russian field artillery was to be used by German units on the eastern front; and as guns were short, four divisions in the West were required to ship all of their artillery to the East and to draw Russian guns in their place. Rundstedt was also required to send large quantities of ammunition for the guns from his depots to the East.[20]

During the late summer, the Germans had been sending each month 20,000 combat-ready replacments from the divisions in the West to fill the divisions in the East. Between September and November, 90,000 men were sent East. On

September 1, 1943, total strength of the western army had fallen to 770,000 including the SS, the Luftwaffe field divisions, service units, and security troops. Part of the reason for the decline after September was that the fear of the Allied invasion ended with the attack on Italy. New recruits were kept in Germany for a full four-month training period under good conditions, rather than being sent to divisions in France, where their training was interrupted with occupation duty.[21]

By September 6, 1943, the western army included twenty-seven poor-quality infantry divisions, most of them with two regiments rather than three; six panzer and motorized divisions with poor equipment; and seven divisions in reserve, three of which had just been formed.[22] The Germans in France obviously were not capable of mobile warfare.

Although the forces in the West included forty divisions, according to Rundstedt, they were being drained of all real fighting power. Even the Twenty-fifth Panzer Division, which had been refitted in Norway prior to its arrival in France in September 1943, was ordered to surrender all of its new Panzer IVs and other German tanks to the Fourteenth Panzer Division in October, when the latter was ordered to Italy. The Twenty-fifth Panzer was reequipped with French tanks. On September 10, 1943, Hitler told Goebbels that the Atlantic Wall formed a strong line of fortifications, but that "there is nothing behind them, nothing but a thin veil of reserves," therefore the invasion must be defeated on the beaches. Hitler was "pretty hopeful" that this could be done.[23]

The Germans had contingency plans worked out in the event that the Allies did attack. These plans indicated the weakness of the potential German response. In the event of an invasion in Brittany, the Germans planned to launch an immediate counterattack with the Twenty-first Panzer Division (newly reformed in France from the Schnell Brigade West and using French tanks), the Ninth and Tenth SS Panzer Divisions (just reaching combat readiness), and a battle group from the 353d Infantry Division, plus some smaller units. The second wave of units to clear up the situation would consist of the Sixtieth Panzer Grenadier Division, the 182d and 189th Reserve Divisions, a battle group from the new Twelfth SS Panzer Division, the Twentieth Mechanized Brigade (three motorized battalions), and smaller units.

If the landing came in Normandy, the same units plus the 715th Infantry Division, the Thirtieth Mechanized Brigade, and other battle groups would be employed. In neither case did the combined first and second waves consist of more than seven divisions. They could not have thrown back a determined Allied landing.[24]

The decline of the army in the West continued. On October 1, 1943, the only trained and equipped mobile divisions were the 384th, 371st, 376th, 356th, and 715th. All of the others were reserve divisions, static divisions, or in the process of formation. This paucity developed as a result of the steady flow of transfers to the East and South, based on the knowledge that the Allies were involved in Italy.

On October 28, 1943, the army in the West had twenty-three divisions on the coast and twenty-three in reserve. Of those on the coast, seventeen were fit only for defense, that is, were occupation divisions; five were only partially capable of defense, leaving only one mobile division in the coastal force. The divisions all had Ost battalions which Rundstedt considered unreliable. All of the coastal divisions were using captured weapons, and there were not enough of those.

Of the twenty-three divisions forming the mobile reserve, two were on the way and eleven were new divisions being formed. The total ration strength, that is, men actually present for duty in the army, navy, and Luftwaffe was 1,370,000 plus service and Hiwis. The total was 1,709,000, more than double the number less than two months previous. Rundstedt still did not feel that this was an adequate force for the defense of the West.[25]

Less than a week later, on November 3, 1943, Hitler issued Directive Number 51, the order to rebuild the army in the West. Thus began an entirely new surge of activity, and the West was placed in top priority for the first time. A steady flow of men and munitions created the force awaiting the Allies in June 1944. The crucial point in Directive Number 51 was that, although there still remained considerable space in Russia for strategic withdrawal and rear-guard actions, an Allied landing would put the enemy right at Germany's throat, the Ruhr industrial section. The objective of the Directive was to create a force that would defeat the anticipated invasion. The panzer and panzer grenadier divisions were to be reinforced, receiving at least ninety-three Panzer IVs or assault guns by December 1943. Each month one hundred new 75mm and 88mm heavy antitank guns were to be sent to the West, in addition to those going to new formations. The troops were to be equipped with antitank rocket launchers, similar to the American bazooka. Each static division was to receive about a thousand additional machine guns. The rebuilding of the Twentieth Luftwaffe, Twelfth SS Panzer Grenadier, and Twenty-first Panzer was to be hurried with additional men and weapons. The reserve divisions were to be filled with recruits.[26]

Hitler's order for one million men for the front on November 27 caused the reclassification of many previously considered unfit for duty to fit for limited service. Those with stomach disorders were formed into battalions and even into a combat division that received special food. Deaf men were formed into ear battalions and assigned to defensive positions. Paring the service units freed 140,000 men, and nondivisional service units produced another 120,000. Hiwis replaced a further 260,000. Placing men unfit for combat on the staffs made 20,000 available, and simply combing through the units produced another 20,000 for a total of 560,000 combat-fit men.[27]

The combing of the rear echelon was accompanied by transfer of men from the navy and air force. The result was a great increase in available men to build new divisions. From October 1943 to June 1944, a stream of new formations, with the equipment promised, began to arrive in the West. Speer's production revolution had provided the weapons. In late 1943, the Twenty-first Wave of divisions (349th, 352d, 353d) was formed and assigned to the West. These divisions were based on the remnants of those worn out on the eastern front that had been fighting as regiments. The replacements came from the combing of service troops, mentioned above, and were fully equipped according to the new division tables, with extra machine guns, artillery, and self-propelled guns.

The Twenty-second Wave (271st, 272d, 275th, 276th, 277th) created under the same conditions as the Twenty-first Wave, was formed in December 1943 and sent to the West.

To thicken the shell of defensive troops, ten occupation divisions had been created and assigned to the West between July 1943 and January 1944 (Forty-seventh, Forty-eighth, Forty-ninth, Seventieth, 242d, 243d, 244th, 245th, 265th, 266th). In late 1943, a group of independent infantry regiments was formed in the West to improve the defense. In January and February 1944, these regiments were combined with the remnants of divisions burned out in the East to form four new divisions of the Twenty-fifth Wave (Seventy-seventh, Eighty-fourth, Eighty-fifth, Ninety-first). In April 1944, the 331st Division was brought from the East for rebuilding, making a total of twenty-one additional infantry and occupation divisions for the West between September 1943 and April 1944.

Five burned-out panzer divisions came from the East (Second, Ninth, Eleventh, Nineteenth, and Lehr), and a new panzer division (116th) was rebuilt from the Sixteenth Panzer Grenadier and the 179th Reserve Panzer Divisions. The Twelfth Panzer SS and Seventeenth SS Panzer Grenadier had completed their training, and the First and Second SS Panzer Divisions came from the East in April and May 1944. The total armored additions between July 1943 and June 1944 were eleven panzer and panzer grenadier divisions. Two parachute divisions were formed in the West, and one from the East was rebuilt. Meanwhile, the drain of units had stopped. Only five divisions were permitted to leave the West after November 1943. Furthermore, in the last year, thirty-seven divisions had been added.

At the time of the invasion in June 1944, there were ten panzer divisions, one panzer grenadier division, sixteen mobile infantry divisions, and twenty-eight static divisions in the West—the most powerful and best-equipped German army assigned to the West since June 1940.

The number of mobile German divisions in the West grew from six in July 1943 to twenty-seven in June 1944. The demand of "1,000,000 men for the front" had nearly been met. The replacement army had produced 968,500 men for new units and replacements in old units in the last six months of 1943. The German army of June 1944 was a far stronger machine than it had ever been before; it was, in fact, at the peak of its power. The combined Allied and Russian offensives of the summer of 1944 soon whittled away its strength, but in June, it was far more powerful in the West than it had been a year before.

Rather than the Allies getting any benefit from the additional year of wear and tear on the German army, the one-year delay had given the Germans an opportunity to build a new group of armies in the West. They were equipped with improved tanks on a more lavish scale than before as a result of the tremendous increase in arms production in late 1943 and early 1944. The delay of a year had not weakened the German army in the West; rather, during that time, the German forces had been considerably reinforced.

17

IMPLICATIONS IN THE POSTWAR WORLD

The Americans believed that a second front was possible in France in 1943. The Russians were demanding a second front as early as 1942. The British preferred a strategy of closing the ring around Germany in the Mediterranean. This dispute created ill feelings among the Allies that, in the case of Russia, extended beyond the war's end. The Americans and the Russians believed that the British refusal to embark on a direct attack lengthened the war and caused additional loss of life. To the British, the one- or two-year delay was essential to ensure against the remotest possibility of failure and, as Churchill often stated, an English Channel filled with floating corpses.

There are several reasons for examining this question thirty years later. Closer scrutiny may provide a better understanding of the deep Russian suspicions of the Western democracies. In addition, the second front issue indicates that even in a democracy a small, strong-willed group of military leaders are able to carry out a policy, if not of deception, at least of straining the truth.

The original plan of April 1, 1942, to attack France in 1943 was and remained a distinct possibility until the commitment of our forces to Italy in September 1943. The position can be stated as follows: (1) At that time, the German army in France was weak and was known to be weak. The static divisions that made up the German garrison in France had no mobility in 1943 and few trained units. (2) The eastern front was absorbing all of the available German forces in 1943, and none could be spared for the West without seriously weakening the German position in Russia. After Kursk in July 1943, there was no German strategic reserve at all. Even before July, the immense Russian buildup in the area would have prevented the Germans from transferring sizable reserves to the West. (3) Adequate Allied forces were available to establish a firm foothold. A considerable number of American and British forces were ready, and more were in reserve in the United States. (4) Shipping was available after June 1942 to bring a million men to Britain as planned. The U-boat threat was under control by January 1943. (5) There were sufficient landing craft to land seven divisions in Sicily in 1943, and these could have been used instead to attack Normandy in 1943. (6) Service troops and air support were available. (7) Allied equipment was comparatively better in 1943 than in 1944.

The reasons for the British reluctance to attack France were complex. For political reasons, Churchill was reluctant because of the effect on the postwar balance of power in central Europe. Churchill wanted a weakened Russia after the war.

Roosevelt and Marshall wished the Western Allies to control as much of Germany as possible after the war. Marshall, in 1943, was concerned regarding the "most unfortunate diplomatic situation" that would occur if the invasion were delayed until the Russians approached the German border.[1] Churchill, on the other hand, was determined that the Allied troops control the Balkans and south central Europe at the end of the war. He dreamed of the Allied armies meeting the Russians somewhere north of Vienna in 1944, with the entire Balkans safely in Western hands behind them, and then jointly with the Russians driving in a western and northern direction against Germany. He feared that an invasion of France would draw German forces away from the East to defend the Ruhr, allowing a rapid Russian advance into the Balkans and central Europe. The American concept of an invasion in northern France was eventually accepted, but only after a year delay that left the Russians supreme in the East.

Politically, that single year was invaluable to the West in the postwar world. To understand the dilemma in which Russia found herself in May 1945, one must imagine that the United States had been overrun from the East Coast as far as the Mississippi River with the enemy within sight of Chicago and actually in the suburbs. The enemy would have penetrated to St. Louis in the following year and leveled the city, cutting all transportation routes between the oil fields in Texas and the rest of the country. In the course of this two-year campaign, the eastern part of the nation would have been laid waste to prevent its use by the enemy, and, as the tide turned, the enemy would destroy more as he retreated. More than fifteen million Americans would have been killed or captured, and we would be dependent industrially on the West Coast. At the end of the war, the United States would be threatened with atomic destruction in the press of her former Allies and even by some outspoken generals of her former comrades in arms.[2]

In very broad general terms, this was the situation of the Soviet Union in 1945. Whether an earlier end of the war would have mitigated these circumstances is questionable. If the Germans had withdrawn from Russia with greater haste, because of an invading army in the West, they would have had less time to destroy the country, and the battles in the cities would have been less costly in terms of destruction and lives.

Above all, the knowledge that the agony was extended purposefully was the most damaging factor in the postwar diplomacy. The devastation gave the Western Allies, who feared the might of a victorious Russia after the war, the opportunity to assemble their military, economic, and diplomatic forces. After World War I a belt of pro-Western nations had been placed between Russia and the rest of Europe: Poland, Finland, Rumania, and the Baltic states. The second time, the Russians proved to be a much tougher nut and forestalled such a repetition of history by the prompt creation of her own border satellites and a vigorous political assault that placed the West on the defensive.

A further political bonus to the West because of the prolongation of the war

was the subjection of Germany to additional bombing. More bombs were dropped on Germany after June 1944 than were dropped in the previous four and a
half years. The really crushing blows began with the thousand-plane raids that
overwhelmed the German defenses and their ability to cope with fires and to
rescue people. Extension of this punishment for a full year reduced the Germans
to a position where they could not threaten the Western Allies for many years to
come.

Despite the obvious political merits of prolonging the war, it was impossible to
admit this policy publicly. Other reasons had to be given for the procrastination.
What better reasons than to invoke the words of the military that more ships,
landing craft, tanks, troops, and planes were needed before tackling the German
army? Therefore, the Allies announced that they did not have sufficient force to
overpower a strong German army in France, even though intelligence reports
available to the top Allied leaders provided them with a nearly perfect picture of
their opponent.

The weakness of the American and British strategy was that neither nation
could foresee in 1943 the rapid recovery of Soviet power after the war. Churchill
dreamed of a postwar Europe with England holding the balance of power and still
thought of a lifeline to a British-ruled India via the Suez Canal. Instead, new
pulses for independence, freedom, and political change made a shambles of the
British Empire, overturned the old order in Europe, and reduced Britain to a
second-rate power, standing by while the United States and Russia divided the
world into respective spheres of influence. An early invasion of France demon-
strating Allied willingness to sacrifice to save Soviet lives might well have
lessened rather than reinforced Russian suspicions of the Western democracies
and led to a more amenable political situation in the postwar world.

The decision to delay was political and not military. There is little printed
evidence relating to the political decision, but the fact that the decision was made
supposedly on military grounds that are not supported under close scrutiny leads
us to search for other reasons. Churchill and Roosevelt directed the war subject
only to a very limited degree of legislative control and to public opinion. Although they received a great deal of advice from the Combined Chiefs of Staff,
the basic strategic decisions were made by the leaders. Churchill went far beyond
that level and intruded in military affairs as detailed as the assignment of units,
the design of tanks, and the timing of battles.

If the West was not ready to attack France in 1943, it was the result of
decisions made by Churchill and Roosevelt. Roosevelt decided to support the
war in the Pacific, far beyond an active defense, at the expense of the European
theater. Both Admiral King and General MacArthur clamored for more troops,
planes, and ships for the Pacific. During the first few months after Pearl Harbor,
these supplies were sent unstintingly to contain the Japanese, but after the Battle
of Midway a stalemate was reached in the central Pacific, and the Japanese halted
at Guadalcanal in their advance to the south. From then on, additional forces
were sent to the Pacific, not to maintain a defensive posture, which was to be the

grand strategy until Germany was defeated, but to go on the offensive. The plea was made that if the offensives were not launched, the islands would become so heavily fortified that their reconquest would be far more difficult. The China Lobby kept continual pressure on Roosevelt to open the Burma Road and to send supplies to Chiang Kai Shek. The end result was that Roosevelt allowed, if he did not order, the diversion of practically the entire American navy to the Pacific, as well as a steady stream of divisions, more than half the shipping, and a lion's share of the landing craft. The craft had been designed by the British for the European war and were, in fact, not suited to the demands of the Pacific. The LST was too slow for the long distances; the LCT lacked seaworthiness; and both were designed primarily for thirty-ton tanks, few of which were needed in the Pacific theater. Far more efficient designs could have been developed for the Pacific to deliver the lighter tanks and vehicles long distances at greater speeds.

Admiral King's attitude may have been based on belief that the British were unwilling to take on Germany, therefore the resources might as well be used in the Pacific. The decision was not King's in the last analysis—it was Roosevelt's. The British Chiefs of Staff were highly critical of the diversions to the Pacific, so the Combined Chiefs of Staff were divided on the issue. Churchill used the Pacific as a trade-off to obtain his wishes in the Mediterranean.

To a lesser degree, the diversion to the Mediterranean further reduced the Allied potential for an invasion in 1943. Because the distances were shorter, troops and ships could have been returned from the Mediterranean until the commitment to Italy in September 1943. Churchill had set his mind on the "soft underbelly" of Europe from the beginning of 1943, and he seldom varied from that course until the final months before June 6, 1944, when he agreed to give complete priority to the major offensive in France. Over and over, when faced with the need to concentrate forces for the attack, the decision was a trade-off; the Americans would send more to the Pacific, and the British would get deeper into the Mediterranean, while the cross-channel attack was postponed because of a lack of resources.

Lack of resources is a convenient phrase that can be used with various rewording to cover practically any problem. All commanders are beset by the nagging fear that they will not have enough of some item at the proper time. With the growth in complexity of war, less able commanders become slaves to their supply officers, who begin to dictate where and when actions can take place on the basis of resources available. Both British and American planners were obsessed with the desire to have more than an ample supply of everything. The need for this enormous excess baggage has been questioned, but even if it were needed, it was all available—including landing craft, materials, troops, vehicles, planes, and ships. All that was needed was the resolution to concentrate the assets in the south of England and give the order to go, rather than spreading the resources across the globe. For the final event in 1944, the planners were told arbitrarily to make enormous cuts, which they did under protest, and the result was still a very heavy oversupply in the initial stages of the invasion. Even in the later phases, the supply shortage was the result of trying to give everyone a share (the old problem of diversion) rather than having enough to carry out the essential drives.

Diversion took other forms. The advocates of air power pressed relentlessly for a greater share of the manpower, shipping, material, and productive capacity of both England and America. Perhaps half of Britain's war effort went into the air war, while about a third of America's effort was so directed. Although these proportions would be difficult to ascertain precisely, the relative share of manpower, shipping, and money gave some indication. What was the total return on the investment? Speer stated that the air war reduced German production by less than 10 percent. The survey made after the war did not show a much more favorable return. The terror from the skies did not reduce the German will to resist any more than it reduced the British will during the early years of the war. In fact, the reverse was true because it made the German civilian a part of the war; he shared in the danger along with the soldier and was transformed into a more committed production worker than his American counterpart.

The air war created a tremendous drain of manpower. This was not a cheap form of warfare in terms of men or machines. To maintain it meant literally pouring the flesh and material of the two nations into the hopper; but pitifully little came out of the other end besides dead and wounded German civilians.

In addition to diversion, poor control was a factor—perhaps one might say lack of resolute command—especially in the shipping situation. The supply of shipping was increasing after June 1942. The ships were available, but were diverted to nonessential duty. In early 1943, the number of ships was so great that the Joint Chiefs of Staff refused to order an increase in production.[3] The submarine was not taking the ships—the Pacific theater was! A ship sent to the Pacific islands might be pressed into use as a floating warehouse and not made available again for months. Despite this drain, even the ships available in the Atlantic were sufficient to improve the supply situation in Europe to the point that rations in England were increased in September 1942.[4] Ships were available in New York with no cargoes, while divisions with complete equipment were delayed in shipment overseas to billets awaiting them in England. A tighter control of the shipping would have produced far better results.

Control of production and training was far better in hand. The British often commented on the concern of American officers for training the army, in contrast to their own method of relegating the preparatory phases to civilian boards. As a result, the British had little concept of lead time and production schedules. Because one hundred LSTs were not available in January 1943 did not mean that they would not be available in April, several months later, if the plan called for them and they were needed. When ROUNDUP was approved in April 1942, the wheels were placed in motion to produce landing capability for this force by April 1943. As we have seen above, the deadlines were met; the craft were produced; the boat and shore regiments were trained to use them; and the divisions had been given practice for the landing. In fact, because of the jurisdictional dispute between the army and the navy, there was a double supply of boat crews, one army and one navy. Nevertheless, the British planners could not be convinced to accept American production schedules and count on delivery. The major obstacle to the cross-channel attack put forth in January 1943 was the need for one hundred LSTs, yet they were available on schedule in April.

Another area where the British lacked confidence was the state of American training. On the basis of a few examples such as the show staged for Churchill in June 1942 and the Kasserine Pass setback, the British concluded that the Americans could not fight the Germans. They were quick to forget their own gallop eastward across the desert with Rommel in hot pursuit on more than one occasion. Of all nations, the British should have been the first to understand that a single defeat is not sufficient evidence to indict an entire army. A poor demonstration by newly formed divisions should not have damned a whole training program, especially in view of the fact that American troops came directly from the obstacle courses in America to enemy-held beaches in Italy and won!

The greatest error of judgment, if it can be called an error, was in the comparison of the Allied forces to the Germans. Allied equipment was not inferior to that of the Germans in 1943. The strength of the German army and the ability of the individuals and units that made up that army were far inferior to the Allies. The Allies could have swept aside this force with little difficulty and made enormous gains before the Germans could have found reserves and moved them to the West. Even if the Germans had made the all-out effort of stripping the East to the point of inviting a Russian steamroller, the Allies could have moved divisions in faster over the beaches than the Germans could move them west by rail. Once landed, the Allied superior mobility would have given them an enormous advantage in the fluid warfare that would have developed.

The question is, did the Allies know this? The British certainly did. In October 1974, the British government permitted the revelation by F. W. Winterbotham that the British had cracked the German code by early 1940. Even before that intelligence source was known, the British had other means of determining the strength of the German army. French spies provided fairly accurate information. They knew that forty trains of fifty cars each were required to move a German infantry division and double that number to move a panzer division. Such major movements, which required thirty-six to seventy-two hours, respectively, of complete use of a rail line, plus the lengthy period needed to load equipment, were easily noted by French spies and account for the accuracy of that area of intelligence. Another source of intelligence was related by Brooke in his diary of May 25, 1940, when he reported the capture of a nearly complete German order of battle: "It gave a complete picture of the Army Groups, Armies, Corps and Divisions of the German Army, with Commanders-in-chief, Chiefs of Staff. Its speedy transmission to the War Office made it possible for the first time to obtain a clear grip on the Order of Battle of the German Army—a grip which was never subsequently lost."[5]

Unfortunately, the Americans relied completely on British intelligence sources. The United States Army created an effective intelligence service under General George V. Strong on May 5, 1942.[6] Many months passed before the American intelligence service was able to provide the American leaders with information directly, and, in the interim, British reports were used.

The Russians, on the other hand, were not dependent on British sources. At the Moscow Conference in August 1942, when Churchill referred to the strength of the occupation army, Stalin replied "that there was not a single German division in France of any value."[7] Stalin knew the German position with great accuracy through the communist sympathizers on the German General Staff who relayed that information to the Russians.

Churchill countered with his information that there were twenty-five German divisions in France at the time and nine of these were first-line.[8] Stalin was closer to the truth, but Churchill's estimate is interesting in view of his condition for a landing in France that "there should be not more than twelve mobile German divisions in Northern France at the time the operation was launched, and that it must not be possible for the Germans to build up more than fifteen divisions in the succeeding two months."[9] When Churchill admitted that there were only nine first-class divisions in all of France, he was also admitting the invalidity of his reason not to invade, for the German forces were not formidable.

After arguing with Churchill on the figures, Stalin finally acceded that if the British would not launch a second front, nothing could be done. He followed up that statement with a formal aide memoire complaining of the lack of the second front "inasmuch as almost all the forces of the German Army, and the best forces to boot, have been withdrawn to the Eastern Front, leaving in Europe an inconsiderable amount of forces, and these of inferior quality."[10]

Stalin did not relax his pressure for long. In February 1943, while the Allies were bogged down in Tunisia and the Germans were bringing the Russian offensive to a halt, he wrote to Churchill that since December 1942 the Germans had transferred twenty-seven divisions including five panzer divisions from France and the Low Countries to the eastern front.[11] Churchill replied on March 11, 1943, that half of the divisions sent from the West to the East after November 1942 had been replaced by divisions from Russia and from new divisions formed in France and that there were then thirty German divisions in France.[12] The British had almost as close a tab on the German divisions as did the Russians, but the two interpreted their quality quite differently.

Even if we put aside all of the possibilities of troop movement that could have become reality had Roosevelt and Churchill followed Marshall's plan of action, the forces available at the conclusion of the Sicilian campaign were still sufficient to create a bridgehead in September 1943 in France rather than in Italy. The facts were no longer remote possibilities because the Italian campaign was launched with the same troops that could have been used in France, and the German weakness was exposed by their inability to drive the Allies back to the sea, even after the transfer to Italy of the cream of the German army in France. The Allies had the strength to land in the face of the German forces. Seven divisions had been landed in Sicily almost in the teeth of units of the Hermann Goering Panzer Division and the Fifteenth Panzer Grenadier Division, both of these far superior to the 716th Infantry Division then holding Normandy. In June 1944, the Allies landed only six divisions against the five German divisions (Twenty-first Panzer, 709th, 716th, 352d, and Ninety-first) holding the same area with five more German panzer divisions available within a few days' reach of the beachhead. Considering the fact that in August 1943 there were only one division on the Normandy Coast and three panzer divisions in all of France, it is very likely that the seven divisions that landed on Sicily would have succeeded in Normandy!

Brooke was aware of the quality, or rather lack of quality, of the German units. In April 1943, he referred to the movement of German divisions as part of a routine exchange of refitted divisions from the West for worn-out divisions from the East. It is quite likely that in their eagerness to involve the United States in the Mediterranean, the British were willing to tell half-truths, for example, the "forty-four divisions" that subsequently formed the occupation army in France referred to in the Casablanca Conference plan were never defined in terms of combat worthiness; and the Americans assumed that all were capable of fighting as first-line divisions.

Thus, the responsibility for the overestimation of German strength in France can be attributed directly to the British high command. That overestimation was the major argument used by the British to oppose Marshall's demands for an immediate attack on France. The reluctance of Stalin to reveal the source of his intelligence while urging on the Allies opens another area of speculation. The simplest answer is that Stalin did not altogether trust his sources, but at the same time he did not wish to risk exposing them. Therefore, his statements regarding the German army were not given appropriate consideration.

Regardless of who believed whom and the interpretation of the facts during the conferences, it is difficult to ignore the issue that all of the Allies were well aware of the strength and weakness of the German forces in France. The British and Americans were also well aware of the strength and weakness of their own forces. Both Churchill and Roosevelt knew that they could launch an invasion in France in 1943 with a good chance of success, but they decided against it, first in July 1942 with the decision to mount the attack on North Africa; second at Casablanca, choosing Sicily as the alternate; and finally at TRIDENT in May 1943 with the decision to pursue the Mediterranean goals for the remainder of the year, turning to France in 1944.

Acceptance of the thesis presented here—that political concerns delayed the French invasion—does very little to change the image that Churchill created in his publications, but it does change the image of Roosevelt. He was not domineered by anyone, but was a man of his own decision. The right-wing press and others pictured Roosevelt as an idealistic tool of the left, who charmed the Russians into behaving in a manner pleasing to the West but detrimental to the long-term interests of the United States. If the thesis is acceptable, a different

Roosevelt emerges, a Roosevelt far more the shrewd politician who exhibited incredible skill in creating a Democratic machine that gave him almost dictatorial powers in the 1930s and elected him to the presidency four times. Although Roosevelt could voice idealistic phrases that caught the minds and hearts of the nation and the world, behind this image was a cool intellect carefully weighing the balance, employing public opinion analysts to measure reactions, and tacking in the wind when the results were not as expected. This Roosevelt was not the tool of any clique or cabal.[13]

The interpretation is therefore plausible that the second front was delayed for political reasons, even though it was militarily possible. While opposing the blatant pleas of Churchill for Balkan adventures and transalpine campaigns, Roosevelt wanted to defeat Germany in the field. He did not want a repetition of World War I with a strong German army still in existence at the time of the surrender. Therefore, one can understand why he accepted the pleas of the insatiable commanders for more men, ships, guns, and supplies as satisfactory reasons for delay. General Marshall, in his role, presented the military facts as he saw them and urged action, but, faced with the final decision to delay, he carried out his orders within the framework. In that light, the diversions to the Pacific, the implied shortage of landing craft (when more than double the required number had been launched), and the drain of resources to subsidiary theaters become understandable.

In the harsh, cold light of 1942, only three years after Stalin had signed a nonaggression pact with Hitler, the decision by Roosevelt and Churchill to allow the two greatest land armies in the world to prolong their agony seemed wise. After the dropping of the atomic bomb in 1945, however, there was no longer any need to fear the Russian army. The loss of life on the eastern front then became as pointless as the dropping of the second bomb at Nagasaki.

NOTES

ABBREVIATIONS USED IN
NOTES AND BIBLIOGRAPHY

CIGS   Chief of Imperial General Staff
DEF   Ministry of Defense Record Series
GHQ   General Headquarters
HM   Her Majesty's
MEF   Middle East Forces
NA   National Archives
PREM   Ministry of Defense Record Series, Operational Papers
OSS   Office of Strategic Services
PRO   Public Record Office
RCT   Regimental Combat Team
SS   Nazi elite troops
WK   Wehrkreise, military district
WO   War Office

Chapter 1

1. Minister of production to the prime minister, October 20, 1942, PREM 3/499/4, PRO.

2. Churchill to Lyttelton, November 9, 1942, PREM 3/499/6.

3. Among the more significant of these books on the German army are: Georg Tessin, *Verbande und Truppen der deutschen Wehrmacht und Waffen SS im Zweiten Weltkrieg, 1939-1945,* 13 vols. (Osnabruck: Biblio, 1965-1977); Burkhart Mueller-Hillebrand, *Das Heer, 1933-1945,* 3 vols. (Frankfurt: Mittler & Sohn, 1956-1969); and Wolf Keilig, *Das Deutsche Heer, 1939-1945,* 3 vols. (Bad Nauheim: Podzun, 1956-1972). Major works on leaders are: Forrest C. Pogue, *George C. Marshall,* vol. 2, *Ordeal and Hope* (New York: Viking, 1967), and vol. 3, *Organizer of Victory* (New York: Viking, 1973); Arthur Bryant, *The Turn of the Tide* (Garden City, N.Y.: Doubleday, 1957); Winston S. Churchill, *The Grand Alliance* (Boston: Houghton Mifflin, 1950), *The Hinge of Fate* (Boston: Houghton Mifflin, 1950), and *Closing the Ring* (Boston: Houghton Mifflin, 1951); and James M. Burns, *Roosevelt: The Soldier of Freedom, 1940-1945* (New York: Harcourt Brace Jovanovich, 1970).

4. J. F. C. Fuller, *The Conduct of War, 1789-1961* (New Brunswick, N.J.: Rutgers University, 1961), pp. 248-49; Jon Kimche, *The Unfought Battle* (New York: Stein and Day, 1968), p. 100.

5. Fuller, *Conduct of War,* pp. 251-55.

6. Hanson W. Baldwin, *Great Mistakes of the War* (London: Harper, 1950), p. 10; Fuller, *Conduct of War,* p. 264.

7. Fuller, *Conduct of War,* pp. 262-66.

8. Ibid., pp. 267-75, 287-88.

9. Richard W. Steele, *The First Offensive, 1942* (Bloomington: Indiana University, 1973), p. 181.

10. Fuller, *Conduct of War,* pp. 262-66.

11. Ibid., p. 269.

12. Kimche, *Unfought Battle,* p. 154.

13. Reginald Bretnor, *Decisive Warfare* (Harrisburg, Pa.: Stackpole, 1969), pp. 23–27.

14. Ibid., p. 48.

15. John Wheldon, *Machine Age Armies* (London: Abelard, 1968), p. 99.

16. Fuller, *Conduct of War*, pp. 255–56; Richard M. Ogorkiewicz, *Armoured Forces* (New York: Arco, 1970), p. 150.

17. Fuller, *Conduct of War*, pp. 70–71.

18. Ibid., p. 256; Wheldon, *Armies*, p. 78; Alistair Horne, *To Lose a Battle* (Boston: Little, Brown, 1969), pp. 43–46.

19. Wheldon, *Armies*, pp. 85–86.

20. Fuller, *Conduct of War*, pp. 255–56.

21. Philip A. Crowl and Edmund G. Love, *Seizure of the Gilberts and Marshalls* (Washington: Department of the Army, 1955), p. 4; Ernest J. King and Walter Muir Whitehill, *Fleet Admiral King: A Naval Record* (New York: Norton, 1952), pp. 327–28.

22. Steele, *First Offensive*, pp. 24–25; Robert E. Sherwood, *Roosevelt and Hopkins: An Intimate History* (New York: Harper, 1948), p. 358.

23. Steele, *First Offensive*, p. 53.

24. Ibid., pp. 54–55, 57–58.

25. Ibid., pp. 61–66, 69–74; King and Whitehill, *Fleet Admiral King*, p. 336.

26. Michael Howard, *The Mediterranean Strategy in the Second World War* (London: Weidenfeld and Nicolson, 1968), pp. 19–20.

27. PREM 3/499/2.

28. Bernard Fergusson, *The Watery Maze* (New York: Holt, Rinehart & Winston, 1961), p. 143.

29. Howard, *Mediterranean Strategy*, pp. 20–21.

30. Steele, *First Offensive*, p. 79; Eisenhower became chief of the War Plans Division on February 16, 1942 (Peter Lyon, *Eisenhower: Portrait of the Hero* [Boston: Little, Brown, 1974], p. 108).

31. Bryant, *Turn of the Tide*, pp. 280, 292.

32. Steele, *First Offensive*, pp. 94–95.

33. Richard M. Leighton, *Global Logistics and Strategy, 1940–1943* (Washington: Department of the Army, 1955), p. 353.

34. Ibid.

35. Maurice Matloff and Edwin M. Snell, *Strategic Planning for Coalition Warfare, 1941–1942* (Washington: Department of the Army, 1953), pp. 210–19; Bryant, *Turn of the Tide*, p. 279; Steele, *First Offensive*, pp. 104–05, 109–10.

36. Dwight D. Eisenhower, *Crusade in Europe* (Garden City, N.Y.: Permabooks, 1952), pp. 61–62.

37. Fergusson, *Watery Maze*, p. 144.

38. Gordon A. Harrison, *Cross Channel Attack* (Washington: Department of the Army, 1951), p. 15; Churchill, *Hinge of Fate*, pp. 314–15.

39. Bryant, *Turn of the Tide*, pp. 277–80.

40. Ibid., pp. 284, 288.

41. Sherwood, *Roosevelt and Hopkins*, p. 523.

42. Bryant, *Turn of the Tide*, pp. 285, 288–89.

43. Ibid., pp. 288, 280.

44. Ibid., pp. 286–87.

45. Ibid., p. 288.

46. Churchill, *Hinge of Fate*, p. 346.

47. Bryant, *Turn of the Tide*, p. 289.

48. Churchill, *Hinge of Fate*, pp. 479–80.

49. Bryant, *Turn of the Tide*, p. 296.

50. Ibid., 300–01, 299, 291.

51. Crowl and Love, *Seizure of the Gilberts and Marshalls*, p. 5.

52. Matloff and Snell, *Strategic Planning*, pp. 231–32.

53. Harrison, *Cross Channel Attack*, p. 24.

54. Bryant, *Turn of the Tide*, pp. 315, 304.

55. Churchill, *Grand Alliance*, p. 545.

56. Military mission in Moscow to director of military intelligence, June 16, June 23, and July 20, 1942, WO 193/651, PRO.

57. Howard, *Mediterranean Strategy*, p. 30; Bryant, *Turn of the Tide*, p. 317; Minutes of the Combined Chiefs of Staff Meeting 23, June 4, 1942 and Meeting 24, June 10, 1942, RG 218, NA.

58. Bryant, *Turn of the Tide*, p. 319.

59. Harrison, *Cross Channel Attack*, p. 25.

60. Howard, *Mediterranean Strategy*, p. 29; Minutes of the Combined Chiefs of Staff Meeting 28, June 20, 1942.

61. Churchill, *Hinge of Fate*, pp. 384–85.

62. Harrison, *Cross Channel Attack*, p. 25.

63. Howard, *Mediterranean Strategy*, pp. 30–31.

64. Harrison, *Cross Channel Attack*, p. 25.

65. PREM 3/333/2.

66. Churchill, *Hinge of Fate*, p. 433.

67. Harrison, *Cross Channel Attack*, p. 26.

68. Churchill, *Hinge of Fate*, p. 434; PREM 3/470.

69. Sherwood, *Roosevelt and Hopkins*, p. 594.

70. Harrison, *Cross Channel Attack*, p. 28; Bryant, *Turn of the Tide*, p. 340; Steele, *First Offensive*, pp. 160–61.

71. Churchill, *Hinge of Fate*, pp. 437–40; PREM 3/470.

72. Harrison, *Cross Channel Attack*, p. 29.

73. Eisenhower, *Crusade*, p. 88.

74. Harrison, *Cross Channel Attack*, p. 29.

75. Minutes of the Combined Chiefs of Staff Meeting 32, July 24, 1942.

76. Paget to Chiefs of Staff, August 7, 1942, WO 199/451.

77. Pogue, *George C. Marshall: Ordeal and Hope*, pp. 347, 349.

78. Eisenhower, *Crusade*, p. 91; Harrison, *Cross Channel Attack*, p. 31.

79. Churchill, *Hinge of Fate*, p. 451.

80. Chiefs of Staff Meeting, November 20, 1942, WO 193/101.

81. Harrison, *Cross Channel Attack*, p. 31.

82. Crowl and Love, *Seizure of the Gilberts and Marshalls*, p. 6.

83. King and Whitehill, *Fleet Admiral King*, p. 380.

84. Ibid., p. 388; Jack Coggins, *The Campaign for Guadalcanal* (Garden City, N.Y.: Doubleday, 1972), pp. 189–90.

85. King and Whitehill, *Fleet Admiral King*, p. 388.

86. Bryant, *Turn of the Tide*, p. 340.

87. Richard M. Leighton, "Overlord Revisited," *American Historical Review* 68 (July 1963): 925.

88. Harrison, *Cross Channel Attack*, p. 22.

89. Leighton, "Overlord," pp. 927–28.

90. Ibid., pp. 928–29; Pogue, *Marshall: Ordeal and Hope,* p. 330.

91. Harrison, *Cross Channel Attack,* p. 22; Leighton, "Overlord," p. 928.

Chapter 2

1. Forrest C. Pogue, *George C. Marshall: Ordeal and Hope* (New York: Viking, 1967), p. 346.

2. Arthur Bryant, *The Turn of the Tide* (Garden City, N.Y.: Doubleday, 1957), pp. 288–91; Maurice Matloff and Edwin M. Snell, *Strategic Planning for Coalition Warfare, 1941–1942* (Washington: Department of the Army, 1953), p. 235.

3. Mark A. Stoler, *The Politics of the Second Front* (Westport, Conn.: Greenwood Press, 1977), p. 165.

4. Bryant, *Turn of the Tide,* p. 400.

5. Winston S. Churchill, *The Hinge of Fate* (Boston: Houghton Mifflin, 1950), p. 649.

6. Bryant, *Turn of the Tide,* p. 401.

7. Churchill, *Hinge of Fate,* p. 652; PREM 3/499/4, PRO.

8. PREM 3/499/4.

9. Printed version, October 24, 1942, PREM 3/499/4.

10. COS (42) 345, PREM 3/499/6.

11. Churchill to Ismay, November 9, 1942, PREM 3/499/6.

12. Churchill to Lyttelton, November 9, 1942, PREM 3/499/6.

13. Dill to Churchill, November 11, 1942, PREM 3/499/6.

14. Churchill, notes, November 16, 1942, PREM 3/499/6.

15. Charles Eade, comp., *The War Speeches of the Rt. Hon. Winston S. Churchill* (Boston: Houghton Mifflin, 1953), 2:350–52.

16. Richard M. Leighton, *Global Logistics and Strategy, 1940–1943* (Washington: Department of the Army, 1955), p. 481.

17. Bryant, *Turn of the Tide,* p. 428.

18. COS meeting, November 20, 1942, WO 193/101.

19. PREM 3/333/11.

20. Churchill to Roosevelt, November 24, 1942, PREM 3/470.

21. PREM 3/470.

22. COS meeting, November 25, 1942, WO 193/101.

23. Stalin to Churchill, November 28, 1942, PREM 3/333/11.

24. Moscow to Foreign Office, December 14, 1942, ibid.

25. Ibid.

26. November 14, 1942, PREM 3/499/5.

27. Bryant, *Turn of the Tide,* p. 428.

28. Churchill to Ismay, November 29, 1942, PREM 3/499/7.

29. COS to Churchill, December 1, 1942, PREM 3/499/7.

30. Eisenhower to Churchill, November 22, 1942, PREM 3/499/5.

31. Bryant, *Turn of the Tide,* p. 434.

32. Frederick Morgan, *Overture to Overlord* (Garden City, N.Y.: Doubleday, 1950), p. 125.

33. Bryant, *Turn of the Tide,* p. 436.

34. Note by Churchill, December 2, 1942, PREM 3/499/7.

35. Churchill, *Hinge of Fate*, p. 657; Bryant, *Turn of the Tide*, p. 433.

36. Jacob to Churchill, December 2, 1942, PREM 3/499/7.

37. Chiefs of Staff, December 3, 1942, ibid.

38. Bryant, *Turn of the Tide*, p. 914.

39. Chiefs of Staff, December 15, 1942, PREM 3/499/7.

40. Minutes of War Cabinet, December 16, 1942, ibid.

41. Bryant, *Turn of the Tide*, p. 437.

42. Telegram 611 (later COS (42) 475), December 23, 1942, PREM 3/499/7.

43. Churchill, memo, December 27, 1942, ibid.

44. Defence Committee, December 29, 1942, ibid.

45. Joint Staff Mission 637, December 30, 1942, ibid.

46. COS (42) 466, December 31, 1942, PREM 3/499/8.

47. Bryant, *Turn of the Tide*, p. 443.

48. Matloff and Snell, *Strategic Planning*, pp. 379-80.

49. Bryant, *Turn of the Tide*, p. 428.

50. Ibid., p. 450; Matloff and Snell, *Strategic Planning*, p. 377.

51. Forrest C. Pogue, *George C. Marshall: Organizer of Victory* (New York: Viking, 1973), p. 19.

52. Gordon A. Harrison, *Cross Channel Attack* (Washington: Department of the Army, 1951), pp. 38-43; Churchill, *Hinge of Fate*, p. 683; Bryant, *Turn of the Tide*, pp. 443-58; Pogue, *Marshall: Organizer of Victory*, pp. 20-30.

53. Leighton, *Global Logistics, 1940-1943*, p. 675; Harrison, *Cross Channel Attack*, p. 43.

54. Leighton, *Global Logistics, 1940-1943*, p. 662.

55. Harrison, *Cross Channel Attack*, p. 43.

56. Jacob, Diary, January 23, 1943, quoted in Bryant, *Turn of the Tide*, p. 458.

57. Michael Howard, *The Mediterranean Strategy in the Second World War* (London: Weidenfeld and Nicolson, 1968), p. 35.

58. Philip A. Crowl and Edmund G. Love, *Seizure of the Gilberts and Marshalls* (Washington: Department of the Army, 1955), pp. 9-10; Ernest J. King and Walter Muir Whitehill, *Fleet Admiral King: A Naval Record* (New York: Norton, 1952), pp. 416-20.

59. Matloff and Snell, *Strategic Planning*, pp. 394-95; Crowl and Love, *Seizure of the Gilberts and Marshalls*, p. 10.

Chapter 3

1. Michael Howard, *The Mediterranean Strategy in the Second World War* (London: Weidenfeld and Nicolson, 1968), p. 36.

2. Ibid.

3. Ibid.

4. Arthur Bryant, *The Turn of the Tide* (Garden City, N.Y.: Doubleday, 1957), p. 492.

5. Ernest J. King and Walter Muir Whitehill, *Fleet Admiral King: A Naval Record* (New York: Norton, 1952), pp. 429-30.

6. Philip A. Crowl and Edmund G. Love, *Seizure of the Gilberts and Marshalls* (Washington: Department of the Army, 1955), p. 11.

7. King and Whitehill, *Fleet Admiral King*, pp. 431-32.

8. Ibid.

9. Ibid., p. 434; Crowl and Love, *Seizure of the Gilberts and Marshalls,* pp. 11–12.

10. Bryant, *Turn of the Tide,* p. 492.

11. Ibid., pp. 493–501.

12. Brooke quoted, ibid., p. 483.

13. Ibid., p. 478; Brooke quoted, p. 501.

14. Ibid., p. 486.

15. Howard, *Mediterranean Strategy,* pp. 36–37.

16. Ibid., pp. 37–38.

17. Winston S. Churchill, *The Hinge of Fate* (Boston: Houghton Mifflin, 1950), p. 941.

18. Forrest C. Pogue, *George C. Marshall: Organizer of Victory* (New York: Viking, 1973), pp. 198–99.

19. Report of the Combined Chiefs of Staff, May 25, 1943, PREM 3/443/4, PRO.

20. Bryant, *Turn of the Tide,* p. 503.

21. Winston S. Churchill, *Closing the Ring* (Boston: Houghton Mifflin, 1951), pp. 35–36.

22. Quoted in Bryant, *Turn of the Tide,* p. 553.

23. Ibid., p. 514.

24. Howard, *Mediterranean Strategy,* p. 45.

25. Churchill, *Closing the Ring,* p. 128.

26. Howard, *Mediterranean Strategy,* pp. 47, 62, 66, 51.

27. Douglas Orgill, *The Gothic Line* (London: Pan Books, 1967), p. 35.

28. Crowl and Love, *Seizure of the Gilberts and Marshalls,* pp. 12–14.

29. Ibid., pp. 14, 17.

30. Churchill, *Hinge of Fate,* p. 792.

31. Howard, *Mediterranean Strategy,* p. 45.

32. Ibid., p. 46.

33. Churchill, *Hinge of Fate,* p. 948.

34. Ibid., pp. 790–92.

35. Ibid., p. 819.

36. Orgill, *Gothic Line,* pp. 23–24.

37. Siegfried Westphal, *The German Army in the West* (London: Cassell, 1951), pp. 135–36.

38. Bryant, *Turn of the Tide,* pp. 507, 521, quote on p. 502.

Chapter 4

1. David Mason, *U-Boat: The Secret Menace* (New York: Ballantine, 1968), p. 13.

2. Wolfgang Frank, *The Sea Wolves* (New York: Ballantine, 1958), Appendix II; Herbert A. Werner, *Iron Coffins* (New York: Holt, Rinehart & Winston, 1969), p. xiv.

3. *Kriegstagebuch des Oberkommandos der Wehrmacht,* 4 vols. (Frankfurt am Main: Bernard und Graefe, 1961–1965), 1:62E.

4. Winston S. Churchill, *Closing the Ring* (Boston: Houghton Mifflin, 1951), p. 5.

5. Stephen W. Roskill, *The War at Sea,* 3 vols. (London: H.M. Stationery Office, 1954–1961), 1:614–16.

6. Mason, *U-Boat,* p. 45; Maurice Matloff and Edwin M. Snell, *Strategic Planning*

for Coalition Warfare, 1941–1942 (Washington: Department of the Army, 1953), Appendix H; Churchill, *Closing the Ring,* p. 9.

7. Frank, *Sea Wolves,* p. 67; Roskill, *War at Sea,* 1:616.

8. Frank, *Sea Wolves,* pp. 70–71.

9. Churchill, *Closing the Ring,* p. 5.

10. Frank, *Sea Wolves,* p. 89; Churchill, *Closing the Ring,* p. 5.

11. Roskill, *War at Sea,* 1:351.

12. Ibid., 1:362; Fred W. Winterbotham, *The Ultra Secret* (New York: Dell, 1974), pp. 126–27.

13. Anthony C. Brown, *Bodyguard of Lies* (New York: Harper & Row, 1975), pp. 54–55, 57.

14. William K. Hancock, ed., *Statistical Digest of the War* (London: H.M. Stationery Office, 1951), pp. 133–34.

15. Roskill, *War at Sea,* 1:464.

16. United States, Department of the Navy, *United States Submarine Losses, World War II* (Washington, Government Printing Office, 1963), pp. 159–60.

17. Roskill, *War at Sea,* 1:460–61.

18. Ernest J. King and Walter Muir Whitehill, *Fleet Admiral King: A Naval Record* (New York: Norton, 1952), pp. 338–39.

19. Frank, *Sea Wolves,* p. 42; Werner, *Iron Coffins,* pp. 47–48.

20. Frank, *Sea Wolves,* pp. 92–93; King and Whitehill, *Fleet Admiral King,* pp. 340–45.

21. Frank, *Sea Wolves,* p. 107; Hancock, ed., *Statistical Digest,* p. 177; Ernest J. King, *U.S. Navy at War, 1941–1945* (Washington: United States Navy Department, 1946), p. 206.

22. Churchill, *Closing the Ring,* p. 9; Matloff and Snell, *Strategic Planning,* Appendix H; Basil Collier, *The Second World War: A Military History* (New York: Morrow, 1967), p. 163; Roskill, *War at Sea,* 1:616.

23. WP (42) 311, PREM 3/499/3, PRO.

24. Donald Macintyre, *The Naval War against Hitler* (New York: Scribner's, 1971), p. 265.

25. Werner, *Iron Coffins,* p. xv.

26. Churchill, *Closing the Ring,* p. 4; Burkhart Mueller-Hillebrand, *Das Heer, 1933–1945,* 3 vols. (Frankfurt: Mittler & Sohn, 1956–1969), 3:103; King, *U.S. Navy,* p. 206.

27. Frank, *Sea Wolves,* p. 111.

28. Winston S. Churchill, *The Hinge of Fate* (Boston: Houghton Mifflin, 1950), p. 879; Macintyre, *Naval War,* p. 321; Arthur Bryant, *The Turn of the Tide* (Garden City, N.Y.: Doubleday, 1957), p. 303.

29. Macintyre, *Naval War,* p. 332.

30. Matloff and Snell, *Strategic Planning,* Appendix H.

31. Peter Lyon, *Eisenhower: Portrait of the Hero* (Boston: Little, Brown, 1974), p. 222; Angus Calder, *The People's War: Britain, 1939–1945* (New York: Pantheon, 1969), pp. 231, 380–81.

32. United States, War Department, *Handbook of German Military Forces,* Technical Manual-Enemy 30-451 (Washington: Government Printing Office, 1945), p. VI, 19.

33. WP (42) 311, July 21, 1942, PREM 3/499/3.

34. October 30, 1942, PREM 3/499/10.

35. Hancock, ed., *Statistical Digest*, p. 176.

36. Matloff and Snell, *Strategic Planning*, Appendix G.

37. Bryant, *Turn of the Tide*, pp. 303–04. Hopkins thought that only forty-four ships got through; see Robert E. Sherwood, *Roosevelt and Hopkins: An Intimate History* (New York: Harper, 1948), p. 544.

38. Bryant, *Turn of the Tide*, pp. 303–04.

39. Robert W. Coakley and Richard M. Leighton, *Global Logistics and Strategy, 1943–1945* (Washington: Department of the Army, 1969), p. 847.

40. Reinhard Gehlen, *The Service* (New York: Popular Library, 1972), p. 55.

41. Charles Eade, comp., *The War Speeches of the Rt. Hon. Winston S. Churchill*, 3 vols. (Boston: Houghton Mifflin, 1953), 2:293.

42. Bryant, *Turn of the Tide*, pp. 303–04.

43. Ibid., pp. 315–19.

44. Frank, *Sea Wolves*, p. 126.

45. Werner, *Iron Coffins*, p. 95.

46. Mason, *U-Boat*, p. 51.

47. Frank, *Sea Wolves*, p. 132.

48. Mason, *U-Boat*, p. 60.

49. Frank, *Sea Wolves*, p. 131.

50. John Kirk and Robert Young, Jr., *Great Weapons of World War II* (New York: Bonanza, 1961), pp. 152–55; King, *U.S. Navy*, p. 257.

51. Roskill, *War at Sea*, 2:92.

52. Hancock, ed., *Statistical Digest*, pp. 133–39.

53. Lord Cherwell to Churchill, October 30, 1942, PREM 3/499/10.

54. Roskill, *War at Sea*, 2:457.

55. Frank, *Sea Wolves*, p. 143.

56. Ibid., p. 149.

57. Eade, comp., *Churchill Speeches*, 2:286.

58. Ibid., 2:306.

59. Coakley and Leighton, *Global Logistics, 1943–1945*, p. 9.

60. Frederick Morgan, *Overture to Overlord* (Garden City, N.Y.: Doubleday, 1950), p. 170.

61. Josef P. Goebbels, *The Goebbels Diaries, 1942–1943*, edited by Jouis P. Lochner (New York: Universal-Award House, 1971), pp. 425, 428.

62. Churchill, *Closing the Ring*, p. 8; Bryant, *Turn of the Tide*, p. 490.

63. Werner, *Iron Coffins*, pp. 101–07; Frank, *Sea Wolves*, p. 159.

64. Werner, *Iron Coffins*, pp. 108–12; Frank, *Sea Wolves*, p. 159.

65. Frank, *Sea Wolves*, pp. 160–61; Werner, *Iron Coffins*, pp. 112–15.

66. Werner, *Iron Coffins*, pp. 119–20.

67. Ibid., pp. 123, 130–34, 143–47, 151; Churchill, *Closing the Ring*, p. 10.

68. Churchill, *Closing the Ring*, p. 10.

69. Werner, *Iron Coffins*, pp. 178, 208; Churchill, *Closing the Ring*, p. 5.

70. Werner, *Iron Coffins*, p. xvii.

71. Churchill, *Closing the Ring*, p. 9; Mueller-Hillebrand, *Das Heer*, 3:103; Matloff and Snell, *Strategic Planning*, Appendix H.

72. Matloff and Snell, *Strategic Planning*, Appendix H.

73. Samuel E. Morison, *The Battle of the Atlantic* (Boston: Little, Brown, 1947), p. 336.

74. Report, April 2, 1943, WO 193/101, PRO.

75. Matloff and Snell, *Strategic Planning,* Appendix G; E. B. Potter, *Nimitz* (Annapolis, Md.: Naval Institute Press, 1976), p. 234; Leighton, *Global Logistics, 1940–1943,* p. 353.

Chapter 5

1. Frederick Morgan, *Overture to Overlord* (Garden City, N.Y.: Doubleday, 1950), p. 92.

2. Bernard Fergusson, *The Watery Maze* (New York: Holt, Rinehart & Winston, 1961), p. 41.

3. Ibid., pp. 41–42; Earl Burton, *By Sea and By Land: The Story of Our Amphibious Forces* (New York: McGraw-Hill, 1944), p. 54.

4. Fergusson, *Watery Maze,* pp. 56–57.

5. Burton, *By Sea,* p. 59.

6. Walter Karig et al., *Battle Report: The Atlantic War* (New York: Farrar & Rinehart, 1946), p. 166; Samuel E. Morison, *Operations in North African Waters* (Boston: Little, Brown, 1955), p. 269.

7. Richard M. Leighton, *Global Logistics and Strategy, 1940–1943* (Washington: Department of the Army, 1955), p. 682.

8. Burton, *By Sea,* pp. 59–62; Morison, *North Africa,* pp. 270–73.

9. Fergusson, *Watery Maze,* pp. 70–72; Burton, *By Sea,* p. 56; Morison, *North Africa,* p. 268; Ernest J. King, *U.S. Navy at War, 1941–1945* (Washington: United States Navy Department, 1946), p. 285.

10. Burton, *By Sea,* pp. 55–56; Fergusson, *Watery Maze,* p. 72.

11. Fergusson, *Watery Maze,* p. 112; Burton, *By Sea,* p. 57.

12. Fergusson, *Watery Maze,* p. 117.

13. Morison, *North Africa,* p. 268; Karig et al., *Battle Report,* p. 166.

14. Fergusson, *Watery Maze,* pp. 113–17; Burton, *By Sea,* p. 60.

15. Robert E. Sherwood, *Roosevelt and Hopkins: An Intimate History* (New York: Harper, 1948), pp. 554-56.

16. Burton, *By Sea,* pp. 59-62; Fergusson, *Watery Maze,* p. 117; Morison, *North Africa,* pp. 267–68.

17. Minutes of the Combined Chiefs of Staff, meeting 22, June 2, 1942, RG 218, NA.

18. Dill to Chiefs of Staff, September 22, 1942, WO 193/487, PRO.

19. Dill to Chiefs of Staff, October 5, 1942, WO 193/487; Coakley and Leighton, *Global Logistics, 1943–1945,* pp. 17–18; Burton, *By Sea,* pp. 84–86.

20. Dill to Chiefs of Staff, November 20, 1942; Air Ministry to Mideast, November 21, 1942; and Porter to Lambe, November 21, 1942, all in WO 193/487.

21. Coakley and Leighton, *Global Logistics, 1943–1945,* pp. 20, 24, 829.

22. Ibid., p. 829; Fergusson, *Watery Maze,* pp. 117–18.

23. Burton, *By Sea,* p. 54; Fergusson, *Watery Maze,* pp. 41, 110, 113.

24. Coakley and Leighton, *Global Logistics, 1943–1945,* p. 829.

25. Morison, *North Africa,* p. 269; Karig et al., *Battle Report,* p. 166.

26. Coakley and Leighton, *Global Logistics, 1943–1945,* p. 75.

27. Burton, *By Sea,* pp. 29, 33; Samuel E. Morison, *Sicily–Salerno–Anzio, January 1943–June 1944* (Boston: Little, Brown, 1954), p. 20.

28. Morison, *Sicily,* p. 29; Fergusson, *Watery Maze,* p. 57; Burton, *By Sea,* p. 52.

29. Leighton, *Global Logistics, 1940–1943,* p. 682; Coakley and Leighton, *Global Logistics, 1943–1945,* p. 829.

30. Leighton, *Global Logistics, 1940–1943,* p. 682; Coakley and Leighton, *Global Logistics, 1943–1945,* p. 829; Fergusson, *Watery Maze,* p. 112.

31. Leighton, *Global Logistics, 1940–1943,* p. 726.

32. Ibid., p. 682.

33. Arthur Bryant, *The Turn of the Tide* (Garden City, N.Y.: Doubleday, 1957), pp. 536–37.

34. Morison, *North Africa,* pp. 266, 270.

35. Fergusson, *Watery Maze,* pp. 41–44.

36. Ibid., pp. 61–65.

37. Ibid., pp. 69, 82.

38. Ibid., p. 181.

39. Ibid., pp. 183–84.

40. Ibid., p. 188.

41. Burton, *By Sea,* pp. 29–32.

42. Kent R. Greenfield et al., *The Organization of Ground Combat Troops: The Army Ground Forces* (Washington: Department of the Army, 1947), p. 85.

43. Ernest J. King and Walter Muir Whitehill, *Fleet Admiral King: A Naval Record* (New York: Norton, 1952), pp. 319–21; Burton, *By Sea,* p. 33.

44. King and Whitehill, *Fleet Admiral King,* pp. 321–22.

45. Greenfield et al., *Organization,* pp. 86, 88; King and Whitehill, *Fleet Admiral King,* pp. 341–42.

46. Greenfield et al., *Organization,* p. 90.

47. William F. Heavey, *Down Ramp: The Story of the Army Amphibian Engineers* (Washington: Infantry Journal Press, 1947), pp. 35–41.

48. Ibid., pp. 65–77.

49. Ibid., pp. 2–3; Roland G. Ruppenthal, *Logistical Support of the Armies,* 2 vols. (Washington: Department of the Army, 1953, 1959), 1:284–85.

50. Heavey, *Down Ramp,* pp. 6–9; Ruppenthal, *Logistical Support,* 1:329.

51. Heavey, *Down Ramp,* pp. 11–14, 17.

52. Ibid., pp. 7, 18–20, 37.

53. Fergusson, *Watery Maze,* p. 223.

54. Heavey, *Down Ramp,* p. 51.

55. Ibid., pp. 47–48.

56. Morison, *North Africa,* p. 29.

57. Bryant, *Turn of the Tide,* p. 404.

58. Morison, *North Africa,* pp. 60–83, 158.

59. Ibid., pp. 137–54.

60. Ibid., pp. 223–38.

61. Ibid., pp. 198–206.

62. Fergusson, *Watery Maze,* pp. 204, 210, 188–90; COS (42), 313th meeting, November 27, 1942, WO 193/487.

63. Morison, *North Africa,* pp. 96–110, 167–73.

64. Fergusson, *Watery Maze,* p. 241.

65. Hanson W. Baldwin, *Battles Lost and Won* (New York: Harper & Row, 1966), p. 196.

66. Morison, *Sicily,* p. 20.

67. Ibid., p. 26.

68. Philip A. Crowl and Edmund G. Love, *Seizure of the Gilberts and Marshalls* (Washington: Department of the Army, 1955), p. 35.

69. Ibid.

Chapter 6

1. John Wheldon, *Machine Age Armies* (London: Abelard, 1968), pp. 131, 135.

2. Basil H. Liddell Hart, *History of the Second World War* (New York: Putnam's, 1970), p. 307.

3. J. N. Kennedy, director of Military Operations to the director of armored fighting vehicles, February 4, 1943, WO 193/540, PRO.

4. Kenneth Macksey, *Tank Warfare* (New York: Stein and Day, 1972), pp. 231–32.

5. Winston S. Churchill, *The Hinge of Fate* (Boston: Houghton Mifflin, 1950), p. 953.

6. F. M. Von Senger und Etterlin, *German Tanks of World War II* (New York: Galahad, 1969), p. 47.

7. Wheldon, *Armies,* p. 136.

8. Kent R. Greenfield et al., *The Organization of Ground Combat Troops: The Army Ground Forces* (Washington: Department of the Army, 1947), p. 429.

9. Wheldon, *Armies,* p. 224.

10. Liddell Hart, *History of the Second World War,* pp. 270–71.

11. Von Senger, *German Tanks,* pp. 45–47.

12. Burkhart Mueller-Hillebrand, *Das Heer, 1933–1945,* 3 vols. (Frankfurt: Mittler & Sohn, 1956–1969), 3:124; Albert Seaton, *The Russo-German War, 1941–1945* (New York: Praeger, 1970), p. 72; Von Senger, *German Tanks,* pp. 37–38; Wheldon, *Armies,* p. 127.

13. Wheldon, *Armies,* p. 127; Seaton, *Russo-German War,* p. 72.

14. Wheldon, *Armies,* p. 101.

15. Von Senger, *German Tanks,* p. 30.

16. Ibid., p. 212.

17. Seaton, *Russo-German War,* pp. 298–99; Von Senger, *German Tanks,* pp. 202–03.

18. Peter Chamberlain and Chris Ellis, *Panzer-Jager* (London: Almark, 1971), p. 4.

19. Peter Chamberlain and Chris Ellis, *British and American Tanks of World War II* (New York: Arco, 1969), p. 105.

20. Ibid., pp. 106–08.

21. Ibid., pp. 108–09.

22. Ibid., pp. 114–17.

23. Ibid., pp. 88–89, 91–94.

24. Ibid., pp. 96–97.

25. Ibid., pp. 138–39.

26. Greenfield et al., *Organization,* p. 73.

27. Ibid., p. 75.

28. Ibid., p. 425; Chamberlain and Ellis, *British and American Tanks,* p. 189.

29. Marshall to Eisenhower, March 12, 1943, and reply, March 18, 1943, WO 204/1290.

30. Chamberlain and Ellis, *British and American Tanks,* pp. 140–41, 147–48.

31. Ibid., p. 142.

32. Greenfield et al., *Organization,* pp. 427–29.

33. Chamberlain and Ellis, *British and American Tanks,* p. 57.

34. Ibid., pp. 60–62.

35. Ibid., pp. 35–36; Military Headquarters Papers, May 21, 1942, WO 197/587.

36. Chamberlain and Ellis, *British and American Tanks,* pp. 37–38.

37. Ibid., pp. 66–68.

38. Ibid., pp. 40, 43–44.

39. Military Headquarters Papers, November 12, 1942, WO 199/587.

40. Chamberlain and Ellis, *British and American Tanks,* p. 140.

41. Ibid., p. 65.

42. Alexander to Churchill, March 23, 1943, WO 193/540.

43. Directorate of Military Operations, January 25, 1943 and February 6, 1943, WO 193/540.

Chapter 7

1. Records of the Oberkommando des Heeres, Reforming Units, 1943–1945, Microfilm, Series GG30 T78, roll 398, frame 299, RG 1027, NA.

2. Records of German Field Commands, Divisions, Tenth Panzer Division, Microfilm, Series GG65 T315, roll 569, frame 1145, RG 1027, NA.

3. Ibid., frames 1145–49, 1156.

4. Ibid., frames 1145, 1177, 1162–63.

5. Ibid., frame 1177.

6. Ibid., frames 1185, 1229, 1230.

7. Ibid., frame 1241.

8. Ibid., frame 1242.

9. Ibid., frame 1244.

10. Ibid., roll 570, frame 210.

11. Ibid., frame 211.

12. Ibid., frame 262.

13. Georg Tessin, *Verbande und Truppen der deutsche Wehrmacht und Waffen SS im Zweiten Weltkrieg, 1939–1945,* 13 vols. (Osnabruck: Biblio, 1965–1977), 3:171.

14. Ibid., 4:36.

15. Ibid., p. 240.

16. Roger J. Bender and Hugh P. Taylor, *Uniforms, Organization and History of the Waffen SS,* 4 vols. (Mountain View, Calif.: Bender, 1971–1976), 3:46.

17. Records of German Field Commands, Divisions, Twenty-fourth Panzer Division, Microfilm, Series GG65 T315, roll 805, frame 5, RG 1027, NA.

18. Ibid., frames 41–42.

19. Ibid., frame 43.

20. Ibid., frame 5.

21. Ibid., frame 9.

22. Ibid., frame 29.

23. Ibid., frames 19–20.

24. Ibid., frames 64, 70.

25. Ibid., frames 8, 65.

26. Ibid., frame 69.

27. Ibid., frame 69; Tessin, *Verbande und Truppen,* 4:240.

28. German Field Commands, Tenth Panzer Division, Microfilm, Series GG65 T315, roll 570, frame 70.

29. Ibid., frame 133.

30. Ibid., frames 95–96, 116.

31. Tessin, *Verbande und Truppen,* 4:160–61.

32. Richard M. Ogorkiewicz, *Armoured Forces* (New York: Arco, 1970), pp. 60–61.

33. H. F. Joslen, *Orders of Battle, Second World War, 1939–1945,* 2 vols. (London: H.M. Stationery Office, 1960), 1:11.

34. Ibid., p. 179.

35. Ibid., pp. 23, 286.

36. Ibid., p. 27.

37. Ibid., p. 29.

38. Ibid., pp. 30–31; for tank data for the divisions, see WO 193/5 and WO 199/587, PRO.

39. WO 193/5 and WO 199/587.

40. Kent R. Greenfield et al., *The Organization of Ground Combat Troops: The Army Ground Forces* (Washington: Department of the Army, 1947), p. 322.

41. Martin Blumenson, *Kasserine Pass* (Boston: Houghton Mifflin, 1967), pp. 224–25.

42. George F. Howe, *The Battle History of the 1st Armored Division* (Washington: Combat Forces Press, 1954), p. 7.

43. Ibid., p. 8.

44. Ibid., p. 9.

45. Ibid., pp. 11, 14–15, 9, 93, 135.

46. George F. Hofmann, *The Super Sixth* (Louisville, Ky.: Sixth Armored Division Association, 1975), pp. 15–17.

47. Ibid., pp. 18–20.

48. Ibid., pp. 21, 23–25, 31–34, 39.

49. Bruce Jacobs, *Soldiers: The Fighting Divisions of the Regular Army* (New York: Norton, 1958), pp. 303–19.

50. Greenfield et al., *Organization,* p. 425.

51. Kenneth Macksey, *Tank Warfare* (New York: Stein and Day, 1972), p. 137.

52. Burkhart Mueller-Hillebrand, *Das Heer, 1933–1945,* 3 vols. (Frankfurt: Mittler & Sohn, 1956–1969), 3:151.

Chapter 8

1. David Bergamini, *Japan's Imperial Conspiracy,* 2 vols. (New York: Morrow, 1971), 2:1234.

2. Kent R. Greenfield et al., *The Organization of Ground Combat Troops: The Army Ground Forces* (Washington: Department of the Army, 1947), p. 38.

3. Ibid., pp. 53–54; Robert R. Palmer, Bell I. Wiley, and William R. Keast, *The*

Procurement and Training of Ground Combat Troops: The Army Ground Forces (Washington: Department of the Army, 1948), pp. 434–35.

4. Palmer et al., *Ground Combat Troops,* p. 444.

5. United States, War Department, Adjutant General, Decimal File, Training, RG 337, NA.

6. *Ours to Hold High: The History of the 77th Infantry Division in World War II* (Washington: Infantry Journal Press, 1947), p. 6.

7. Adjutant General, Decimal File; *Ours to Hold High,* p. 9.

8. *Ours to Hold High,* p. 11.

9. Ibid., pp. 10–12.

10. Ibid., pp. 12–14.

11. Ibid., pp. 14–17.

12. Ibid., pp. 17–21.

13. Ibid., p. 18.

14. Ibid., pp. 21–22.

15. United States, War Department, Unit History Data Cards, Organization and Directory Section, Operations Branch, Operations and Training Division, Adjutant General's Office, RG 407, NA.

16. Paul L. Schultz, *The 85th Infantry Division in World War II* (Washington: Infantry Journal Press, 1949), pp. 7–9; Harry J. Goodyear, comp., *History of the 3rd Battalion, 338th Infantry Regiment, 85th Infantry Division, World War II* (n.p.: Campus Publishing Co., 1946), p. 11.

17. Unit History Data Cards; Goodyear, *3rd Battalion,* p. 10; Schultz, *85th Infantry,* pp. 10–12.

18. Schultz, *85th Infantry,* pp. 16–19; Goodyear, *3rd Battalion,* p. 13.

19. Schultz, *85th Infantry,* pp. 23–25.

20. Ibid., pp. 24–25.

21. Ibid., pp. 26–28, 32.

22. Ibid., p. 33.

23. Ibid., pp. 33–41.

24. Palmer et al., *Ground Combat Troops,* p. 440.

25. Ibid., p. 438.

26. Ibid., p. 458.

27. Robert E. Sherwood, *Roosevelt and Hopkins: An Intimate History* (New York: Harper, 1948), p. 592.

28. Palmer et al., *Ground Combat Troops,* p. 457.

29. *Ours to Hold High,* p. 19.

30. Winston S. Churchill, *The Hinge of Fate* (Boston: Houghton Mifflin, 1950), p. 323.

31. Sherwood, *Roosevelt and Hopkins,* p. 592.

32. Arthur Bryant, *The Turn of the Tide* (Garden City, N.Y.: Doubleday, 1957), pp. 332–33.

33. Martin Blumenson, *Kasserine Pass* (Boston: Houghton Mifflin, 1967), p. 309.

34. Erwin Rommel, *The Rommel Papers,* edited by Basil H. Liddell Hart (New York: Harcourt Brace, 1953), pp. 398, 366.

35. Ibid., p. 407.

36. Josef P. Goebbels, *The Goebbels Diaries, 1942–1943,* edited by Louis P. Lochner (New York: Universal Award House, 1971), pp. 349, 356, 430–31.

37. Siegfried Westphal, *The German Army in the West* (London: Cassell, 1951), p. 165.

38. Palmer et al., *Ground Combat Troops,* p. 455.

39. Wolf Keilig, *Das Deutsche Heer, 1939-1945,* 3 vols. (Bad Nauheim: Podzun, 1956-1972), 3:101, p. 6; Burkhart Mueller-Hillebrand, *Das Heer, 1933-1945,* 3 vols. (Frankfurt: Mittler & Sohn, 1956-1969), 3:50-51.

40. Georg Tessin, *Verbande und Truppen der deutschen Wehrmacht und Waffen SS im Zweiten Weltkrieg, 1939-1945,* 13 vols. (Osnabruck: Biblio, 1965-1977), 5:264, 7:56-58, 165-66.

41. Records of German Field Commands, Divisions, Sixty-fifth Division, Microfilm, Series GG65 T315, roll 1037, frames 603-04, RG 1027, NA.

42. Ibid., frame 602.

43. Ibid., frames 543, 545.

44. Ibid., frame 545.

45. Ibid., frame 556.

46. Ibid., frames 542-43.

47. Ibid., frame 542.

48. Ibid., frame 545.

49. Ibid., frame 547.

50. Ibid., frame 546.

51. Ibid., frame 406.

52. Ibid., frame 331.

53. Ibid., frames 395, 402.

54. Ibid., frame 391.

55. Ibid., frames 160-61.

56. Ibid., frames 157-59.

57. Ibid., frame 41.

58. Ibid., frame 263.

59. Ibid., frames 111, 193, 154-55.

60. Ibid., frame 111.

61. Ibid., frame 112.

62. Ibid., frames 110, 69-70.

63. Ibid., frames 87-92.

64. Ibid., frame 68.

65. Ibid., frames 42-43.

66. Ibid., frame 71.

67. Ibid., frames 761-72.

68. Ibid., frames 719-26.

69. Ibid., frames 42-43.

70. Ibid., frames 318-19.

71. Ibid., frame 97.

72. Ibid., frame 1037.

73. Ibid., frame 758.

74. Ibid., frame 42.

75. Ibid., frame 776.

76. Ibid., frame 708.

77. Ibid., frames 702-03.

78. Ibid., frames 630-33.

79. Ibid., frame 621.
80. Ibid., frame 633.
81. Ibid., frames 680, 687.

Chapter 9

1. *The Reserve Officers' Training Corps Manual, Infantry*, 4 vols., 24th ed. (Harrisburg: Military Service Publishing Co., 1942), 3:698.
2. Ibid.; Ian Hogg and John Weeks, *Military Small Arms of the Twentieth Century* (Northfield, Ill.: Digest Books, 1973), p. 4.37.
3. Ibid., pp. 5.62, 5.25.
4. *ROTC Infantry Manual*, 3:698.
5. Ian Hogg, *Grenades and Mortars* (New York: Ballantine, 1974), p. 122.
6. Kent R. Greenfield et al., *The Organization of Ground Combat Troops: The Army Ground Forces* (Washington: Department of the Army, 1947), p. 290.
7. Ibid., p. 293.
8. Ibid., pp. 338–39.
9. John R. Galvin, *Air Assault: The Development of Airmobile Warfare* (New York: Hawthorne, 169), pp. 87–88.
10. Greenfield et al., *Organization*, p. 341.
11. Hal Burton, *The Ski Troops* (New York: Simon and Schuster, 1971), p. 110.
12. T/0 Infantry Battalion, January 13, 1943, WO 32/10400, PRO.
13. H. F. Joslen, *Orders of Battle, Second World War, 1939–1945*, 2 vols. (London: H.M. Stationery Office, 1960), 1:131.
14. John Batchelor and Ian Hogg, *Artillery* (New York: Scribner's, 1972), p. 22.
15. Joslen, *Orders of Battle*, 1:131.
16. Ibid., p. 127.
17. Ibid., pp. 89, 350; J. B. M. Frederick, *Lineage Book of the British Army: Mounted Corps and Infantry, 1660–1968* (Cornwallville, N.Y.: Hope Farm Press, 1969), pp. 150, 189, 289.
18. Joslen, *Orders of Battle*, 1:351, 362.
19. Burkhart Mueller-Hillebrand, *Das Heer, 1933–1945*, 3 vols. (Frankfurt: Mittler & Sohn, 1956–1969), 3:58–59.
20. Records of the Oberkommando des Heeres, Reforming Units, 1943–1945, Microfilm, Series GG30 T78, roll 398, frames 368296–97.
21. Ibid., frames 368298 and 368262.
22. Mueller-Hillebrand, *Das Heer*, 3:235; Wolf Keilig, *Das Deutsche Heer, 1939–1945*, 3 vols. (Bad Nauheim: Podzun, 1956–1972), 1:15, p. 15.
23. German OKH, Reforming Units, Microfilm, Series GG30 T78, roll 398, frames 368116–18.
24. Ibid., frame 368229.
25. Ibid., frame 368230.
26. Ibid., frame 368241.
27. Keilig, *Das Deutsche Heer*, 1:15, p. 16; Mueller-Hillebrand, *Das Heer*, 3:227.
28. Guy Sajer, *The Forgotten Soldier* (New York: Harper & Row, 1971), p. 170.
29. Ibid., p. 206.
30. Werner Haupt, *Die 260. Infanterie-Division, 1939–1944* (Bad Nauheim: Podzun, 1970), pp. 166, 169–70, 196–97.
31. Ibid., p. 167.

32. Werner Haupt, *Geschichte der 134. Infanterie-Division* (Weinsberg: Herausgegeben vom Kameradenkreis der ehemaligen, 134. Inf.-Division, 1971), pp. 166, 174.

33. Albert Seaton, *The Russo-German War, 1941–1945* (New York: Praeger, 1970), pp. 391, 384.

34. OSS Report File OB 19S, NA.

35. German OKH, Reforming Units, Microfilm, Series GG30 T78, roll 398, frame 368234.

36. Mueller-Hillebrand, *Das Heer,* 3:153.

37. Keilig, *Das Deutsche Heer,* 1:15, p. 40.

38. Mueller-Hillebrand, *Das Heer,* 3:111–12.

39. German OKH, Reforming Units, Microfilm, Series GG30 T78, roll 398, frames 368233–37.

40. Mueller-Hillebrand, *Das Heer,* 3:116.

41. Robert R. Palmer, Bell I. Wiley, and William R. Keast, *The Procurement and Training of Ground Combat Troops* (Washington: Department of the Army, 1948), p. 442.

42. German OKH, Reforming Units, Microfilm, Series GG30 T78, roll 398, frame 368360.

43. Mueller-Hillebrand, *Das Heer,* 3:120–21.

44. Seaton, *Russo-German War,* pp. 390–91.

Chapter 10

1. John Quick, *Dictionary of Weapons and Military Terms* (New York: McGraw-Hill, 1973), p. 422; Bernard Fitzsimons, *Warplanes and Air Battles of World War II* (New York: Beekman, 1973), p. 52.

2. Bryan Cooper and John Batchelor, *Bombers, 1939–1945* (London: Marshal Cavendish, 1974), pp. 42–43, 52; Quick, *Dictionary,* p. 212.

3. Alfred Price, *Luftwaffe* (New York: Ballantine, 1969), p. 92.

4. Gavin Lyall, ed., *The War in the Air: The Royal Air Force in World War II* (New York: Ballantine, 1970), p. 206; Adolf Galland, *The First and the Last: The Rise and Fall of the German Fighter Forces, 1938–1945* (New York: Ballantine, 1957), pp. 124–25.

5. Galland, *The First and the Last,* p. 125.

6. Edward Jablonski, *Flying Fortress* (Garden City, N.Y.: Doubleday, 1965), pp. 310–11.

7. Quick, *Dictionary,* p. 275.

8. Jablonski, *Flying Fortress,* p. 89.

9. Galland, *The First and the Last,* p. 143.

10. Ibid., p. 148.

11. Ibid., pp. 141–42; Martin Caidin, *Black Thursday* (New York: Dutton, 1960), pp. 25–26; Price, *Luftwaffe,* p. 97.

12. Martin Caidin, *ME 109* (New York: Ballantine, 1968), pp. 116–28; William Green, *War Planes of the Second World War,* 10 vols. (Garden City, N.Y.: Doubleday, 1960–1973), 1:153–55.

13. Green, *War Planes,* 1:97–100.

14. John Kirk and Robert Young, Jr., *Great Weapons of World War II* (New York: Bonanza, 1961), p. 16.

15. Caidin, *ME 109,* p. 112.

16. Price, *Luftwaffe*, p. 121.

17. Galland, *The First and the Last*, p. 149.

18. Ibid., pp. 188, 150–52.

19. Ibid., pp. 188, 129; Price, *Luftwaffe*, pp. 94–95.

20. Galland, *The First and the Last*, pp. 157–59.

21. Ibid., pp. 166, 168.

22. Caidin, *Black Thursday*, p. 199.

23. Galland, *The First and the Last*, p. 179.

24. Caidin, *Black Thursday*, pp. 56–57.

25. Galland, *The First and the Last*, p. 188.

26. Price, *Luftwaffe*, p. 127; Galland, *The First and the Last*, p. 180; Caidin, *Black Thursday*, pp. 275–78.

27. Roger A. Freeman, *Mustang at War* (Garden City, N.Y.: Doubleday, 1974), p. 66; John Batchelor and Bryan Cooper, *Fighter: A History of Fighter Aircraft* (New York: Scribner's, 1973), p. 101.

28. Green, *War Planes*, 4:170–77.

29. Ibid., pp. 136–37; Freeman, *Mustang at War*, pp. 11–17.

30. Green, *War Planes*, 4:136–38.

31. Ibid., pp. 140–43.

32. James Campbell, *The Bombing of Nuremberg* (Garden City, N.Y.: Doubleday, 1974), p. 188.

33. John Wheldon, *Machine Age Armies* (London: Abelard, 1968), p. 139.

34. Albert Seaton, *The Russo-German War, 1941–1945* (New York: Praeger, 1970), p. 402.

35. Lyall, ed., *War in the Air*, p. 202; Campbell, *Bombing of Nuremberg*, pp. 142, 170–72; Wheldon, *Armies*, p. 138.

36. Batchelor and Cooper, *Fighter*, p. 86; Richard Humble, *War in the Air, 1939–1945* (London: Salamander, 1975), p. 11.

37. Wheldon, *Armies*, pp. 137–42.

38. Green, *War Planes*, 2:97–98; John Vader, *Spitfire* (New York: Ballantine, 1969), pp. 90–91.

39. Green, *War Planes*, 2:104–05.

40. Vader, *Spitfire*, p. 135; Green, *War Planes*, 2:105.

41. Green, *War Planes*, 2:108–10.

42. Lyall, ed., *War in the Air*, pp. 215–19.

43. Fitzsimons, *Warplanes*, p. 82; *Kriegstagebuch des Oberkommandos der Wehrmacht*, 4 vols. (Frankfurt am Main: Bernard und Graefe, 1961–1965), 2:613, 1227; Terence Robertson, *Dieppe: The Shame and the Glory* (Boston: Little, Brown, 1962), p. 389.

44. *Kriegstagebuch*, 3:122.

45. Caidin, *Black Thursday*, pp. 49–50.

46. Price, *Luftwaffe*, p. 95.

47. Humble, *War in the Air*, p. 6.

48. Wheldon, *Armies*, pp. 137–38.

49. Peter C. Smith, *The Stuka at War* (New York: Arco, 1971), pp. 12–14; David Mason, *U-Boat: The Secret Menace* (New York: Ballantine, 1968), pp. 199–201, 237.

50. Price, *Luftwaffe*, p. 34.

51. Smith, *Stuka*, p. 16; Batchelor and Cooper, *Fighter*, p. 83.

52. Page Shamburger and Joe Christy, *The Curtiss Hawk Fighters* (New York: Sports Car Press, 1971), p. 49.

53. Quick, *Dictionary*, p. 217.

54. Shamburger and Christy, *Hawk Fighters*, pp. 73-76.

55. Freeman, *Mustang at War*, p. 23.

56. Batchelor and Cooper, *Fighter*, p. 127.

57. Kirk and Young, *Great Weapons*, pp. 24-27.

58. Shamburger and Christy, *Hawk Fighters*, p. 73.

59. Batchelor and Cooper, *Fighter*, p. 243; Kirk and Young, *Great Weapons*, pp. 20, 23.

60. Albert Speer, *Inside the Third Reich* (New York: Macmillan, 1970), pp. 331-32.

Chapter 11

1. Richard M. Leighton, *Global Logistics and Strategy: 1940-1943* (Washington: Department of the Army, 1955), p. 724.

2. Ibid., p. 733.

3. Alfred Vagts, *Landing Operations* (Harrisburg: Military Service Press, 1946), p. 40.

4. Leighton, *Global Logistics, 1940-1943*, p. 733.

5. Vagts, *Landing Operations*, p. 40.

6. United States, War Department, *Staff Officers Field Manual, Enemy Forces: Organization, Technical and Logistical Data*, Field Manual-Enemy 101-10 (Washington: Government Printing Office, 1942), p. 49.

7. WO 193/855, PRO.

8. *Kriegstagebuch des Oberkommandos der Wehrmacht*, 4 vols. (Frankfurt am Main: Bernard und Graefe, 1961-1965), 3:265-335.

9. *Staff Officers Field Manual, Enemy Forces*, 101-10, p. 48.

10. United States. War Department, *The German Armored Division*, Information Bulletin No. 18 (Washington: Government Printing Office, 1941), p. 20.

11. Kent R. Greenfield et al., *The Organization of Ground Combat Troops: The Army Ground Forces* (Washington: Department of the Army, 1947), pp. 282, 285-86.

12. Secretary of War to Churchill, PREM 3/55/2, PRO.

13. Vagts, *Landing Operations*, p. 41; Leighton, *Global Logistics, 1940-1943*, pp. 723.

14. Werner Haupt, *Geschichte der 134. Infantrie-Division* (Weinsberg: Herausgegeben vom Kameradenkreis der ehemaligen, 134. Inf.-Division, 1971), p. 166.

15. United States. War Department. *Handbook of German Military Forces*, Technical Manual-Enemy 30-451 (Washington: Government Printing Office, 1945), p. VI, 20.

16. WO 32/10400.

17. Haupt, *134. Infantrie-Division*, pp. 173, 175.

18. Leighton, *Global Logistics, 1940-1943*, pp. 736-37.

19. Forrest C. Pogue, *George C. Marshall: Organizer of Victory* (New York: Viking, 1973), pp. 80-81.

20. Kenneth Strong, *Intelligence at the Top* (Garden City, N.Y.: Doubleday, 1969), p. 64.

21. Greenfield et al., *Organization*, p. 203.

22. Robert R. Palmer, Bell I. Wiley, and William R. Keast, *The Procurement and*

Training of Ground Combat Troops (Washington: Department of the Army, 1948), p. 226.

23. Charles B. MacDonald, *The Mighty Endeavor: American Armed Forces in World War II* (New York: Oxford, 1969), p. 251.

24. Greenfield et al., *Organization,* pp. 203, 209, 213.

25. PREM 3/55/7.

26. January 23, 1941, PREM 3/55/2.

27. Churchill to Ismay, December 27, 1942, PREM 3/190/3.

28. Ismay to Churchill, December 30, 1942, ibid.

29. PREM 3/54/9.

30. Winston S. Churchill, *Closing the Ring* (Boston: Houghton Mifflin, 1951), pp. 682-83.

31. Strong, *Intelligence,* p. 64.

32. Lucas K. Truscott, *Command Missions: A Personal Story* (New York: Dutton, 1954), p. 544.

33. George F. Hofmann, *The Super Sixth* (Louisville, Ky.: Sixth Armored Division Association, 1975), p. 449.

34. Millard Fillmore Hospital, *Annual Report for 1975* (Buffalo, N.Y.: n.p., 1976), passim.

35. Burkhart Mueller-Hillebrand, *Das Heer, 1933-1945,* 3 vols. (Frankfurt: Mittler & Sohn, 1956-1969), 3:217-19; Wolf Keilig, *Das Deutsche Heer, 1939-1945,* 3 vols. (Bad Nauheim: Podzun, 1956-1972), 2:101, V, p. 66.

36. WO 204/2042.

Chapter 12

1. Fred W. Winterbotham, *The Ultra Secret* (New York: Dell, 1974), passim.

2. Letter to author from Miss G. L. Beech, PRO, March 1, 1978.

3. Anthony C. Brown, *Bodyguard of Lies* (New York: Harper & Row, 1975), p. 20.

4. Ibid., p. 21.

5. Ibid., pp. 21-23; Winterbotham, *The Ultra Secret,* pp. 34, 51-52.

6. Winterbotham, *The Ultra Secret,* p. 73.

7. Ibid., pp. 38-42.

8. Ibid., pp. 51-52, 351.

9. Ibid., p. 52.

10. Walter Warlimont, *Inside Hitler's Headquarters, 1939-1945* (New York: Praeger, 1964), p. 641.

11. American Telephone and Telegraph Company, *Telephone and Telegraph Statistics of the World, January 1, 1938,* Comptroller's Department, Chief of Statistics Division (n.p.: n.p., 1939), pp. 5-6.

12. United States, Department of Commerce, *Historical Statistics of the United States: Colonial Times to 1957* (Washington: Government Printing Office, 1960), pp. 484, 486.

13. OSS Report, File OB1955, NA.

14. Ibid., OB3066, OB2382, OB3768, OB3518, OB3227S, OB5234.

15. Ibid., OB3094.

16. Ibid., 22424.

17. *Kriegstagebuch des Oberkommandos der Wehrmacht,* 4 vols. (Frankfurt am Main: Bernard und Graefe, 1961-1965), 2:1383.

18. OSS Report, File 23408; *Kriegstagebuch,* 2:1390.

19. OSS Report, File 23803S; *Kriegstagebuch,* 2:794.

20. OSS Report, File 27198C.

21. Ibid., 26550C.

22. Ibid., 26855.

23. Winterbotham, *The Ultra Secret,* p. 178.

24. Review by MI 14 to director of military intelligence, March 23, 1943, WO 193/855, PRO.

25. Pierre Accoce and Pierre Quet, *Master Spy: A Man Called Lucy* (New York: Coward, McCann & Geoghegan, 1972), pp. 8–9.

26. Winston S. Churchill, *The Hinge of Fate* (Boston: Houghton Mifflin, 1950), p. 479.

27. OSS Report, File 23928S.

28. Winterbotham, *The Ultra Secret,* p. 42.

29. Ladislas Farago, *The Game of Foxes* (New York: Bantam, 1971), pp. 745–53.

30. *Kriegstagebuch,* 3:852.

31. OSS Report, File OB2940C.

32. Farago, *Game of Foxes,* p. 762.

33. Brown, *Bodyguard of Lies,* p. 102.

34. Farago, *Game of Foxes,* p. 762.

35. Brown, *Bodyguard of Lies,* pp. 73–74.

36. Terence Robertson, *Dieppe: The Shame and the Glory* (Boston: Little, Brown, 1962), p. 33.

37. Ibid., pp. 34–37, 49–73.

38. Brown, *Bodyguard of Lies,* p. 73.

39. Stephen W. Roskill, *The War at Sea,* 3 vols. (London: H.M. Stationery Office, 1954–1961), 2:241.

40. Brown, *Bodyguard of Lies,* pp. 74–75.

41. Robertson, *Dieppe,* pp. 113–15, 125–26.

42. Ibid., pp. 130–34; Brown, *Bodyguard of Lies,* pp. 79–81.

43. *Kriegstagebuch,* 2:1280–81; Warlimont, *Hitler's Headquarters,* p. 247.

44. Robertson, *Dieppe,* p. 176; Brown, *Bodyguard of Lies,* p. 85.

45. Intelligence Report, August 10, 1942, WO 106/4196.

46. Georg Tessin, *Verbande und Truppen der deutschen Wehrmacht und Waffen SS im Zweiten Weltkrieg, 1939–1945,* 13 vols. (Osnabruck: Biblio, 1965–1977), 9:74–75, p. 176; Brown, *Bodyguard of Lies,* p. 85.

47. Mountbatten to Brooke, November 1, 1942, WO 106/4115.

48. Robertson, *Dieppe,* pp. 387–88.

49. Brown, *Bodyguard of Lies,* p. 87.

50. Records of German Field Commands, Divisions, Tenth Panzer Division, Microfilm, Series GG65 T315, roll 570, frames 413–15, RG 1027, NA.

51. Brown, *Bodyguard of Lies,* pp. 178–80.

52. Report on Jubilee by J. H. Roberts, commander of the Second Canadian Division, WO 106/4197.

53. Brown, *Bodyguard of Lies,* p. 87.

54. August 20, 1942, PREM 3/256, PRO.

55. Winterbotham, *The Ultra Secret,* p. 246.

56. Brown, *Bodyguard of Lies,* p. 81.

57. *Kriegstagebuch,* 2:609.

58. German Field Commands, Tenth Panzer Division, Microfilm, Series GG65 T315, roll 570, frame 466.

59. Robertson, *Dieppe,* p. 386.

60. Roskill, *War at Sea,* 2:251.

61. Churchill to Ismay, December 21, 1942, and reply December [?], 1942, PREM 3/256.

62. August 10, 1942, WO 106/4196.

63. WO 106/4197.

64. Report, August 30, 1942, ibid.

65. Appendix A, 3 h, August 10, 1942, WO 106/4196.

66. Churchill to Ismay, December 6, 1942, PREM 3/256.

67. Warlimont, *Hitler's Headquarters,* p. 253.

68. Brown, *Bodyguard of Lies,* p. 233.

69. Lord Beaverbrook was convinced that the raid was arranged to discredit the second front. See A. J. P. Taylor, *Beaverbrook* (New York: Simon and Schuster, 1972), p. 538.

Chapter 13

1. Earl Alexander of Tunis, *The Alexander Memoirs, 1940-1945,* edited by John North (New York: McGraw-Hill, 1961), p. 37.

2. Ibid., p. 65.

3. *Kriegstagebuch des Oberkommandos der Wehrmacht,* 4 vols. (Frankfurt am Main: Bernard und Graefe, 1961-1965), 3:144, entry for February 19, 1943.

4. George F. Howe, *Northwest Africa: Seizing the Initiative in the West* (Washington: Department of the Army, 1957), p. 475.

5. Lucas K. Truscott, *Command Missions: A Personal Story* (New York: Dutton, 1954), p. 537.

6. Fred W. Winterbotham, *The Ultra Secret* (New York: Dell, 1974), pp. 149-51.

7. WO 204/936, PRO.

8. Truscott, *Command Missions,* p. 537.

9. Daily Report, North African Theater of Operations, January 29, 1943, Operations Division, War Department General Staff in Project Decimal File, 1942-1945, RG 165, NA.

10. Ibid., March 26, 1943; *Kriegstagebuch,* 3:1416.

11. Winterbotham, *The Ultra Secret,* p. 135.

12. Martin Blumenson, *Kasserine Pass* (Boston: Houghton Mifflin, 1967), p. 305; Anthony C. Brown, *Bodyguard of Lies* (New York: Harper & Row, 1975), p. 132.

13. Dwight D. Eisenhower, *Crusade in Europe* (Garden City, N.Y.: Permabooks, 1952), pp. 158, 182.

14. Blumenson, *Kasserine Pass,* p. 306.

15. Winterbotham, *The Ultra Secret,* p. 148.

16. Blumenson, *Kasserine Pass,* p. 131.

17. Daily Summary, February 13, 1943, Plans and Operations Division, War Department, RG 165.

18. Cable Log, February 13, 1943, Allied Force Headquarters, Chief of Staff, in the Walter Bedell Smith Collection, Eisenhower Library, Abilene, Kansas.

19. Ibid., February 4, 1943, Message 208, Eisenhower Library.

20. WO 106/2726.

21. Blumenson, *Kasserine Pass,* p. 131.

22. WO 201/2174.

23. G-2 Report 90, February 5, 1943, WO 204/3961.

24. WO 201/2174.

25. I. S. O. Playfair and C. J. C. Molony, *The Mediterranean and the Middle East,* vol. 4 (London: H.M. Stationery Office, 1966), p. 288.

26. Ibid.; Blumenson, *Kasserine Pass,* p. 131.

27. Records of German Field Commands, Divisions, Tenth Panzer Division, Microfilm, Series GG65 T315, roll 570, frames 354–62, RG 1027, NA.

28. *Kriegstagebuch,* 3:115, entry for February 10, 1943.

29. Playfair and Molony, *Mediterranean,* p. 288.

30. German Field Commands, Tenth Panzer Division, Microfilm, Series GG65 T315, roll 570, frames 363, 368–78.

31. Truscott, *Command Missions,* p. 152.

32. WO 106/2726.

33. WO 175/53.

34. GSI Daily Intelligence Summary, GHQ MEF, February 14, 1943, WO 201/2174.

35. Howe, *Northwest Africa,* pp. 403–04; Blumenson, *Kasserine Pass,* p. 124.

36. Blumenson, *Kasserine Pass,* pp. 121, 124–26, 128.

37. Ibid., p. 129.

38. G-2, 25, AFHQ in the field, February 15, 1943, WO 204/3961.

39. Blumenson, *Kasserine Pass,* p. 127; Playfair and Molony, *Mediterranean,* p. 289; Truscott, *Command Missions,* p. 153.

40. Playfair and Molony, *Mediterranean,* pp. 189–90; Basil H. Liddell Hart, *History of the Second World War* (New York: Putnam's, 1970), pp. 402–03; Howe, *Northwest Africa,* p. 403.

41. Howe, *Northwest Africa,* pp. 411–16; Blumenson, *Kasserine Pass,* pp. 149–53.

42. Blumenson, *Kasserine Pass,* pp. 155–63; Howe, *Northwest Africa,* pp. 417–24.

43. Cable Log, Allied Force HQ, February 5 and 8, 1943, Smith Collection, Eisenhower Library.

44. Howe, *Northwest Africa,* pp. 425–35; Blumenson, *Kasserine Pass,* pp. 190–91; Playfair and Molony, *Mediterranean,* pp. 293–94; Truscott, *Command Missions,* p. 538.

45. Playfair and Molony, *Mediterranean,* p. 292; Howe, *Northwest Africa,* p. 424; Blumenson, *Kasserine Pass,* p. 203.

46. Howe, *Northwest Africa,* pp. 439–40.

47. Ibid., pp. 439–56; Blumenson, *Kasserine Pass,* pp. 230–31; Liddell Hart, *History of the Second World War,* p. 407.

48. Ronald Lewin, *Rommel as Military Commander* (New York: Ballantine, 1970), p. 260; Blumenson, *Kasserine Pass,* pp. 254–55; Howe, *Northwest Africa,* p. 456.

49. Howe, *Northwest Africa,* pp. 460–65; Blumenson, *Kasserine Pass,* pp. 268–69; Playfair and Molony, *Mediterranean,* p. 299.

50. Howe, *Northwest Africa,* pp. 469–70; Playfair and Molony, *Mediterranean,* pp. 300–01.

51. Howe, *Northwest Africa,* p. 477; Blumenson, *Kasserine Pass,* pp. 303–04.

52. Howe, *Northwest Africa,* p. 478.

53. Ibid., p. 478.

54. Lewin, *Rommel,* pp. 259–60.

Chapter 14

1. Dwight D. Eisenhower, *Crusade in Europe* (Garden City, N.Y.: Permabooks, 1952), pp. 240-41.

2. Kent R. Greenfield et al., *The Organization of Ground Combat Troops: The Army Ground Forces* (Washington: Department of the Army, 1947), p. 199.

3. Robert R. Palmer, Bell I. Wiley, and William R. Keast, *The Procurement and Training of Ground Combat Troops* (Washington: Department of the Army, 1948), p. 433.

4. Richard M. Leighton, *Global Logistics and Strategy, 1940-1943* (Washington: Department of the Army, 1955), pp. 144-51.

5. Greenfield et al., *Organization*, p. 393.

6. Ibid., pp. 394, 220.

7. Ibid., pp. 221-23.

8. Ibid., pp. 223-25.

9. Ibid., p. 225.

10. Ibid., p. 161.

11. Ibid., p. 177.

12. Maurice Matloff and Edwin M. Snell, *Strategic Planning for Coalition Warfare, 1941-1942* (Washington: Department of the Army, 1953), pp. 394-95.

13. Leighton, *Global Logistics, 1940-1943*, Chart 15.

14. Ibid., pp. 732, 703.

15. Arthur Bryant, *The Turn of the Tide* (Garden City, N.Y.: Doubleday, 1957), p. 260.

16. Ibid., pp. 260-61.

17. Review of the Home Forces, September 8, 1942, WO 199/451, PRO.

18. Winston S. Churchill, *The Hinge of Fate* (Boston: Houghton Mifflin, 1950), p. 927.

19. Memorandum, May 13, 1942, WO 199/453.

20. Memorandum, June 2, 1942, WO 193/234.

21. CIGS Conference, July 3, 1942, WO 199/453.

22. Memorandum, July 31, 1942, PREM 3/55/3.

23. Memorandum, August 1, 1942, WO 193/2 and WO 199/451.

24. Churchill, *Hinge of Fate*, pp. 748-49.

25. Forrest C. Pogue, *George C. Marshall: Organizer of Victory* (New York: Viking, 1973), p. 15.

Chapter 15

1. Burkhart Mueller-Hillebrand, *Das Heer, 1933-1945*, 3 vols. (Frankfurt: Mittler & Sohn, 1956-1969), 3:117.

2. Records of the Oberkommando des Heeres, Reforming Units, 1943-1945, Microfilm, Series GG30 T78, roll 398, frames 368262-64, RG 1027, NA.

3. Basil H. Liddell Hart, *History of the Second World War* (New York: Putnam's, 1970), p. 243.

4. Mueller-Hillebrand, *Das Heer*, 3:78-79.

5. Ibid., p. 80.

6. Ibid.

7. Ibid., p. 79.

8. Ibid., p. 80.

9. Ibid., pp. 98–102.

10. Ibid., pp. 132–34.

11. *Kriegstagebuch des Oberkommandos der Wehrmacht,* 4 vols. (Frankfurt am Main: Bernard und Graefe, 1961–1965), 3:1416.

12. Georg Tessin, *Verbande und Truppen der deutschen Wehrmacht und Waffen SS in Zweiten Weltkrieg, 1939–1945,* 13 vols. (Osnabruck: Biblio, 1965–1977), 9:240.

13. Ibid., p. 210.

14. *Kriegstagebuch,* 3:117.

15. Ibid., p. 237.

16. Ibid., p. 238.

17. Ibid., p. 241.

18. Ibid., pp. 265–335.

19. Ibid., pp. 254–55.

20. Ibid., p. 261.

21. Ibid., p. 1550.

22. Ibid., p. 100.

23. Albert Seaton, *The Russo-German War, 1941–1945* (New York: Praeger, 1970), pp. 396–98.

24. Ibid., pp. 370–80.

25. Mueller-Hillebrand, *Das Heer,* 3:115.

26. Tessin, *Verbande und Truppen,* 8:338.

27. *Kriegstagebuch,* 3:260.

28. Tessin, *Verbande und Truppen,* 4:226.

29. *Kriegstagebuch,* 3:1037, 1129, 1559; Wolf Keilig, *Das Deutsche Heer, 1939–1945,* 3 vols. (Bad Nauheim: Podzun, 1956–1972), 2:15, p. 60.

30. Mueller-Hillebrand, *Das Heer,* 3:117.

31. Ibid., p. 155.

32. Nicola Pignato, *Armi Della Fanteria Italiana Nella Seconda Guerra Mondiale* (Parma: Emanno Albertelli, 1971), pp. 9–10.

33. Ibid., pp. 8–9.

34. Mueller-Hillebrand, *Das Heer,* 3:117.

35. Tessin, *Verbande und Truppen,* 4:10.

36. Mueller-Hillebrand, *Das Heer,* 3:117.

37. Ibid., pp. 98–102, 109–11.

38. Ibid., pp. 110–11; Seaton, *Russo-German War,* pp. 297–98.

39. Seaton, *Russo-German War,* p. 391.

40. Meuller-Hillebrand, *Das Heer,* 3:114; German OKH, Reforming Units, Microfilm, Series GG30 T78, roll 398, frame 368260.

41. German OKH, Reforming Units, Microfilm, Series GG30 T78, roll 398, frame 368263.

42. Werner Haupt, *Geschichte der 134. Infanterie-Division* (Weinsberg: Herausgegeben vom Kameradenkreis der ehemaligen, 134. Inf.-Division, 1971), pp. 157–64, 166.

43. German OKH, Reforming Units, Microfilm, Series GG30 T78, roll 398, frames 368268–77.

44. Mueller-Hillebrand, *Das Heer,* 3:140.

45. German OKH, Reforming Units, Microfilm, Series GG30 T78, roll 398, frames 367255–60.

46. *Kriegstagebuch,* 3:773, 1153.

47. Milton Shulman, *Defeat in the West* (New York: Dutton, 1948), p. 93.

48. Mueller-Hillebrand, *Das Heer,* 3:140.

49. *Kriegstagebuch,* 3:817, 765.

50. Ibid., pp. 1141, 1235.

51. Mueller-Hillebrand, *Das Heer,* 3:136.

52. Tessin, *Verbande und Truppen,* 9:134.

53. Mueller-Hillebrand, *Das Heer,* 3:140-41; Jurgen Thorwald, *The Illusion* (New York: Harcourt Brace Jovanovich, 1975), pp. 180-81, 220-25.

54. Shulman, *Defeat in the West,* p. 94.

55. Seaton, *Russo-German War,* pp. 392-93.

56. Ibid., p. 393.

57. Mueller-Hillebrand, *Das Heer,* 3:113.

58. Ibid.

59. *Kriegstagebuch,* 3:1153.

60. Seaton, *Russo-German War,* p. 394.

61. Mueller-Hillebrand, *Das Heer,* 3:114-15.

62. Seaton, *Russo-German War,* p. 401; Albert Speer, *Inside the Third Reich* (New York: Macmillan, 1970), p. 639.

63. Speer, *Third Reich,* pp. 262-63; Seaton, *Russo-German War,* p. 397.

64. *Kreigstagebuch,* 1:87E.

65. Speer, *Third Reich,* p. 264.

66. Alan Clark, *Barbarossa: The Russian-German Conflict, 1941-1945* (New York: New American Library, 1966), p. 349.

67. Speer, *Third Reich,* p. 263.

68. Clark, *Barbarossa,* pp. 350-51.

69. Speer, *Third Reich,* pp. 369-71.

70. Mueller-Hillebrand, *Das Heer,* 3:182.

Chapter 16

1. *Kriegstagebuch des Oberkommandos der Wehrmacht,* 4 vols. (Frankfurt am Main: Bernard und Graefe, 1961-1965), 1:87E.

2. Burkhart Mueller-Hillebrand, *Das Heer, 1933-1945,* 3 vols. (Frankfurt: Mittler & Sohn, 1956-1969), 3:136; Gordon A. Harrison, *Cross-Channel Attack* (Washington: Department of the Army, 1951), p. 145; United States, War Department, *Handbook of German Military Forces,* Technical Manual-Enemy 30-451 (Washington: Government Printing Office, 1945), pp. I, 3-4.

3. Mueller-Hillebrand, *Das Heer,* 3:152.

4. Ibid.

5. Ibid., pp. 132-34, 149.

6. Albert Seaton, *The Russo-German War, 1941-1945* (New York: Praeger, 1970), pp. 390-91.

7. Mueller-Hillebrand, *Das Heer,* 3:117.

8. *Kriegstagebuch,* 3:759-60.

9. Josef P. Goebbels, *The Goebbels Diaries, 1942-1943,* edited by Jouis P. Lochner (New York: Universal Award House, 1971), p. 453.

10. Mueller-Hillebrand, *Das Heer,* 3:117.

11. Ibid.

12. *Kriegstagebuch*, 3:827.

13. Ibid., p. 1556; Georg Tessin, *Verbande und Truppen der deutschen Wehrmacht und Waffen SS im Zweiten Weltkrieg, 1939–1945,* 13 vols. (Osnabruck: Biblio, 1965–1977), 7:148.

14. *Kriegstagebuch*, 3:1556; Tessin, *Verbande und Truppen,* 8:152.

15. *Kriegstagebuch*, 3:1161; Tessin, *Verbande und Truppen,* 3:147.

16. Mueller-Hillebrand, *Das Heer,* 3:32.

17. Basil H. Liddell Hart, *The German Generals Talk* (New York: Morrow, 1948), pp. 232, 238.

18. *Kriegstagebuch*, 3:817.

19. Ibid., pp. 1087, 1091, 1053.

20. Ibid., p. 828.

21. Mueller-Hillebrand, *Das Heer,* 3:136, 145.

22. *Kriegstagebuch*, 3:1551, 1091.

23. Goebbels, *Diaries*, p. 487.

24. *Kriegstagebuch*, 3:1230–31.

25. Wolf Keilig, *Das Deutsche Heer, 1939–1945,* 3 vols. (Bad Nauheim: Podzun, 1956–1972), 3:204, 1943, p. 3.

26. Mueller-Hillebrand, *Das Heer,* 3:150.

27. Ibid., pp. 134–36.

Chapter 17

1. Forrest C. Pogue, *George C. Marshall: Organizer of Victory* (New York: Viking, 1973), p. 194.

2. Peter Lyon, *Eisenhower: Portrait of the Hero* (Boston: Little, Brown, 1974), p. 448.

3. Richard M. Leighton, "Overlord Revisited," *American Historical Review,* 68 (1963), 932–33.

4. Lyon, *Eisenhower,* p. 222.

5. Arthur Bryant, *The Turn of the Tide* (Garden City, N.Y.: Doubleday, 1957), p. 96.

6. Dwight D. Eisenhower, *Crusade in Europe* (Garden City, N.Y.: Permabooks, 1952), p. 50.

7. Winston S. Churchill, *The Hinge of Fate* (Boston: Houghton Mifflin, 1950), p. 479.

8. Ibid.

9. Winston S. Churchill, *Closing the Ring* (Boston: Houghton Mifflin, 1951), p. 77.

10. Churchill, *Hinge of Fate,* pp. 480, 490–91.

11. Ibid., p. 745.

12. Ibid., p. 748.

13. John Gunther, *Roosevelt in Retrospect* (New York: Pyramid, 1962), pp. 336–37, 366.

BIBLIOGRAPHY

Manuscript Sources

GERMANY

Records of German Field Commands, Divisions, Tenth Panzer Division, Microfilm, Series GG65 T315, rolls 569 and 570, RG 1027, NA.
Records of the Oberkommando des Heeres, Reforming Units, 1943–1945, Microfilm, Series GG30 T315, roll 398, RG 1027, NA.
Records of German Field Commands, Divisions, Sixty-fifth Infantry Division, Microfilm, Series GG65 T315, roll 1037, RG 1027, NA.
Records of German Field Commands, Divisions, Twenty-fourth Panzer Division, Microfilm, Series GG65 T315, roll 805, RG 1027, NA.

GREAT BRITAIN

Papers of the Minister of Defense, the ULTRA papers, RG DEFE 3, PRO.
Ministry of Defense, Operational Papers, RG PREM 3, PRO.
War Office, War of 1939 to 1945, PRO.
    Registered Papers, General Series, RG WO 32.
    Directorate of Military Operations and Intelligence, RG WO 106.
    War Diaries, North African Forces, RG WO 175.
    Directorate of Military Operations, Collation Files, RG WO 193.
    Military Headquarters Papers, British Expeditionary Force, RG WO 197.
    Military Headquarters Papers, Home Forces, RG WO 199.
    Military Headquarters Papers, Middle East Forces, RG WO 201.
    Military Headquarters Papers, Allied Forces Headquarters, RG WO 204.

UNITED STATES

War Department
    General and Special Staff Operations Division Project Decimal File 1942–1945, North African Theater of Operations, Daily Reports, RG 165, NA.
    Plans and Operation Department, Daily Summary Subject File, 1941–1947, RG 165, NA.
    Records of the U.S. Joint Chiefs of Staff and Combined Chiefs of Staff, Minutes of the Combined Chiefs of Staff, RG 218, NA.
    Records of the Adjutant General's Office, Decimal File, RG 337, NA.
    Unit History Data Cards, Organization and Directory Section, Operations Branch, Operations and Training Division, Adjutant General's Office, RG 407, NA.
Office of Strategic Service, File of Reports, NA.
Allied Force Headquarters, Chief of Staff, Cable Log, Walter Bedell Smith Collection, Eisenhower Library, Abilene, Kansas.

Printed Sources

Accoce, Pierre, and Pierre Quet. *Master Spy: A Man Called Lucy*. New York: Coward, McCann & Geoghegan, 1972.

Addington, Larry H. *The Blitzkrieg Era and the German General Staff, 1865–1941*. New Brunswick, N.J.: Rutgers University, 1971.

Alexander of Tunis, Earl. *The Alexander Memoirs, 1940–1945*. Edited by John North. New York: McGraw-Hill, 1961.

Ambrose, Stephen E. *The Supreme Commander*. Garden City, N.Y.: Doubleday, 1970.

American Telephone and Telegraph Company. *Telephone and Telegraph Statistics of the World, January 1, 1938*. Comptroller's Department. Chief of Statistics Division. n.p.: n.p., 1939.

Badoglio, Pietro. *Italy in the Second World War*. London: Oxford, 1948.

Baldwin, Hanson W. *Battles Lost and Won*. New York: Harper & Row, 1966.

———. *Great Mistakes of the War*. London: Harper, 1950.

Batchelor, John, and Bryan Cooper. *Fighter: A History of Fighter Aircraft*. New York: Scribner's, 1973.

———, and Ian Hogg. *Artillery*. New York: Scribner's, 1972.

Behrens, Catherine. *Merchant Shipping and the Demands of War*. 2 vols. History of the Second World War, Civil Series. London: H.M. Stationery Office, 1955.

Bekker, Cajus. *Hitler's Naval War*. London: Zebra Books, Kensington Publishing Corp., 1977.

Belote, James H., and William M. Belote. *Titans of the Seas*. New York: Harper & Row, 1975.

Bender, Roger J., and Hugh P. Taylor. *Uniforms, Organization and History of the Waffen SS*. 4 vols. Mountain View, Calif.: Bender, 1971–1976.

Bergamini, David. *Japan's Imperial Conspiracy*. 2 vols. New York: Morrow, 1971.

Blumenson, Martin. *Kasserine Pass*. Boston: Houghton Mifflin, 1967.

Bolitho, Hector. *The Galloping Third: The Story of the 3rd, the King's Own Hussars*. London: Murray, 1963.

Bretnor, Reginald. *Decisive Warfare*. Harrisburg: Stackpoole, 1969.

Brown, Anthony C. *Bodyguard of Lies*. New York: Harper & Row, 1975.

Bryant, Arthur. *Triumph in the West, 1943–1946*. Garden City, N.Y.: Doubleday, 1959.

———. *The Turn of the Tide*. Garden City, N.Y.: Doubleday, 1957.

Burns, James M. *Roosevelt: The Soldier of Freedom, 1940–1945*. New York: Harcourt Brace Jovanovich, 1970.

Burton, Earl. *By Sea and by Land: The Story of Our Amphibious Forces*. New York: McGraw-Hill, 1944.

Burton, Hal. *The Ski Troops*. New York: Simon and Schuster, 1971.

Caidin, Martin. *Black Thursday*. New York: Dutton, 1960.

———. *ME 109*. New York: Ballantine, 1968.

Calder, Angus. *The People's War: Britain, 1939–1945*. New York: Pantheon, 1969.

Campbell, James. *The Bombing of Nuremberg*. Garden City, N.Y.: Doubleday, 1974.

Carell, Paul. *Invasion: They're Coming*. New York: Bantam, 1964.

Carmichael, Thomas N. *The Ninety Days*. New York: Bernard Geis Associates, 1971.

Chamberlain, Peter, and Chris Ellis. *British and American Tanks of World War II*. New York: Arco, 1969.

———. *Panzer-Jager*. London: Almark, 1971.

Churchill, Winston S. *Closing the Ring*. Vol. 5 of *The Second World War*. Boston: Houghton Mifflin, 1951.

————. *The Grand Alliance*. Vol. 3 of *The Second World War*. Boston: Houghton Mifflin, 1950.

————. *The Hinge of Fate*. Vol. 4 of *The Second World War*. Boston: Houghton Mifflin, 1950.

Clark, Alan. *Barbarossa: The Russian-German Conflict, 1941-1945*. New York: New American Library, 1966.

Cline, Ray S. *Washington Command Post: The Operations Division*. United States Army in World War II. Washington: Department of the Army, 1951.

Coakley, Robert W., and Richard M. Leighton. *Global Logistics and Strategy, 1943-1945*. United States Army in World War II. Washington: Department of the Army, 1969.

Coggins, Jack. *The Campaign for Guadalcanal*. Garden City, N.Y.: Doubleday, 1972.

Collier, Basil. *Defence of the United Kingdom*. History of the Second World War, Military Series. London: H.M. Stationery Office, 1957.

————. *The Second World War: A Military History*. New York: Morrow, 1967.

Cooper, Bryan, and John Batchelor. *Bombers, 1939-1945*. London: Marshall Cavendish, 1974.

Craven, Wesley F., and James L. Cate. *The Army Air Force in World War II*. 7 vols. Chicago: University of Chicago, 1948-1951.

Crowl, Philip A., and Edmund G. Love. *Seizure of the Gilberts and Marshalls*. United States Army in World War II. Washington: Department of the Army, 1955.

Davies, W. J. K. *German Army Handbook, 1939-1945*. New York: Arco, 1974.

Eade, Charles, comp. *The War Speeches of the Rt. Hon. Winston S. Churchill*. 3 vols. Boston: Houghton Mifflin, 1953.

Eisenhower, Dwight D. *Crusade in Europe*. Garden City, N.Y.: Permabooks, 1952.

Erickson, John. *The Road to Stalingrad: Stalin's War with Germany*. New York: Harper & Row, 1975.

Esposito, Vincent J. *The West Point Atlas of American Wars*. Vol. 2. New York: Praeger, 1959.

Farago, Ladislas. *The Game of Foxes*. New York: Bantam, 1971.

Fergusson, Bernard. *The Watery Maze*. New York: Holt, Rinehart & Winston, 1961.

Fitzsimons, Bernard. *Warplanes and Air Battles of World War II*. New York: Beekman, 1973.

Frank, Wolfgang. *The Sea Wolves*. New York: Ballantine, 1958.

Frederick, J. B. M. *Lineage Book of the British Army: Mounted Corps and Infantry, 1660-1968*. Cornwallville, N.Y.: Hope Farm Press, 1969.

Freeman, Roger A. *Mustang at War*. Garden City, N.Y.: Doubleday, 1974.

Fuller, J. F. C. *The Conduct of War, 1789-1961*. New Brunswick, N.J.: Rutgers University, 1961.

Funk, Arthur L. *The Politics of Torch*. Lawrence, Kan.: University Press of Kansas, 1974.

Galland, Adolf. *The First and the Last: The Rise and Fall of the German Fighter Forces, 1938-1945*. New York: Ballantine, 1957.

Galvin, John R. *Air Assault: The Development of Airmobile Warfare*. New York: Hawthorn, 1969.

Gehlen, Reinhard. *The Service*. New York: Popular Library, 1972.

Goebbels, Josef P. *The Goebbels Diaries, 1942-1943*. Edited by Louis P. Lochner. New York: Universal-Award House, 1971.

Goodyear, Harry J., comp. *History of the 3rd Battalion, 338th Infantry Regiment, 85th Infantry Division, World War II*. n.p.: Campus Publishing Co., 1946.

Gray, Carl R. *Railroading in Eighteen Countries*. New York: Scribner's, 1955.

Great Britain. Admiralty. *The Royal Marines: The Admiralty Account of their Achievements 1939–1943*. n.p.: n.d.

———. War Office. *German Order of Battle, 1944*. London: Hippocrene, 1975.

———. War Office. *War Time Tank Production: Command Paper 6865*. London: H.M. Stationery Office, 1946.

Green, William. *War Planes of the Second World War*. Vols. 1, 2, and 4. Garden City, N.Y.: Doubleday, 1971–1973.

Greenfield, Kent R. et al. *The Organization of Ground Combat Troops: The Army Ground Forces*. United States Army in World War II. Washington: Department of the Army, 1947.

Gregory, Barry. *British Airborne Troops, 1940–1945*. Garden City, N.Y.: Doubleday, 1975.

Guderian, Heinz. *Panzer Leader*. New York: Ballantine, 1957.

Gunther, John. *Roosevelt in Retrospect*. New York: Pyramid, 1962.

Hall, Hessel D. *North American Supply*. History of the Second World War, Civil Series. London: H.M. Stationery Office, 1955.

———, C. C. Wrigley, and J. D. Scott. *Studies of Overseas Supply*. History of the Second World War, Civil Series. London: H.M. Stationery Office, 1956.

Hancock, William K., ed. *Statistical Digest of the War*. History of the Second World War, Civil Series. London: H.M. Stationery Office, 1951.

Harrison, Gordon A. *Cross Channel Attack*. United States Army in World War II. Washington: Department of the Army, 1951.

Haupt, Werner. *Die 260. Infanterie-Division, 1939–1944*. Bad Nauheim: Podzun, 1970.

———. *Geschichte der 134. Infanterie-Division*. Weinsberg: Herausgegeben vom Kameradenkreis der ehemaligen, 134. Inf.-Division, 1971.

Heavey, William F. *Down Ramp: The Story of the Army Amphibian Engineers*. Washington: Infantry Journal Press, 1947.

Hess, William. *B-17 Flying Fortress*. New York: Ballantine, 1974.

Hofmann, George F. *The Super Sixth*. Louisville, Ky.: Sixth Armored Division Association, 1975.

Hogg, Ian. *Grenades and Mortars*. New York: Ballantine, 1974.

———, and John Weeks. *Military Small Arms of the Twentieth Century*. Northfield, Ill.: Digest Books, 1973.

Hohne, Heinz. *The Order of the Death's Head*. New York: Ballantine, 1971.

Horne, Alistair. *To Lose a Battle*. Boston: Little, Brown, 1969.

Howard, Michael. *The Mediterranean Strategy in the Second World War*. London: Weidenfeld and Nicolson, 1968.

Howe, George F. *The Battle History of the 1st Armored Division*. Washington: Combat Forces Press, 1954.

———. *Northwest Africa: Seizing the Initiative in the West*. United States Army in World War II. Washington: Department of the Army, 1957.

Humble, Richard. *War in the Air, 1939–1945*. London: Salamander, 1975.

Irving, David. *The Rise and Fall of the Luftwaffe*. Boston: Little, Brown, 1973.

Jablonski, Edward. *Flying Fortress*. Garden City, N.Y.: Doubleday, 1965.

Jacobs, Bruce. *Soldiers: The Fighting Divisions of the Regular Army*. New York: Norton, 1958.

Joslen, H. F. *Orders of Battle, Second World War, 1939–1945*. 2 vols. History of the Second World War, Military Series. London: H.M. Stationery Office, 1960.

Kahn, Ely J., and Henry McLemore. *Fighting Divisions*. Washington: Infantry Journal Press, 1945.

Karig, Walter, et al. *Battle Report: The Atlantic War*. New York: Farrar & Rinehart, 1946.

Keilig, Wolf. *Das Deutsche Heer, 1939–1945*. 3 vols. Bad Nauheim: Podzun, 1956–1972.

Kimche, Jon. *The Unfought Battle*. New York: Stein and Day, 1968.

King, Ernest J. *U.S. Navy at War, 1941–1945*. Washington: United States Navy Department, 1946.

———, and Walter Muir Whitehill. *Fleet Admiral King: A Naval Record*. New York: Norton, 1952.

Kirk, John, and Robert Young, Jr. *Great Weapons of World War II*. New York: Bonanza, 1961.

Koltunov, G. A. "Kursk: The Clash of Armour," in *Tanks and Weapons of World War II*. Edited by Beekman House. New York: Beekman, 1973. Pp. 81–97.

Kriegstagebuch des Oberkommandos der Wehrmacht. 4 vols. Frankfurt am Main: Bernard und Graefe, 1961–1965.

Leighton, Richard M. *Global Logistics and Strategy, 1940–1943*. United States Army in World War II. Washington: Department of the Army, 1955.

———. "Overlord Revisited." *American Historical Review*, 68 (1963), 919–37.

Lewin, Ronald. *Rommel as Military Commander*. New York: Ballantine, 1970.

Liddell Hart, Basil H. *The German Generals Talk*. New York: Morrow, 1948.

———. *History of the Second World War*. New York: Putnam's, 1970.

———. *Strategy-The Indirect Approach*. London: Faber, 1954.

———. *The Tanks*. 2 vols. New York: Praeger, 1959.

Lyall, Gavin, ed. *The War in the Air: The Royal Air Force in World War II*. New York: Ballantine, 1970.

Lyon, Peter. *Eisenhower: Portrait of the Hero*. Boston: Little, Brown, 1974.

MacDonald, Charles B. *The Mighty Endeavor: American Armed Forces in World War II*. New York: Oxford, 1969.

Macintyre, Donald. *The Naval War against Hitler*. New York: Scribner's, 1971.

Macksey, Kenneth. *Tank Warfare*. New York: Stein and Day, 1972.

Mason, David. *U-Boat: The Secret Menace*. New York: Ballantine, 1968.

Matloff, Maurice, and Edwin M. Snell. *Strategic Planning for Coalition Warfare, 1941–1942*. United States Army in World War II. Washington: Department of the Army, 1953.

Millard Fillmore Hospital. *Annual Report for 1975*. Buffalo, N.Y.: n.p., 1976.

Miller, John, Jr. "The Casablanca Conference and Pacific Strategy," *Military Affairs*, 13 (1949), 209–15.

Morgan, Frederick. *Overture to Overlord*. Garden City, N.Y.: Doubleday, 1950.

Morison, Samuel E. *The Battle of the Atlantic*. Vol. 1 of The History of United States Naval Operations in World War II. Boston: Little, Brown, 1947.

———. *Operations in North African Waters*. Vol. 2 of The History of United States Naval Operations in World War II. Boston: Little, Brown, 1955.

————. *Sicily-Salerno-Anzio, January 1943-June 1944*. Vol. 9 of The History of United States Naval Operations in World War II. Boston: Little, Brown, 1954.

Mueller-Hillebrand, Burkhart. *Das Heer, 1933-1945*. 3 vols. Frankfurt: Mittler & Sohn, 1956-1969.

Ogorkiewicz, Richard M. *Armoured Forces*. New York: Arco, 1970.

Orgill, Douglas. *The Gothic Line*. London: Pan Books, 1967.

Ours to Hold High: The History of the 77th Infantry Division in World War II. Washington: Infantry Journal Press, 1947.

Palmer, Robert R., Bell I. Wiley, and William R. Keast. *The Procurement and Training of Ground Combat Troops*. United States Army in World War II. Washington: Department of the Army, 1948.

Pignato, Nicola. *Armi Della Fanteria Italiana Nella Seconda Guerra Mondiale*. Parma: Ermanno Albertelli, 1971.

Playfair, I. S. O., and C. J. C. Molony. *The Mediterranean and Middle East*. Vol. 4. History of the Second World War, Military Series. London: H.M. Stationery Office, 1966.

Pogue, Forrest C. *George C. Marshall: Ordeal and Hope*. Vol. 2. New York: Viking, 1967.

————. *George C. Marshall: Organizer of Victory*. Vol. 3. New York: Viking, 1973.

Potter, Elmer B. *Nimitz*. Annapolis, Md.: Naval Institute Press, 1976.

Price, Alfred. *Luftwaffe*. New York: Ballantine, 1969.

Quick, John. *Dictionary of Weapons and Military Terms*. New York: McGraw-Hill, 1973.

The Reserve Officers' Training Corps Manual, Cavalry. Harrisburg: Military Service Publishing Co., 1942.

The Reserve Officers' Training Corps Manual, Infantry. 4 vols. 24th ed. Harrisburg: Military Service Publishing Co., 1942.

Robertson, Terence. *Dieppe: The Shame and the Glory*. Boston: Little, Brown, 1962.

Rommel, Erwin. *The Rommel Papers*. Edited by Basil H. Liddell Hart. New York: Harcourt, Brace, 1953.

Rosinski, Herbert. *The German Army*. New York: Praeger, 1966.

Roskill, Stephen W. *The War at Sea*. 3 vols. History of the Second World War, Military Series. London: H.M. Stationery Office, 1954-1961.

Ruppenthal, Roland G. *Logistical Support of the Armies*. 2 vols. United States Army in World War II. Washington: Department of the Army, 1953, 1959.

Sajer, Guy. *The Forgotten Soldier*. New York: Harper & Row, 1971.

Schultz, Paul L. *The 85th Infantry Division in World War II*. Washington: Infantry Journal Press, 1949.

Seaton, Albert. *The Russo-German War, 1941-1945*. New York: Praeger, 1970.

Shamburger, Page, and Joe Christy. *The Curtiss Hawk Fighters*. New York: Sports Car Press, 1971.

Sherwood, Robert E. *Roosevelt and Hopkins: An Intimate History*. New York: Harper, 1948.

Shulman, Milton. *Defeat in the West*. New York: Dutton, 1948.

Smith, Peter C. *The Stuka at War*. New York: Arco, 1971.

Speer, Albert. *Inside the Third Reich*. New York: Macmillan, 1970.

Steele, Richard W. *The First Offensive, 1942*. Bloomington, Ind.: Indiana University, 1973.

Stoler, Mark A. *The Politics of the Second Front*. Westport, Conn.: Greenwood Press, 1977.

Strong, Kenneth. *Intelligence at the Top*. Garden City, N.Y.: Doubleday, 1969.

Taylor, A. J. P. *Beaverbrook*. New York: Simon and Schuster, 1972.

Tessin, Georg. *Verbande und Truppen der deutschen Wehrmacht und Waffen SS im Zweiten Weltkrieg, 1939-1945*. 13 vols. Osnabruck: Biblio, 1965-1977.

Thorwald, Jurgen. *The Illusion*. New York: Harcourt Brace Jovanovich, 1975.

Truscott, Lucas K. *Command Missions: A Personal Story*. New York: Dutton, 1954.

United States. Department of Commerce. *Historical Statistics of the United States: Colonial Times to 1957*. Washington: Government Printing Office, 1960.

————. Department of the Navy. *United States Naval Aviation, 1910-1970*. Washington: Government Printing Office, 1970.

————. Department of the Navy. *United States Submarine Losses, World War II*. Washington: Government Printing Office, 1963.

————. War Department. *Enemy Air-Borne Forces*, Special Series No. 7. Washington: Government Printing Office, 1942.

————. War Department. *The German Armored Division*, Information Bulletin No. 18. Washington: Government Printing Office, 1941.

————. War Department. *Handbook of German Military Forces*, Technical Manual-Enemy 30-451. Washington: Government Printing Office, 1945.

————. War Department. *Staff Officers Field Manual, Enemy Forces: Organization, Technical and Logistical Data*, Field Manual-Enemy 101-10. Washington: Government Printing Office, 1942.

Vader, John. *Spitfire*. New York: Ballantine, 1969.

Vagts, Alfred. *Landing Operations*. Harrisburg: Military Service Press, 1946.

Von Senger, F. M., und Etterlin. *German Tanks of World War II*. New York: Galahad, 1969.

Warlimont, Walter. *Inside Hitler's Headquarters, 1939-1945*. New York: Praeger, 1964.

Wedemeyer, Albert C. *Wedemeyer Reports!* New York: Henry Holt, 1958.

Werner, Herbert A. *Iron Coffins*. New York: Holt, Rinehart & Winston, 1969.

Westphal, Siegfried. *The German Army in the West*. London: Cassell, 1951.

Wheldon, John. *Machine Age Armies*. London: Abelard, 1968.

White, B. T. *German Tanks and Armored Vehicles, 1914-1945*. New York: Arco, 1968.

Winterbotham, Fred W. *The Ultra Secret*. New York: Dell, 1974.

INDEX